Research Methods in Psychology

CANADIAN EDITION

Research Methods in Psychology

From Theory to Practice

Ben Gorvine

Karl Rosengren

Lisa Stein

Kevin Biolsi

Shayna Rusticus

OXFORD
UNIVERSITY PRESS

OXFORD
UNIVERSITY PRESS

Oxford University Press is a department of the University of Oxford.
It furthers the University's objective of excellence in research, scholarship,
and education by publishing worldwide. Oxford is a registered trade mark of
Oxford University Press in the UK and in certain other countries.

Published in Canada by
Oxford University Press
8 Sampson Mews, Suite 204,
Don Mills, Ontario M3C 0H5 Canada

www.oupcanada.com

Library and Archives Canada Cataloguing in Publication
Title: Research methods: from theory to practice / Ben Gorvine, Karl Rosengren, Lisa Stein,
Kevin Biolsi, Shayna Rusticus.
Names: Gorvine, Ben, author. | Rosengren, Karl Sven, author. | Stein, Lisa (Editor), author. |
Biolsi, Kevin, author. | Rusticus, Shayna, author.
Description: Canadian edition. | Includes bibliographical references and index.
Identifiers: Canadiana (print) 2019019250X | Canadiana (ebook) 20190192526 | ISBN 9780199033874
(softcover) | ISBN 9780199039210 (loose leaf) | ISBN 9780199033881 (EPUB)
Subjects: LCSH: Psychology—Research—Methodology. | LCSH: Psychology—Research—Canada—Methodology. |
LCSH: Social sciences—Methodology. | LCSH: Social sciences—Canada—Methodology.
Classification: LCC BF76.5 .G67 2020 | DDC 150.72/1—dc23

Cover image: Klaus Vedfelt/Stone/Getty Images
Cover design: Sherill Chapman

1 2 3 4 — 23 22 21 20

Brief Contents

Contents

CHAPTER 14   Publishing Your Research [Online]

CHAPTER 15   Neuroscience Methods [Online]

Preface

Research Methods in Psychology: From Theory to Practice is designed primarily for students who want to or will be expected to conduct research or for those who want to understand research as it occurs from the "inside." As its name suggests, this text guides students through the entire research process—from learning about the wide range of current methods to the first step of developing a research question and through the final stage of writing up and presenting or publishing results.

Our first goal for this book is to provide beginning researchers with the knowledge and skills they need to begin ethical, creative research. Although this book focuses primarily on psychological research, its content is relevant for anyone interested in doing research in the social and behavioural sciences. Our second and closely related goal for this book is to help students become not only producers of research, but also educated consumers of the research they encounter daily in online news sources, blogs, social media, and printed newspapers and magazines. These reports often provide brief snippets from actual research, but with an unstated marketing bias. We believe that every educated adult in our society should know when to trust these accounts and how to evaluate them.

Given the large number of research methods books on the market, someone could reasonably ask why another book on this topic is necessary. Because three of us have taught research methods and helped redesign the research methods classes at our universities, we feel there is a need for a novel approach to this course. In our experience, we have found that the majority of current research methods texts are not written with the notion that students will conduct their own research projects, nor do they provide beginning students with much guidance about becoming involved in research.

In contrast, *Research Methods in Psychology: From Theory to Practice* delves into the practical challenges that face new researchers. We start at the beginning with practical tips on how to select a research topic and find relevant research articles and then guide students through each stage of the research process, ending with detailed information on writing up your research results, presenting research at conferences, and finding the right publication outlet for research, a topic we think will be particularly valuable as more and more undergraduates work toward these goals.

We also include two chapters on statistics. This may seem odd given that most colleges and universities require a separate statistics course prior to a research methods course. However, we have seen that many students taking research methods need at least a refresher, if not a more comprehensive review, of statistical material. Additionally, a number of colleges and universities are moving toward an integrated sequence of statistics and research methods courses, an approach we feel is quite productive. These statistics chapters provide up-to-date information about current controversies regarding the continued use of null hypothesis testing with a view to what the future might hold for data analysis, while also providing students with a requisite understanding of the traditional model. We also present material on research over time (or developmental approaches), neuroscience, qualitative research, case study approaches, single-case experimental designs, and meta-analysis. Although we acknowledge that few undergraduates will use these methods in their undergraduate careers, we feel this information will make them better critical consumers of research wherever they encounter it.

FEATURES

Research Methods in Psychology: From Theory to Practice contains a number of distinct features. Each chapter begins with an **Inside Research** section that highlights research that is being conducted by researchers across Canada. Their shared experiences about their research studies, struggles, and career choices help demystify and personalize the research process and capture some of its inherent excitement for students. A **Chapter Abstract** presents an overview of what will be covered in the chapter, along with a list of **Learning Objectives** specific to the chapter. A **Flowchart** depicts the organization of the research process and important choice points. The flowchart in Chapter 1 provides an overview of the entire research process, emphasizing iterative aspects of research. Flowcharts in subsequent chapters zoom in on sections of the initial flowchart relevant to the material covered in the chapter.

Each chapter includes at least one **Media Matters** section that analyzes and evaluates how a particular research study or general topic relevant to the chapter is portrayed in the mass media. **Practical Tips** boxes highlight central concepts introduced in each chapter, and a **Chapter Summary** recaps the key issues. Two pedagogical elements conclude each chapter. The first is **End-of-Chapter Exercises**, which offer a series of questions that readers can use to test their understanding of the content presented in the chapter and to push themselves beyond the text to consider wider applications of the material. The second is a list of **Key Terms** defined in the **Marginal Glossary** within each chapter. Although many terms are specific to research methods and analysis, others come from diverse areas of psychology to broaden students' understanding of the field.

Our **Accompanying Instructor's Manual** not only presents standard material such as chapter outlines, slides, and exam questions, but also includes details and examples regarding how to conduct data analysis in SPSS and R. These analyses are based on the examples provided in the chapters.

ORGANIZATION

Whereas many instructors like to assign chapters in a textbook in the order in which they appear, our own experience has taught us that this can be difficult in a research methods class, especially one that requires students to conduct mini research projects. In a sense, to be a skilled researcher and critical consumer of research, you need to know all of the material covered in this book to start with. This is clearly not practical or possible. For this reason, we have designed chapters to stand alone as references for a particular method or issue, so that they might be used in an order that best fits an instructor. We have also placed a chapter on ethics early in the book and presented material on ethics throughout the text to reflect our belief that ethical concerns should be considered throughout the research process. In our own research methods courses, we include in almost every class a brief discussion of ethical issues relevant to a particular method or gleaned from a recent press account.

ACKNOWLEDGEMENTS TO THE US EDITION

A book like this takes some time and a lot of help! We are particularly thankful for Jane Potter at Oxford University Press for convincing us that we should write this book. We are grateful to Lisa Sussman at Oxford University Press for her careful editing of the text and for guiding us through the entire process. We also thank the many reviewers and students who read drafts of chapters, as well as the many students who have taken our research methods classes. Your thoughts and comments have undoubtedly made this a better book! We thank the following reviewers:

Michael D. Anes, Wittenberg University

Suzette Astley, Cornell College

Jodie Baird, Swarthmore College

Levi R. Baker-Russell, University of Tennessee

Cole Barton, Davidson College

Timothy Bickmore, Northeastern University

Caitlin Brez, Indiana State University

Kimberly A. Carter, California State University, Sacramento

Janessa Carvalho, Bridgewater State University

Herbert L. Colston, University of Wisconsin–Parkside

Elizabeth Cooper, University of Tennessee, Knoxville

Katherine Corker, Kenyon College

Randolph R. Cornelius, Vassar College

Amanda ElBassiouny, Spring Hill College

Catherine Forestell, The College of William & Mary

Judith G. Foy, Loyola Marymount University

Ronald S. Friedman, University at Albany, State University of New York

Kathleen Geher, State University of New York, New Paltz

Frank M. Groom, Ball State University

David Haaga, American University

William Indick, Dowling College

Mark A. Jackson, Transylvania University

Kulwinder Kaur-Walker, Elizabeth City State University

Victoria Kazmerski, Pennsylvania State University, Erie

Marina Klimenko, University of Florida

Nate Kornell, Williams College

Rebecca LaFountain, Pennsylvania State University, Harrisburg

Huijun Li, Florida A&M University

Stella G. Lopez, University of Texas at San Antonio

William McKibbin, University of Michigan, Flint

Lindsay Mehrkam, University of Florida

Kathryn Oleson, Reed College

Bonnie Perdue, Agnes Scott College

Bill Peterson, Smith College

Thomas Redick, Purdue University

Monica Riordan, Chatham University

Melissa Scircle, Millikin University

Elizabeth Sheehan, Georgia State University

Angela Sikorski, Texas A&M University Texarkana

Meghan Sinton, College of William and Mary

Mark Stellmack, University of Minnesota

Janet Trammell, Pepperdine University

Andrew Triplett, Loyola University, Chicago

Laura Butkovsky Turner, Roger Williams University

Barbara J. Vail, Rocky Mountain College

Luis A. Vega, California State University, Bakersfield

John L. Wallace, Ball State University

Mark Whiting, Radford University

Ryan M. Yoder, Indiana University–Purdue University, Fort Wayne

Finally, we thank all of our families. Ben thanks Amy for her endless patience with the length and scope of this project and her invaluable help in designing several of the figures in the chapter on experimental methods. He also thanks his daughters, Emma and Sophie, for their love and for providing the motivation to push through this project. Karl thanks Sarah for listening to many crazy research ideas and helping to turn them into more practical ones, as well as providing support on a daily basis. Karl also thanks his daughters, Emily and Julia, for their love and support. Lisa thanks Daniel for his constant encouragement, invaluable IT support, and take-out dinners and Madeline, Emma, and Owen for making everything worthwhile. Kevin thanks Carol, Lauren, and Megan for their love, encouragement, and support.

WHY A CANADIAN EDITION?

The Canadian edition of *Research Methods in Psychology: From Theory to Practice* offers a Canadian perspective on conducting research in psychology. This has two key advantages. First, by emphasizing Canadian-specific content and language, most notably in regard to Canadian research ethics, this text will be more relevant to students and instructors in Canada. Second, by highlighting Canadian researchers and incorporating Canadian research examples throughout the text, it exposes students to the amazing work that is being conducted in our own country.

ACKNOWLEDGEMENTS TO THE CANADIAN EDITION

Even adapting an existing book takes a considerable amount of time and effort by many. I am thankful for Dave Ward at Oxford University Press for the opportunity to adapt this book into a Canadian edition. I am also grateful to Elizabeth Ferguson and Mariah Fleetham for their editing of the book and assistance through the entire process of this adaptation. I would also like to thank two student assistants, Kyla Javier and Thomas Hughes, for their help in identifying potential Canadian researchers to profile in this book and for searching out Canadian research to use as examples throughout the book. I am very grateful to each of the researchers who agreed to be profiled in the Inside Research boxes at the start of each chapter. I would like to thank the students in my research methods classes, who through their successes and struggles helped me identify particular content areas to expand on and include in this adaptation. I would also like to thank the reviewers who read drafts of chapters. Your thoughts and comments have undoubtedly made this a better book! We thank the following reviewers:

Kelly Arbeau, Trinity Western University
Craig Blatz, MacEwan University
Connie Boudens, University of Toronto
Michael Emond, Laurentian University
Ken Fowler, Memorial University of
    Newfoundland
Stephen W. Holborn, University of
    Manitoba
Guy Lacroix, Carleton University
Harvey Marmurek, University of Guelph
Jennifer Ostovich, McMaster University
Kendall Soucie, University of Windsor

Finally, I would like to thank Chris for his support and encouragement through this process, and my children, Evan, Kaylee, and Amy, for their love and support.

Introduction to Research Methods

1

Chapter Contents

INSIDE RESEARCH: Carla MacLean

Instructor, Department of Psychology, Kwantlen
Polytechnic University

As an undergraduate at the University of Victoria, I was not initially charmed by the research process. Like anything that is difficult to master, conducting good research is challenging. However, as my interest in psychology grew, so too did my research skills, and now working with others to conduct research is one of the things I enjoy most in my career. My interests are diverse, yet at the core of my research pursuits is a quest to understand how we might maintain accuracy or reduce bias in people's assessments of situations, information, and one another. I typically pursue these core interests in the applied areas of eyewitness memory and professional decision making (e.g., industrial incidents, forensic events, the legal system).

My goal is to explore topics that are interesting to both psychologists and the broader public, to stimulate discussions, and to generate psychologically based strategies for issues found in the world outside the lab. It is not difficult to find such topics. In collaboration with talented colleagues and students, I have

continued

researched such things as the effect of knowledge and expectation on professionals' and witnesses' observations of people, places, and events, as well as psychologically based incident report forms and investigation tools.

Over the years, conducting research has taught me to be measured and organized in how I approach new problems, both inside and outside of the lab—this is a powerful life skill. I encourage you to embrace the challenge of research, think critically, and enjoy the process!

Carla MacLean has interests in the strengths and weaknesses of human memory, as well as judgment and decision making. Much of her research has real-world application, focusing on eyewitness memory as well as context effects and motivation on professionals' judgments. Her research methods include both experiential and computer-based designs.

Research Focus: Professional experience and judgment, as well as eyewitness memory

THE RESEARCH PROCESS

This flowchart provides an overview of the research process, emphasizing the iterative aspects of research. Flowcharts in subsequent chapters zoom in on sections of this flowchart relevant to the covered material.

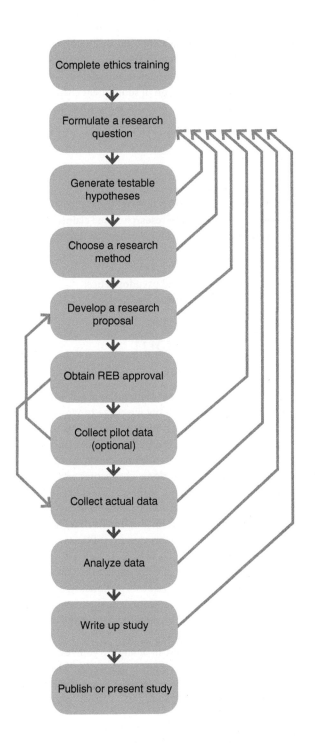

Chapter Abstract

In this chapter, we discuss the importance of research methods and their relevance not only to the scientific process but also to daily life. We explore various approaches to evaluating the constant stream of reports of research findings in the media and advertising, as well as results published in scholarly journals. We present examples of fraudulent and questionable ethical practices to help develop a healthy skepticism of all research findings. Finally, we introduce the fundamental distinction between science and pseudoscience and present a flowchart depicting the research process that will guide the organization of subsequent chapters.

LEARNING OBJECTIVES

By the end of this chapter, you should be able to:
- Explain the importance of understanding research methods.
- Describe methods for evaluating the quality of research-based claims.
- Provide examples of cognitive biases and explain how they can influence our decision making.
- Identify the three goals of science.
- Differentiate between the scientific method and pseudoscience.
- Describe the difference between applied and basic research.

WHY YOU SHOULD CARE ABOUT RESEARCH METHODS

There are three main reasons why you should know something about research methods. First, such knowledge helps you better understand how we come to know the truth of the information we are presented with on a daily basis, ranging from claims that it is better to buy organic food to claims that listening to music while studying will not improve your exam scores. How can you tell whether the results of research studies or claims made in the media are justifiable and believable? In the past few years alone, companies and researchers have claimed that listening to Mozart boosts IQ; wearing magnetic bracelets reduces pain and motion sickness and promotes better balance; drinking coffee and red wine promotes health; drinking pomegranate juice reduces cholesterol and boosts heart health; and drinking diet soda may increase women's risk for depression. Are any of these claims true? How would you find out?

Second, understanding research methods will be directly applicable to many of your other psychology courses. The content of these courses (e.g., social, personality, or clinical psychology) have advanced from years of research that have developed the theories and current trends you will learn about in those fields. Further, you will be required to read and interpret research studies conducted in these fields as part of your studies.

Finally, understanding research methods can aid in many of your everyday decisions. In terms of both physical and psychological well-being, a deeper knowledge of methods can help you make good healthcare decisions. In terms of being a consumer, this knowledge can help you evaluate advertising claims made about a new car, television, or computer so that you can make the best possible choice.

Another good reason to know about research is so that you can conduct your own research. Doing research can be a fun, creative, and rewarding experience, but becoming a skilled researcher requires a certain amount of knowledge. Our hope is that by reading this book, you will acquire the knowledge you need to be a better consumer of research and to conduct your own research project.

METHODS FOR EVALUATING CLAIMS

One way to evaluate research claims made by researchers, reporters, or healthcare-related websites is to simply accept them at face value because they are based on the opinions of experts. After all, the claim must be supported by some expert for it to appear in the news or on the Internet, right? However, increasing numbers of individuals are getting their news online or through social media, and this has allowed for increasing instances of fake news—*made-up content that is presented as real news.*

Do you blindly trust experts cited in a newspaper or online? Can you tell whether an image you are seeing is authentic or fabricated? How do you know who you can trust? Many reports do not even mention a specific expert, so how can you determine whether the report and reporting provide an accurate description of trustworthy results?

A second approach for evaluating claims is to read and evaluate the actual research. But often you will find competing accounts that are difficult to interpret without extensive knowledge of a particular field of study. How, then, do you evaluate the claims found in different sources and come to your own conclusion? This evaluation process becomes easier as you gain experience and learn to judge the quality of the research and conclusions.

A third method for evaluating claims is to search for similar results, or converging evidence, about claims made in news releases (in print or online) and original research. **Converging evidence** refers to results from multiple research investigations that provide similar findings. But when you begin to search for converging results, you may be confronted with a diverse set of facts and opinions that can be difficult to sort out.

converging evidence
Results from multiple research investigations that provide similar findings.

Finally, you could conduct your own research project to test the claims, but many individuals do not have the knowledge or resources to conduct such tests. Much of this book is targeted to help you design and conduct your own research project.

The Extraordinary Coffee Bean

As an introduction to evaluating particular claims that appear in the media, we present two reports about coffee and consider how you might evaluate their accuracy. We examine issues of expertise, reading, and evaluating past research; the importance of finding convergent evidence; and particular aspects to look for in a report of a research finding.

For many years, reports about the health benefits of caffeine have circulated in the media. A *New York Times* article highlighted in Figure 1.1 suggests that caffeine consumers have a lower death rate than individuals who abstain from caffeine. Should we trust Jane Brody and

Having Your Coffee and Enjoying It Too
By JANE E. BRODY [NY TIMES, June 25, 2012]

A disclaimer: I do not own stock in Starbucks nor, to my knowledge, in any other company that sells coffee or its accoutrement. I last wrote about America's most popular beverage four years ago, and the latest and largest study to date supports that earlier assessment of coffee's health effects. Although the new research, which involved more than 400,000 people in a 14-year observational study, still cannot prove cause and effect, the findings are consistent with other recent large studies. The findings were widely reported, but here's the bottom line: When smoking and many other factors known to influence health and longevity were taken into account, coffee drinkers in the study were found to be living somewhat longer than abstainers. Further, the more coffee consumed each day—up to a point, at least—the greater the benefit to longevity. The observed benefit of coffee drinking was not enormous—a death rate among coffee drinkers that was 10 percent to 15 percent lower than among abstainers. But the findings are certainly reassuring, and given how many Americans drink coffee, the numbers of lives affected may be quite large.

FIGURE 1.1   The benefits of coffee.

her reporting? How can we know whether the research she reported really supports the claim that is being made?

There are multiple ways to evaluate the report. First, you could try to find out who conducted the original research. Was it a trained, objective researcher or someone hired by Starbucks or some other coffee supplier? The blurb in Figure 1.1 does not contain this information, but if you look at the original press report (Brody, 2012), you will find that Dr. Neal Freedman and his colleagues conducted the study. Dr. Freedman is listed as an epidemiologist at the National Cancer Institute, and the research was published in the *New England Journal of Medicine*. He seems like a trained researcher, so perhaps we should accept the findings. But **skepticism** is a good trait when reading newspapers or websites, and we will explore in the next section why trusting the experts may or may not be a good thing.

Second, you could dig for converging evidence from other websites or news outlets. Do multiple sites provide converging evidence? Unfortunately, not all of them will cover the same aspects of a story. The media story "Should You Swap Your Regular Coffee for Green Coffee Extract? (Stieg, 2019) suggests that green coffee beans (beans that are un-roasted and unprocessed, as is typically done for regular coffee) contain high levels of chlorogenic acid, which acts as an antioxidant, and can help you lose weight and poten-tially protect against diabetes and heart disease. The compound has been extracted from the bean and turned into a powder or supplement that can be taken orally. The story cites a Dr. Luis Cisneros-Zevallos throughout the article. Is he an expert on caffeine and weight loss? Should we automatically accept his claims because he is a doctor? How should we evaluate these two reports, and should we drink coffee or take green coffee bean supple-ments, or both?

skepticism The process of applying critical thinking in evaluating the truth of a claim.

Third, you could use knowledge of research methods to help you evaluate the claims. We will go into this approach in more detail shortly. Here, we describe potential approaches you can use as you encounter research claims reported in the media.

Trust the Experts

Trusting the experts is a common strategy. After all, *The New York Times* and other newspapers would not report inaccurate or wrong information, would they? One piece of information to help you determine accuracy is whether the news report is based on an original research study, an interview with the lead researcher, or some secondary source. Even if the report lists the journal that published the research, you still cannot be sure it is based on the original data. Many scientific journals (or periodicals with scientific-sounding names) publish secondary reports of research, meaning they are not the original source. The problem with using secondary sources is the further you get from the primary source, the less accurate the information becomes.

If the press release quotes the lead researcher, you can generally assume that the report is based on the original research and not some secondary source. But how can you tell whether the lead researcher is trustworthy? Generally, if researchers are faculty members or scientists at known universities or research institutes (such as the Institute of Cancer Research or the Canadian Institutes of Health Research), you can assume they are highly qualified experts in their particular field. But even experts have biases and vested interests, and some skepticism is always warranted (see "Media Matters: The Persistent Autism–Vaccine Myth"). For example, it is always useful to know who paid for the research. Did Dr. Freedman and his colleagues receive payment by coffee producers or suppliers to conduct their research?

Even researchers from respected universities sometimes cross the line. In 2010, the Stanford University School of Medicine confronted scandals involving conflict-of-interest issues

secondary source An article or reference in which the author describes research that has previously been published.

primary source An article or reference that describes the results of original research that was conducted by the author(s) of the article.

MEDIA MATTERS

The Persistent Autism–Vaccine Myth

When Andrew Wakefield claimed in 1998 that he had found a link between the onset of autism and the measles, mumps, and rubella (MMR) vaccine, he set off a public opinion firestorm that burns in the media to this day. Although Wakefield's findings did not hold up under scrutiny, some parents shunned not only the MMR vaccine but *all* vaccines for their children and encouraged others to follow their example.

Wakefield's mythical autism–vaccine connection stands as a powerful cautionary tale of what can happen when fraudulent research meets mass media amplification and parents desperate to find an explanation for their children's suffering. In the past 15 years, the anti-vaccination movement has rallied around Wakefield. It has contributed to an increase in outbreaks of measles, mumps, and whooping cough in Europe, the United States, and Canada, because some parents have refused to vaccinate their children (Chai, 2014; Gross, 2009; Hiltzik, 2014).

Newspaper headlines and broadcast news trumpeted Wakefield's research linking autism and the MMR vaccine,

continued

citing its appearance in *The Lancet*, a prestigious peer-reviewed medical journal. The research was based on 12 children with intellectual disabilities, 9 of whom were showing some signs of autism (Deer, 2011). Wakefield reported that the parents had noted the onset of some of the children's behavioural symptoms immediately after receiving the MMR vaccine, and he presented these observations as fact (Deer, 2011). As Brian Deer (2011) detailed in an investigative report in the *British Medical Journal*, the paper is rife with discrepancies, including falsified data and misreported or changed time frames, symptoms, and diagnoses.

What Wakefield did not reveal in the article or in his subsequent press conference was his work on a rival measles vaccine (Gross, 2009). He had received funding in 1997 from a Norfolk lawyer with whom he was working on a lawsuit against the manufacturers of the MMR vaccine (Deer, 2011).

The Lancet published a retraction of Wakefield's paper in 2010. Britain's General Medical Council banned Wakefield from practising medicine (Hannaford, 2013), citing unprofessional conduct. Over the next few years, a range of media outlets denounced Wakefield's research and conduct (e.g., "Aftermath of an Unfounded Vaccine Scare," 2013).

But the damage had been done. Parental online groups continue to support Wakefield's claims. A Health Canada survey of 1,029 Canadians conducted in 2017 revealed that 5 per cent of parents reported having "low" trust in vaccinations and that 12 per cent had refused or delayed getting some vaccinations. Only 48 per cent reported having "no doubts or concerns about vaccinating my child" (Health Canada, 2018).

As a response to the anti-vaccination movement, two provinces within Canada—Ontario and New Brunswick—now require parents to provide proof of vaccination for school registration. There is also a growing media backlash to the anti-vaccination movement. Interestingly, posts on social media regularly encourage parents to vaccinate their children, pointing to reports on the surge in cases of measles and whooping cough (e.g., Ingraham, 2015). Perhaps media will, in the end, put out the fire it helped to create.

with a number of prominent researchers. In one instance, a psychiatrist allowed a pharmaceutical company to ghostwrite a book on pharmacology. Another case involved 12 Stanford physicians who accepted relatively large sums of money (some more than $100,000) for speaking engagements involving talks about the drugs made at that pharmaceutical company (Reid, 2010). It is important, especially if a particular drug or product is being advocated, to determine who is sponsoring the research and whether the researcher has a bias, vested interest, or conflict of interest that should make you skeptical about the validity, or accuracy, of the findings.

You can usually determine the source of a researcher's funding by checking the original publication and the researcher's website. Although investigators are typically required to disclose this information, some unethical researchers fail to provide it or, in some cases, as did members of the Stanford faculty, say they did not know it was required.

Unfortunately, sometimes even well-known researchers from respected universities engage in fraud. In 2011, Diederik Stapel, a prominent and widely published social psychologist, admitted he had faked data about research findings on stereotyping, discrimination, advertising, and situations where individuals appeared to prefer negative feedback to praise (Aldhous, 2011). His research was reported in a number of top scientific journals, including *Science*, one of the most prestigious publications on science news and research. A number of junior researchers alleging scientific misconduct uncovered Stapel's fraud. Close investigation of the data in many of these studies suggested a number of anomalies, including surprisingly large experimental effects and data that lacked any outliers. Within Canada, there have been 78 identified instances of Canadian researchers who have committed fraud through fabricating data, misusing grant money, or otherwise engaging in questionable ethical practices (Robinson, 2016). Due to Canadian privacy laws, the identities of these researchers and the specifics of their wrongdoing are not made public.

In the case of Stapel, this highlights the idea that knowledge of research methods can help you evaluate the validity of research claims. If the data look too good to be true—or the claims too shocking or grandiose—they probably are. It also underscores the idea that you should approach press releases and even research published in high-quality scientific journals with a skeptical eye. Although the vast majority of research is conducted and published following appropriate standards, the message is that you should not always assume the expert is right.

Read and Evaluate Past Research

Another way to evaluate claims is to search out and read the published research on the topic. With a strong background in research methods, you are in a better position to recognize particular flaws in the design, method, analysis, or inferences drawn from the data that might make it difficult to trust the claims made by an author, manufacturer, or researcher. As with looking for converging reports across different popular press outlets, such as *CBC News* and the *Globe and Mail*, it is always useful to examine a number of research articles to evaluate a particular claim. Chapter 3 includes more detail about how to find and evaluate relevant research articles. Researchers do not always agree—and if they do not, you will need to track down more articles to evaluate the validity of an overall claim.

Search for Convergence

As mentioned previously, another good way to evaluate a claim made in the media or scholarly journals is to look for converging evidence. Ideally, you want to find multiple websites or research articles that provide the same or similar information and conclusions. This does not always lead to a simple answer. In some cases, if an equal number of studies support or refute the claim, you may be left with no clear conclusion. Yet, with specific research findings, a person knowledgeable about research and methodology will look to see whether the results have been replicated. **Replication** occurs when researchers achieve the same or highly similar results after repeating a study or experiment. Although you should still be skeptical if the original researcher is the only one to replicate the results, if the results hold up over time and are reported by independent laboratories and researchers, you can be fairly confident of their validity.

replication The process through which either the original researcher or the researchers from an independent laboratory repeat the investigation and obtain the same or highly similar results.

How to Evaluate the Quality of Reported Research

Several pieces of information will help you evaluate the quality of the research that backs up an article's claims. First, does the article list the names of the researchers? If it does, you can use this information to determine whether the lead researcher has basic qualifications and experience.

Second, does the article, website, or press release identify where the research was conducted? Although research is conducted at different types of institutions (academic and non-academic), knowing the particular institution can help you determine whether the researchers have the necessary resources and support structure to conduct high-quality research. Yet you should avoid assuming that all findings coming from a well-known research institution are of the highest quality. As we emphasized earlier, it is *always* useful to evaluate research reports with a critical view. However, one of the problems with advanced training in many disciplines is that individuals become hypersensitive to flaws in research, setting standards that are unattainable by even the most thoughtful, careful researchers. If possible, determine what can be learned or taken away from any research article, even after you have taken design flaws into account. Conducting your own research will eventually help you understand the practical considerations of all research and the fact that all researchers must make compromises.

Third, has the research been published (and if so, in what type of journal?), or is it based on preliminary findings? Often, researchers will present preliminary findings at national and international conferences where other researchers can comment on and evaluate them through a peer-review process. It is common to see press releases based on findings reported at conferences. But in other cases, researchers may go straight to the media with what they think is a novel or "hot" finding, bypassing the review process that occurs when a finding is presented in a scientific forum or journal. You should always be skeptical about research that reports preliminary findings that have not been either presented at a scientific conference or published in a respected journal.

Preliminary Findings.   In fact, there are many instances where a study's preliminary results are not supported when the entire data set is collected. In a number of famous cases, researchers went straight to reporters, who championed what they thought was a breakthrough finding, only to find out that the researchers' claims based on preliminary data could not be verified. One such example is "cold fusion" (Taubes, 1993), the idea that a nuclear reaction can occur at room temperature, which opened up the possibility of cheap, almost limitless energy. Ultimately, repeated failures to replicate the results led the scientific community to dismiss the claim, after large sums of research funds were expended. As this example suggests, a crucial aspect of good science is ensuring that results can be replicated, especially if they seem too good to be true or go against the bulk of established theory and research. It is important to realize, however, that breakthroughs do occur in science, and novel findings are often slow to be accepted. Thus, although skepticism can serve to police a scientific discipline, if taken to an extreme it can also impede the advance of science.

Published Research.   Different types of publications serve as outlets for disseminating research. Researchers generally try to publish in high-quality scientific and scholarly journals, which are collections of scholarly papers published by academic or research organizations. Most journals have standards for acceptance that guarantee a certain level of quality for the research found between their covers. By and large the highest-quality research will be published in journals that have a peer-review process. Peer-reviewed journals send any submitted article out to knowledgeable researchers or scholars in the same field. The reviewers (usually a minimum of two) evaluate the manuscript in terms of the adequacy of overall writing, research methods, statistical analyses, and inferences drawn from the study.

Recognizing higher-quality journals becomes easier as you gain expertise in your chosen field. High-quality journals usually reject many more research studies than they publish, with some journals having rejection rates as high as 95 per cent. But the rejection rate is only one of a number of factors that experts in a field use to evaluate journals. Other factors include the

peer-reviewed journals Scholarly journals whose editors send any submitted article out to be evaluated by knowledgeable researchers or scholars in the same field.

journal's impact factor (a measure of how frequently articles in the journal are cited in a particular year), expertise of the journal editor and editorial board (these individuals choose reviewers and make decisions about what to publish in the journal), and the scope of the journal (does it target a narrow scientific or more general audience?). A research study published in a less-prestigious journal may signal that the researcher made a number of compromises, which made determining the validity of the conclusions difficult. For example, to keep the costs of conducting a research project within budget, a researcher may choose to have a relatively small number of participants or use a less-desirable method or technology for collecting the data. These choices may in turn lead the reviewers to question the strength of the conclusions that can be drawn from the research.

How Cognitive Biases and Heuristics Affect Your Judgment

Regardless of whether you are evaluating a newspaper report, website blurb, or journal article, it is important to realize that a number of factors influence the judgments and decisions that people make (Kahneman, 2011). These factors also influence you as you evaluate the validity of various claims and as you construct, design, and conduct your own research. These factors may also affect participants in your research studies as they respond to questions and situations that you have created. Daniel Kahneman and other researchers (Gilovich, Griffin, & Kahneman, 2002; Kahneman, Slovic, & Tversky, 1982) have outlined several of these factors, labelled cognitive biases and heuristics.

Cognitive biases are ways of thinking that push you to respond in a particular way in certain situations. Heuristics are mental shortcuts that often help us find adequate but less-than-perfect solutions to difficult problems. Sometimes these ways of thinking and simple procedures lead to highly effective problem solving, but at other times they yield surprisingly bad decisions. Many are related and operate in similar ways to influence how we process information and make decisions. It is worth noting that all of these cognitive biases and heuristics operate outside of our conscious control. Unfortunately, ample evidence suggests that an awareness and understanding of a particular bias or heuristic does not protect you from it (Kahneman, 2011). However, we argue that being conscious of these biases and heuristics can help you recognize when they might be active and counteract them with deliberate, conscious processes.

A variety of biases and heuristics can influence individuals evaluating and conducting research. One overarching framework for explaining these biases and heuristics is the cognitive miser model. This model refers to decision making where we attend to only a small amount of information, using as much prior information and experience as possible (Fiske & Taylor, 2013). Said another way, it suggests that individuals tend to avoid actively engaging with information to understand claims or solve problems unless they are particularly motivated to do so (i.e., they take the easy way out). Although the cognitive miser model can occasionally lead to appropriate decisions, you can easily imagine how not evaluating all of the information on a certain topic could lead to crucial errors. You can overcome this bias in your own research by reading the background literature as thoroughly as possible. The more you know about past research in an area, the less likely you will be to draw on a small amount of information in making important decisions.

The availability heuristic (Kahneman, 2011) describes how an individual overestimates the likelihood of an event that comes easily to mind, making it more difficult for a researcher to consider important any information that is not as prominent. For example, selective reporting by the media of dramatic yet relatively rare events, such as a child abduction, may lead us

cognitive bias An approach to thinking about a situation that may lead you to respond in a particular manner that may be flawed.

heuristic Mental shortcuts that assist people in finding adequate but often imperfect solutions to difficult problems.

cognitive miser model A cognitive bias that leads individuals to attend to only a small amount of information to preserve mental energy.

availability heuristic A cognitive process that leads individuals to overestimate the likelihood of events that come easily to mind.

discounting base-rate
information A
cognitive bias that leads
individuals to favour
anecdotal evidence over
more detailed
information that is
available.

to believe such events occur much more frequently than they actually do. A similar bias involves **discounting base-rate information** in favour of anecdotal evidence (Kahneman, 2011). This bias occurs when you make a decision, such as buying a new car, based on a friend's experience (good or bad) rather than on detailed source knowledge, as might be found in *Consumer Reports'* yearly evaluation of cars.

One of the most powerful and well-documented heuristics is **anchoring**, the tendency to use a particular value as the basis for estimating an unknown quantity, even if the starting value given is entirely arbitrary. In the original demonstration of this concept, Tversky and Kahneman (1974) asked students whether the percentage of African nations in the United Nations was larger or smaller than one of two given anchors: 10 per cent or 65 per cent. Students who saw the anchor of 10 per cent gave an average estimate of 25 per cent, whereas those who saw the anchor of 65 per cent gave an average estimate of 45 per cent.

anchoring A heuristic that leads individuals to use a particular value as a base for estimating an unknown quantity and adjust their estimate based on that quantity, even if the value given is entirely arbitrary.

Anchoring has been shown to have powerful effects in real-world contexts. For example, a study of real estate agents who were asked to assess the value of an actual house on the market showed that providing two different values for the asking price of the same house—even when accompanied with a range of other information—had a major impact on the realtors' estimates; those given the larger anchor had much higher estimates of the home's value, whereas those given the smaller anchor had much lower estimates. This occurred despite the realtors' belief that the asking price had not affected their self-reported estimates (Northcraft & Neale, 1987). From a research perspective, being aware of the anchoring heuristic can help you design and construct better survey or interview questions. Similarly, knowing about this heuristic can help you evaluate whether the results in someone else's research may have been influenced by this approach.

Framing is a similar bias that can influence respondents who are answering questions on a survey or interview. This bias is caused by the manner in which a question is "framed," or worded. **Framing effects** occur when what might be thought of as inconsequential changes in the wording in a question influence the decision a respondent makes (Kahneman, 2011). For example, a patient may be more likely to agree to a particular medical procedure when it is framed as having an 85 per cent chance of success than when it is presented as having a 15 per cent chance of failure. There has been considerable focus on the impact of framing a choice in terms of a positive (a gain frame) or negative (a loss frame) perspective in the fields of social psychology (e.g., Higgins, 2000), medicine (e.g., Armstrong, Schwartz, Fitzgerald, Putt, & Ubel, 2002), and economics (e.g., Kahneman & Tversky, 1979).

framing effect A
cognitive bias caused
by seemingly
inconsequential
differences in wording in
a question or problem
that lead respondents to
vary their choices.

As another example of the framing effect, consider the two survey questions in Table 1.1. The way in which the response options are presented in these two versions of the question could result in different patterns of responding among individuals merely because of the way in which the response options are framed. When constructing surveys, or even the next time you fill out a survey, pay attention to how the questions are being framed and how that could impact your responses.

Table 1.1   Example of the framing effect in a survey question.

Example 1: How many hours per week do you watch TV?

0 hours	1–2 hours	3–4 hours	5 or more hours

Example 2: How many hours per week do you watch TV?

0 hours	1–9 hours	10–19 hours	20 or more hours

Two other notable cognitive biases are the tendency to infer causality from randomly correlated events and to perceive order in random events. We refer to these two effects more generally as the causality bias (Rosengren & French, 2013), or the tendency to assume that two events are causally related because of proximity of time and place, when in fact no such causal relation is present. A number of fascinating websites document many meaningless correlations, including http://tylervigen.com. This site, developed by Harvard student Tyler Vigen, reports that the divorce rate in Maine is highly correlated with the US per-capita consumption of margarine and that the US per-capita consumption of cheese is highly correlated with the number of people who have died becoming tangled in their bedsheets. Although the connections suggested by these correlations are likely coincidental, the website serves as a warning to researchers and consumers of research that just because a finding is statistically significant, it is not necessarily meaningful. Likewise, we should be careful about inferring causality from correlations.

One last bias worthy of noting is confirmation bias, which is the tendency to give the most weight to information that supports your claim or viewpoint, potentially discounting or ignoring information that goes against your viewpoint. An example of this problem is captured in Tim O'Brien's cartoon depicting a researcher who has just blown up his laboratory equipment (see Figure 1.2). Even though his experiment clearly failed, he justifies the outcome, saying, "I totally meant to do that." In this case, the existing view could be that the researcher is a highly skilled, competent chemist, and the only way the information (the explosion) can

> causality bias The tendency to assume that two events are causally related because of proximity of time and place, when in fact no such causal relation exists.

> confirmation bias The tendency to give the most weight to information that supports your theory, potentially discounting or ignoring data that go against your strongly held theoretical bias.

"I totally meant to do that."

FIGURE 1.2   Tim O'Brien cartoon showing confirmation bias in interpretation of data.

support that viewpoint is if this outcome is interpreted as intentional. Confirmation bias illustrates the importance of thinking about your own biases (both common sense and scientific) and how these biases might influence (in positive and negative ways) the design of your research studies, how you interpret your results, and especially how you handle information that goes against your viewpoint. As new researchers, it is important to keep this bias in mind when researching a topic or question that you plan to study so that you do not just look for research evidence that supports your hypothesis. You should also look for evidence that may contradict your hypothesis. If you can then successfully discredit this conflicting evidence (e.g., identify flaws in the research design), it will make your argument in support of your hypothesis that much stronger.

This discussion of cognitive biases and heuristics should not lead you to conclude that your own judgments are always flawed or incorrect. Rather, we hope this serves as a cautionary tale, an antidote to the cliché that you should always "follow your gut." Even highly experienced researchers can fall prey to biases and heuristics. We argue that a background knowledge of cognitive biases and heuristics can make individuals better consumers of knowledge and better researchers, regardless of their field of study. Ultimately, in the same way that we encourage you to be skeptical of reports that you encounter in the popular media, you should be equally skeptical of your own quick judgments and evaluations.

Conducting Your Own Research to Evaluate Claims

We believe that conducting your own research is the best way to gain a more sophisticated understanding of research and the potential problems associated with a particular research study. When you attempt to do research on your own, you become acutely aware of practical issues that may lead to a flawed research process.

Researchers must compromise on issues involving participant selection or experimental design because of a number of different constraints, which can include a lack of resources, difficulty in obtaining the desired population, or concerns with the safety and confidentiality of participants. For these and other reasons, no research study is perfect. Therefore, a knowledgeable researcher or consumer of research must learn to evaluate whether the limitations in the study make it difficult to draw reasonable conclusions from the data. In some cases, flaws in the research may render conclusions provided by the researchers questionable. But in most cases, issues with the way a research study is designed and carried out may mean only that the results should not be generalized much beyond the context of the original study. Much of the rest of this book is devoted to teaching you how to design and conduct your own research project. Yet, even if you do not go on to conduct research yourself, the material in this book should help you become an educated consumer of research.

DISTINCTION BETWEEN SCIENCE AND PSEUDOSCIENCE

pseudoscience
Practices, beliefs, or claims that are presented as scientific but do not have a scientific basis or empirical support.

Many scientists like to think that the boundary between science and **pseudoscience**—practices, beliefs, or claims that are presented as scientific but actually have no scientific basis or empirical support—is clear-cut and that these two approaches to inquiry are easy to identify. However, this is not always the case. An example of a claim based on pseudoscience that at first appeared scientific was subliminal advertising and the claim that buying behaviour could be influenced through receiving visual or auditory information that is below our level of conscious perception. Through the use of the scientific approach, including the overall goals of science and the scientific method, pseudoscientific claims such as this can be distinguished from true science; often because when put to the test, pseudoscientific claims fail to demonstrate scientific evidence in support of their claim (such as subliminal advertising) or they are unable to be tested scientifically through the scientific method.

The Goals of Science

The goals of science can be placed into three broad categories: to describe, to explain, and to predict. Consider how these goals apply to the health benefits of coffee mentioned previously:

- *Description.* What happens when we look at death rates between individuals who regularly consume coffee and those who abstain from coffee? We see that, on average, people who drank coffee had longer lifespans. With this goal, we are only interested in identifying or describing the relationship or effect that we see.
- *Explanation.* Why do people who drink coffee have longer lifespans than those who do not drink coffee? With this goal, we want to go beyond just describing what we see and attempt to provide a reason to explain the relationship or effect. Could it be that the antioxidants that are found in coffee are what leads to greater longevity?
- *Prediction.* What do we predict would happen if we were to consume other foods that had the same levels of antioxidants that are found in coffee? Could this also lead to greater longevity? With this goal, if we know there is a relationship between two variables, we can use this to predict certain outcomes in new samples (we would expect that if we collected coffee consumption habits in a new sample of individuals, those drinking coffee would also tend to live longer) or in new contexts (predicting that the consumption of other foods that have antioxidants would also lead to greater longevity).

These three goals—to describe, explain, and predict—interact in complex ways. For example, we use descriptions and explanations to help us make predictions, and we use explanations and predictions to help us design studies that allow for novel descriptions. In many ways, these goals set science apart from pseudoscience, but more importantly, the characteristics of the scientific method differentiate these two approaches.

The Scientific Method

Good science differs from pseudoscience in its use of a strict set of principles referred to as the scientific method. This approach requires that research be objective, consistent (or reliable), conducted in a public manner, and based on established procedures and past knowledge.

Objective. The first key aspect of the scientific method is its emphasis on objectivity. From a research perspective, objectivity refers to the idea that researchers strive for the truth rather than attempt to find results that support their own beliefs or theory. Pseudoscience often comes disguised as science. For example, wearable magnets, such as in bracelets or rings, are worn for their expected ability to alleviate pain and other health concerns. The idea behind static magnetic field therapy is that the molecules within our bodies have small amounts of magnetic

scientific method An approach that seeks to generate explanations for observable phenomena with an emphasis on objectivity and verifiable evidence.

objectivity Approaching knowledge as a quest for the truth, rather than as an attempt to find results that support one's own beliefs or theory.

energy in them and certain health problems happen because these magnetic fields are out of balance. Having a magnet placed on one's skin is believed to correct this imbalance and improve health (Wheeler, 2017). However, research testing the efficacy of magnetic bracelets has generally not found support for these claims (e.g., Szabo, Szemerszky, Dömötör, Gresits, & Köteles, 2017). Yet these alternative therapy bracelets have been worn by professional athletes and celebrities who have endorsed their healing benefits (Weathers, 2015).

The ideal of objectivity requires that research be conducted in a way that produces unbiased results. Objectivity is most easily understood when contrasted with subjectivity, which stems from an individual's own beliefs, experiences, and interpretations. In science, researchers try hard to be objective and not allow their own beliefs, emotions, or biases to interfere with the pursuit of greater knowledge. Although complete objectivity is impossible, the research enterprise should be driven as much as possible by data rather than your own biases. For example, testimonial evidence (particularly from celebrities) should send up a red flag.

In lieu of valid empirical evidence, a company may resort to high-profile anecdotes in hopes of persuading consumers of their pseudoscientific claims. As the cognitive psychologist Keith Stanovich (2012) argues, testimonials are incredibly persuasive but also harmful to society, leading to investments of time and resources in disreputable products and ideas. Stanovich notes that claims from such vivid testimonial evidence can overwhelm people's weighting of solid, scientifically grounded data.

subjectivity
Approaching knowledge from the standpoint of an individual's own beliefs, experiences, and interpretations.

Consistent.   A second key aspect of the scientific method involves reliability, which refers to the idea that an investigation should yield consistent findings if researchers use the same procedures and methods again and again. Ideally, it is important to determine whether research can be replicated within a research group, as well as across independent research teams. If a result is obtained only by a single researcher or single research team working in one laboratory—and cannot be confirmed by other, independent laboratories—then there is reason for skepticism. Often the difference between pseudoscience and science comes down to the fact that science, if performed correctly, yields results that can be replicated widely, whereas pseudoscience is more likely to yield results that are not replicable.

reliability The idea that an investigation or measurement tool should yield consistent findings if researchers use the same procedures and methods repeatedly.

Public.   The third important characteristic about science is that it exists in the public realm. Results from experiments and investigations are discussed within laboratory groups, presented at national and international conferences, and published in journals. Many of these journals (including many online ones) employ rigorous procedures to evaluate the importance of the research, the quality of the research methods, and the validity of any claims made by researchers.

Even after an article has been published, other researchers will often attempt to replicate the study or question the methods used or the validity of interpretations drawn from the data. In many ways, the scientific approach involves a relatively constant stream of evaluation and criticism. Pseudoscientific claims will often not be open for public discussion, and the methods used (and even the actual data) may not be provided for scrutiny and evaluation in a public way.

Based on Established Principles and Past Knowledge.   A fourth aspect that separates science from pseudoscience is the central role of explanation in science. That is, the explanation given for a phenomenon must be based on established principles and past knowledge. In contrast, pseudoscientific claims often provide explanations that are not testable or are based on an individual's claims that cannot be supported by actual data and rigorous testing. Often individuals promoting pseudoscience ask the consumer to "believe" them and their story. For example, when professional athletes or celebrities endorse products (such as magnetic bracelets) they ask consumers to blindly trust their personal opinion about the health properties of the bracelets and to buy the bracelets.

In summary, science seeks to accurately describe phenomena in the world, to provide a rational explanation for these phenomena, and to use the information gained through research to make predictions about future events or situations. Good science is grounded in skepticism, acknowledges the limitations of methods and interpretations, and asks both the general public and the scientific community to examine the data, evaluate the research, replicate the findings, and ultimately judge the validity of the claims.

DISTINCTION BETWEEN APPLIED AND BASIC RESEARCH

Scholars and researchers often make the distinction between applied and basic research. Applied research generally seeks to address a practical issue or problem. This type of research is thought to have more immediate value because it focuses on real-world problems and attempts to find specific solutions to those problems. Research designed to make solar energy panels more efficient and economical is one example of applied research. Within psychology, investigations into the efficacy of a particular kind of behavioural intervention for children with attention-deficit hyperactivity disorder would be an example of applied research.

Basic research strives to advance knowledge within a particular area of science. Basic research may focus on testing a particular theory or the exploration of a particular phenomenon. An example of basic research within psychology would be investigating the process of language acquisition: How do humans acquire the capacity to perceive, understand, and use language to communicate? The goal of this research is to simply increase the amount of knowledge on this topic and not to actually come up with a practical solution to a problem.

The line between applied and basic research is not always clear and straightforward. Applied research often fails to find solutions to vexing problems, and basic research often yields findings that solve long-standing practical problems. Both kinds of research can provide real value to society. For example, basic psychological research on judgment and decision making has led researchers to rethink applied problems in education ("Why don't students understand evolution?"), medicine ("Why don't people do what their doctors tell them to do?"), and economics ("Why do people buy lottery tickets?"). Stanovich (2012) argues that it is a mistake to view the distinction between applied and basic research solely in terms of whether the research has practical applications. He suggests that the distinction is mainly one of time: "Applied findings are of use immediately . . . However, there is nothing so practical as a general and accurate theory" (p. 110).

THE RESEARCH PROCESS AND ORGANIZATION OF THIS BOOK

Figure 1.3 provides an overview of the research process and also, for the most part, the organization of this book. Note that the flowchart presents arrows going down the centre to illustrate the most efficient pathway from the start of a research project to final write-up. However, virtually no research project follows this pathway. Rather, most projects involve a highly iterative

applied research
Research that generally seeks to address a practical issue or problem.

basic research
Research that strives to advance knowledge within a particular area of science.

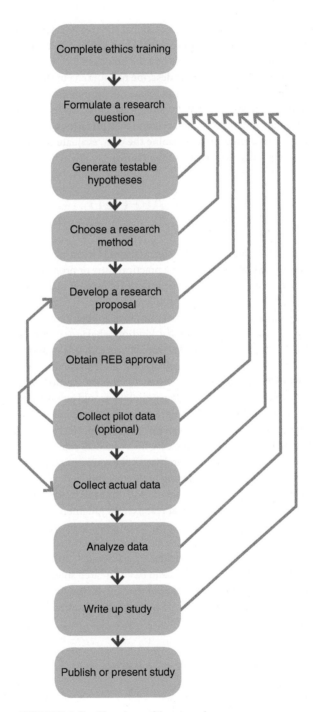

FIGURE 1.3   Flowchart of the research process.

process captured by the arrows that circle back up the chart. These arrows are meant to convey the idea that as researchers progress through the research process, questions and issues pop up that cause them to reconsider previous plans. These questions and issues can lead to a reformulation of the original research question or a change in the overall research design or procedures.

We emphasize that the research process is open and non-linear, with many different choices that can alter the focus or direction of the project. Each of these steps also requires a set of choices and tasks that we will describe in the chapters to come. In our view, the first step of the research process involves ethics training. Chapter 2 addresses ethical issues and aspects of ethics training, as well as the often disturbing history of research that has led to our current ethical standards. Chapter 3 leads you through the process of choosing an area of research and formulating a research question. Chapter 4 explains how to generate a testable hypothesis, identify variables of interest, and begin to design an experiment. Chapter 5 discusses developing your research proposal, in particular how to obtain a sample, choose measures, conduct a power analysis, and formulate an analysis plan.

Chapter 6 addresses the design and construction of interviews and surveys, which are becoming increasingly popular with the advent of online technology. Chapter 7 focuses on experimental designs, which are widely considered the gold standard for scientific inquiry. Chapter 8 covers variations on standard experimental designs, including quasi-experimental, factorial, and single-case approaches. Chapter 9 presents the major types of non-experimental designs—meaning designs that do not apply an experimental control, such as observation, case studies, archival research, and meta-analysis. Chapter 10 explores research over age and time, which examines developmental changes that take place over study participants' lifespans. Chapters 11 and 12 lead you through the process of analyzing and interpreting your raw data and drawing appropriate conclusions through the use of statistics. Finally, Chapter 13 describes how to accurately report your results in a clear, readable article or poster format and to identify your target audience.

Two additional chapters are available online. Chapter 14 offers tips on presenting your research to the wider scientific community at conferences and in the pages of scholarly journals, while Chapter 15 introduces basic methods and techniques in neuroscience, an area of research with increasing prominence in psychology and related fields.

PRACTICAL TIPS

Practical Tips for Research Methods

1. Be an educated and critical consumer of research reports wherever you encounter them.

2. Learn how to evaluate sources of information.

3. Do not trust a single source—look for converging information from a variety of sources.

4. Realize that cognitive biases and heuristics influence researchers, participants, and you.

CHAPTER SUMMARY

Through our analysis of sample media reports, it should be apparent that knowledge of research methods is invaluable to vetting the barrage of research findings that confront people daily. Strategies such as identifying the researchers, their funding, and their motives, as well as reading and evaluating past research, should help you determine what findings are reliable and which are not. Remember, every reported research finding requires a critical eye. Knowledge of research methods will also provide a template for conducting your own research, a subject we delve into in later chapters.

End-of-Chapter Exercises

1. You recently came across a news article entitled "Weekend Warrior? Your Two-Day Exercise Is Just as Good to Reap Health Benefits: Study" (see Chai, 2017). How could you assess the accuracy of this claim?
2. Find a news article or media claim on a topic of interest to you. Discuss whether this article/claim appears to be based on science or pseudoscience. What kinds of features should you look for?
3. Researchers from Cornell University and University of Jena in Germany conducted a study that appeared in the journal *Environment and Behavior* in December 2015. Results showed that diners ordered significantly more items, including alcoholic beverages, when served by wait staff with a high body mass index compared with wait staff with a low body mass index. Several news outlets, including the *Wall Street Journal* and *USA Today*, ran stories on the study. Do you think

the findings are noteworthy or valid? Why or why not? What bias might the researchers suffer from?
4. Although researchers have shown that there is no evidence to support Andrew Wakefield's claim that the measles, mumps, and rubella vaccine leads to autism, the belief that it does remains strong. What biases and heuristics might influence the continued belief that vaccines cause autism? How might you as a researcher or scientific writer counteract those beliefs?
5. As we discussed in this chapter, it is important to obtain converging evidence to support research claims. Why might people so often avoid doing just that? Why do we prefer the one-off study to looking critically at scientific claims?
6. In addition to learning about how to conduct a research study, how else could learning about research methods be beneficial?

Key Terms

anchoring, p. 12
applied research, p. 17
availability heuristic, p. 11
basic research, p. 17
causality bias, p. 13
cognitive bias, p. 11
cognitive miser model, p. 11
confirmation bias, p. 13

converging evidence, p. 5
discounting base-rate information, p. 12
framing effect, p. 12
heuristic, p. 11
objectivity, p. 15
peer-reviewed journals, p. 10
primary source, p. 7

pseudoscience, p. 14
reliability, p. 16
replication, p. 9
scientific method, p. 15
secondary source, p. 7
skepticism, p. 6
subjectivity, p. 16

Conducting Ethical Research

2

Chapter Contents

INSIDE RESEARCH: Chris Lovato

Have you ever wondered why people do what they do? Why they make certain choices—both good and bad? What motivates their actions? Growing up, I was fascinated by psychology and read my father's old college psych textbooks over and over again. As an undergraduate psychology major, my goal was to become a clinical psychologist because I wanted to help people be the best they could be.

After entering graduate school, I discovered that I had a passion for health behaviour research, particularly applied research in real-world settings. I wanted to study the ways in which we can support positive health behaviours in settings such as schools, worksites, and communities. I pursued this interest both through my course work, a specialization in program evaluation, and working as a research assistant.

Professor, School of Population and Public Health, University of British Columbia

continued

After finishing my doctorate in educational psychology, I joined a research centre at the University of Texas Health Science Center in Houston. As a research associate, I worked with senior faculty on a range of school, worksite, and community health promotion programs and developed my own program of intervention research in tobacco control. I was later recruited to San Diego State University where I was director of Student Health Promotion, Student Health Services, and a faculty member in the School of Public Health. While in that position I conducted research in the areas of tobacco control, sexually transmitted infections, and skin cancer. All of this fostered a new interest in health promotion in college populations.

After five years in this position, cupid's arrow struck—I met the love of my life and left my faculty position. I moved to Vancouver, British Columbia, where I joined a research centre as a visiting scholar. Although it was difficult for me to be without a permanent position, it was an experience that confirmed the passion I have for being a researcher. During that time of being a "non-paid employee," I felt no different about my work. I continued to conduct unfunded research, write research papers, study, and be involved in scholarly activities. After two years, I applied for and was appointed as faculty in the School of Population Health where I am now located and enjoying my work as a researcher and teacher of program evaluation.

My current research focuses on evaluating the impact of health programs and policies, particularly in the areas of health promotion and health services. I am currently conducting a study that is assessing the effectiveness of interventions to enhance physician engagement in the workplace. I am also a collaborator on three health promotion studies.

Chris Lovato has combined her interests in public health, psychology, education, and program evaluation to investigate the effectiveness of interventions designed to change behaviours at the individual, organizational, and community levels. She uses both quantitative and qualitative methods in her research. She is recognized for her work on evaluating public health and health service programs.

Research Focus: Public health, health promotion, behaviour change

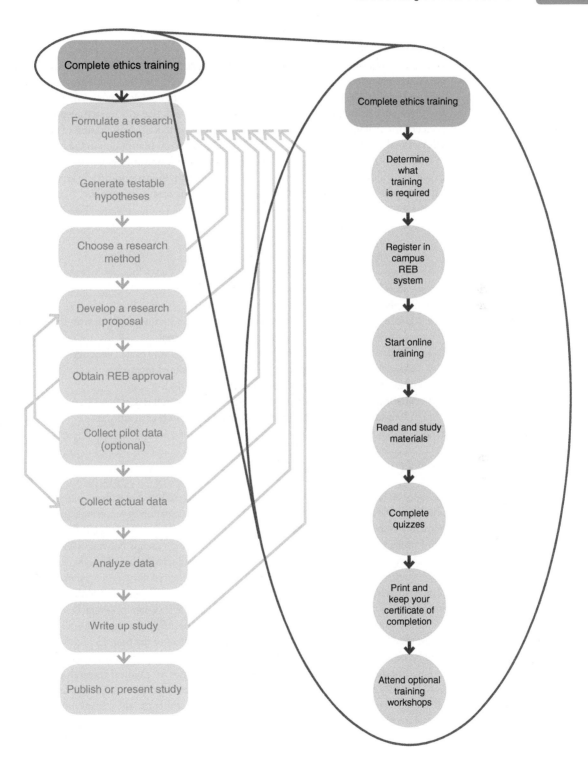

Chapter Abstract

In this chapter, we provide some historical context for the evolution of ethical standards in social science research, introduce the basic ethical framework that guides research in psychology, and explain the function and role of research ethics boards (REBs). We present, in detail, the three core principles that guide ethical research practice in Canada: respect for persons, concern for welfare, and justice. We end the chapter with a brief discussion of ethical research with animals. This chapter provides the foundation for our instruction in the research process. We believe that ethical principles are central to the conduct of good scientific research in psychology and that researchers must have a thorough understanding and knowledge of ethical principles *before* beginning any other aspects of the research process.

LEARNING OBJECTIVES

By the end of this chapter, you should be able to:

- Explain the purpose of research ethics.
- Discuss the three core ethical principles for conducting research with human participants, as stated in the Tri-Council Policy Statement.
- Explain the role of informed consent, including some of its challenges.
- Describe some of the potential benefits and risks of research.
- Describe the role of research ethics boards (REBs).
- Distinguish between the three categories of research risk.
- Describe the "Three Rs" that guide ethical research with animals.

HISTORY OF ETHICS

In 1946, an international military tribunal was conducted in Nuremberg, Germany, where 23 physicians and scientists stood trial for their willing participation in war crimes and crimes against humanity before and during World War II. They were accused of inflicting a range of horrific and lethal procedures on prisoners being held in concentration camps between 1933 and 1945. The medical experiments these physicians and scientists conducted included freezing experiments; malaria experiments; mustard gas experiments; bone, muscle, and nerve regeneration and bone transplantation; sterilization experiments; typhus experiments; and incendiary bomb experiments. More specifically, some prisoners were forced to stand in tanks of ice water for several hours to research the prevention and treatment of hypothermia, while other healthy prisoners were infected with malaria to test the effectiveness of various drugs. At the conclusion of the trial, 15 of the defendants were found guilty; seven were given the death penalty, and eight were imprisoned (Leaning, 1996).

Up until this point, there were virtually no guidelines for medical research or experimentation. Doctors and researchers relied on informal professional codes of conduct and personal ideas about right and wrong. However, after the Nuremberg trials, ethical standards were put into place in response to these abuses of research participants by doctors and scientists. Subsequently, a statement was put forth that outlined the duties and responsibilities involved in conducting research on human participants; most notably, participants must be competent, have full knowledge of the research, and have freely volunteered to participate in the research. This statement is known as the Nuremberg Code.

FIGURE 2.1   Main defendants at the Nuremberg trials. Front from left: Rudolf Hess, Joachim von Ribbentrop, Hermann Goering, and Wilhelm Keitel.

The Nuremberg Code of 1947

The Nuremberg Code of 1947 comprised 10 standards that guided ethical research involving human beings. The first standard asserted that participants must not only consent to participate in the experiment, but also have the legal capacity to give consent. For instance, prisoners, minors, and people with intellectual disabilities could not participate in experiments. This resulted in the seemingly common sense principles of respect for persons, beneficence, and justice informing the 10 standards of the code and the ensuing three core principles that guide Canadian research ethics (Unger, 2011).

> **Nuremberg Code of 1947** A group of 10 standards that guide ethical research involving human beings.

The Declaration of Helsinki

The horrific and cruel experiments conducted in the name of science during World War II led to a proactive investigation of practices worldwide. As a result, the World Medical Association produced an ethics statement on human experimentation in 1964 known as the Declaration of Helsinki. The declaration broadened the Nuremberg Code guidelines, stating "It is the mission of the doctor to safeguard the health of the people." The document also made an important distinction between therapeutic and non-therapeutic clinical studies—in other words, research conducted to help sick patients versus experiments performed for purely scientific goals—and created rules governing both types of endeavours (Katz, 1972).

> **Declaration of Helsinki** Formalized in 1964, this international proclamation broadened the Nuremberg Code guidelines from 1947, stating "It is the mission of the doctor to safeguard the health of the people."

Tri-Council Policy Statement

In 1998, Canada's three key federal funding agencies—the Canadian Institutes of Health Research (CIHR), the National Sciences and Engineering Research Council of Canada (NSERC), and the Social Sciences and Humanities Research Council of Canada (SSHRC)—jointly produced the Tri-Council Policy Statement: Ethical Conduct for Research Involving Humans (TCPS) to guide the ethical conduct of research involving human participants (CIHR, NSERC, & SSHRC, 2018). This document outlines the three core principles that guide research conducted in Canada:

- *Respect for persons*, which dictates that researchers protect the autonomy of participants, obtain their informed consent, and treat them with courtesy
- *Concern for welfare*, which reinforces researchers' obligation to do no harm and at the same time maximize the study's potential benefits
- *Justice*, which calls for the fair administration of carefully considered procedures and non-exploitive selection of participants so that people of all races, ethnicities, and incomes can benefit from research and share in its burdens

The TCPS, which was revised in 2010 and then again in 2014 and 2018, and is now referred to as the *TCPS 2*, aims to provide guidance on how researchers can conduct research that upholds these core principles. Actually putting these principles into practice can, at times, be challenging, and the interpretation of the nuances of the principles are sometimes open to debate.

RESPECT FOR PERSONS

The principle of respect for persons implies that individuals who participate in research should be making a voluntary and informed decision as to their participation. This means that potential participants should understand the purpose of the research and any risks or benefits to their participation, as fully as reasonably possible. This is achieved through the process of informed consent.

Consent forms should be written in clear language that is appropriate for the age or reading level of your participants. This form is required to include the following information:

- Invitation to participants to participate in research
- Evidence that participation is voluntary
- Description of what participants will be asked to do
- Assurance that participants' responses and personal information will be kept confidential after they are collected
- Risks and benefits to the participants
- Costs to participants or payments expected
- Alternatives, if any, to participation
- A place for participants' and researchers' signatures

Researchers normally handle the issue of confidentiality by collecting data anonymously or by removing identifying information from the participants' data (resulting in deidentified data), storing data on a password-protected computer or in a locked file cabinet, and allowing access only to research team members. It is also best to store any information that connects participants to their data in a separate location, such as a password-protected file or a separate locked file cabinet.

Participant Coercion

In recruiting participants, researchers must pay special attention to the potential for coercion—the act of taking away someone's voluntary choice to participate through either negative or positive means. Coercion presents an interesting challenge to the principle of respect for persons because it can slip by undetected. General agreement exists that participation in research should always be voluntary, but what about the seemingly harmless case in which a researcher who is teaching a class wants to recruit from students within the course? (This is a common occurrence in a university setting.) The coercive element is that students may feel compelled to participate in the research as a requirement to do well in the class or to please their professor—even if they are given assurances to the contrary.

Consequently, researchers typically build a "firewall" between themselves and potential participants so that they do not know, for example, which students choose or refuse to participate (i.e., the students' identities are kept anonymous). Often instructors will ask a colleague who is not teaching the course, or a research assistant, to request the students' participation and collect the actual data, which are then deidentified.

The compensation of participants presents another potentially coercive situation. More researchers are paying people to complete surveys, participate in interviews, or take part in experiments. Researchers believe that this approach improves participant recruitment, helps recruit a more diverse sample, leads participants to take their participation more seriously, and assists with participant retention in studies with multiple sessions. However, data on this issue are not entirely clear. One reason is that potential benefits of incentives can interact in complex ways with particular research questions. From an ethical perspective, compensation should correspond to what is being asked of participants. If the compensation is "too good to refuse," then prospective participants might feel they cannot possibly turn down the study. For example, a $50 payment for a 10-minute survey would likely fall into this category.

So how should you decide whether to pay your participants? And, if you do decide to pay participants, what is the right amount? Luckily, many other researchers have already addressed this issue. Look for related research in your area that has already been published; check the methods section for whether the researchers paid their participants and, if so, how much. You can also ask your instructor or call your local research ethics board representatives and ask them for advice, because they have likely encountered similar questions.

One final case of coercion involves the recruitment of patients/participants by the same individuals who are conducting the research. For example, is it ethical for doctors to recruit their own patients to participate in research that drug companies are paying the doctors to conduct? Many physicians see no problem with this, arguing that it is both common practice and the only way to recruit the right sample of participants. In fact, recruitment of patients has become a relatively common practice among clinical psychologists. Yet many other behavioural scientists see this as potentially coercive or a conflict of interest because researchers are often in positions of authority over people they are trying to recruit. In these situations, chances that participants could give completely voluntary, informed consent are slim. In the field of psychology, this most often comes up in psychotherapy outcome research. As with recruiting students in a class, the underlying concern is that patients might feel obligated to participate as a condition of the treatment or to please their therapist. Again, the best safeguard is to create a firewall so that someone other than the treating psychologist requests participation and protects the identity of participants, as well as those who choose not to

coercion The act of taking away someone's voluntary choice to participate through either negative or positive means.

participate. In some cases, this can be a greater challenge than in a classroom study because of the particular requirements surrounding confidentiality for patients.

Special Populations

Working with special populations can also create unique ethical challenges for researchers trying to uphold the principle of respect for persons. We will briefly consider three categories—prisoners/detainees, children, and Indigenous people—to provide insight into the ethical issues related to conducting research with these groups.

Prisoners.   Research with prisoners poses obvious ethical challenges; given the prisoner's state of incarceration, it is even more critical to ensure that any decisions to participate in research are truly voluntary. The *TCPS2* only provides limited guidance on research with this population, and current policies and practices vary across provinces (Silva, Matheson, & Lavery, 2017). The two key issues regarding prisoners centre on unequal power relationships and its impact on voluntary participation, and challenges in protecting the confidentiality of prisoners who participate in research (Silva et al., 2017).

Children.   Also discussed within the *TCPS2*, research with children presents both legal and developmental issues that interface with ethical concerns. From a legal standpoint, a minor cannot provide consent to participate in research. As a result, the consent process in research with children takes on an additional layer: a parent or legal guardian must provide the legal *consent* for participation, and the child must provide *assent* to participate (i.e., they must still agree to take part in the study). If a child is too young or for any reason has trouble understanding and responding to verbal or written information (e.g., the child is an infant or has some disability), only parental consent is required.

From a developmental standpoint, child assent must be acquired with language and techniques that are understandable and appropriate for the child's age. With preschool-age children, assent is typically acquired verbally, but with older children and adolescents, assent often resembles the formal, written consent process. In research with children, both the legal consent *and* the child's assent must be obtained to move forward. In narrow circumstances, a waiver of parental consent may be allowed—but only when circumstances make it evident that obtaining such consent is impossible (e.g., in the case of child neglect or abuse) and researchers have made assurances of protection for the child participants.

Indigenous People.   In applying the three core principles from the *TCPS2* when working with Indigenous people, there is a greater emphasis on the principle of concern for welfare and, in particular, capitalizing on the benefits of the research for the Indigenous community more broadly. Researchers need to seek engagement with the community and relevant service organizations to discuss the level of community involvement in the research in the form of a research agreement—and even whether it is appropriate to conduct the research in question, particularly if the community or group does not directly involve knowledge-bearers in the community. Researchers also need to be aware of, and respect, relevant customs and codes of practice among Indigenous peoples, such as their custom to pass on cultural knowledge through oral histories rather than written histories. Further, researchers need to be aware of limitations of what knowledge can be shared publicly and who owns the data once it has been collected. These discussions must occur before the

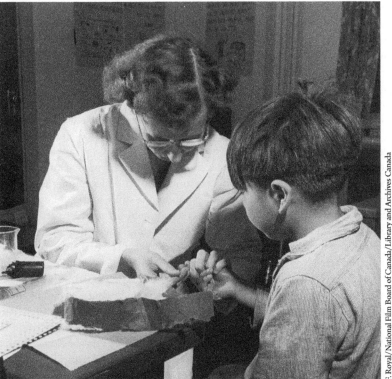

F. Royal/National Film Board of Canada/Library and Archives Canada

FIGURE 2.2   A nurse takes a blood sample from a child at the Alberni Indian Residential School in 1948, one of six residential schools where the Canadian government performed nutritional experiments on Indigenous children without their knowledge or consent (Mosby, 2013). How has Canada's history of unethical experimentation influenced the principles of the *TCPS2*?

research is conducted and be documented within the research agreement. In some cases, it could be inappropriate to use a formal written consent procedure with Indigenous individuals, and the *TCPS 2* does allow for this flexibility regarding cultural customs.

Deception

The use of deception in research continues to be one of the most controversial and lively areas of discussion for research ethics boards and ethicists. Deception is generally categorized as being either moderate or mild, with the requirement that more moderate forms of deception include a thorough debriefing at the conclusion of the study. Deception usually takes one of two forms: **active deception**, in which participants are given false information, and **passive deception**, in which some details of a study are withheld. Whether active or passive, deception is only considered justifiable by the significance of the research—the question being answered must be important enough to allow for the temporary breach of ethics.

Beyond the cost–benefit analysis of the research's importance, deception is viewed as justifiable only if a researcher can demonstrate that no other methods are available to study the given topic. For example, Claude Steele and Joshua Aronson (1995) performed a groundbreaking

active deception The giving of false information to study participants.

passive deception The withholding of some study details from participants.

stereotype threat The activation of a negative belief about a particular group that influences members of that group to underperform in certain situations.

priming The presentation of cues to push thinking in a certain direction.

debrief To give participants study information that was initially withheld and the reasons why the information was withheld.

demonstration of the concept of stereotype threat—the activation of a negative belief about a particular group that influences members of that group to underperform in certain situations. These researchers found that black Americans underperformed on the verbal portion of the Graduate Record Examination (GRE) compared to a sample of white peers when they were primed—given cues that push their thinking in a certain direction—before taking the test that their racial group tends to do poorly on such exams. In this study, it was important that participants did not know they were being primed. The priming is only effective if it is done covertly—that is, deception is necessary. It is hard to envision any other way to study this phenomenon, because if participants knew about the priming, the study would undoubtedly lose its effectiveness.

At the conclusion of a study, researchers should debrief their participants. Debriefing involves explaining the purpose of the study, explaining the use of deception (if any), providing an opportunity for participants to ask questions about the study, and enabling the researcher to address any harm to the participant that may have resulted from their participation in the study. As noted by Harris (1988), "the purpose of debriefing is to remove any misconceptions and anxieties that the participants have about the research and leave them with a sense of dignity, knowledge, and a perception of time not wasted." Debriefing can either be conducted as a face-to-face interview with the participants, or if the study is straightforward or was conducted online, it may consist of a written summary of the study's purpose and hypotheses.

Any study that involves deception must be followed with a debriefing. These should be done as a face-to-face session so that participants can be given study information that was initially withheld and the reasons for doing so. Further, participants should be given the opportunity to ask questions and reconfirm their consent now that the true purpose of the study and the reason for the deception has been revealed. In some cases, a funnel debriefing may be used in which the researcher will ask a series of questions about the study, starting broad and getting more specific, to identify whether the participant had any suspicions about the true nature of the study prior to revealing and discussing the deception.

funnel debriefing During the debriefing session, the researcher asks the participant a series of questions, starting broad and getting more specific, to identify if the participant had any suspicions about the true nature of the study.

CONCERN FOR WELFARE

The principle of concern for welfare relates to the consideration of a person's quality of life and the impact that research may have on a person's physical, mental, economic, and social circumstances. When planning a research study, researchers need to identify the potential risks and benefits to participants. The benefits are then weighed against the risks in a risk–benefit analysis. The aim is to maximize the benefits while minimizing the risks, including taking steps to ensure that participants are not exposed to unnecessary risks. Although it can be challenging trying to balance the risks, which are more immediate and measurable, with benefits, which could be only potential benefits that occur in the future, this analysis is critical to the ethics of research. In considering the overall welfare of participants, the potential research outcomes and benefits must outweigh the risks.

risk–benefit analysis A comparison of the risks and benefits associated with a research study. It is used to determine whether the study is worth conducting or if the risks are too high.

Benefits for Participants and Society

Benefits of the research generally relate to direct benefits to the participant. However, there can also be potential benefits to society; for instance, the knowledge gained through the research may improve educational or medical practices. For instance, the Canadian Longitudinal Study on Aging was designed to explore the process of aging and the factors that play into successful aging (Raina et al., 2009), and thus has the potential to inform Canadian healthcare practice.

For participants, benefits can include material benefits, such as monetary payment, gift cards, entry into a raffle for a gift card or prize, or course credit. Other benefits include knowledge about the topic or research process in general or treatment for a health problem. At times participants themselves may receive no direct benefits from participating in research. This is fine, as long as the knowledge gained from the research is considered beneficial to society at large. In this case, consent forms may merely state "Although there are no direct benefits to individual participants, knowledge gained from this research will greatly enhance our knowledge of [ ]."

Research Risks

Potential research risks that can occur while participating in a study can include physical harm, psychological harm, social harm, economic harm, or legal harm.

- *Physical harm.* Risks that involve physical pain or discomfort, injury, or illness that occurs during the course of the research.
- *Psychological harm.* Risks that relate to the experience of mental distress during or after participation in a study. This can include feelings of stress, anxiety, worry, embarrassment, loss of self-esteem, and so on.
- *Social harm.* Risks that could impact a participant's relationship or standing within their community and may involve embarrassment, loss of respect, or stigmatization. A breach of confidentiality could potentially lead to such social risks, especially if the topic of the research was sensitive (e.g., mental health).
- *Economic harm.* Risks that involve any monetary cost to participants, such as the cost of travel, parking, childcare, and so on that could be incurred as a result of participation in the research.
- *Legal harm.* Risks that could involve criminal prosecution or civil lawsuit as a result of a participant disclosing illegal behaviours. Because researchers in psychology often study areas of human behaviour where they are likely to encounter illegal activities, the question of what to do if you discover such behaviours in the course of research is a thorny one. In many cases, the ability to study a particular topic (e.g., illicit drug use, underage drinking) depends on the assurance of participants' confidentiality or anonymity.

The truth is, *all research has risks.* Do not under- or overstate the risks in the consent form or application. For example, if your research requires hours of mind-numbingly boring responses on a keyboard, merely note "This research involves no more than minimal risk; there is no more risk than encountered in everyday life." Do not say, "This research involves no more than minimal risk; however, you may get bored, fall asleep, and hit your head on the keyboard."

JUSTICE

Justice signifies equitability and a sense of fairness. The principle of justice requires that research should fairly and equitably distribute the benefits and burdens of the research. This means that certain segments of the population, such as those who are disadvantaged or vulnerable, should not have to be unfairly burdened with the risks of research. It also means that benefits of research should be equally shared and promoted. The Indigenous Literary Studies Association, which was formed in 2013 at the University of British Columbia, represents a group of Indigenous and settler scholars who promote and celebrate Indigenous literature through an annual scholarly event (Samson, 2018). This association has helped emerging Indigenous writers and has raised awareness regarding the types of ethical issues that need to be adhered to in the researching and teaching of Indigenous literatures in Canada (e.g., issues around the ownership and interpretation of data).

WHY ETHICS MATTER

One useful way to think about ethics and research is that ethical conduct in research reflects the social responsibility that the researcher has to society at large. Ideas about social responsibility do change as a society's ethics evolve, however; for instance, child labour in Canada was once common, but now laws ban this practice. When researchers follow best practices from an ethical standpoint, they help maintain the relationship of trust between the researcher and society.

Practically speaking, ethics in psychology refers to adhering to the standards outlined in the *TCPS 2*. Many psychologists treat these standards as well established, when in truth they are not. As we discuss later in this chapter, examples of questionable ethical practices by researchers makes the maintenance of this trust all the more essential (see "Media Matters: David Reimer"). The onus for maintaining the bond of trust falls squarely on the shoulders of the researcher. But to fulfill this obligation, researchers must understand ethical standards and

MEDIA MATTERS

David Reimer

Of all the ethical violations in research throughout history, one of the cruelest is the case of David Reimer, an unwitting subject of one researcher's experiment gone very wrong. Reimer's treatment by an ambitious "expert" stands as a cautionary tale of what can happen when researchers care more about their theories than their participants.

Bruce Reimer and his twin brother, Brian, were born in 1965 to a young couple in Winnipeg and were, by all accounts, normal baby boys. At the age of eight months, they underwent circumcision at a nearby hospital. The doctor used an electrocautery needle instead of a scalpel and inadvertently burned off Bruce's penis (Colapinto, 2000); reconstructive surgery was not advanced enough at that time to restore it (Walker, 2004).

Janet and Ron Reimer visited several doctors, none of whom offered solutions. Distraught and unsure of where to turn, the Reimers saw by chance a television show featuring a researcher named Dr. John Money, a sexologist at Johns Hopkins University (BBC Horizon, 2005). Money was a pioneer in the new field of sex change surgery, and he appeared alongside a transgender woman.

"[Money] was very charismatic, seemed highly intelligent, and seemed very confident of what he was saying," Janet recalled. And I thought, 'Here's our answer, here's our salvation, here's our hope'" (BBC Horizon, 2005).

Janet wrote to Money explaining her son's condition, and he invited them to bring Bruce to his gender identity clinic in Baltimore. What Money didn't tell the Reimers was that he had long searched for such a case to prove his theory about "nurture over nature" in sexual identity (Colapinto, 2000). Money believed that gender was basically neutral for the first two years of life and that principles. Without this background, researchers cannot make ethically sound judgments in designing, implementing, analyzing, and disseminating their findings.

Ethics are not stable, universal principles; rather, they evolve over time and depend on the particular context in which the research is being conducted. Although some philosophers (e.g., Kant, Sartre) have argued that our actions should be guided by moral imperatives based on universal laws such as the Golden Rule (treat others as you would like to be treated), many others argue that ethics are socially mediated, not a universal code of conduct. Although the ethical principles outlined in this chapter are designed to provide a base for making ethical decisions, how these principles are interpreted and enforced varies from university to university, from community to community, from province to province, and from country to country. This variation makes cross-cultural research particularly challenging because what is or is not viewed as ethical may vary extensively across cultures. As an example, differences exist between Canada and the United States regarding the use of placebo controls and the types of research that can be conducted with children (Millum, 2012). In Canada, placebo trials cannot be conducted if there exists a treatment that is known to be effective, while in the United States such trials can be conducted. In regards to research with children, within Canada, this research is only permitted when it is considered minimal risk. Alternatively, research that is slightly above minimal risk can be conducted with children in the United States. These differences can potentially have an impact on what research topics are being studied and whether there can be collaborations across countries.

Part of being a good researcher is consciously thinking about the ethical aspects of your own research and design. Most researchers will say that, in general, you should not lie to participants in your research or to your colleagues or to the public in writing up your research, or that

environment could make a baby adopt either a male or a female sexual identity. The Reimers gave him the perfect experiment for his hypothesis, complete with the built-in matched control of Brian. Money proposed raising Bruce as a girl and giving him estrogen supplements. Money told the couple that they must never reveal the truth to their children or the experiment would fail. They agreed and renamed Bruce as Brenda (Colapinto, 2004).

Money's hypothesis soon turned out to be flawed, although Janet followed his instructions to socialize Bruce as a girl. At age 2, Brenda tore off her dresses, and as she grew she developed a clear preference for Brian's toys. When she went to school she had trouble making friends, got into physical fights, and was ridiculed by peers for her boyish manners and gait. By the time she was 10, Brenda expressed sexual attraction for girls (Walker, 2004).

"It was so obvious to everyone, not just to me, that she was just masculine," Janet said (BBC Horizon, 2005).

Money, meanwhile, met with the Reimer twins every year and recorded his observations that the gender reassignment was succeeding, despite all evidence to the contrary. His textbook *Man & Woman, Boy & Girl*, written with the psychiatrist Anke A. Ehrhardt, included a chapter on the success of Bruce/Brenda, and the case became famous (Money & Ehrhardt, 1972).

When the Reimer twins were in their early teens, a local psychiatrist convinced the parents to reveal the truth. Brenda changed his name to David and began to dress like a boy. He received testosterone injections and had several surgeries to return to his male state. "Suddenly it all made sense why I felt the way I did. I wasn't some sort of weirdo. I wasn't crazy," he said (Colapinto, 2004). The media began reporting on Reimer when another researcher inspired him to go public with his tragic experiences.

Unfortunately, David's newfound sense of self was short-lived. Although he eventually married a woman, David struggled with depression and was devastated by Brian's death at the age of 37. He wound up separated from his wife, unemployed, and financially destitute. David committed suicide in 2004.

you should not make up data or steal others' ideas. But most, if not all, research includes ethical grey areas that a researcher should consider. For example, sometimes participants decide they do not want to complete a study. Is it ethical to reward those who complete the study? If so, when does the size of the reward become coercive? Is it ethical to punish participants who leave a study early by deducting funds from the payment, taking away course credits, or requiring them to do some other more onerous activity? Many issues related to participant recruitment, informed consent, and other research procedures and standards are somewhat controversial and not clear-cut. The final decision about whether a proposed study has adhered to ethical standards is made by a research ethics board.

RESEARCH ETHICS BOARDS

research ethics board (REB) A committee, consisting of faculty and community members, that has been established to review and approve research proposals within a university.

Any institution where researchers receive funding from the tri-council funding agencies must have a **research ethics board (REB)**. REBs consist of at least four faculty members belonging to the institution who have content, research methods, or ethics expertise, and at least one member of the community who does not have an affiliation with the institution. The REB reviews and approves research proposals and ensures that they are adhering to the *TCPS 2* ethical guidelines. Many institutions require that faculty and students are familiar with these guidelines by having them complete the *TCPS 2* Course on Research Ethics. This is a free, online tutorial that is available at https://tcps2core.ca/welcome. Once this tutorial has been completed you are able to print off a certificate of completion. You may be asked to complete this tutorial and submit a copy of the certificate as a requirement of your course.

Categorizing Research Risk

exempt research Research that does not require research ethics board review.

Before starting any research, you need to submit the research proposal to the REB for review, generally via an online submission system. Although the specific requirements may vary from institution to institution, the REB application process will generally require that you provide information about the identification of participants and how they will be recruited, details about informed consent, the research materials, and a summary of the intended research project, including the specific aims, background and importance, and methods. Additionally, you need to determine what kind of review is needed, which is based on the level of risk involved. There are three categories of risk: exempt research, minimal risk research, and greater than minimal risk research.

Exempt research does not require formal ethical review. It often includes work evaluating educational practices in established educational settings. The course evaluations that you likely have to do at the end of each course you take would be an example. Under certain conditions, it may also include the use of survey, interview, or observational procedures where participants are not identified (have you ever been asked to complete an anonymous survey at a shopping mall?) or research that involves the observation of public behaviour. An example that has raised some ethical questions is a study by Middlemist, Knowles, and Matter (1976), where they investigated how invading men's personal space in a public washroom would impact their speed and flow of urine. Unbeknownst to bathroom goers, an observer in the bathroom was keeping note of which urinals men chose and their patterns of urination. Unsurprisingly, men preferred to keep their distance from one another, and the closer they were to one another the longer it took for urination to start. Then, to test these observations

Table 2.1 REB criteria for assessing research risk and type of review.

		Research Risk		
		Low	Medium	High
Group Vulnerability	High	Greater than Minimal Risk (Full REB Review)	Greater than Minimal Risk (Full REB Review)	Greater than Minimal Risk (Full REB Review)
	Medium	Minimal Risk (Delegated Review)	Greater than Minimal Risk (Full REB Review)	Greater than Minimal Risk (Full REB Review)
	Low	Minimal Risk (Delegated Review)	Minimal Risk (Delegated Review)	Greater than Minimal Risk (Full REB Review)

experimentally, they manipulated the bathroom setting by having a confederate stand next to the bathroom goer or by placing out of order signs next to some of the urinals to create different levels of personal space. An observer was again taking notes of urination patterns. The entire study was conducted without the participants being aware they were being observed. This study has raised a number of ethical concerns, such as whether this was an unjust invasion of the men's privacy, if it could have resulted in potential discomfort to the men (especially if they discovered they were being watched), and the fact that they were never informed that they were part of a study (Koocher, 1977).

Minimal risk research includes research in which potential risk to participants is not greater than what would be expected in daily life. Research that falls within this category can be assigned for a delegated review by the REB. This means that the research can be reviewed and approved by a single member of the REB rather than having to undergo a full board review, which may only happen once or twice a month. Approval generally happens a lot quicker for studies in this category.

minimal risk research Research that does not pose risks that are greater than risks encountered in daily life.

Greater than minimal risk research refers to research that poses risks to participants that would be greater than what one would expect in their everyday life. The determination of whether the research risk is greater than minimal risk relates to an assessment of both the level of research risk (type, likelihood of occurrence, and magnitude of risk) and the vulnerability of the intended participants (see Table 2.1). Research that involves deception would also be classified as greater than minimal risk. All research in this category requires a full REB review.

greater than minimal risk research Research that may pose substantial risk to participants and requires a full REB review.

CONFLICT OF INTEREST

Yet another set of interesting ethical issues arises around questions of **conflict of interest** for researchers. Although the research process is held out as impartial, researchers who are funded by agencies with a particular stake in the results provoke, at minimum, the appearance of a conflict of interest that can call into question the capacity of the researcher to do the work with required objectivity.

Questions around conflict of interest often arise when corporate funding undergirds particular research—for example, when a drug company commissions a study on the effectiveness of a particular medication. Researchers are encouraged in such circumstances to be aware of

conflict of interest A situation in which financial or other considerations may compromise or appear to compromise a researcher's judgment in conducting or reporting research.

and mitigate any conflicts of interest to the extent possible. Ultimately, however, the only "remedy" for such a conflict is full disclosure so that the community of scholars can account for the conflict in vetting the research findings.

An interesting example comes from Anxiety Canada (Grant, 2017). The not-for-profit organization recruited a team of psychiatrists and other medical professionals to sit on a panel to develop a set of guidelines for managing anxiety, post-traumatic stress, and obsessive-compulsive disorders. The psychiatrics sought out, and received, financial support for this work from several leading pharmaceutical companies. Although the conflict of interest was disclosed and the drug companies were not involved in the guideline paper, legitimate concerns still exist regarding the recommended guidelines and whether they are free of bias. Such financial conflicts of interest are commonplace in the development of clinical practice guidelines (Grant, 2017).

EXAMPLES OF ETHICAL VIOLATIONS IN PSYCHOLOGY

Throughout psychology's history, there have been several examples of questionable ethical practices. Two of the most well-known examples are the cases of Stanley Milgram, who performed a series of experiments on obedience from 1963 to 1965, and Philip Zimbardo, who carried out a prison simulation study at Stanford University in 1971.

Milgram wanted to explore the justifications given by accused Nazi war criminals at the Nuremberg trials for acts of genocide committed during World War II. In particular, Milgram wanted to know how easy it would be to convince ordinary people to commit atrocities. (The short answer: pretty easy.) Milgram's original study deceived participants about the purpose of the research. Researchers told participants they were taking part in an experiment on memory and learning, but the researchers were really examining how far participants would go in obeying researchers' demands. When they first arrived at Milgram's laboratory, participants met with a researcher in a lab coat and were introduced to another participant, a middle-aged man named Mr. Wallace. (In fact, Mr. Wallace was an accomplice in the study, called a **confederate**.) The researcher had Mr. Wallace and the participant draw slips of paper to determine who would be the "teacher" and who would be the "learner"; in truth, all participants were teachers and Mr. Wallace was always the learner. Then the researcher attached electrodes to Mr. Wallace that were connected to an imposing-looking "shock" machine, and he told participants to administer shocks of varying levels to Mr. Wallace, depending on how he performed on a test of word pairs.

As Mr. Wallace got answer after answer wrong, the researcher urged participants to deliver higher and higher voltages. At a certain level, Mr. Wallace would scream in pain (although he was pretending—he was not receiving any shocks) and volunteers would become upset. As the experiment continued, Mr. Wallace twitched and writhed, at one point begging the researcher to stop the study (Milgram, 1963). Yet, in response to commands to continue, about 65 per cent of the participants delivered shocks all the way to what they believed was the maximum amount: 450 volts. The research protocol generated considerable short-term stress and potential long-term harm for those who complied and administered the highest shock level. Many psychologists found Milgram's studies unethical, in particular his callous observations of the obvious suffering of the participants while they decided whether to continue shocking the subject (Baumrind, 1964). More recent evidence has even suggested that Milgram did not debrief all his participants, as claimed, and that many of the participants have experienced lasting negative effects as a result of their participation in the study (Brannigan,

confederate A person (accomplice) who is part of an experiment or study (but unknown to the participants) and plays a specific role in setting up the experimental situation.

Nicholson, & Cherry, 2015). Others, however, insisted that Milgram had provided invaluable information about obedience to authority, especially in light of the Nuremberg trials and in trying to understand how people could inflict such harm on other human beings. Thus, this particular case highlights a balance that must be made between risks of harm experienced by a participant and the gain in knowledge that can be made from the outcome of a study.

Even more controversial was Zimbardo's Stanford Prison Experiment (SPE; Haney, Banks, & Zimbardo, 1973a, 1973b), which involved a group of 24 young male college students who had agreed to take part in a study on the psychological effects of prison life. Researchers randomly divided participants into guards and prisoners, the latter of whom were led to cells in the "Stanford County Jail," which was really a basement laboratory (Haney, Banks, & Zimbardo, 1973a). Guards donned uniforms and sunglasses and carried clubs. After searching, stripping, and delousing prisoners, the guards forced them to wear smocks, rubber sandals, nylon stocking caps (to simulate shaved heads), and heavy ankle chains—all designed to make prisoners feel powerless, emasculated, uncomfortable, and oppressed.

Zimbardo soon observed a dramatic shift in behaviour among members of both groups. Although they had not received any specific training, the guards made up their own set of rules, such as demanding prisoners do push-ups for perceived insubordination. The guards grew increasingly abusive. The prisoners responded in turn by rebelling, ranging from verbal taunts, to placing mattresses against doors, to tearing off their smocks and nylon caps. One by one, prisoners began to show signs of extreme emotional distress, such as sobbing, screaming, and refusing to eat. Within a matter of days, Zimbardo reported, the prisoners were "disintegrated, both as a group and as individuals. . . . The guards had won total control of the prison, and they commanded the blind obedience of each prisoner" (Zimbardo, 1999). Zimbardo ended the study, which he had planned to run for two weeks, after six days.

While many criticisms have been put forth regarding the methodology of the SPE, including demand characteristics, ecological validity, inability to voluntarily leave the experiment, and selection bias, a recent exposé by Blum (2018) has presented evidence that the entire experiment was fraudulent. Audio evidence from previously published recordings of Zimbardo and interviews that Blum conducted with the study participants has revealed that the guards had been coached on what to say or do to be cruel (Blum, 2018). Further, many of the participants, when interviewed by Blum, indicated that they were faking, or playing up, some of their behaviours. The SPE has made some influential conclusions regarding how human behaviour can be influenced by external circumstance; however, these recent revelations significantly challenge what, if anything, can be concluded from this study.

Neither Milgram's nor Zimbardo's experiment would muster ethical approval today, thanks to sweeping changes to ethical standards instituted in the past 25 years. However, researchers have devised ways to ethically modify these designs to determine whether their results can be replicated. For instance, Burger (2009), a professor at Santa Clara University, conducted a replication of the Milgram study and found comparable results. However, Burger added several safeguards to his design so that it would pass ethical tests. First, in his design, the hypothetical shock levels only went up to 150 volts (rather than the 450 volts in Milgram's study). This much lower cutoff was based on analysis of Milgram's data, which indicated that knowing what a participant would do up to 150 volts would provide good predictive information about what he or she would likely do next; actually putting participants through the potential stress of a manipulation up to 450 volts was unnecessary. Second, Burger screened out potential participants who might have an adverse reaction to the study. Third, participants were given repeated written reminders that they were free to withdraw from the study at any time and that they would still be paid. Fourth, experimenters gave participants a sample shock so that they

Chuck Painter/Stanford News Service. Courtesy of the Special Collections and University Archives, Stanford University

FIGURE 2.3   The Zimbardo experiment.

could see the generator was real, but the sample shock had 15 volts (as opposed to 45 volts in Milgram's design). Fifth, participants were informed immediately after the study that no real shock had been administered; in the original Milgram study, it is unclear how much time elapsed between the end of the study and when participants were told of the deception. Finally, a clinical psychologist monitored the study and was empowered to end the study early if undue stress was observed. This replication provides evidence that ethical, creative scientists can often devise ways to conduct research that might otherwise be considered unethical in ways that are, in fact, ethical by modern standards.

Lest you think that contemporary psychologists no longer involve themselves in ethically questionable enterprises, we offer a more recent example involving a controversy about a Facebook study that intentionally skewed the content of participants' news feeds to be more positive or negative than normal to manipulate their moods. Although academic psychologists served as consultants for the study, details of the research emerged indicating that a Cornell University ethics board did not preapprove the study (as would be the normal procedure) but was instead consulted after the fact (Sullivan, 2014). Much of the public uproar stemmed from the revelation that participants in the study were offered no option for informed consent. Although the cases of Milgram and Zimbardo have become historical footnotes, this final recent example highlights that the struggle and debate in the field around what constitutes ethical conduct are ongoing.

ETHICAL CONSIDERATIONS FOR RESEARCH WITH NON-HUMAN ANIMALS

There are considerable ethical issues related to using non-human animals in research. These issues include whether animals should be used in research at all, what kinds of research should or should not be allowed with animals, what particular species of animals are appropriate for

Egoreichenkov Evgenii/Shutterstock

FIGURE 2.4   Views about what is acceptable research on animals both inside and outside the research laboratory have changed over time.

use in research, and what levels of care and treatment should be required. Similar to changes that have occurred in our ethical perspectives on the treatment of human subjects, views about research on animals both inside and outside the research laboratory have changed greatly over time. Generally, non-human animals used in research are treated better today than they were 50 years ago. Additionally, acceptable research methods today are somewhat more restricted than in the past, especially in the case of the use of non-human primates in research.

Why Use Animals in Research?

The best place to start a discussion of non-human animal research is to ask, "Why should research with animals be conducted at all?" The first reason is that animal research can provide a useful model for exploring the impact of some event on health and behaviour that can be applied to humans. For example, we have gained substantial knowledge from animal research about how particular diseases progress and how these diseases might be effectively treated. We have also learned from animal models about the impact of impoverished environments (e.g., nutritional or maternal deprivation), detrimental environments (e.g., exposure to drugs, pollution, or toxins), and enriched environments (e.g., stimulating environments that encourage physical activity). Although it is possible to investigate some of these issues with humans, studies with animals can be more highly controlled, enabling greater causal inferences. In many cases, animal research can answer important research questions about improving humans' health and well-being that cannot be effectively studied using other methods.

Another reason for using animals in research is that it allows the exploration of research questions that cover long periods of the lifespan and even across generations. By studying animals that reach maturity quickly and have relatively short lifespans, such as mice, we can examine important questions related to the interaction of genes and environments and how this interaction plays out over time. These animal models also enable the exploration of whether particular influences might impact the next generation. For example, researchers have found that male mice that have experienced severe stress have sperm with altered RNA (Gapp et al., 2014). When the sperm of these mice are used to fertilize an egg, the resulting offspring show behavioural and metabolic differences related to the altered RNA. This dramatic finding would be impossible and unethical to explore in humans.

What Animals Are Used in Research?

The vast majority (~95 per cent) of psychological research using animals is conducted with rodents (e.g., mice, rats; Speaking of Research, n.d.). Researchers studying various aspects of perception use different animal models to examine particular subjects, such as the development of vision (e.g., fish, cats) and hearing (e.g., chinchillas). Non-human primates have been used to study a wide range of topics, including the causes and treatments of particular diseases, visual processing, and the impact of different types of deprivation and enrichment. Over time, the use of non-human primates in research has declined, in part because of the cost of research, changing views of how these animals should be treated, and increased pressure from animal rights groups. However, as laboratory research with non-human primates has declined, researchers have been using field observations of primates in natural habitats. Thus, animal research should not be equated with invasive laboratory procedures.

How Are Animals Protected?

The **Canadian Council on Animal Care** (**CCAC**) is a national organization, funded by the CIHR and NSERC, that is responsible for protecting the health and well-being of animals being used in research. Based on a concept first published in 1959 on ethical decision making in the use of animals (Russell & Burch, 1999), the CCAC encourages the "Three Rs" tenet for the use of animals in research: replacement, reduction, and refinement. Within each institution, animal care committees review research proposals involving the use of animals and ensure they adhere to the Three Rs:

- *Replacement* refers to avoiding the use of animals completely (such as by using simulation methods instead) or using lower, less sentient animals (e.g., invertebrates as a means of replacing more sentient animals, such as mice, in research). At one point in time, baboons were used in crash tests for cars. Now, crash test dummies are used instead.
- *Reduction* relates to designing studies that require fewer animals being used. Careful planning should be conducted prior to the start of a study to ensure that the appropriate number of animals are used and that procedures are standardized and highly controlled to minimize the number of animals required.
- *Refinement* refers to the modification of experimental procedures so that any pain and distress experienced by animals is minimized.

The protection of animals involved in research goes well beyond the research situation because the researchers (and institution) are responsible for providing a home for the animals when they are not directly involved in a research project.

As with all research, the choice of methods and whether to involve non-human animals should be determined by the research question and ethical considerations. It is also important to realize that animal research has led to breakthroughs in our knowledge about diseases, interventions, and interactions between genetics and the environment.

Canadian Council on Animal Care (CCAC) The national organization responsible for protecting the health and well-being of animals being used in research, teaching, and testing throughout Canada.

Three Rs The principles of replacement (avoiding use of animals), reduction (minimizing use of animals), and refinement (modifying treatment of animals) that guide research being conducted with animals.

Practical Tips for Conducting Ethical Research

1. Always consider your obligations to society at large as the backdrop for any research that you conduct.

2. Keep the three core principles for research from the Tri-Council Policy Statement 2 in mind as you design your research.

3. Be aware of the rules and regulations that apply to your particular research.

4. Consult with your REB if you are unclear as to whether your activities require ethical approval or if they fall under the exempt research category.

CHAPTER SUMMARY

The first issue you must grapple with as a researcher is recognizing the importance and complexity of ethical guidelines. Research ethics are hardly precise—they are constantly evolving and depend on the particular context in which the research is conducted. As you have learned, the history of research has experienced instances that are marred by arrogance, thoughtlessness, and disregard for the welfare of participants by researchers all over the world. Benchmarks such as the Nuremberg Code, the Declaration of Helsinki, and the *TCPS 2* were designed to set limits on the power of researchers over their participants and institute safeguards for people not able to speak for themselves. The three core principles outlined in the *TCPS 2*—respect for persons, concern for welfare, and justice—provide guidance to researchers to ensure they protect the welfare of their participants. We hope that as you move forward in the research process, you will keep in mind that your first goal should be to conduct an ethical study.

End-of-Chapter Exercises

1. Complete the *TCPS 2* Course on Research Ethics. This tutorial is available at https://tcps2core.ca/welcome.

2. Anyone who conducts psychological research is required to do online training. Some see it as valuable, whereas others see it as a waste of time. What are the benefits and problems of this model? To what extent do you feel ethical issues are clear? Do you think discussion and debate about them are important? Is online training likely to be effective in improving the ethical behaviour of researchers? Why or why not?

3. The ethical problems that placebo groups can present are often underappreciated. What is the specific ethical challenge that a placebo (a treatment that has no therapeutic effect) control group may present in a research design? Under what circumstances should researchers worry, and when should they be less concerned? Given the power of a placebo group in a research design, are there ever circumstances where the ethical concerns could rule out the use of the placebo altogether?

4. In January 2012, researchers manipulated the news feeds of approximately 700,000 Facebook users. Some users were shown positive content while others were shown negative content. The succeeding posts made by these users were then analyzed to see if they were influenced by the content they were exposed to. (Albertson & Gadarian, 2014). Do you think this study violated any ethical principles? Why or why not?

5. Would the ethical violations experienced by David Reimer and his family happen today? Do you think that the more open online atmosphere regarding ethical training and issues prevents egregious violations, or at least makes it harder for them to occur?

6. For each of the following research scenarios, indicate whether it would be classified as exempt research, minimal risk research, or greater than minimal risk research. Explain your choice.

   a. A group of researchers is interested in studying body image in women. In one group, women will complete the body image measures after viewing advertisements with female models. In a second group, women will complete the measures after viewing advertisements of neutral objects.

   b. A university is interested in examining students' perceptions of the learning environment for the purposes of program review. They will have staff members internal to the university administer a learning environment survey to the students at the end of the academic year.

   c. A researcher is interested in studying depression among older adults in nursing homes. The researcher will visit local nursing homes to recruit residents to complete a measure of depression.

   d. A group of researchers is interested in studying whether the wording of rating scale survey items has an impact on the quality of data obtained. They have developed three different types of response anchors for a measure of readiness for residency. Medical residents will be randomly assigned to complete one of the three survey versions.

   e. A team of researchers is interested in studying the bystander effect. They have a confederate, who is either a young women or young man, stand by a car that is pulled over on the road with the hood up. The researchers will record the number of helpful interventions made by members of the public.

Key Terms

active deception, p. 29

Canadian Council on Animal Care (CCAC), p. 40

coercion, p. 27

confederate, p. 36

confidentiality, p. 26

conflict of interest, p. 35

debrief, p. 30

Declaration of Helsinki, p. 25

deidentified data, p. 26

exempt research, p. 34

funnel debriefing, p. 30

greater than minimal risk research, p. 35

informed consent, p. 26

minimal risk research, p. 35

Nuremberg Code of 1947, p. 25

passive deception, p. 29

priming, p. 30

research ethics board (REB), p. 34

risk–benefit analysis, p. 30

stereotype threat, p. 30

Three Rs, p. 40

Tri-Council Policy Statement, p. 26

Starting Your Research

3

Chapter Contents

INSIDE RESEARCH: Christopher Green

I have studied a lot of different areas of psychology. For my master's degree I did a multivariate analysis of people's perceptions of art. My doctoral training was focused mostly on experiments in memory, but for my dissertation I wrote computer programs that simulate the ways in which people solve logic problems. After I became a professor, I started working on the history of psychology, so I did my research in libraries and archives, reading the old mail and diary entries of important figures from the past, like William James and John Dewey. A few years ago, I started doing something called "digital history" (where we use computers to analyze huge historical databases—like every article published in several different journals across a half-century of time). I am currently focused on how psychologists' statistical practices have changed since World War II.

Professor, Department of Psychology, York University

Courtesy of Christopher Green

continued

What I have learned about methodology from working in these different areas is that what appears in methods textbooks is not a fixed body of knowledge that defines the limits of what you can do. It is, instead, a mere catalogue of the methods that people have used in the past frequently enough that they have confidence in the methods' ability to produce useful answers to their questions. It is good material to know before you set out on your own, but there are always new kinds of questions that no one has asked before. You shouldn't let what is in the textbook limit your vision of what you can do. New kinds of problems, new kinds of technology, and sometimes just new ways of looking at the world can call for new methods to be developed. You have to think about them carefully, and you have to work hard to develop them into precise tools, but new methods are always possible and often necessary.

Christopher D. Green is a professor of psychology at York University in Toronto. He has written *Early Psychological Thought: Ancient Accounts of Mind and Soul* (with Philip R. Groff, 2003) and *Psychology and Its Cities: A New History of Early American Psychology* (2019). He has been president of the Society for the History of Psychology, and he edited the *Journal of the History of the Behavioral Sciences*.

Research Focus: History of psychology, statistical practice in psychology

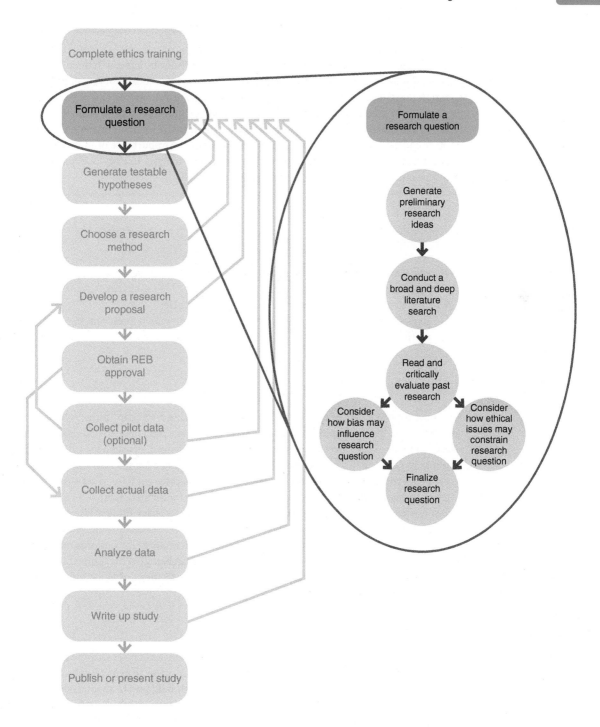

Chapter Abstract

In this chapter, we will guide you through the process of choosing a research topic and narrowing your ideas to a specific question. We start with helping you locate sources of ideas and inspiration for research topics—including books, journal articles, classes, and ongoing research projects—and then give you tips on how best to glean information from them, in particular how to most effectively read journal articles. We delve into the foundation of theory, touching on its broad categories in psychology, and then discuss the importance of theory in defining your research question, hypotheses, methodology, and analysis strategy. We conclude with how to avoid common problems in starting your research.

LEARNING OBJECTIVES

By the end of this chapter, you should be able to:

- Identify sources for research ideas.
- Describe the main sections of a typical research article.
- Explain what a theory is and how it can guide your research questions, hypotheses, methodology, and analyses.

CHOOSE A RESEARCH TOPIC

The most daunting task of the research process is choosing a topic to study. Psychology is a vast field full of unanswered questions. This can make the choice of a specific topic overwhelming—even for seasoned researchers. Experienced researchers often work on multiple projects, all in various stages of completion, ranging from the idea and design stages to data collection, analysis, and the final write-up. Often, different lines of research will serve to cross-fertilize one another, providing novel directions for further research.

But novice researchers do not have that luxury. Trying to pick your first research topic can be paralyzing. The good news is you do not have to come up with an amazing, grand, new idea, just some area of human behaviour that you would like to explore. The best way to approach it is through questions: What is interesting to you as a human being? What is one thing you have always wondered about? What makes people behave the way they do? What follows are a few ideas and resources to get you started.

Take a Variety of Psychology Classes

Although it may seem like obvious advice, psychology classes offer a great source of ideas for research topics. We advise students early in their academic career to experiment with different classes; you never know what may pique your interest and could lead to an interesting research topic. As you take classes and do your readings for these classes, think about how it relates to your everyday experiences in working and interacting with people. Does it fit? Are there observations that do not seem to coincide with what you have been reading and learning? Observations by one of this book's authors of his children interacting with photographs and small toys went against a particular theoretical perspective. It led him to collaborate with other researchers to investigate these behaviours in more controlled settings (see DeLoache, Pierroutsakos, Uttal, Rosengren, & Gottlieb, 1998; DeLoache, Uttal, & Rosengren, 2004).

Hit the Books

Our next suggestion is to read broadly, because no research idea is truly novel—it either builds on past research or attempts to repudiate past research. But what should you read? Introductory textbooks for general topics that you find interesting, or textbooks from previous psychology courses, provide a good place to look for ideas that can help you narrow your research focus. When you find a topic that interests you, track down some of the classic studies mentioned in the text. These articles should help frame the research in a broader theoretical context. Then, find some more recent scholarly articles on the topic.

Search for Research Articles

In the era of the Google search, many students are content to find research articles through the "brute force" methodology of a keyword search—either directly into a search engine like Google Scholar or using the keyword search feature in a database such as PsycINFO. Although this method may yield many hits, it is often inefficient, either requiring that you (1) know all (or at least many of) the relevant keywords or (2) are willing to sift through dozens, or even hundreds, of potential references to cull the most relevant.

PsycINFO A database specific to psychology journals and related references.

   Although it is not practical for us to list all of the possible ways to find research articles, here are several alternative strategies to simply searching by keywords:

1. *Use the advanced search features on PsycINFO.* When simple keyword searching yields too many results, the advanced search features can be extremely useful. For example, you can designate that you are only interested in articles from a particular range of years (useful if you are only looking for the most current work on a topic) or specify that you only want peer-reviewed material. You can also specify the type(s) of articles you are seeking (e.g., only empirical studies or only meta-analyses—statistical reports on the findings found across several studies) or narrow your search to only look at research with particular age groups.
2. *Use the keyword listings to target your search.* For any given article that you find on PsycINFO, a list of keywords will often be provided just below the abstract. The keywords serve as clues for how the particular piece of work is classified and organized along with similar works. For example, an article on peer rejection for children with attention-deficit hyperactivity disorder might include keywords like "Attention-Deficit Disorder with Hyperactivity," "Friendship," "Peer Relations," and "Psychosocial Development." Once you identify the main keywords for an article of interest, conducting a more targeted PsycINFO search with those keywords as your search terms can be helpful for finding similar articles.
3. *Look at the cited references for relevant articles that you locate.* One handy feature of PsycINFO is that, for any article you locate, you can follow a link to see the references that are cited in that particular piece of work. If an article is relevant to your particular research focus, then it is likely that at least some of the articles cited in the article will also be relevant. In effect, you can benefit from the diligence of previous researchers in identifying the important literature on a topic.

4. *Follow a particular cited reference or author forward in time.* PsycINFO and Google Scholar also make it easy to take a particular reference—or a specific author—and follow the work forward in time. In other words, when you find an article that is important to the research you are doing, you can look to see who has subsequently cited that article. (This is the flipside of the strategy mentioned in number 3.) In this way, you will be able to see related work that has occurred since the publication of a particular article.

5. *Consult with a reference librarian.* Librarians are trained to find information quickly and efficiently. A brief meeting or consultation with a reference librarian may help you better define your key search terms and find the material you need. Librarians will also point you to resources and services that you may not be aware exist. For example, most libraries offer an interlibrary loan service that, with some lead time, can track down articles and books at other institutions.

The Art of Reading Research Articles

Once you have located research articles published in high-quality journals, one of your biggest challenges will be the task of reading the articles. Like many difficult tasks, proficiency in reading this work comes from repeated exposure and practice. That said, there are some strategies and questions to ask that can help as you begin to read research literature. See the Appendix for a summary of these questions.

We recommend that you become a non-linear reader. Unlike other works that you may read, it often does not make sense to read a research article from front to back in the way that you would read a novel. Instead, it is more than acceptable (and often advisable) to skip around and cull the article for key pieces of information. In your first run through, start with a quick reading, where you search for key phrases and information (e.g., "The goal of this research is . . ." "Our hypotheses were . . ." "Major implications include . . ."). If the article is relevant to your topic and interests, then you can go back and do a thorough reading for details.

To know what to look for, you must first understand the basic anatomy of a research article. Although there is some minor variability in formatting across different journals, most research articles are split into four broad sections: introduction, method, results, and discussion. In addition to these sections, most articles begin with an **abstract**—a brief summary of the article's purpose, methods, major findings, and implications—and end with a reference section that contains a list of other works that were used in designing the particular research.

abstract A brief summary of a research article's purpose, methods, and major findings. Abstracts are typically about 150 to 300 words in length.

Abstract.   A good place to start reading any article is the abstract, but resist the temptation to stop there. The abstract will give you a brief overview of the topic, findings, and implications of the article. It can be an invaluable tool for screening an article (and making an initial determination as to whether it is worth reading further or whether the article relates to your interests and questions). But be warned: It does not provide enough information to allow for a thorough understanding of the work. You may need to go beyond the abstract to fully determine the relevance of an article to your interests.

literature review A summary of previous research that has been done on the topic, typically located in the introduction of the paper.

Introduction/Literature Review.   Typically, the introduction of the paper starts by broadly articulating the problem or issue being studied, summarizing the previous work that has been done on the topic—known as a **literature review**—and explaining how the current work fits in and answers specific questions to advance our knowledge in the given area of research. The end of the introduction includes the particular hypotheses or predictions of the researchers. After reading this section, you should be able to answer the following questions: (1) What are the problem areas—both broad and specific—that have led the researchers to study this problem and generate hypotheses? Why does the topic matter? (2) What are the central research questions? (3) What is the research hypothesis?

Method. The method section lays out the specifics of how the research was conducted. It is incumbent on the researchers to describe their methods in enough detail that other researchers can attempt to replicate the findings (as part of the larger scientific research cycle). Traditionally, this section is further subdivided into participants, materials, and procedures sections. The participants section describes who was studied; the materials section describes what measures, instruments, and techniques were used; and the procedures section details how it was done. After reading the method section, you should be able to answer the following questions: (1) Who is being studied (sample size and demographics)? (2) What are the key variables that were measured in the research? If the study is experimental, you should also be able to identify the independent and dependent variables. (See Chapter 4 for a more detailed discussion of these concepts.) (3) How have the researchers operationalized those variables (i.e., defined them in measurable terms)? (4) What methods are used to collect the data, and what sorts of controls are in place to deal with potential sources of error and confounding variables? How do the methods allow for distinguishing among various possibilities?

Results. The results section is the heart of the research article. You should plan on reading this section, even if you do not understand all of the statistical analyses being used. The results section gives you the raw, complete findings without the researchers' interpretation or spin. As such, it is an important place to begin your own evaluation of what the research has found, before you read the researchers' take on the meaning of their work. After reading the results section, you should be able to answer the following questions: (1) Broadly speaking, what are the methods of data analysis—qualitative, quantitative, or both? (2) Based on the analyses, what did the researchers find with respect to each of their hypotheses? Were their hypotheses supported?

Discussion. The discussion section of the article is where the authors offer their interpretation of the findings and how they believe the results should be understood and applied. A well-written discussion section not only articulates the meaning of the findings but also explains how the findings fit into the larger context of other work in the area. In addition, the discussion section will typically spell out the limitations of the research and make particular recommendations for future work in the area. After reading the discussion section, you should be able to answer the following questions: (1) What are the major conclusions of the authors? What are the implications for this area of research? (2) Are the conclusions reasonable and well-grounded in the actual findings? (3) What are the caveats and major limitations of the research?

References. The list of references is at the end of an article, but this can be an invaluable source of related works. If you determine that a particular article is relevant to your interests/topic, then the reference section should be used as a springboard for finding additional materials. For an excellent and detailed resource to assist you in deeper reading of research literature, we suggest *Reading and Understanding Research* by Locke, Silverman, and Spiruduso (2010).

Get Involved in an Ongoing Research Project

Probably the most effective way for coming up with a new research idea is to get involved in an ongoing research project or research lab. If you are at a college or university where the faculty regularly conducts research, one of the best places to start is to look at faculty or department webpages. If the description of their research looks interesting, read some of their papers. Then try to set up an appointment to meet with them about their research. If they have a research lab, you can ask about the research being conducted in the lab and whether there may be opportunities to volunteer with the lab. There may even be opportunities for paid research assistant positions within some labs. Faculty members generally have a quota of how many students they will take on and perhaps other criteria, such as having completed a research methods course. If your first choice does not have any positions available, try a different faculty member.

Working in a research laboratory can be extremely helpful for gaining experience in the research process and seeing the process unfold from idea generation to design, implementation, and then analysis and reporting of results. As a part of a research team, you may have the chance to observe the interplay of theory and data, the challenges of getting a study to run smoothly, the excitement of processing the first couple of participants in a new study, the thrill of running the initial statistical data analyses to examine the results, and the potential challenges faced when the data contradict or fail to support the original hypotheses. These are the kinds of things that make conducting research much more fun than merely being a consumer of research.

Even better than getting involved in just one laboratory is working or volunteering in two or more laboratories during your undergraduate years. This provides you with multiple potential recommenders should you decide to apply to graduate school and also exposes you to multiple subareas within psychology. Since you never know what you might find interesting, breadth of exposure is better the earlier you are in your psychology education.

Most students start their research careers working in research labs on the projects being studied by faculty members. Under a faculty member's supervision, you would get the opportunity to slowly develop content knowledge and experience with one or more research areas and methodologies. You may then choose to continue on in the lab and complete an honour's thesis, and possibly carry on to complete a master's degree and a Ph.D. As an undergraduate student, it is much more common for you to adopt a topic provided by your faculty supervisor than to select your own topic.

Not all research is fun and games, however, and not all laboratory research experiences are the same. Make sure that your experience involves more than simply data coding or data entry. Although these relatively low-level tasks are necessary parts of the research process, they can be time consuming and monotonous. Ideally, you should try to work in a laboratory that provides you with a wide range of research experience and has some sort of regular laboratory meeting, where the mechanics of research are discussed along with more theoretical issues. Many laboratory meetings also include reading and discussing current research in the field related to ongoing projects.

Research can also be frustrating. Many times the data analyses do not yield clear or even interpretable results, which can lead to hours of searching for methodological or theoretical reasons to explain the results. But overall, faculty members who do research enjoy what they are doing and are deeply committed to investigating a certain set of research questions. If you are part of a well-functioning research program, you should find the research process challenging but intellectually rewarding. Gaining experience in a research laboratory has also become expected for students interested in pursuing advanced degrees in psychology and related fields.

LET THEORY GUIDE YOUR RESEARCH

Once you have identified an area of research that interests you, you must determine in what ways theory will guide your research inquiry. The debate around the role of theory in psychological research is long-standing, and there is no singular, authoritative answer to the question. Some researchers say that theory drives their research methods, whereas others say their methods are not informed by an underlying theory.

Although there is no consensus that a theoretical framework is an essential prerequisite to conducting psychological research, having theory available can facilitate the research process. In this section, we discuss the ways in which theory can help define your initial research questions, hypotheses, methodology, and analysis strategy. Although theory offers clear benefits in all of these areas, adhering to a particular theoretical framework can come with pitfalls, which we also consider.

The Role of Theory in Forming Research Questions

Theory can be invaluable as you form your initial research questions. Although we have already discussed some places where your initial research questions may emerge, using previous research and reading the work of theorists who have come before is an effective approach for setting your initial research agenda. Because your research questions and interests will often be broad and ambitious, a theory can help you focus and narrow the scope of that inquiry. The downside of this narrowing, however, is the risk that a given theory may limit your inquiry too much by restricting the types of questions you might ask. This interplay between the focus that a theory can provide and the restrictions that it may impose highlights both the risks and the benefits of using theory in the early stages of the research process.

In some cases, having the theory—or at least competing theoretical ideas—is essential for guiding research from the onset. A good example of this comes from the seminal work of Michelene Chi (1978). Chi was interested in determining whether maturity or knowledge (expertise) was the central driving force for cognitive development in the area of memory recall; essentially, she wanted to test the effects of what is popularly known as "nature versus nurture" on memory by looking at whether older adults had better recall (which would confirm the nurture theory) because they were trained experts, as opposed to children. Chi's study involved the theory of domain-specific expertise—the view that people can develop different areas of expertise, such as in language or mathematical skills, to different degrees. She speculated that this kind of area-specific expertise might override the traditional "deficits" of younger children in the area of memory. To determine which was more important, she pitted child chess experts against college-age novices in a task to recall pieces on a chessboard and found that the child experts performed at a higher level. In contrast, on a traditional number recall task, the college students performed at a superior level to the child experts. The research questions around the role of knowledge, expertise, and maturation would never have been asked without the theory to drive the initial inquiry.

The frameworks that theories provide can also define a research agenda at the most basic level. A vivid example of this can be seen in the contrast between the approaches of traditional clinical psychology, which integrates science, theory, and practice to treat patients' psychologically based distress, and positive psychology, the scientific study of strengths and virtues that enable individuals and communities to thrive. Each approach offers a fundamentally different set of values about the nature of human strength and deficit. Whereas clinical psychology has traditionally studied mental health and illness from the perspective of pathology (the

research question The central question(s) you are seeking to answer in your research study. It may ask what, how, or why something is happening.

domain specific The idea that knowledge or expertise in different areas is not based on an underlying general capability, but rather determined by particular capabilities or experiences within an area.

clinical psychology The area of psychology that integrates science, theory, and practice to treat patients' psychologically based distress.

positive psychology An area of psychology that focuses on studying the strengths and virtues that enable individuals and communities to thrive.

causes and effects of disease), proponents of positive psychology have argued that the focus of inquiry should be on human strength, intelligence, and talent (Seligman & Csikszentmihalyi, 2000). As a consequence, the very questions that a traditional clinical psychology researcher might ask (e.g., about the causes of depression) differ from the questions a researcher coming from positive psychology would posit (e.g., about the ways in which resilience and optimism can buffer an individual from depression).

Whatever the possible constraints using theory present, it is also important to consider whether any question can ever truly be approached atheoretically (without using theory). Although some might worry that using a theory to form initial research questions unnecessarily focuses your framing of the issues, others might question the very existence of an atheoretical research question. Even if you are not using a formalized theory, all researchers are driven by a set of background assumptions and personal motivations based on our fundamental ideas about how the world works, and these ideas inevitably inform how we address a research question. Consider the powerfully stated philosophical notion that underlies the work of the early twentieth-century behaviourist John Watson: "Give me a dozen healthy infants, well-formed, and my own special world to bring them up in, and I'll guarantee to take any one at random and train him to become any type of specialist I might select—doctor, lawyer, artist, merchant-chief, and yes, beggar-man and thief" (Watson, 1913). To the extent that we are

MEDIA MATTERS

Being Mindful in the MindUP program

An example of a positive collaboration between psychology research and the media is the MindUP™ program. This program, which was started by actress Goldie Hawn to assist children to be more caring and less stressed, has research evidence backing up its success (Allen, 2015). Used primarily within elementary school classrooms, the program teaches children a number of mindfulness practices, which include breathing and moving exercises. Recently this program has garnered a lot of media attention since Goldie Hawn has teamed up with her daughter, Kate Hudson, in a Fabletics fundraiser to raise money for the program (Kanter, 2018). Hawn has also been promoting the program through presentations across the world, including at the Forbes Women's Summit in New York City (Pomerantz, 2014) and the World Government Summit in Dubai (Elsa, 2018).

One of the lead researchers on this project, Kimberly Schonert-Reichl, from the University of British Columbia, has said "It's one of the first studies of its kind to investigate the value of a social and emotional learning program that incorporates mindfulness techniques for children's well-being using a variety of scientific measures, including both biological and neurological tests" (Allen, 2015). In a randomized controlled trial involving Grade 4 and 5 students who were randomly assigned to either mindfulness training or a regular social responsibility program, students receiving the mindfulness training showed improved cognitive control, greater empathy, perspective taking, mindfulness, and reduced self-reported symptoms of depression and aggression (Schonert-Reichl et al., 2015). The data collected included self-report and peer-report surveys, tests of cognitive abilities, and saliva collected from the students to analyze their cortisol levels (an indicator of stress).

The MindUP program has a theoretical basis in four core pillars: social–emotional learning, mindful awareness, positive psychology, and neuroscience (see https://mindup.org). The program revolves around 15 lessons focused on promoting mindfulness and perspective taking, and includes activities such as "brain breaks," which focus on guided breathing exercises multiple times a day. Currently the program is used in schools in 12 different countries around the world.

always working from pre-existing ideas, an honest self-assessment of your own assumptions and biases is an important part of the research process.

Figure 3.1 provides an example of how a theory can lead to different interpretations of data. Each of the three finalist captions from the *New Yorker* leads to a completely different interpretation of the cartoon, with one focusing the reader on the age of the batter, one equating baseball and chess (provided by a prominent social psychologist), and one providing a relatively bad pun.

Theory May Shape Hypotheses

In addition to its role in the formation of research questions, theory also has a function in shaping hypotheses, or predictions about the outcome of a research study (i.e., an answer to your research question). The assumptions embedded within a particular theory can help to define the particular predictions that you, the researcher, might make about a given topic.

John Klossner/The New Yorker Collection/The Cartoon Bank

Let's walk him and pitch to the bishop."

FIGURE 3.1   *New Yorker* cartoon showing how "theory" can alter the interpretation of "data."

An illustration from a well-known area of psychological inquiry is instructive here. Festinger's (1957) elegant articulation of cognitive dissonance—the notion that we are uncomfortable holding conflicting cognitions (thoughts) simultaneously and that we are motivated to reduce this discomfort (or "dissonance") by changing our existing cognitions to bring about a more consistent belief system—has spawned numerous studies examining the role of such dissonance in changing attitudes and beliefs. The theory of dissonance has led to predictions that would otherwise be seen as counterintuitive—for example, one such hypothesis was that individuals who were paid less to complete a monotonous task would report that the task was more important than those who had been paid more. The researchers found that participants who were not paid well and spent a lot of time on a very boring project justified their effort by suggesting the project was important (Festinger & Carlsmith, 1959).

Theory and Methodology Reinforce One Another

The interplay between theory and methodology—the specific procedures or techniques that are used to identify, collect, and analyze information about a topic—is also an interesting area to consider. First, it is important to make a distinction between *method* and *methodology*. A method is the tool that is used to collect your data to answer your research questions—for example, using surveys to collect data. A methodology is the justification for using a particular research method, as well as a lens that will guide how the data will be analyzed. It is the broader strategy that is used in a research approach and can apply several different methods in the testing of a research hypothesis.

On the one hand, theory can both define and lead to the selection of a particular methodology. On the other hand, advances in methodology can drive changes in theory (and practice). First, consider the ways in which theory defines and leads to the selection of a particular methodology. Two popular methodological approaches serve as good examples. The first comes from the study of infant cognitive development, the "preferential-looking" paradigm. In studies that use looking-time methodology, babies are presented with an object, photo, or short

hypothesis
A statement that predicts the outcome of your research study. It specifies a predicted answer to your research question.

cognitive dissonance
The idea that we are uncomfortable holding conflicting thoughts simultaneously and that we are motivated to reduce this discomfort (or "dissonance") by changing our existing thoughts to bring about a more consistent belief system.

methodology The specific procedures or techniques that are used to identify, collect, and analyze information about a topic.

method The tools that are used to collect research data (e.g., surveys).

habituation
Diminished response to
a stimulus that comes
about through repeated
exposure to that
stimulus.

event (called a "novel visual event") until they tire of looking at it—this is known as habituation. They are then presented with a variation of the event that differs from the first event in some particular manner, and the amount of time they spend looking at the variation is measured. The assumption is that if infants look for a longer time at the variation of the event, then they are discerning something important about the event. This methodology has been used to argue that babies possess an understanding of basic physics by presenting them with "impossible" physical events (Spelke, 1985). In these studies, infants are first habituated to normal physical events, such as a ball dropping. Then researchers compare their looking time with that of another dropping event. In the control condition, the ball drop follows normal physical laws (e.g., principles of gravity and solidity), and in the experimental condition infants witness an impossible event (e.g., the ball falls and then appears below a solid surface).

Although it may sound simplistic, the theory that leads researchers to select the preferential-looking methodology is the underlying notion that babies are smart and they come into the world equipped with numerous understandings about how their environment works. Without that basic assumption, a researcher would not be inclined to use the preferential-looking methodology in the first place.

A second example of how theory can define and lead to the selection of a particular methodology comes from the intersection of developmental psychology and behavioural genetics. In an effort to parse out the relative contributions of genetic and environmental factors in development, for a number of years researchers have used a "twin-study" methodology in which they measure twins raised in the same family environments on a variety of characteristics. Both monozygotic (identical) and dizygotic (fraternal) twins are studied because monozygotic twins share nearly 100 per cent of their genetic material, whereas dizygotic twins share, on average, only 50 per cent.

The paradigm involves comparing the two different types of twins on traits, with the notion that any similarity between the monozygotic twins above and beyond the dizygotic twins should be a result of genetic factors (Neale & Cardon, 1992). Just as the preferential-looking methodology discussed previously is based on a theory that infants are innately intelligent, twin-study methods are also based on a fundamental theoretical assumption—that a range of behaviours and traits are largely genetically determined. As with the looking-time methodology, without that assumption, a researcher would be unlikely to be interested in selecting a twin-study methodology.

Interplay between Theory and Analysis Strategy

Although theory can influence research questions, hypotheses, and methodologies in fundamental ways, its impact is perhaps most profound in the ways that it shapes how researchers analyze their data. The theoretical orientation of many researchers governs the approach they take to data analysis. In this case, your pre-existing theory dictates the predictions you have for your study, and these in turn influence the ways in which you go about analyzing your data. At a more practical level, considering your analysis strategy as you develop your research question can prevent confusion and frustration when you run your analyses.

Not all researchers will say that their analysis is driven by their theoretical orientation or even their research question. For example, researchers working with infants tend to use a limited number of methodologies, and these methodologies (e.g., habituation) are accompanied by a particular data analysis approach (e.g., the looking times in the experimental and control conditions are examined using a *t* test). Greater detail about different data analysis approaches are discussed in Chapters 11 and 12.

t test A statistical approach that compares the difference between the means of two groups.

AVOID COMMON PROBLEMS IN STARTING YOUR RESEARCH

Probably the biggest challenge we see students face is coming up with the initial idea for research, whether it be for a paper or for a class research project. Although we provided some methods and ideas for generating research ideas at the beginning of this chapter, we also advise you to research a topic that you find fun and interesting. This will make the task of searching for relevant literature, reviewing research that has been done before, and defining your own research question much easier and more rewarding.

Often novice researchers believe they must do something completely new and different. This is an impossible task and most (honest) seasoned researchers will tell you that their own research builds on and extends from previous research, rather than being completely new and original. So think of your own research in this same way: Think about extending existing research in a novel direction rather than trying to come up with a research idea that will save the world or win you a Nobel Prize. But at the same time, you want to extend previous work in important ways. So, we would generally advise you to avoid a minimalist approach—often referred to as "incremental" research—that merely extends the age range of participant populations used in past research or examines a novel participant population, unless these extensions can be justified on theoretical or methodological grounds as important contributions.

One other common problem we find is that novice researchers often attempt to measure too many things, which leads to complex designs and often uninterpretable results. It is generally best, especially in an initial foray into a research area, to examine a small number of variables. Answering one research question always leads to others, and for most researchers this becomes a lifelong process. We hope it will become that for you as well.

PRACTICAL TIPS

Practical Tips for Starting Your Research

1. When deciding on your first research topic, make sure it is a doable project—do not try to win the Nobel (or Ig Nobel) Prize by being overly ambitious or grandiose.

2. Be prepared to make mistakes and learn from them—your second research project will be better than your first.

3. Do a thorough reading of the literature—you should become an expert on the topic.

4. Look for key sections of a research article rather than reading the entire article from start to finish.

5. Get involved in a faculty member's research—join a research lab.

6. Look for opportunities in research labs that provide you with a full range of research experiences.

7. Spend some time thinking about your own theoretical biases and how they might influence you as a researcher.

CHAPTER SUMMARY

Starting any new project can be difficult, and this is especially true in research. However, the array of suggestions listed in this chapter should help you find a topic that engages and sustains your interest throughout the process. Once you discover that topic, using targeted research tools to investigate scholarly journal articles and books will save you time and yield much better, faster results than a general online search. Just as important in coming up with a research question is recognizing the central role that theory plays in all research and understanding how it can help you in the next step: choosing a design.

End-of-Chapter Exercises

1. Look up some of the faculty members on your school's webpage. What types of research activities are they involved in? How many have current research labs?

2. Using PsycINFO or Google Scholar, find an article on a research topic of interest to you. Does this article have all six sections discussed in this chapter? Briefly describe the type of information included in each section.

3. We have argued throughout this chapter about the importance of drawing on a theory to guide your research. Discuss the advantages and disadvantages to using theories to develop your research questions and hypotheses.

4. Many students are interested in the topic of whether listening to music helps or hinders them while studying. Using PsycINFO or Google Scholar, find a theory that attempts to explain the relationship between music and memory. Briefly describe the key ideas proposed by the theory.

Key Terms

abstract, p. 48

clinical psychology, p. 51

cognitive dissonance, p. 53

domain specific, p. 51

habituation, p. 54

hypothesis, p. 53

literature review, p. 48

method, p. 53

methodology, p. 53

positive psychology, p. 51

PsycINFO, p. 47

research question, p. 51

t test, p. 55

Focusing Your Question and Choosing a Design

4

Chapter Contents

INSIDE RESEARCH: Tony Vernon

Professor emeritus of psychology, University of Western Ontario

Although I am a Canadian, I grew up in England. My father—Philip E. Vernon—was conducting a lot of cross-cultural research in those days, primarily in the area of intelligence and mental abilities, and it was not unusual for me to spend my summer holidays overseas wherever his research took him: Jamaica, Africa, and Canada, to name a few. I did not participate in his research, of course, but from an early age I was fascinated with the tests he used and especially those that he devised himself. This was the main factor that led me to pursue studies and eventually a Ph.D. in areas of psychology related to measurement and the assessment of individual differences, broadly defined.

Over the years, my own research has focused on intelligence and speed of information processing, biological correlates of intelligence, behavioural genetics, and human personality. Individual

continued

differences in personality continue to fascinate me, and my students' research has looked at such diverse topics as the Big 5, emotional intelligence, humour styles, mental toughness, leadership, and—most recently—the dark triad and other dark-side traits. In much of this work we have used behaviour genetic methodology, which allows us not just to assess the phenotypic (or observed) correlations between different personality traits but also to tease apart the extent to which these correlations are attributable to common genetic or environmental factors that the traits have in common. It may not happen in my lifetime but I hope that this research will contribute to the eventual identification of specific genes and environmental factors that affect our behaviour and our personalities.

Tony Vernon is Professor Emeritus in the Department of Psychology at the University of Western Ontario where he has worked since receiving his Ph.D. from the University of California at Berkeley in 1981. He has published extensively in the areas of intelligence and personality and is a past president of the International Society for the Study of Individual Differences. He was also editor-in-chief of the journal *Personality and Individual Differences* from 2006 to 2015.

Research Focus: Intelligence and personality

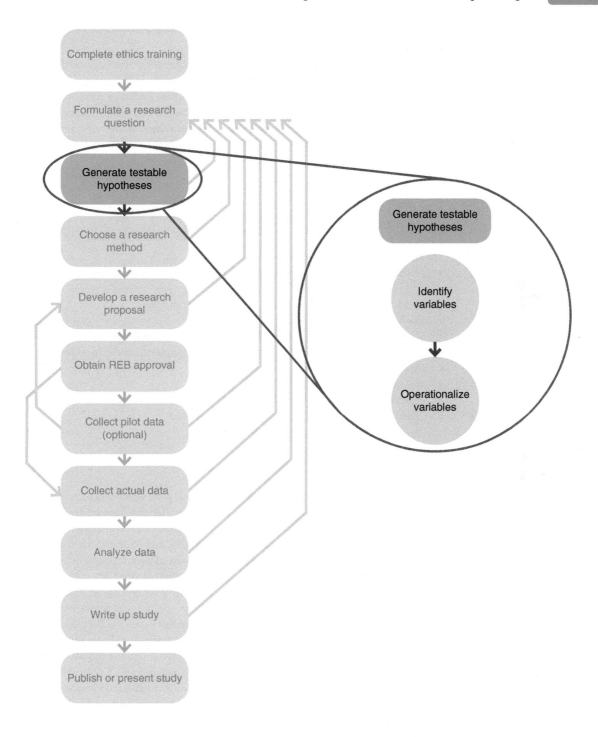

Chapter Abstract

Once you have chosen an area of study and narrowed the scope of your research to a specific question or set of questions, the time has come to more clearly define your goals. The next step is to create hypotheses, identify variables of interest, evaluate particular methods, and begin to design the experiment or research study. We start this chapter with the problem of defining the goal of your research, then we will discuss general issues related to choosing a research methodology, and finish with a discussion of two very important concepts in research: reliability and validity.

LEARNING OBJECTIVES

By the end of this chapter, you should be able to:

- Distinguish between a research question and a research hypothesis, and be able to correctly state both.
- Define and identify independent and dependent variables.
- Operationally define variables.
- Compare and contrast quantitative and qualitative research approaches.
- Discuss the advantages and disadvantages of experimental and non-experimental methods.
- Define reliability and validity.
- Describe the different methods of assessing reliability.
- Describe the different sources of validity evidence.

DEFINE YOUR GOAL

operationalizing The process by which a researcher strives to define variables by putting them in measurable terms.

validity Overall, this concept refers to the idea that your measurements and methodology allow you to capture what you think you are trying to measure or study.

reliability The idea that an investigation or measurement tool should yield consistent findings if researchers use the same procedures and methods repeatedly.

The first step in your research endeavour is defining your goal, which will require you to specify your research question(s) and hypotheses. As we suggested in Chapter 3, how you go about this will be informed, at least in part, by your review of previous research literature and theories, your experience working in research labs with others, and your own ideas and ingenuity. The quality of your research question determines the rest of your research—for better or for worse—so doing a thorough, thoughtful job at the outset is essential.

Defining a research question in the abstract is difficult, so we will use an example to anchor our discussion throughout this chapter. Our example comes from a controversial product that has been popular among parents of young children in recent years: the *Baby Einstein* videos.

Suppose you are interested in testing the claim that such products boost the intelligence of young children. How would you begin to tackle this question? In the following sections, we will discuss the steps involved in designing your study: how to frame a research question and form testable hypotheses, operationalize and define your variables, choose your methodology, and weigh the benefits and limitations of both quantitative and qualitative approaches. Along the way, we will also consider the issues of validity and reliability that are central to the choices you make as a researcher. Validity refers to the extent to which your measures and methodology accurately enable you to capture the "reality" of the behaviour or concept that you are investigating—in other words, are you actually studying what you claim to be studying? Reliability refers to the consistency of your chosen measures and methodological approach—that is, is your approach dependable? Can you obtain the same or similar results if you repeat your study or specific measurements?

Define the Research Question

Articulating the initial question ("Do *Baby Einstein* videos boost young children's intelligence?") is just the beginning. The real challenge is to put the question in terms that are testable, falsifiable (able to be proven wrong), and definable in scope.

Form a Testable Hypothesis.   An important step in formulating your research project is crafting a specific and testable hypothesis that will guide your investigation. In our *Baby Einstein* example, we might believe that the videos work—but such a hypothesis is too vague to test (see "Media Matters: Baby Geniuses"). A testable hypothesis must be specific in its prediction. We could hypothesize that a group of children exposed to several hours of the videos per week (for some specified amount of time) will show higher levels of intelligence on a standardized measure than children who spend several hours watching non–*Baby Einstein* videos. This hypothesis is testable because it makes a particular prediction that can be supported or refuted through the collection of relevant data or information.

Ensure Your Hypothesis Is Falsifiable.   There must be a way to know whether your hypothesis is false, that is, if the videos do not boost intelligence. In the case of a study where you are measuring gain versus no gain, it is not difficult to see how a hypothesis could be falsifiable; the best way to falsify the idea that the videos boost intelligence would be to show no significant measurable gains in intelligence scores for children who are exposed to the videos.

However, some theories in the history of psychology have defied falsifiability. Among them are Sigmund Freud's personality elements in his structural theory of personality (id, ego, superego). Freud's concepts of the id, ego, and superego are unconscious processes that are loosely defined, which makes them difficult, if not impossible, to measure objectively.

As another example, Jean Piaget, a noted developmental psychologist, hypothesized key constructs of assimilation (the taking in of new information and incorporating it into our existing ideas) and accommodation (the taking in of new information and it modifying or changing our ideas), which are for the most part untestable.

Both of these examples involve unconscious, unobservable, and unmeasurable processes that are difficult, if not impossible, to study empirically. Researchers would struggle and likely fail to construct a testable hypothesis for an experiment that would falsify their existence. Yet the lack of falsifiability of these concepts does not mean that they are untrue. Rather, their lack of falsifiability places them outside the realm of scientific inquiry.

It is possible that with methodological innovations, concepts once considered unfalsifiable may, in fact, become falsifiable. Freud's notion of the unconscious serves as a fascinating example. Although at one time many psychologists would have asserted that we could not verify the unconscious, today many argue that the Implicit Association Test (Greenwald, McGhee, & Schwartz, 1998) can potentially measure implicit cognition, that is, thoughts and attitudes about which a person is not consciously aware. A relatively new technique used by social psychologists, the Implicit Association Test (IAT) measures reaction time to investigate the strength of association between people's mental representations. While the IAT test may have promise as a measure of implicit bias, there are critics who call into question the psychometric reliability and validity of the test. From a methodological standpoint, however, the bottom line is that this technique provides an opportunity for supporting or falsifying at least some

falsifiable The concept that researchers can test whether the hypothesis or claim can be proven wrong.

assimilation A concept of Piaget's (a cognitive developmental psychologist) that refers to a process where internal mental structures take in new information and fit it in with existing structures (schemas).

accommodation A concept of Piaget's (a cognitive developmental psychologist) that refers to a process where internal mental structures change as a function of maturation and taking in new information.

Implicit Association Test A test of implicit cognition that measures participants' reaction time to investigate the strength of association between people's mental representations.

Baby Geniuses

Unlock the "little genius" within your infant! Increase the cognitive development of your toddler, who will be counting numbers and decoding language before you know it! Your baby can learn to read! Such were the initial claims of companies selling video products (and later, a variety of tools) that pioneered the so-called "baby genius industry" in the late 1990s and early 2000s.

Most media outlets ignored these extraordinary statements at first, even if the videos proved immediately popular with parents. Scant early reports on the baby genius phenomenon focused on the trend of younger and younger children being immersed in electronic media. One newspaper article cited a 2003 study of young children's media habits by the Henry J. Kaiser Family Foundation, which showed that 32 per cent of children aged 6 months to 2 years were watching Baby Einstein videos. According to one mother, "You want to make sure you're doing everything you can for your child, and you know everyone else uses 'Baby Einstein,' so you feel guilty if you don't" (Lewin, 2003).

By 2006, however, baby genius products had come under intense media scrutiny. The Campaign for a Commercial-Free Childhood (CCFC) filed a complaint with the Federal Trade Commission against the Walt Disney Company, which by then owned Baby Einstein, and the Brainy Baby Company for false and deceptive advertising. Although the Federal Trade Commission decided not to take action, Disney removed some product testimonials from its website and said that it would better substantiate its educational claims in the future (CCFC, 2007).

Vitalinka/Shutterstock

Then, in 2007, the *Journal of Pediatrics* published a study by researchers at the University of Washington (Zimmerman, Christakis, & Meltzoff, 2007), which issued a press release for the study suggesting that regular viewing of the videos might even cause harm to children. The correlational study was based on telephone interviews of approximately 1,000 parents of children aged 2 to 24 months. The authors concluded that for every hour per day spent watching baby DVDs and videos, infants aged 8 to 16 months understood an average of six to eight fewer words than babies who did not watch them (Pankratz, 2007).

Media and parenting blogs jumped on results of the University of Washington study. The chief executive officer of Disney, Robert Iger, subsequently demanded that the university retract the press release, a request the university rejected. Yet a couple of years later Disney offered a full refund to consumers who bought *Baby Einstein* videos from 2004 to 2009, eventually paying out $100 million; the company also stopped claiming that the products were educational (Martin, 2011). Consumers from both Canada and the United States were offered the reimbursement (Mclean, 2009).

aspects of Freud's notion of cognitive processes outside of conscious awareness. It also highlights the importance of making your own evaluation of a test or measure prior to selecting it for use in your research.

operational definition A clearly specified definition of your variables, stated in observable and measurable terms.

Operationally Define Your Variables

In forming your hypotheses, you are specifying the variables you intend to test in your research and providing an operational definition for each of these variables. In the case of *Baby Einstein*, the glaring challenge involves the definition of intelligence. If we want to test whether watching particular videos makes children smarter, then we first must agree on what we mean by "smarter." In psychology, the question of how to best define intelligence has a narrative almost as long as the history of the field itself. For example, should we conceptualize and measure intelligence as a single, unified factor (Spearman, 1904); as two broad areas of interrelated abilities (Horn & Cattell, 1967); or as a series of independent domains (Gardner, 1983)? Generally, variables can be operationally defined in multiple ways, so it is essential that you clearly specify how you intend to operationalize your variables for your study. And when you are reading about research being conducted by others, it is equally important to pay attention to how they have operationally defined the variables they used.

For our *Baby Einstein* study, we would have to pick our operationalization of intelligence as a precondition for designing our study. Do we want to hypothesize that the videos increase Spearman's notion of general measures of intelligence? Or perhaps that they enhance fluid intelligence (i.e., speed of processing) in Horn and Cattell's terms? Or maybe the videos are most effective for the domain of musical intelligence, as defined by Gardner. Once we select our preferred definition of intelligence, we would be ready to select a measurement tool to use with our participants—in this case, some sort of intelligence test. We would also need to operationalize the exposure to the video content. Although this is an easier task than defining intelligence, it would be equally important to clearly define what it means to receive a "dosage" of the videos (i.e., how much time watching the video, on how many different occasions).

CHOOSE A RESEARCH METHODOLOGY

Researchers choose a particular research design for many different reasons. Some researchers always use the same methodology in all or almost all of their research, whereas other researchers use a wide variety of research designs. There is no single best design that should be used in all circumstances. The key point to keep in mind is that your research question should always drive the choice of methodology and *should interest you*.

Choosing a research design requires you to consider several issues. The first issue concerns the point at which you are entering the research process. Are you investigating a relatively understudied set of behaviours, or are you attempting to forge a new direction in a well-established field? Often researchers working in understudied or less well-established areas use designs that are exploratory and that enable the researcher to isolate a small number of variables from the myriad variables that could be investigated for more in-depth study. For example, researchers just starting in a new domain of inquiry might use an observational design or open-ended interviews to help narrow and define the research question. In his classic research on the stickleback fish, Tinbergen (1951) began with natural observations that helped him develop more specific hypotheses, which he could then test in highly controlled experiments.

Second, researchers in more established fields might use a relatively small number of experimental designs that are accepted by the majority of researchers in a particular field. For example, much of the research on how infants reason about the world uses a standard methodology known as habituation (see Bornstein, Mash, Arterberry, & Manian, 2012). In this particular design, infants are repeatedly presented with a set of stimuli that share important features (e.g., a set of male faces). After repeated exposures, the infants become bored and look less at the stimuli (i.e., they become "habituated"). Once the infants' looking time decreases below a predetermined criterion, researchers change the stimuli for one group (known as the experimental group) of infants, for example, by replacing male faces with female faces. If infants recognize the change in stimuli, their looking time generally increases (i.e., they become "dishabituated"). A second group of infants (the control group) will receive additional examples of the original stimuli set (e.g., more male faces), and generally they will continue to be "bored" by the repeated exposures. We will discuss this type of experimental design in more detail in Chapter 7. The main idea is that researchers may use particular designs because they are the established ones in a particular discipline, with the notion that they have been vetted by the scientific community (meaning they are assumed to be both valid and reliable designs, concepts we will examine shortly).

Other issues that influence your choice of design include the cost of doing the research, whether you have the proper tools or technology available, and, of course, whether the research you are interested in can be done in a manner that is ethical and safe to study.

Obviously, you cannot use your preferred research design if you do not have the financial resources or technology available. But you can often devise low-cost methods using simpler technologies to creatively address the same or a related research question. One thing to remember, however, is that no design is perfect and no single research study can provide the final, definitive evidence that answers your research question. It is also the case that using multiple designs can help establish the validity of a particular finding.

Yet another issue depends on whether your research question is attempting to understand (1) a *relation* between two or more variables or (2) what *causes* a particular behaviour or outcome. A correlational design is used when your research question seeks to establish whether there is a correlation, or relation, between your variables. If a correlation is found it means that if there is an increase or decrease in one variable there will be a corresponding change in the other variable. Alternatively, a causal design is used when your question seeks to establish whether there is a cause-and-effect relationship between your variables and whether one variable can be demonstrated to cause a change in the other variable.

Quantitative Research Approaches

When selecting a design, researchers can choose from quantitative or qualitative research. Quantitative research is any systematic study that yields numerically measured data. In quantitative research designs, measurement is typically determined a priori, that is, before the study is conducted. In quantitative research, statistical analyses are used to answer the questions at hand. Although use of statistics defines quantitative research, quantitative research can be either experimental or non-experimental. The choice of a particular methodology often depends on available resources and the nature of the question being asked, because some questions are more amenable to one over the other. Discussion of the advantages and limitations of experimental and non-experimental approaches follows.

Experimental Methods. Experimental methods are often held up as the gold standard for scientific research because they possess a set of powerful advantages. Such methods refer to a group of approaches where the environment of the research setting is tightly controlled and often (although not always) conducted within a formal laboratory setting. Within that controlled environment, the conditions are carefully crafted so that any differences found between groups can be attributed to the intentional manipulations of the independent variable(s) to which the participants are exposed. In addition to this level of control, the experimental method includes the important technique of random assignment—assigning participants by chance to either an experimental group (the participants who receive the

correlational design
A research design that seeks to understand how different variables are related to one another.

causal design
A research design that seeks to understand what causes or explains a certain phenomenon.

quantitative research The use of numerical data and statistical techniques to examine questions of interest. Or, research that results in data that can be numerically measured.

random assignment
The assignment of participants to different conditions in an experiment by methods that rely on chance and probability so that potential biases related to assignment to conditions are removed.

experimental group In an experimental design, the set of participants that receives the intervention or treatment with the goal of determining whether the treatment impacts the outcome.

experimental treatment) or a control group (the participants who do not receive the experimental treatment).

This procedure enables the experimenter to assume that any differences in individual characteristics among the participants will be randomly distributed across the two groups. The random distribution across groups on the variables of interest should lead the groups to be highly similar at the start of the experiment. And, by accommodating pre-existing differences between participants, an experimenter can be more confident that whatever differences do emerge are a result of the actual experimental manipulation.

Consider an experiment designed to investigate the impact of a new drug on children's attention. The experimental group would receive the new drug and the control group would not receive the drug. As participants are recruited to the study, they would be randomly assigned to either the experimental group (and receive the drug) or the control group (and not receive the drug). Using random assignment, existing individual differences among children in attention should be equally distributed in both the experimental and the control group. Thus, the experimenter would expect to find highly similar attention levels in both groups at the start of the study. If the experimenter finds that, after taking the new drug for some time, children in the experimental group have higher attention levels than those of the control group, they can infer that the drug has an impact on attention levels. We provide a much more detailed explanation of experimental designs in Chapter 7.

What might an experimental design to examine the effectiveness of *Baby Einstein* videos look like? Although we will discuss an actual study shortly, we will first discuss the broad parameters of an experimental approach to the topic. Imagine a study where a group of young children and their parents are recruited and randomly divided into two groups: (1) an experimental group where the children come to a laboratory setting and watch the videos with their parents for a designated amount of time every week for several months and (2) a control group where the children come to the laboratory setting with their parents for an equivalent amount of time and are simply instructed to interact and play during the sessions. Because the company claims that the videos increase vocabulary, at the end of the visits both groups of children are tested on their understanding of a list of vocabulary words. Although other procedures could be implemented to tighten this design—and the actual research does, in fact, have additional controls in place—the basic features of the experimental method can be seen here: conditions that differ only in terms of the variable of interest (watching the videos) and random assignment of participants to one of those conditions.

The example just given contains two major constructs, or variables, that are relevant to our study. The first is the independent variable, a factor that is manipulated or systematically varied in an experiment. The independent variable typically forms the groups (also called levels) that you want to compare. It is the factor that you are hoping will have an effect on the dependent variable, which is the response of interest that the experimenter thinks is influenced by the independent variable. A good way to remember the difference between an independent and a dependent variable is that a person's score on the dependent variable will *depend* on what group they were in on the independent variable. In our *Baby Einstein* study, the independent variable is the exposure to the videos (or lack of exposure for the control group; thus, creating two groups), and our dependent variable is vocabulary learning.

A major advantage of an experimental setup, assuming it has been done with proper care, is that it is a causal design and you *can*, in fact, draw conclusions about causality. In other words, if you find that the children in the video group have greater vocabulary retention, you can assert that the videos caused this greater learning.

control group In an experimental design, the set of participants who do not receive the experimental treatment (or who receive an inert version). This group is compared with the experimental group.

independent variable A variable manipulated by the experimenter to observe its effect on a dependent variable.

dependent variable The factor of interest being measured in the experiment that changes in response to manipulation of the independent variable.

ecological validity
A measure of the degree to which the conclusions drawn from a research study can be applied to real-life situations.

A major, frequently cited disadvantage of experimental methodology is its artificiality. This concern relates to the concept of ecological validity—the extent to which the study captures the reality of the topic. When a topic is studied in a controlled laboratory setting, critics assert that lack of resemblance to the "real world" may call the applicability of the results into question. Although this is not a trivial concern and one that researchers must take seriously, some have argued that such a critique may be overstated because it ignores the very purpose of experimental methods: "the artificiality of scientific experimentation is not a weakness but actually the very thing that gives the scientific method its unique power to yield explanations about the nature of the world" (Stanovich, 2013, p. 105).

non-experimental methods A group of research approaches that do not attempt to manipulate or control the environment, but rather involve the researcher using a systematic technique to examine what is already occurring.

Non-experimental Methods.

Non-experimental methods comprise a group of approaches that do not attempt to manipulate or control the environment, but rather involve the researcher using a systematic technique to examine what is already occurring. In a non-experimental study, the researcher designs ways to measure phenomena as they naturally occur.

Non-experimental methods have some primary advantages. The first is one of ecological validity. Essentially, when you observe and measure a phenomenon as it naturally occurs, you can be assured that your data are a reasonably unadulterated reflection of reality. Second, it is often impossible—logistically, ethically, or both—to experimentally manipulate some phenomena. For example, if you want to study the health effects of chronic smoking, you are unable to systematically assign people to a heavy smoking group so that you can compare them with more moderate smokers or non-smokers. Researchers also cannot randomly assign a participant to variables such as age or gender. In such cases, your best bet is to use non-experimental methods to discern relationships and trends.

Non-experimental methods also have some disadvantages. One major limitation involves the determination of causality. When using non-experimental methodology, researchers cannot conclusively assume causal relationships between variables, even if they are fairly certain about the nature of such relationships. The reason for this goes back to one of the advantages of experimental methods. In an experimental design, you benefit from the ability to randomly assign participants to carefully controlled conditions so that you can attribute any difference between participants to the experimental manipulation. Without this careful control and random assignment (which allows you to assume that your groups are equivalent), any relationships between variables that you discover are purely correlational; we can say that particular phenomena are associated, but we cannot state the direction of that association or whether the association may be caused by some third, unmeasured variable.

Let's return to the *Baby Einstein* example as an illustration. Imagine that we conducted a non-experimental study to examine the relationship between exposure to the videos and babies' word learning. In our study, we took two already existing groups of babies—one whose parents played the videos for their children for the past few months and a second who have never seen the videos. We find that the group of babies who have been exposed to the videos have learned a significantly greater number of words than the babies who have not been exposed. Can we conclude that the videos are responsible for this difference—that is, that they caused the babies to learn more words?

As tempting as that conclusion might be, the answer is no. Without experimental control and random assignment, we cannot be sure that the differences between the groups are not a result of some third variable, some other factor related to both of the relevant variables at hand (video watching and word learning). For example, there may be pre-existing differences between the groups of parents and babies who are likely to use the videos versus those who do not use them. Parents of babies who view the videos may be more verbal with their children in the first place or may have access to other resources that the parents of the non–video users do not have.

The other major limitation to non-experimental research is that the data derived from such studies do not allow you to draw conclusions about directionality of effects. Although the *Baby Einstein* example may be less relevant here, consider another example from the intelligence literature: the positive association between intelligence and socio-economic status. Although it is well established that higher levels of intelligence are associated with higher levels of income, what is the direction of this effect? Is it that being more intelligent in the first place helps you to get a job and accrue resources that put you in a higher socio-economic bracket? Or does socio-economic advantage supply you with resources (books, access to high-quality education) that foster higher levels of intelligence? One possibility is bidirectionality—that is, the causal arrow may go in both directions. But without the benefit of an experimental design (which would be hard to envision with this topic), we are left to speculate about the nature of this association.

Qualitative Research Approaches

Whereas quantitative research focuses on obtaining information that can be "quantified" or counted, qualitative research emphasizes words and meaning (Willig, 2012). That is, qualitative researchers are generally interested in participants' subjective experience; they try to understand the way participants experience some event and what the experience means to them. Often these researchers will examine behaviour in context, focusing on language and actions to understand how participants make sense of a particular event. This richness in data, which is a key strength of qualitative research, comes from the different methods that are typically used in qualitative research. The three most common of these are participant observation, in-depth interviews, and focus groups. Interviews and focus groups are expanded on in Chapter 6, and participant observation is explained in more detail in Chapter 8. The detail and richness of data that come with using these methods also come at a cost. Qualitative data is much more time consuming to collect and analyze compared to quantitative data.

Similar to there being multiple research designs within quantitative research, the same is true for qualitative research. The choice of qualitative design will depend on key philosophical assumptions regarding the nature of reality (ontological assumption), how knowledge is known or acquired (epistemological assumption), the roles of values in research (axiological assumption), and the procedures used in the process (methodological assumption; Creswell & Poth, 2018). Researchers' stance on these assumptions will inform their theoretical perspective and will guide how, and on what, they will focus their research. A detailed discussion of the various theoretical perspectives and methodologies that qualitative researchers can draw upon are beyond the scope of this book, but interested readers are referred to *Qualitative Inquiry and Research Design* by Creswell and Poth (2018). We will, however, provide two examples of qualitative studies to provide some context for this approach.

Our first example comes from Yang and colleagues (2011), who wanted to examine the impact of tai chi, a Chinese martial art involving slow, patterned movements and meditation, on practitioners' quality of life. These researchers conducted semi-structured interviews with eight tai chi practitioners and examined their experiences practising tai chi using a social constructionist theoretical perspective, which focuses on the ways in which the participants

bidirectionality In a cause-and-effect relationship between two variables, both variables can act as the causal variable. For example, higher intelligence may cause one to be in a higher socio-economic bracket and being in a higher socio-economic bracket may cause one's intelligence to increase; the effect goes both ways.

qualitative research Research that results in data that are non-numerical and are analyzed for meaning or patterns.

social constructionism A theoretical perspective that examines how participants derive meaning from their lived experiences.

derive meaning from their lived experiences. The interviews were coded and analyzed for common themes among the participants. One theme that emerged from this study was that many older adults who regularly practised tai chi felt that it provided a strong sense of spiritual well-being. Direct quotes from the participants are often used to provide evidence for the themes derived in the analysis of qualitative data. For instance, one participant in the Yang and colleagues (2011) study was quoted as saying "it's very different to quiet your mind and not be thinking about things . . . I don't know how to explain it . . . it can be very spiritual" (p. 7).

A second example comes from a study by Carla Rice (2007), who used a **post-structural feminist** theoretical perspective to understand Canadian women's experiences of feeling fat. Rice was interested in exploring how women's bodies and identities were shaped through cultural and social norms. She conducted interviews with 81 women to obtain their body histories and coded these histories into common themes. *Learning size differences* was one theme that emerged from this study and captured how women were socialized by family and peers to recognize that different body sizes were valued differently, which perpetuated an anti-fat attitude among many of the women.

post-structural feminism A theoretical perspective that seeks to explore and understand how individuals are shaped and experienced through cultural and social norms.

What these two examples share in common is their focus on collecting rich narrative data and seeking to understand the meaning participants ascribed to their experiences. When presenting the results of qualitative data, the goal can be to merely describe the data or to uncover the meaning of an experience from the data (Willig, 2012). Researchers taking the former perspective attempt to capture the quality and richness of participants' experience "in their own words." In contrast, researchers taking a more interpretative view try to go beyond the words and descriptions to find hidden or non-obvious meanings derived from the experience. Within psychology, descriptive accounts generally dominate. However, in both of the examples just presented, the researchers went beyond description to explore what tai chi practice meant to the older adults (Yang et al., 2011) and how women had been socialized to view their bodies (Rice, 2007).

ADVANTAGES OF MULTIPLE APPROACHES AND METHODS

Because quantitative and qualitative approaches, and experimental and non-experimental methods, all have their own strengths and weaknesses, the ultimate research strategy is often to employ multiple approaches and methods to study any given topic. In studying our *Baby Einstein* videos, why not conduct qualitative research as well as use a more quantitative approach? Why not use non-experimental and experimental methodologies that look at children and parents both in their natural environment and in the laboratory setting? Using multiple methods does require more time and resources, but it can provide a fuller picture of the topic you wish to study.

mixed methods research Research that uses both quantitative and qualitative data within a single study.

exploratory design A mixed methods research design that first collects and analyzes qualitative data then uses these findings to inform the quantitative data collection.

Mixed methods research is a research methodology that uses both qualitative and quantitative research together in a single study or set of related studies. The rationale for this type of design is that by using both approaches, in combination, a better understanding of the research problem or issue can be obtained than through either approach alone. In a mixed methods study, the data can be "mixed" a number of ways. For instance, if a topic is a relatively new area of research, it may be best to use a qualitative approach to get "the lay of the land" and then, once you have a good sense of the issue, follow up with a more structured quantitative methodology (referred to as an **exploratory design**). For instance, for her Ph.D. thesis, one of the authors of this text used this design, which first involved a qualitative study to explore men's perceptions of their body image and then a quantitative study that developed and tested a new measure for assessing the areas of concern that were identified by the men in the qualitative study. Alternatively, an explanatory design first collects quantitative data then follows up with a qualitative design to more deeply explore the results of the quantitative data. Finally, a convergent design will first collect and analyze quantitative and qualitative data separately, but will then integrate the results together, often in the discussion section. It is important to remember that no single design or approach is perfect, and ultimately your research question should drive the choice of design.

As discussed in Chapter 1, a key aspect of the scientific method involves the notion that results can be replicated. We discussed the importance of this idea with respect to replicating results using the same methods over time and with different experimenters, especially ones from independent laboratories. In fact, Daniel Kahneman has argued that psychologists should routinely work with other researchers in their field who work in other independent laboratories to replicate each other's research (Yong, 2012). But another important way to provide support for a research finding is to obtain converging evidence for that finding using a variety of different methodological approaches. Replication of results involves the related concepts of reliability and validity.

explanatory design
A mixed methods research design that first collects and analyzes quantitative data then follows up the findings with a more in-depth qualitative study.

convergent design
A mixed methods research design that collects and analyzes the quantitative and qualitative data separately, but then integrates the results together.

RELIABILITY AND VALIDITY

The concepts of reliability and validity are two of the most important concepts in research methods. Reliability is generally defined as a measure of the consistency of results obtained using the same or similar measures. Imagine stepping on a scale and getting a reading of your weight. If you were to step off the scale and then step back on, you would expect to see the same weight. This indicates that you are getting a consistent, or reliable, reading from the scale. If the reading was to change each time you stepped on the scale, you would not know what your real weight was and the scale would be of little use.

Another way to think of reliability is in terms of measurement error. Measurement error is the random or chance fluctuations that impact data during the measurement process. Reliability and measurement error are inversely related. A measure that is reliable, and is providing consistent results, would have little measurement error; for example, the scale that gives you a consistent reading. Conversely, a measure that has low reliability has high measurement error; it is this measurement error that leads to inconsistent results, and why an unreliable scale would give you different readings each time you stepped on it. Validity, in contrast, is a measure of whether a variable or assessment actually captures what it is supposed to capture; for instance, a scale is meant to be a measure of how much you weigh.

Figure 4.1 shows how the general concepts of reliability and validity relate to one another. As shown in the first target, the three arrows are clustered together; this consistency in hitting the target in nearly the same spot indicates that the shooter is very reliable, but since the arrows did not hit the bullseye, it indicates that the shots were not accurate—they are not valid. In the middle target, the arrows are clustered together, and they hit the centre of the target. This indicates that the shooter is both reliable and valid in their aim. Finally, the third target shows three arrows in three different locations and none of them have hit the bullseye. This indicates that the shooter is neither reliable nor valid in their aim. Thus, you can see that these concepts are related but not equivalent. Basically, you must have reliability in order to

measurement error
The difference between the actual or true value of what you are measuring and the result obtained using the measurement instrument.

Table 4.1   Types of reliability.

Term	Definition	Example
Reliability	A general measure of the consistency of your assessment, usually measured by specific types of reliability.	If measures of infant intelligence are reliable, then one should be able to obtain the same intelligence score over different assessments. Reliability is often assessed by examining the correlation between scores on different assessments. If the correlation approaches $r = 1.0$, the two assessments are highly reliable.
Test–retest	A measure of the consistency of results obtained using the same assessment tool on multiple occasions.	If you measure an infant's IQ today, how likely are you to obtain the same score tomorrow or at some later date using the same test? It is typically measured by calculating the correlation between the two different scores measured at two different times. Researchers must be careful to consider effects that arise from repeated testing. Taking the same test twice can lead individuals to change their responses—because they have learned something or because their views have changed.
Alternate forms	A measure of the consistency of results obtained on different but equivalent forms of the same assessment tool.	You design two forms of your infant IQ measure that involve different but equivalent items. If you have high reliability, the results you obtain using the different forms should yield the same values (as measured by a correlation between the scores obtained on the two forms).
Inter-rater reliability	A measure of agreement in the scores provided by two or more different raters.	Two different experimenters make independent assessments of an infant's IQ; to what extent are the scores from one experimenter consistent with those obtained by the other experimenter? Generally assessed using a statistic known as kappa (κ).
Internal consistency	A measure of how much the scores on items within an assessment yield the same values—to what extent are items within the assessment correlated with each other? Two common ways of assessing internal consistency are through the split half and Cronbach's alpha methods.	You design your infant IQ measure with multiple items that assess "numerosity" (having a general sense of number, even at a young age). If you have high internal consistency, then one item that reflects a greater sense of numerosity will yield similar values as a second item that also reflects a greater sense of numerosity.
Split half	Within a test, this is a measure of internal consistency where the scores on half the items on an assessment are correlated with the scores on the other half of the assessment.	In an IQ test made up of 100 items, to what extent do the scores obtained on a random selection of 50 items correlate with those obtained on the remaining 50 items?

Term	Definition	Example
Cronbach's alpha (α)	Within a test, this is a measure of internal consistency that measures the average correlation between all items in the assessment.	An IQ test with a high α-value is one where the items with the assessment tool are all highly correlated with one another.
	This measure is equivalent to obtaining the average of all possible split-half reliabilities.	

have validity. If you can't measure something consistently, how could it be valid? However, it is possible to measure something reliably but for it to be way off topic and not valid, such as in the first target.

There are four common approaches that researchers use to assess the reliability of a particular measure. Test–retest reliability assesses the stability of a measure over time and involves correlating the scores from the same measure taken at two different points in time. Alternate forms reliability assesses the similarity between two versions of the

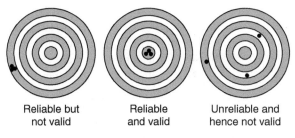

Reliable but not valid   Reliable and valid   Unreliable and hence not valid

FIGURE 4.1   Concepts of reliability and validity.

same measure and involves correlating the scores from two different versions of a scale or assessment designed to measure the same construct. Inter-rater reliability assesses the consistency in ratings between two raters observing the same behaviour and involves correlating the ratings given by two raters. Internal consistency reliability assesses the degree to which items within an assessment are consistent with one another and measure the same thing. Table 4.1 lists common types of reliability, definitions, and examples.

While reliability looks at the precision with which you measure something, validity looks at how accurately you are measuring what you think you are measuring. Validity has a long history, and the way in which we view validity has changed over the years (Sireci, 2016). Further, not everyone agrees on a single definition of validity and, as a result, researchers tend to talk about many different types of validity. We align our views of validity with those that are endorsed in the *Standards for Educational and Psychological Testing* (AERA, APA, & NCME, 2014). In this sixth revision of the *Standards*, validity is defined as "the degree to which evidence and theory support the interpretations of test scores for proposed uses of tests" (p. 11). And when we say "test," we mean this to include any measure, tool, or survey that collects quantitative data. Validity is viewed as a unitary concept in that there are not different "types" of validity, but rather different types of validity *evidence* that all support the intended uses of test scores. The five sources of validity evidence presented in the *Standards* are as follows:

- Evidence based on test content
- Evidence based on response processes
- Evidence based on internal structure
- Evidence based on relations to other variables
- Evidence based on consequences of testing

test–retest reliability Correlation of the scores from the same measure that is taken by the same group of respondents at two different points in time.

alternate forms reliability Correlation of the scores from two different versions of the same measure that is taken by the same group of respondents.

inter-rater reliability Correlation of the ratings made by two different raters observing the same behaviour.

internal consistency The degree to which the items within a measure assess various aspects of the same construct.

evidence based on test content The degree to which the content of a test measures what it is intended to measure.

construct underrepresentation A construct is measured too narrowly and its measurement does not include all relevant aspects of the construct.

construct irrelevant variance A construct is measured too broadly and its measurement includes aspects that are not part of the construct.

evidence based on response processes The degree to which the mechanisms underlying what people think, feel, or do when responding to test items or tasks matches the construct the test or task is trying to measure.

evidence based on internal structure The degree to which test items and components match the structure of the underlying construct.

factor analysis A statistical technique that examines the relationships between items in a scale. This approach is useful for determining whether a scale measures a single variable or multiple ones.

evidence based on relations to other variables The degree to which a test/construct is related to other external variables.

Evidence based on test content refers to how well the content of a test measures the construct it is intended to measure. For instance, if you were to write a quiz on the content of this chapter, then the quiz should consist of questions that will assess how well you know the content in this chapter. The quiz should cover all topics covered in this chapter and not, for instance, just focus on this section on validity. It should also only assess the content of this chapter and not include questions on areas outside of this chapter, such as questions on research ethics. This refers to the concepts of **construct underrepresentation** and **construct irrelevant variance**. The former refers to a measure that is too narrowly focused and fails to include key aspects of the construct, while the latter refers to a measure that is focused too broadly and includes aspects that are not part of the construct one is trying to measure (DeVellis, 2017).

Evidence based on response processes examines the cognitive processes that test takers engage in when completing a test. Examining evidence based on response processes involves looking at the mechanisms underlying what people think, feel, or do when responding to test items or completing tasks and whether this matches what was intended (Hubley & Zumbo, 2017). This can be useful in understanding ways in which items may have unknown, multiple, or unintended interpretations. For instance, Canadians may know that a toque is a knit hat, but other cultural groups may be unfamiliar with this word.

Evidence based on internal structure refers to how well items and components match the structure of the underlying construct. If, for instance, you were interested in studying student perceptions of the learning environment and your theoretical framework posits that the learning environment is a single dimension, then you would want to demonstrate that the items on this measure are all measuring a single construct. If, however, your theoretical framework suggests that the learning environment consists of multiple dimensions, then you would want to provide evidence that the items do in fact measure multiple dimensions. **Factor analysis** is a statistical technique that is commonly used to identify the underlying structure of a construct as it examines the pattern of correlations underlying a set of items.

Evidence based on relations to other variables examines the relationships among the test/construct and other external variables. This source of validity evidence can be further subdivided based on the type of external variable that is being assessed. If compared to other measures that are intended to assess the same or similar constructs, you would expect them to correlate with one another; such correlations are referred to as **convergent evidence**. For example, Tony Vernon (see the Inside Research box at the beginning of this chapter) and colleagues (2016) examined the relationship between the **general factor of personality (GFP)** and the **dark triad** (a cluster of three antisocial personality traits: Machiavellianism, narcissism, and psychopathy). As hypothesized, they found significant negative correlations between GFP and both Machiavellianism and psychopathy, which provides evidence of convergent validity. Sometimes it is important to demonstrate that two variables are not related to one another—that they are distinct constructs. This form of evidence is referred to as **discriminant evidence**. Generally, evidence of discriminant validity is demonstrated by showing that two variables do not correlate with one another. Often, measures of **socially desirable responding** are used to provide evidence of discriminant validity.

Another way in which a relationship between variables can be assessed is in how well test scores can predict an external criterion. This is different from the discussion of convergent and discriminant evidence above in that the criterion is distinct from the test scores, and the test scores are intended to predict performance on the criterion. For instance, high school grades are commonly used to predict performance in university and are thus used to inform decisions on who to accept into university; thus, university performance is the criterion and high school grades would be the predictor variable. This type of evidence is further divided based on *when* the criterion variable is being measured. If the predictor variable and criterion are measured at the same point in time, it is referred to as concurrent evidence. If the criterion is measured at a point in the future, it is referred to as predictive evidence. High school and university are spaced years apart; thus, using high school grades to predict later performance in university would be an example of predictive evidence.

Evidence based on consequences of testing involves examining the interpretations and uses of test scores and their resulting intended (and unintended) consequences. If we consider high-stakes educational testing as an example, consequences of testing can be positive (e.g., increased teacher professional development), negative (e.g., test anxiety), intended (e.g., greater accountability), and unintended (e.g., narrowing of the curriculum; Blazer, 2011). In providing evidence based on the consequences of testing, it is important to consider each of these four outcomes and the impact they could have on the interpretation and use of test scores.

Although not a true type of validity evidence, you may come across claims of face validity. Face validity assess whether the items on a test appear, on the surface, to measure what they purport to measure. For instance, you would expect a math exam to have math questions on it or a customer service survey to ask questions about customer service. However, just because the items look like they are measuring what they claim to, this is not considered sufficient empirical evidence to support the validity of the test scores. Some "bad" measures may look like they have face validity (e.g., think about the various surveys you find in magazines or on Facebook), and other "good" measures may not look like they have face validity. The Minnesota Multiphasic Personality Inventory-2 (MMPI-2), a measure of personality, contains many items that would not appear to be valid indicators of personality. For instance, the item "I enjoy detective mystery stories" is an indicator of the suppression of aggression. However, these items have been shown to empirically discriminate among different personality traits. So while face validity cannot be used as a legitimate source of validity evidence, it can have value in terms of how acceptable individuals find the items, which could increase their willingness to complete the items.

There are two additional types of validity evidence that are worth mentioning at this point, and will be discussed in more detail in Chapter 7. Internal validity assesses whether a particular variable is the actual cause of a particular outcome. Internal validity is particularly important in an experimental design. When a study has high internal validity, you can be confident in demonstrating a cause-and-effect relationship between two variables. High internal validity can be achieved through good experimental control and the elimination of possible confounding variables. External validity refers to the degree to which the conclusions drawn from a particular set of results can be generalized to other samples or situations. External validity is important when you want to extend your findings beyond your specific study to a broader population or context or to a real-world application. Examples and definitions of the different types of validity are provided in Table 4.2.

To conclude our discussion of reliability and validity, there are three important points to take away. First, when speaking about reliability and validity, it is in reference to the scores produced from the measure and not the measure itself. A measure cannot be valid or invalid. Rather, it is the scores produced from the measure that can be valid or invalid. To demonstrate this, imagine that your instructor has created a quiz to assess your knowledge of the content in this chapter. Your score on this quiz should be an accurate indicator of your content knowledge. If, however, your instructor takes this same quiz and instead administers it to a class of introductory psychology students as a measure of their knowledge of introductory

convergent evidence The degree to which two constructs that theoretically should be related to one another are related.

general factor of personality A single dimension of personality.

dark triad A cluster of three antisocial personality traits: Machiavellianism, narcissism, and psychopathy.

discriminant evidence A lack of correlation between two constructs that should not be related to one another.

socially desirable responding The tendency of individuals to respond in a way that will be viewed favourably by others.

concurrent evidence The degree to which test scores predict a criterion variable measured at the same point in time.

predictive evidence The degree to which test scores predict a criterion variable measured at a future point in time.

evidence based on consequences of testing Evidence that examines the interpretations and uses of test scores and their resulting intended and unintended consequences.

internal validity An assessment of whether a particular variable is the actual cause of a particular outcome.

confounding variables Variables that are not accounted or controlled for in your study that could act as an alternative explanation for your research findings.

external validity A measure of the degree to which the conclusions drawn from a particular set of results can be generalized to other samples or situations.

psychology, would that give an accurate indicator of their knowledge? Clearly the answer is no. Has the quiz changed? No. But the way in which the quiz is being used and the meaning of the scores has changed.

Second, claims of reliability and validity are not yes or no questions. Scores are not reliable/unreliable or valid/invalid. Rather, both are measured on a continuum and are a matter of degree. You can have a measure that is highly reliable, moderately reliable, somewhat reliable, and so on.

Finally, reliability and validity are distinct but related concepts. Reliability is about consistency, while validity is about accuracy. You can have reliability without validity, but not the other way around. In order for a measure to produce valid scores, it must be reliable. However, reliability on its own it not sufficient to demonstrate the validity of scores. You must provide additional validity evidence via other means.

RAISING CHILDREN'S INTELLIGENCE: WHAT WORKS?

Now that we have spent the better part of this chapter using the *Baby Einstein* videos as an example, you might be curious as to what the research has actually found in terms of the extent to which these videos boost young children's intelligence. Although a variety of researchers have examined this issue, a study by DeLoache and colleagues (2010) is representative of the findings.

In their study, a group of 12- to 18-month-old children were placed in one of three experimental conditions: (1) a video with interaction condition, where the parent and child watched the video together at least five times per week for a four-week period (for a total of at least 10 or more hours in 20 or more separate episodes of viewing); (2) a video with no interaction condition identical to the first condition, except parents did not watch the video with the child; or (3) a parent-teaching condition where children were not exposed to the videos, but parents were instructed to try to teach the 25 words featured on the video however they wanted. There was also a fourth control condition with no intervention, which provided a baseline for natural vocabulary growth.

The operationalization of intelligence was simple (and not as lofty as the grand debates alluded to earlier in this chapter): the number of new words learned by the children after a four-week period. The findings, although perhaps disappointing to promoters of the *Baby Einstein* series, were clear: The children who viewed the video in the four-week conditions did not learn any more words than did the control group. In fact, the most word learning occurred in the no-video parent-teaching condition (supporting what many parents intuitively know—that in-person interaction with one's children is irreplaceable).

The merits of the *Baby Einstein* product aside, this study illustrates some of the central principles discussed in this chapter: the importance of operationalizing your variables clearly, the challenges of selecting a research approach and set of methods, and the consequences of those choices for the validity and reliability of your study. In this case, DeLoache and colleagues opted for an experimental design with a relatively straightforward operationalization of intelligence that allowed for a direct test of one of the claims of the *Baby Einstein* product. Of course, their particular set of choices would not be the only way to study the issue, and it is always worth considering the benefits of other methods (non-experimental methods and qualitative approaches) that might yield other insights about the effectiveness of such products.

Table 4.2   Different sources of validity evidence.

Term	Definition	Example
Evidence based on test content	The degree to which the content of a measure assesses what it is intended to measure.	Does the IQ assessment you designed measure all aspects of intelligence, or does it only measure verbal, spatial, or quantitative intelligence?
Evidence based on response processes	The degree to which the mechanisms underlying what people think, feel, or do when responding to items or tasks matches what was intended.	Do infants' responses to the IQ assessment you designed actually indicate their level of intelligence?
Evidence based on internal structure	The degree to which the items on a measure match the underlying structure of the construct.	Do the items on the IQ assessment match the underlying theoretical structure the assessment is based on?
Evidence based on relations to other variables	The degree to which the scores on a measure are related to other external variables.	Does the IQ assessment correlate in predictable ways to other variables?
Convergent validity	The degree to which two assessments designed to measure the same construct or behaviour actually do measure the same thing.	Is intelligence as measured by the Stanford–Binet Intelligence Scale highly correlated with intelligence as measured by the Wechsler Adult Intelligence Scale?
Discriminant validity	The degree to which two assessments designed to measure different constructs or behaviours are in fact measuring different things.	Does a high school achievement test measure something different than the Stanford–Binet Intelligence Scale, or is performance on both assessments highly correlated?
Predictive validity	The degree to which an assessment correlates with a future measure of a construct or behaviour.	Is "IQ" measured in infancy highly correlated with measures of intelligence assessed in later childhood and even adulthood?
Concurrent validity	The degree to which an assessment is correlated with an outcome measure at present.	Is "IQ" as measured by the Stanford–Binet Intelligence Scale highly correlated with performance on a problem-solving task given in the same testing session?
Face validity	The degree to which a measure "appears" to assess the behaviour of interest.	Do other people agree that the intelligence assessment you designed actually measures intelligence?
Internal validity	The degree to which a particular variable is actually the cause of a particular outcome.	Does watching *Baby Einstein* videos boost intelligence? Or do the parents who play these videos for their children do other things that are actually the cause of any increases in intellectual performance?
External validity	The degree to which the conclusions drawn from the results of an investigation can be generalized to other samples or situations.	Do the results obtained in a study of the efficacy of *Baby Einstein* videos to boost intelligence in middle-class infants generalize to children from different classes and cultures?

Practical Tips for Focusing Your Question and Choosing a Design

1. Define a reasonable goal for your research, one that is doable given your time and resources.

2. Spend time considering your own background assumptions and theoretical perspective and how they might influence your research.

3. Spend time thinking about how to operationalize your key concepts and how they can fit into a testable hypothesis.

4. Do not let the design drive your research. Make sure your research question drives your choice of design.

5. Do not be afraid to experiment with different methodologies.

6. Consider whether more than one design might be useful for providing converging evidence for your results.

CHAPTER SUMMARY

Our hypothetical *Baby Einstein* study in this chapter illustrates the issues involved in defining your goal once you have decided on an area of research that interests you. Knowing the assumptions and background theory behind your research will help you shape your research questions and hypotheses. Keep in mind that your research question and what you hope to answer in that question—whether you are looking to demonstrate a correlational or causal relationship—will also aid you in determining which methodological approach to take and which design to use, whether quantitative, qualitative, experimental, non-experimental, or a combination of all of them. Regardless of the approach chosen, the reliability and validity of the approach and measures chosen should also be considered.

End-of-Chapter Exercises

1. Imagine you are interested in conducting a study that will examine the effects of motivation on academic performance.
   a. Translate this into a research question.
   b. Translate this into a research hypothesis.
   c. What is your independent variable? Your dependent variable?
   d. Provide an operational definition for both of these variables.
   e. Describe how you could conduct this study using (i) an experimental research design and (ii) a non-experimental research design.

2. For each of the scenarios below, identify the independent and dependent variables.

   a. A group of 40 participants are selected and randomly assigned to participate in a three-month yoga program or a three-month tai chi program. At both the beginning and the end of the three months the participants are weighed and complete a measure of stress.

   b. Participants watched a 10-minute clip of cat videos either alone or with others and then rated how funny the video clip was.

   c. Several sections of an introductory psychology class were split into two groups. One group was required to purchase a paper textbook while the other group was required to purchase an e-book version of the textbook. At the end of the course, the marks between the two groups were compared.

d. An instructor wanted to test whether the method used to form groups for in-class activities would lead to better outcomes. In one section of an introductory research methods course she assigned students into groups. In another section of the same course she let students self-select into groups. At the end of the course she had students complete a set of measures on group dynamics, satisfaction, and performance.

3. Provide operational definitions for the following variables:
   a. stress
   b. love
   c. body image

d. motivation
e. relationship satisfaction
f. narcissism

4. Quantitative and qualitative research approaches are often presented as contrasting methodological approaches, with quantitative methodologies dominating the field of psychology in recent years. Why do you think quantitative methods have enjoyed such popularity among researchers? If you were asked to make the case for qualitative approaches, what might you say? What benefits of qualitative research might be underappreciated?

5. Imagine you have just developed a new measure of introversion. What types of reliability and validity evidence would you want to provide for this measure? Briefly describe how you would collect this evidence.

Key Terms

accommodation, p. 61

alternate forms reliability, p. 71

assimilation, p. 61

bidirectionality, p. 67

causal design, p. 64

concurrent evidence, p. 73

confounding variables, p. 74

construct irrelevant variance, p. 72

construct underrepresentation, p. 72

control group, p. 65

convergent design, p. 69

convergent evidence, p. 73

correlational design, p. 64

dark triad, p. 73

dependent variable, p. 65

discriminant evidence, p. 73

ecological validity, p. 66

evidence based on consequences of testing, p. 73

evidence based on internal structure, p. 72

evidence based on relations to other variables, p. 72

evidence based on response processes, p. 72

evidence based on test content, p. 72

experimental group, p. 64

explanatory design, p. 69

exploratory design, p. 68

external validity, p. 74

factor analysis, p. 72

falsifiable, p. 61

general factor of personality, p. 73

Implicit Association Test, p. 61

independent variable, p. 65

internal consistency, p. 71

internal validity, p. 74

inter-rater reliability, p. 71

measurement error, p. 69

mixed methods research, p. 68

non-experimental methods, p. 66

operational definition, p. 62

operationalizing, p. 60

post-structural feminism, p. 68

predictive evidence, p. 73

qualitative research, p. 67

quantitative research, p. 64

random assignment, p. 64

reliability, p. 60

social constructionism, p. 67

socially desirable responding, p. 73

test–retest reliability, p. 71

validity, p. 60

Developing Your Research Proposal

5

Chapter Contents

INSIDE RESEARCH: Jayne Gackenbach

I began my university education in the 1960s as a mathematics major at a small technical college, but got caught up with the counterculture rebellion and eventually graduated with a degree in journalism. I've had an interest in both science and social action for most of my life, and these dual passions drove me to pursue first a master's thesis on feminism and then doctoral training in experimental psychology and a doctoral dissertation on lucid dreams. In 1988, I immigrated to Edmonton, Alberta. I taught at various schools in the area until I got a full-time position at MacEwan University, from which I retired a year ago as a professor emeritus. In 1992, I was invited to present my work on lucid dreaming to the Dalai Lama at a conference on sleeping, dreaming, and dying. I am also a past-president of the International Association for the Study of Dreams.

Courtesy of Jayne Gackenbach

Professor emeritus, Psychology Department, MacEwan University

continued

Many years later, my interests turned to video game play when my son got a Nintendo. Specifically, I wanted to know how these experiences of digital realms affected dreams. I have used various scales to assess people's use of games and their experience with dreams. There are laboratory approaches in dream research, but they are very expensive, and so much of the scientific research into dreams relies on self-report. Over the last quarter century, beginning with a personal interest in graduate school, I've shown how important dreams are to memory systems, and how video game play can have an effect on dreams and the development of consciousness. As I had my first experiences with digital life through video games and also saw how online experiences were increasingly pervading society around me, I was inspired to explore how those virtual worlds might impact our private experiences of the night.

Jayne Gackenbach's most recent research endeavours combine her dream and technology interests, examining the dreams of video game players. She has released two related books. One was co-written with her gamer son, Teace Snyder, on the effects of video game play: *Play Reality*. She also has an edited book, *Video Game Play and Consciousness*, from NOVA publishers.

Research Focus: Gaming and dreams, which has been expanded on in more recent years to include social media usage

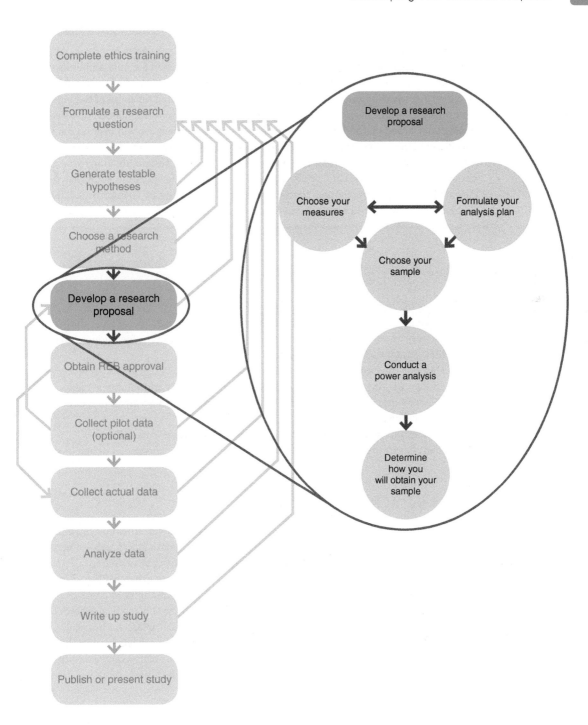

Chapter Abstract

Once you begin to develop your proposal, you have finally reached the nuts-and-bolts stage of designing a research study. In Chapter 4, we discussed the initial steps of how to define and shape your research questions and hypotheses. We also reflected on some of the big-picture decisions you will need to make as you grapple with the numerous trade-offs involved in selecting your broad methodological approach. In future chapters, we will explore the various specific methodologies and designs at your disposal. Before you consider these specific designs, however, you must address four key aspects of research design: obtaining your sample, choosing your measures, conducting a power analysis, and formulating your analysis plan. Although we present these four aspects in a particular order, they are all interrelated. It is helpful to think about them in a simultaneous rather than sequential fashion.

LEARNING OBJECTIVES

By the end of this chapter, you should be able to:
- Explain why it is important to have a representative sample.
- Identify examples of probability and non-probability sampling techniques and discuss their advantages and disadvantages.
- Describe the four scales of measurement.
- Explain why the scale of measurement, and the reliability and validity evidence available for a measure, are important to consider when selecting a measure for your study.
- Explain the purpose of conducting a power analysis.
- Explain why an analysis plan should be developed prior to data collection.
- Identify various constraints that may impact your choice of research design or sample.

OBTAIN YOUR SAMPLE

Before you launch almost any study in psychology, you must determine how you will obtain participants. Although this may seem easy, the availability of certain individuals—for instance, left-handed cello players with at least five years' experience playing in an orchestra—may constrain your research. Whether you are located in a large, diverse urban setting or in a more homogeneous rural college or university setting may affect your ability to conduct research. For example, if you wish to study children or adults with certain medical disorders (e.g., autism, schizophrenia), you are more likely to find them in urban areas near hospitals or medical schools. Leave yourself adequate time to recruit your sample, especially since the process can be time intensive. For student-based class research projects, plan to give yourself at least two to three weeks to collect your data. More typical research projects often require several months of data collection.

Populations versus Samples

population The entire group of individuals relevant to your research.

You must first consider the population that will be the focus of your study. The **population** refers to the entire group of individuals relevant to your research. Note that a population in this sense is a moving target that always depends on your research question. For example, if you want to study attitudes that students hold about financial aid at a particular university, then the population of interest would be all of the students at that given university—not all of the students at many universities or across the country. If you are studying the level of boredom (or excitement) students reading this textbook for a particular class experience around research methods, then all the students in that class form the population of interest—not all the students in the university.

In considering potential participants, you must decide which criteria you will use to include or exclude individuals from the population of interest. This is an essential step in developing your research proposal and enables you to refine the specific definition of your population. For example, if you are studying depressed men, the inclusion criteria might be that participants are men between the ages of 35 and 44 with diagnosed major depressive disorder. By extension, you are excluding younger and older men and all women.

In almost all research studies, studying the entire population of interest is not a possibility. If your population is a single class (as in our example of readers of the unnamed exciting textbook), then perhaps your study can involve that entire population. But, more commonly, psychological research populations are too large or spread across too many geographical regions, making them impractical to study in their entirety. Imagine trying to study all depressed adults in Canada, all married couples in the Prairies, or all middle school students in Vancouver. In such cases, we focus our research on a **sample**—a subset of individuals drawn from the population.

sample A subset of individuals drawn from the population of interest.

Representative Samples

In selecting a research sample, most researchers try to gather a representative sample, one that shares the essential characteristics of the population from which it was drawn. For instance, one of the authors of this textbook often demonstrates sampling in his undergraduate statistics course with candy. He gives students a pack of M&Ms and asks them to compare the distribution of the different colours (red, green, orange, yellow, blue, brown) in their individual bags with the distribution of colours across all manufactured M&Ms as reported by Mars, Inc. The idea is that each snack pack is a sample of the larger population of manufactured M&Ms and—unless there is reason to believe that the packaging process is systematically biased toward certain colours—each individual bag serves as a **representative sample** of that larger population.

representative sample A sample that shares the essential characteristics of the population from which it was drawn.

Do I Need a Representative Sample?   Why should we worry about getting a representative sample? The answer brings us back to the discussion of external validity from Chapter 4, and it wholly depends on your research topic. If your goal is to make an externally valid conclusion that applies to the outside world, then having a representative sample matters. For example, if you want to show the efficacy of a particular form of psychotherapy for people with anxiety disorders, then you will need a representative sample of individuals with anxiety disorders. If you fail to have a representative sample, your conclusions cannot be extended generally to people suffering from anxiety disorders.

Not all research, however, requires representative samples. Imagine you are studying a perceptual phenomenon such as the well-known Stroop effect. The Stroop effect is a delay in reaction time that occurs when the name of a colour is printed in a colour different from the word itself (e.g., the word "RED" is printed in blue ink). When people are asked to report the colour of the mismatched print, their reaction time is slower than if the word and colour match (i.e., the word "RED" is printed in red ink). This perceptual interference phenomenon would arguably not differ across various segments of the population, since many researchers of perceptual phenomena assert that they are relatively universal. A researcher examining the Stroop effect might not be concerned about gathering a representative sample. However, even in this example the research results might vary as a function of literacy or education levels. Members of a college or university community tend to think they and their peers represent the general population. However, only about 24 per cent of 20 to 24 year olds are enrolled in degree-granting institutions (Statistics Canada, 2017). Be careful about assuming you are studying a universal process that holds for all samples or populations.

The Undergraduate "Problem"?   Related to the representative sample debate, psychological researchers are often criticized for their overreliance on undergraduates from introductory psychology participant pools. Although these students provide a convenient sample, using them to examine a research question for which they do not represent the general population can harm the validity of your findings. This might not be a major concern if you were studying perceptual phenomena such as the Stroop effect, but you would be more concerned if you were studying people's attitudes toward current events.

Henrich, Heine, and Norenzayan (2010) have argued that "WEIRD" samples (Western, educated, industrialized, rich, and democratic) may be among the least representative groups when we are looking for samples that resemble humans on a global level (see "Media Matters: WEIRD Science"). In their analysis, WEIRD samples are often outliers in a broad range of domains, from spatial reasoning to self-concept. As a result, Henrich and colleagues contend that some of psychology's claims about human nature based on this unusual subpopulation are problematic at the least. However, opinions about the significance of this problem range widely. An analysis by Cooper, McCord, and Socha (2011) argued that undergraduate students are virtually identical to comparison groups of other adults in terms of personality (using the classic Big 5 personality dimensions: openness, conscientiousness, extraversion, agreeableness, and neuroticism) and politics. If so, WEIRD samples may not be as big a deal as previously thought.

Regardless of where researchers land on these issues, most agree that you must be vigilant in considering whom you will study and what conclusions you can legitimately draw based on your samples. You should always consider how your sample might influence your ability to generalize to other samples and the population of interest.

Labelling Populations

Labelling your populations of interest, regardless of their origins and characteristics, requires some thought and care. The truth is, members of any group may not agree on a proper label. Some individuals, for instance, like to be referred to as "Hispanic," "First Nations," or "East Indian," whereas others prefer "Latinx," "Indigenous," or "South Asian." We recommend asking a few members of the sample group, someone close to them, or an organization advocating for their needs how they want to be identified. If this is not practical or possible, find out as much as you can about the target population, including its history of labels. However, be aware that journal editors may request particular labels when you submit work for publication (see Chapter 14 online).

Many researchers are interested in studying groups that differ in some way from the typical, healthy undergraduate. As with any population, it is important to define your population of

WEIRD Science

How similar are human beings in the way they think and process the world? Although we look different, form different communities, and observe different rituals, underneath it all we must share the same cognitive mechanisms. In other words, a brain is a brain, no matter whether it lives in Borneo or Toronto. Right?

For decades, almost all psychology researchers would have answered a resounding "yes!" to that question. They assumed that findings from studies conducted with test participants in the industrialized West were generalizable to all human beings.

But, as Henrich and colleagues (2010) suggested, perhaps claims about participants from WEIRD countries cannot, in fact, be generalized to the global population. Their study, which appeared in the journal *Behavioral and Brain Sciences*, concluded that participants from WEIRD countries tend to be more individualistic, analytic, concerned with fairness, existentially anxious, and less conforming than those from non-WEIRD societies.

At first, media response to their findings consisted mainly of commentary on psychology and academic websites, such as PLoS blogs, many of which passionately endorsed the study. "If you have one blockhead colleague who simply does not get that surveying his or her students in 'Introduction to Psychology' fails to provide instant access to 'human nature,' this is the article to pass along," proclaimed one blogger on *Neuroanthropology.net* (Downey, 2010).

Aside from a *New York Times* article that also supported the study's findings (Giridharadas, 2010), commentary stayed in the blogosphere until almost three years after the study was published. Then *Pacific Standard*, a magazine covering environmental, socio-political, and public policy issues, published an in-depth article that traced the research of Joe Henrich, one of the lead authors, from his early days as a graduate student through the researchers' reaction to the WEIRD study (Watters, 2013).

Slate magazine ran an article written by a behavioural neuroscientist who applied the WEIRD theory to a study on the loss of virginity and subsequent sexual satisfaction in adulthood (Brookshire, 2013). The participants were—you guessed it—undergraduate students. Brookshire discussed brain development in adolescence and the dangers of extrapolating outcomes from these young participants to the general population. She argued that although some studies conducted with WEIRD populations may be generalized (at least to the rest of the WEIRD population), those concerning topics such as sexuality and social punishment should not be.

At this point the WEIRD theory remains a minority psychological opinion that requires further confirmation. However, the study's implications could be enormous for researchers, who would have to spend a great deal more time and money expanding their participants beyond the convenient pool of undergraduate students. Stay tuned.

interest when you design your study and select participants, but these special populations require even deeper consideration than others.

Generally, when researchers refer to "non-standard" or "atypical" populations, they mean participants who vary in important ways from the general population. Although we use these labels to explain particular research issues, you should always be extremely careful and respectful about how you refer to research participants in any study. Aside from offending members of the group you hope to study, using labels viewed as insulting by your participants may influence their honesty and willingness to provide accurate information or participate at all. Using particular labels may convey unintended messages to both the readers of your work and the group you are studying.

Probability Samples

random sampling
A method in which
every member of a given
population has an equal
chance of being selected
into a sample.

Researchers often argue for the need to do **random sampling**—a method in which every member of a given population has an equal chance of being selected into the sample. This approach offers the most straightforward method for obtaining a representative sample. To return to our M&M example, imagine you have a giant barrel of 10,000 candies, but rather than counting all the M&Ms of different colours, you want to estimate the distribution by taking a subset of those M&Ms. To select a random sample (suppose you want 100 in your sample), you would need a methodology in which every M&M in the barrel has an equal chance of being selected for your sample, perhaps by shaking up the barrel and then dipping in a scoop to select 100 candies. Sampling methods for which the probability of each person being selected into the sample is known are referred to as **probability sampling** methods.

probability sampling
Sampling methods for
which the probability of
a person being selected
into a sample is known.

Generally speaking, for random sampling to work, you must replace samples that you draw from a population so they do not affect the overall probability that others will be selected. The easiest way to understand this is with a standard deck of cards. Suppose you want to take a random sample of cards from the deck. You shuffle the deck after selecting each card. If you do not replace the card you selected each time before selecting the next one, then the probability of selecting any subsequent card increases each time. Your chance of selecting any given card the first time is 1/52, and it becomes 1/51 the second time, 1/50 the third time, and so forth.

You would not select the same person from the population more than once, because this would violate statistical assumptions about the independence of observations and potentially skew your results. His or her replacement into the population (i.e., putting the person back into the metaphorical deck so that he or she can be selected again) retains the equal probability of selecting any given member. When dealing with large populations, researchers often do not worry about replacement, because the probability changes minimally as each individual is selected into the sample.

Problems with Random Sampling.

Although random sampling is viewed as the gold standard for selecting participants, there are often practical barriers to assembling a truly random sample. Successful random sampling assumes that you are able to identify each individual in your population of interest and have complete access to this population. If you sample students at a university, the population is known and listed in a centralized place, and you could conceivably use the registrar's records to randomly select your sample.

However, many populations are not so thoroughly indexed and organized. For example, what if you wanted a random sample of the residents of the city of Winnipeg? There is no single comprehensive record of the city's entire population, so you would have to use incomplete methods. Traditionally, researchers would use the phone book for randomly selecting participants. Although this method is somewhat dated, we can still use it to illustrate the point.

A phone book included an extensive listing of many of the city's residents, but also systematically excluded some groups of individuals. Historically, phone books were thought to undersample those from lower-income brackets who might not be able to afford a home phone (Taylor, 2003). Although that bias may still be a factor today, phone books are also limited in utility because they include only landlines and, therefore, exclude the ever-growing group of people who use only cell phones. They also exclude individuals who choose not to be listed in the phone book. Depending on your research questions, individuals with unlisted numbers may respond differently than those who list their numbers (Moberg, 1982; Roslow & Roslow, 1972). Basically, using a phone book to gather a random sample will leave you with a biased sample because the listings themselves are a biased population. This example highlights the dilemma of random sampling in the real world.

Alternatives to Random Sampling.   Whereas true random sampling can be either impractical or impossible, alternative methodologies offer some of the benefits of random sampling. Following are a few of many such methodologies.

   Stratified random sampling, one of the most common alternatives, divides a population into homogeneous groups, called strata, along some key dimension (for example, race/ethnicity) and then randomly samples a predefined number or proportion of individuals from within each of the strata. This approach may ensure greater representativeness because relatively smaller groups are represented among your strata in proportion to the original population. This methodology is often used to ensure that minority groups are adequately represented in a sample. Say that only 5 per cent of your population of M&Ms is red. In true random sampling, it is possible that in a sample of 100 M&Ms you might end up with only one or two red candies, or even zero. A stratified random sampling approach would guarantee that 5 per cent of your sample will consist of red M&Ms—in other words, that you will continue sampling M&Ms until you reach that 5 per cent threshold. In some cases, you may want to use an oversampling approach, in which you intentionally overrecruit underrepresented groups into your sample to ensure that you will have enough representation of those groups to make valid research conclusions. To return to our obsession with M&Ms, if your sample is only 100 M&Ms and five red M&Ms will not be enough to draw valid conclusions, then you might oversample the red M&Ms (deciding, for example, to ensure that 20 per cent of your sample is red). For a real-life example of the importance of sampling, see "Media Matters: The $1 Million Netflix Prize."

stratified random sampling A technique whereby a population is divided into homogeneous groups, called strata, along some key dimension (e.g., race/ethnicity), and then random samples are drawn from within each of the strata.

oversampling The intentional overrecruitment of underrepresented groups into a sample to ensure there will be enough representation of those groups to make valid research conclusions.

MEDIA MATTERS

The $1 Million Netflix Prize

The importance of sampling was highlighted in a contest put on by Netflix in 2006. The contest aimed to create an algorithm that would improve movie recommendations by at least 10 per cent over its current algorithm (Lohr, 2009). The first to come up with the algorithm would win a $1 million prize. Thousands of teams stepped up to the plate to tackle the problem and were provided with a data set containing over 100 million movie ratings of almost 18,000 movie titles provided by approximately 480,000 Netflix subscribers

(Bennett & Lanning, 2007). They were to use this data set to create a model that would predict a separate sample of 3 million ratings.

It took nearly three years before this 10 per cent threshold was reached. Although individual teams were able to make small gains in their predictions, they struggled to increase the success rate to the 10 per cent criterion. It wasn't until teams began joining forces, combining their different ideas and using different sampling strategies, that they began to achieve real progress.

In 2009, BellKor's Pragmatic Chaos—an alliance of three teams that included statisticians, machine learning experts, and computer engineers from Canada, the United States, Austria, and Israel—finally won the contest with an algorithm that improved the accuracy of the predictions by 10.05 per cent (Lohr, 2009). The team owed their success to the different ways in which they sampled their data (Van Buskirk, 2009). For instance, they discovered that the length of time between watching a movie and rating the movie, and the day of the week that the movie was rated, were important factors in creating a more successful model.

Non-probability Samples

non-probability sample A sample in which members of the population are not all given an equal chance of being selected.

What about situations when gathering a representative sample does not matter? In such cases, random sampling (or its variations) may not be required, and a non-probability sample—one in which members of the population are not all given an equal chance of being selected—may be an appropriate option.

convenience sampling A method of sampling that makes use of the most readily available group of participants.

One of the most common ways to acquire a non-probability sample is through convenience sampling. Many undergraduate students (particularly in research methods courses) use this method because, as the name suggests, it draws on the most readily available group of participants. In a convenience sample, you typically recruit people who are easily accessible. For example, you could obtain a convenience sample of undergraduates by using your university's research participant pool or asking friends who live on campus to participate in your survey on attitudes toward cannabis use.

snowball sampling A method of sampling in which participants are asked to help recruit additional participants.

A related type of non-probability sampling is snowball sampling, in which participants are asked to help recruit additional participants. Although snowball sampling is a non-systematic approach (like convenience sampling), it does have the potential advantage of helping a researcher access a difficult or hidden population. If you were conducting a study of undocumented immigrants, for example, a snowball sample might be the best way to gather a sample of reasonable size.

self-selection An instance where participants electively place themselves into a particular sample (or they opt out of participation).

With any sort of non-probability sample, you should always be aware of the hazards of self-selection—that is, that participants select themselves into a particular sample (or opt out of participation). Ultimately, you cannot avoid the phenomenon of self-selection in sampling. The best a researcher can do is try to account for it by understanding and, in some cases, measuring the factors that might lead participants to opt in or out.

Online Samples

One of the most prominent and popular ways to collect samples today is online. Numerous online resources offer a ready source of participants, such as the Mechanical Turk (MTurk) platform. Although social science researchers have used MTurk for only a few years, it has become increasingly popular because of its low-cost, large participant pool and convenient system for recruitment and compensation.

Other online systems for generating surveys, such as SurveyMonkey and Qualtrics, have also grown in popularity and in some cases offer services for gathering samples. Both SurveyMonkey and Qualtrics also provide extensive tools for constructing, structuring, and presenting your survey. You can choose from a variety of question or item types, including rating scales, multiple-choice questions, and open-ended questions, and determine whether items are presented in fixed or randomized orders. You can also allow the survey to branch off into customized sets of questions for respondents who answer a question in a particular way. For example, if you are studying dating behaviour, you might ask different follow-up questions for respondents who indicate their last dating experience was positive compared with those who rated it as negative.

One concern that is often raised about online samples is the extent to which they may (or may not) be representative of their intended populations. Emerging evidence suggests that many of these samples—especially MTurk—do a reasonably good job of representing the demographic diversity of the larger population. In fact, Buhrmester, Kwang, and Gosling (2011) argue that the diversity of the MTurk sample surpasses other standard Internet samples and many US college samples. They argue that although MTurk may not be effective for sampling specific targeted populations, it does a pretty good job of population random sampling. However, it should be noted that the bulk of MTurk workers are from the United States (75 per cent), with only 1 per cent of workers residing in Canada (Difallah, Filatova, & Ipeirotis, 2018).

Similarly, Scherpenzeel and Bethlehem (2011) contend that as larger portions of the population go online, the concern that online participants cannot represent the larger population has diminished. They do point out, however, that certain segments of the population will be easier to sample online than others (e.g., young, working, single people are more readily accessed online than elderly or non-Western populations).

On the whole, the evidence indicates that online samples are here to stay and that they do an acceptable job, at least in some domains, of providing diverse, representative samples. Depending on your research question, however, you may want to collect multiple samples from different populations with the hope of providing converging evidence for your findings. It might be useful to see whether the results you obtain using MTurk are similar to or different from those obtained from a group of psychology undergraduates.

CHOOSE YOUR MEASURES

Once you have determined how you will obtain your sample, the second step in establishing your research proposal is figuring out which measures you will use. Although your selection of measures will vary greatly depending on your research topic and the age and characteristics of your sample, there are some overarching considerations for how you go about this task. We discuss two of those broad topics here: determining your scale of measurement and considering the reliability and validity of your chosen instruments.

Remember, when you choose measures for your research, you do not need to reinvent the wheel. There may already be established measurement tools available for many topics you come up with, and many of these tools have a significant base of research to support their validity and reliability. For example, the Beck Depression Inventory is a widely used self-report measure to assess depression (Beck, Ward, Mendelson, Mock, & Erbaugh, 1961). You should always search the prior work on your topic before you begin to hammer out the specifics of your research proposal.

As you choose your research measures, you will also need to consider the issue of **measurement error**. Any given instrument will exhibit some difference between the actual or true value of what you are measuring and the result obtained using the measurement instrument. This difference, or error, is something that researchers must accept, because no single measurement

measurement error The difference between the actual or true value of what you are measuring and the result obtained using the measurement instrument.

instrument can ever be perfect. Some measurement tools are better than others, and this can be assessed by looking at the available reliability and validity evidence for the tool, but awareness of the ever-present problem of measurement error is essential for thoughtful research design.

For instance, research has found that older adults tend to slow down their walking speed when they talk more often than younger adults do when talking and walking. This dual-task effect, a situation where one task (e.g., talking) interferes with another (e.g., walking), has been found in older adults to be related to street-crossing behaviour (Neider et al., 2011) and an increased risk of falling (Beauchet et al., 2008; Bootsma-van der Wiel et al., 2003). Measuring walking speed is relevant to this discussion.

A traditional, low-cost way to measure walking speed is to have two individuals record walking speed over a set distance with stopwatches. If you try to do this with a partner, you will quickly see that this approach can be prone to errors. If the distance is relatively short, say 10 metres, and the observers are not synchronized at the start and finish, then the measurement error could exceed what you might expect from the manipulation—in this case the addition of the second task. You can fix some of these problems by automating the timing with an electronic system that is triggered in the same way for each participant. But even these systems are not perfect. In fact, no measurement system is truly perfect.

As a researcher, you must consider the amount of error that is built into your measurement tool. Even measures such as reaction time that are captured by key presses on a computer are influenced by aspects of technology, such as the responsiveness of the key press, the refresh rate of information on the computer screen, and the speed of the computer processor. Although improvements in technology and computer processing speeds reduce many of these issues, they will never go away completely.

Scales of Measurement

Although an introductory statistics textbook would cover the issue of scale of measurement extensively, here we define the four scales of measurement and only briefly discuss the benefits and detriments of each one. We cover the scales in ascending order of complexity—nominal, ordinal, interval, and ratio. The more complex scales contain more information, and interval and ratio scales are often preferred for research instruments because they contain the most quantitative information. See Table 5.1 for a summary of characteristics of each of these scales.

nominal scale The most basic measurement, when scale points are defined by categories.

Nominal Scale.   The most basic measurement scale is a nominal scale, which is defined by categorical measurements. When a measurement is categorical, the values assigned to the different categories have no numerical meaning—that is, the numbers mark information about the category, but nothing else. Nominal data answer questions about "how many" rather than "how much." In other words, nominal data can be examined by looking at how many different categories there are and the frequencies of occurrences in these different categories. For example, if you are tallying votes for preferences for ice cream (chocolate, strawberry, vanilla), then you might assign a 1 to chocolate, a 2 to strawberry, and a 3 to vanilla. This allows you to count the number of people who prefer either chocolate or strawberry, but the actual numerical values of 1 and 2 are arbitrary.

ordinal scale A scale possessing the properties of identity and magnitude such that each value is unique and has an ordered relationship to the other values on the scale.

Ordinal Scale.   The second type of measurement scale is an ordinal scale, which has the properties of identity and magnitude. Each value is unique and has an ordered relationship to the other values on the scale. What distinguishes an ordinal scale from other, more powerful,

Table 5.1 The four basic scale types.

Scale Type	Characteristics	Examples
Nominal (categorical)	Responses are unordered categories. Although responses might be assigned numbers for coding purposes (e.g., Liberal = 1, Conservative = 2), the numerical assignments are arbitrary.	Political party affiliation (Liberal, Conservative, New Democratic Party, Green) Sex (male, female, other) Religious affiliation (Christian, Jewish, Buddhist, Hindu, Muslim, etc.)
Ordinal (rank order)	Responses are ordered categories ("greater than" or "less than" relationships make sense).	Rankings of students according to aggressiveness Preference rankings (e.g., "I like X most, Y second most, . . .") Likert items (e.g., a 5-point response scale from "strongly disagree" to "strongly agree"; are often treated as interval scales*)
Interval	Responses are numerical and the differences between points on the scale are numerically meaningful.	Temperature in degrees Celsius or Fahrenheit IQ test scores Many scales in behavioural research Likert items (e.g., a 5-point response scale from "strongly disagree" to "strongly agree")
Ratio	Responses are interval and there is a meaningful 0 value. Ratios (e.g., response X is twice that of response Y) have meaning for these types of scales.	Length Reaction time Temperature in degrees Kelvin (where there is an absolute 0) Amount of money earned

* Considerable debate exists regarding whether Likert-type items should be treated as ordinal or interval when analyzing data.

scales is that the numbering of values reflects information only about rank—it does not tell you anything about the value of the distance between ranks. In other words, the distance between each rank may differ from point to point. Consider an ordinal scale of measurement where you ask a preschool teacher to rank her students from the most to the least aggressive. When the teacher ranks Noah as the most aggressive, Samantha as second, and Emma as third, we cannot assume that the "distance" between Noah and Samantha and that between Samantha and Emma is uniform. Noah may be much more aggressive than any other student in the class, and there might be a big drop-off between Noah's and Samantha's aggression. Further, it could be that Samantha and Emma are almost equal in their aggression, with Samantha having only a slight edge. The rank orders tell us nothing about the distance from one rank to the next.

Interval Scale.   Like the ordinal scale, the interval scale contains rank order information, but it also has the property of equal intervals between points. What this means is that a score of 4 is a single unit greater than a score of 3, and the size of the interval between 4 and 3 is the same as the size of the interval between 3 and 2. Treating measurements as interval scales is

interval scale A scale containing rank order information, as well as the property of equal intervals between points; it does not contain an absolute zero point.

common in psychological research. A well-known example is the IQ score, where each point on the scale is an equivalent unit (i.e., the distance between 100 and 110 is the same as the distance between 90 and 100). Another important feature of this scale is that it does not have a meaningful absolute zero point. For example, temperature in degrees Celsius is measured on an interval scale. When it is zero degrees Celsius outside, this does not mean that there is a lack of temperature; rather the zero value is just used as the indicator for the temperature at which water freezes and does not represent a measurement of no temperature.

ratio scale A scale sharing all the properties of an interval scale (rank order information and equal interval), but also containing a meaningful absolute zero point, where zero represents the absence of the thing that is being measured.

Ratio Scale.   Finally, the ratio scale contains the most quantitative information. It shares all the properties of an interval scale, and it has a meaningful absolute zero point, where zero represents the absence of the thing that is being measured. Whereas most psychological constructs that we choose to measure do not contain such an absolute zero point (as in the example of IQ, there is no "0," representing the absence of intelligence), a variety of basic measurements are, in fact, ratio scales. Examples include measurements of time, speed, and length—that is, the length of 0 on a ruler represents the absence of any length. A ratio scale allows you to compare measurements in terms of ratios. For example, if you were measuring how long two different groups needed to complete a task, you could note that participants in group 1 responded, on average, twice as quickly as participants in group 2.

Select Your Scale

parametric test
A statistical test that requires that the measurement scale of your data be interval or ratio and makes strong assumptions about the distribution of measurements in your population.

The big question you should ask yourself in choosing your scale is, "How will I statistically think about the data I collect?" The form in which you collect the data will determine how— and even *whether*—you will be able to use certain statistical approaches to analyze your data. In the worst-case scenario, the data you collect may turn out to be unanalyzable. Your answer to the above question will help you make the right choice and avoid excruciating headaches down the road.

non-parametric test
A statistical test that makes few assumptions about the population distribution and may be applied to nominal and ordinal measurements.

When analyzing data, researchers often have a choice between various parametric and non-parametric tests. Parametric tests (e.g., *t* tests) require that the measurement scale be interval or ratio and make strong assumptions about the distribution of measurements in your population. Non-parametric tests (e.g., chi-square) make few assumptions about the population distribution and may be applied to nominal (names or categories) and ordinal (order) measurements. We discuss both types of tests at greater length in Chapter 12. But the truth is that researchers try to select measures that enable parametric analyses (interval and ratio data) whenever possible. Of course, some research will dictate the measurement scale you can use, and it is not possible to measure everything using interval or ratio measures. Certain information is inherently categorical and must be scaled that way. For instance, if we conduct a study of different types of psychotherapy and count the number of people who comply with treatment for the different types, then the type of therapy (e.g., cognitive-behavioural, psychodynamic, humanistic) is a categorical variable.

Likert-type ratings
Items that ask participants to rate their attitudes or behaviour using a predetermined set of responses that are quantified. An example would be a 5-point rating scale that asks about level of agreement from 1 (strongly disagree) to 5 (strongly agree).

There is some controversy about whether a common type of measurement in psychological research, called Likert-type ratings of attitudes, can, in fact, be considered an interval scale. An example of a Likert-type item would be, "I feel anxious when I am going to speak in front of a group of people." Participants respond on something like a 1-to-5 scale, with 1 representing "strongly disagree" and 5 representing "strongly agree." Critics such as Jamieson (2004) have argued that we abuse Likert-scale ratings when we treat them as interval data, because we cannot, in fact, assume that the intervals between the values are equal (i.e., that the distance between "strongly disagree" and "disagree" is the same as the distance between "agree" and "strongly agree"). These critics contend that we should instead be treating Likert-type data as ordinal. However, other researchers have demonstrated empirically that, when several individual items are combined and are analyzed as a scale, it is acceptable to treat these items as interval data and analyze them as such (Carifio & Perla, 2008). Although we cannot resolve this controversy here (and most researchers do treat such measures as interval), it is important to be aware of the debate surrounding this issue.

Reliability and Validity

A final crucial consideration in selecting your measures brings us back to our discussion of reliability and validity in Chapter 4. Ideally, any measures you use should be high in both validity and reliability, meaning they should capture what they are intended to measure (validity), and they should yield consistent results (reliability). The best measures do both well, although there is often an interesting interplay between reliability and validity.

Some steps intended to make a measure yield more valid data, so that it represents the "real thing" as closely as possible, might harm its reliability and vice versa. For example, if you wanted to measure a complex construct such as creativity, you might assume you could find a fairly reliable measure—such as counting the number of solutions that a participant generated in response to a particular problem. The difficulty with this measure, however, is that the definition of creativity as fluency of ideas in problem solving is likely only one piece of the true construct. A more valid measurement might involve an evaluation of the novelty of each individual solution. Although this would be a more valid way to measure creativity, reliably measuring novelty is challenging.

Again, you do not need to reinvent the wheel. A search through the literature can yield a treasure trove of previously established measures that provide both reliable and valid data. Searching through the literature for an existing measure of your variable(s) should be your first step before deciding to develop your own measure. That way you can benefit from the efforts of others and will have existing evidence for the reliability and validity of the measure to gauge its quality. Developing a new measure from scratch requires considerable work, and you cannot be certain of its quality as it will have no evidence of its reliability and validity until it has been tested.

CONDUCT A POWER ANALYSIS

Once you have determined your sample and your measures, two more important steps remain in developing your proposal: conducting a power analysis and formulating an analysis plan. Researchers are inclined to cut corners in these steps, frequently bypassing them altogether. In fact, conducting a power analysis has become a regular practice in psychological research only within the past couple of decades.

The primary reason that researchers skip these steps is simple: You cannot begin your study without a sample and a set of measures, but you can always go back after completing your study to determine your level of power and to design an analysis plan. We argue that although you *can* perform research without conducting a power analysis and designing an analysis plan up front, researchers who follow best practices (and hence generate the best research) make these steps a part of the planning process.

Prospective versus Retrospective Power Analysis

statistical power The probability that your study will be able to detect an effect in your research, if such an effect exists.

What exactly does it mean to conduct a power analysis? Statistical power refers to the probability that your study will be able to detect an effect in your research (such as a difference between groups or a relationship between two variables), if such an effect exists. The latter point is important—that power refers *only* to your ability to detect effects that are actually present. If your study does not elicit the hypothesized effect, no amount of statistical power can help you. Power is typically reported as a coefficient that represents the probability of being able to detect the effect. So, a power of .60 means that you have a 60 per cent chance of detecting an effect of a given size, assuming that one exists.

prospective power analysis A series of computations that help you determine the number of participants you will need to successfully detect an effect in your research.

There are two primary ways to go about a power analysis: prospectively (a priori) and retrospectively (post hoc). We prefer a prospective power analysis, because it suggests that you are thinking about the issue of power as you design your study. A prospective analysis involves a computation that helps you determine the number of participants you will need to successfully detect an effect in your research. Although there is no hard and fast rule about what your power should be, psychology researchers should strive for a power of .80 (80 per cent chance of detecting a real effect of a given size).

effect size The magnitude of an effect (such as a difference of means or a relationship between two variables).

One challenge in doing a prospective power analysis is that it requires that you know the effect size of the phenomenon that is being studied before you conduct the research. Effect size, as the name suggests, measures the magnitude of a particular effect. To determine the power needed to detect an effect, you must know the size of that theoretical effect. As you might expect, a small or moderate-size effect will require a larger sample size to get adequate statistical power, whereas a larger effect requires a relatively smaller sample, because the effect itself is easier to detect.

retrospective power analysis A series of computations that help you determine how much power you had in a study after the fact.

When researchers do not know the magnitude of an effect before conducting their research, they may rely instead on a retrospective power analysis, where they can report how much power they had in their study after the fact. Thus, although it is preferable in principle to take the a priori approach, doing so requires that you are either studying an effect where previous research has already established an effect size or you have firm theoretical grounding to make an educated guess about the likely effect size. If you are dealing with an entirely new area, you always have the option to do a pilot study first to get a handle on the effect size. Ultimately, however, these extra steps lead some researchers to give up on prospective power analysis altogether. Chapter 11 includes a more in-depth discussion of both effect size and statistical power.

Why Does Power Matter?

It is worth considering the real-world implications of underpowered research that might fail to detect meaningful effects. Imagine, for example, that you are conducting research on a new psychotherapeutic intervention for panic disorder. An underpowered study that fails to detect whether your treatment approach is effective could prevent individuals and therapists from hearing about a highly effective treatment. For individuals struggling with panic disorder and for the therapists who work with them, this would be a tangible and tragic consequence of this frequent oversight in psychological research methods.

FORMULATE AN ANALYSIS PLAN

The final step of developing your proposal is a particularly interesting topic to end with, because it is rife with disagreement about best practices. Formulating an analysis plan requires a specific strategy for what sorts of analyses you will conduct. For example, if you plan to examine differences in performance between two groups, then you will need to apply one type of statistical analysis. However, if you want to look at the relationship between two variables, you must use a different statistical technique (see Chapters 11 and 12). Your analysis plan should be laid out before collecting data. Almost all researchers plan their selection of sample and measures (although admittedly to varying degrees), and most would agree on the wisdom of conducting a power analysis, even if many do not do it. In contrast, not all researchers would agree they should formulate their analysis plan at the beginning of the research process *and then stick to it.*

The argument in favour of including an analysis plan in your proposal is that it may help to keep "false positives" in your research findings to a minimum. What does this mean? You want your hypothesis—*not* the significant statistical results you may gather—to drive your research and analyses. Statistical significance is central to being able to report your research findings, and the temptation to maximize your chances of reaching statistical significance in your analyses is considerable. Holding yourself to an analysis plan is one way to combat this temptation.

In contrast, is there anything wrong with data exploration? Should researchers really constrain themselves from looking at analyses that had not been conceptualized at the beginning of the process after the fact? What you think of the issue even shapes how you refer to the practice. Consider, for example, the terms *data mining* or *data fishing* as opposed to *data exploration.* Exploration sounds like a full, worthwhile (and even noble) undertaking, whereas mining and fishing sound a bit suspect and imply some rule breaking.

Although we cannot resolve this debate for you here (because ultimately there is no single correct answer), we can offer some general (and less controversial) recommendations. First, it is a good idea to have an analysis plan as you formulate your research proposal, even if you do not intend to stick to that plan strictly throughout your research. Thinking carefully about how you will analyze your data will lead to a more thorough study design and will ensure that you will be able to get the answers you seek. It may help you realize that you should collect different data or that you do not actually need some of the data you are collecting. Considering the type of data your study will generate and how you will answer your questions with particular statistical techniques can only lead to more carefully constructed research.

Second, be aware that if you decide to explore your data for potentially statistically significant findings *after* your study is completed, you are leaving yourself open to the appearance of "*p*-Hacking"—the process of deliberately manipulating factors in your research to maximize your chance of uncovering a statistically significant finding ($p < .05$). *p*-Hacking can include a variety of actions, such as dropping groups, specific cases, or variables from an analysis or adding analyses that were not part of an initial plan.

Simmons, Nelson, and Simonsohn (2011) argue that whatever steps you take, you should aim for transparency (i.e., letting the scientific community know what you have done so that your work can be fairly evaluated). They do not suggest that *p*-Hacking is acceptable as long as you talk about it; rather, they contend that you must disclose fully any steps you undertake that may either intentionally or unintentionally enhance your chances of uncovering statistically significant findings. They also suggest that the burden to show that results did not emerge out of "arbitrary analytic decisions" (Simmons et al., 2011, p. 1363) lies with the researcher. The greater your ability to show that your analysis plan was well considered at the outset of your research, the more defensible your findings will be in the end.

statistical significance An indicator of the probability of obtaining an effect size as large as (or larger than) the one you obtained; also indicates that the differences between groups are not due to sampling error.

p-Hacking The process of deliberately manipulating factors in your research to maximize your chance of uncovering a statistically significant finding ($p < .05$).

THE ART OF JUGGLING CHOICES

In a perfect world, you could always choose the best research design and participant population to address your research question. However, researchers rarely operate in such a world. When conducting research, you are always faced with making difficult choices, making compromises, and trying to come up with the best solutions for less-than-optimal situations. Sometimes recruiting your desired participant population will be difficult or nearly impossible. Often your research will be constrained by time and resources.

Participant Recruitment Issues

Many research studies require a particular participant population to address the research question of interest. The more specialized the population, the more difficult recruiting participants will be. What do you do if you cannot find the desired number of participants (or anyone) to participate in your study? First, you can offer some type of incentive. Many researchers today routinely pay participants to participate in research. This often leads to greater participation rates and fewer "no shows" and also helps with recruiting a more diverse sample. The payment should be approved by the research ethics board (see Chapter 2) and should not be so large as to be viewed as coercive. Many researchers offer a raffle for a gift card or some other prize to keep overall costs of the study down. University students are often given bonus course credit for their participation in studies.

Another approach is to go where the participants are. If you are interested in children, go to daycare centres or the homes of children that you know or have contacts with. If you are interested in individuals with Parkinson's disease, find support groups that focus on that disease. If feasible, consider "moving" the laboratory to a place that is convenient or easily accessible for the participant population you are interested in. We know several researchers who study older adults and set up satellite laboratories in malls, as well as others who have gone to retirement communities. If none of these approaches works, it is time to rethink your research question, design, or participant population.

Time Constraints

A few different types of time constraints exist. If you are an undergraduate student collecting data for your research methods course, you may have only have a few weeks to collect your data. You may have to alter your participant population or methods so that you can finish on time. Experienced researchers also confront time constraints. Some research, such as on seasonal affective disorder, is best done during the winter months when the disorder is prevalent. Other research that uses undergraduates is best done during the academic year. Thus, researchers working on a particular problem or using a particular participant population must time their research appropriately. If you cannot meet the time constraints, you may need to rethink your research question, design, or participant population.

Money Constraints

Research can cost a lot of money, including payment to research participants, travel expenses for participants or experimenters, and the cost of materials or stimulus preparation. These costs can add up quickly, especially if you require a large sample. You can keep participant costs down by offering participants a chance to win money or a gift card in a raffle, but this approach might not be as successful as paying each participant individually for recruiting the number of participants you need.

More and more researchers are using online approaches to obtain relatively large samples at a relatively small cost. For example, Amazon's MTurk (discussed earlier in this chapter) is an online crowdsourcing resource where researchers can pay a relatively small amount of money to individuals willing to complete surveys online for funds they can then use on Amazon.

Because of the growing trend of researchers copyrighting their measures, you may need to purchase copies of questionnaires or established measures. Once a measure has been copyrighted, other researchers generally cannot use that measure without paying a fee. You are faced with the choice of coming up with your own measure, one that is potentially less desirable and less well established, or finding some way to pay for the copyrighted material. Again, if you cannot meet the monetary constraints, you may need to rethink your research question, design, or participant population.

Equipment Constraints

Some researchers love to use high-tech data collection and coding techniques that can be very costly. For example, researchers using the sophisticated technique of functional magnetic resonance imaging may need to pay up to $400 per hour for machine time to collect data. Researchers studying brain activity using event-related potentials often require systems costing a few hundred thousand dollars. Obviously, the cost of this equipment is well beyond that of a beginning researcher, but most research will require at least a computer and specific software for generation of materials, data storage, and data analysis. Most, if not all, research requires some equipment. What if you cannot afford it? Or what if you are collecting data in a remote location and cannot transport the desired equipment? Once again, you are faced with choices that pit the optimal against the obtainable.

Make the Best Choices

How does one juggle these different constraints to design and implement the best research study possible? It is difficult. But remember that there is no perfect study. Do the best you can with the resources you have. Often your constraints stimulate creative, low-cost, and low-tech solutions that are just as reliable and valid as expensive, high-tech solutions. Just do not forget about reliability and validity in the decision-making process.

Another option to consider is collecting converging evidence using a variety of different methods. This approach may help you get around some of the constraints and ultimately provide better data. For example, if you decide to run your survey on MTurk to collect a large number of participants at a relatively low cost, consider a companion survey with another sample population that may cost more to collect but will provide more information on other potentially important characteristics.

PRACTICAL TIPS

Practical Tips for Developing Your Research Proposal

1. Be sure to leave yourself adequate time to recruit your sample.

2. Clearly define your population of interest, giving thought to the criteria for inclusion and exclusion.

3. Consider the ways in which your sample needs to be representative (or not), and select your sampling methodology accordingly.

4. Choose your measurements, keeping in mind both the scale of those measurements and the issues of validity and reliability. Do not reinvent the wheel—it is typically best to use existing measures.

5. Consider conducting a prospective power analysis to determine how many participants you need in your study before you begin collecting data.

6. Formulate a general analysis plan before you begin collecting data.

CHAPTER SUMMARY

With research question and hypotheses in hand, you have moved on to the task of designing your research proposal, which will keep you in good stead when it comes time to launch your study. The proposal process begins with the challenge of obtaining representative participant samples so that you can create valid conclusions that will apply to broad groups of people.

Approximations of random sampling—considered the gold standard for gathering participants—have grown easier in recent years thanks to online systems such as MTurk, which offer a low-cost, large pool of participants. You may also choose from alternative methods, such as stratified random sampling, oversampling, and snowball sampling.

Next, you must select a scale of measurement—nominal, ordinal, interval, or ratio—depending on the complexity of information your study requires. Above all, your measure should gather data that are both valid (well founded and reflecting the real world) and reliable (consistent).

Conducting a power analysis will tell you the probability that your research will be able to detect an effect. Researchers complete a power analysis either before or after designing the study (although preferably before).

The final step in your design should be formulating an analysis plan. This is a specific strategy for what sorts of analyses you will conduct.

End-of-Chapter Exercises

1. The issue of obtaining a representative sample (i.e., a sample that accurately represents your population of interest) presents substantial challenges for researchers. As important as this issue may be for some research studies and topics, it may not be an issue for all psychological research. As a prospective researcher, what criteria would you use to determine whether a representative sample is necessary for a given study?

2. Many researchers draw their samples from undergraduate research pools. What are the advantages to doing this? What are the disadvantages? Identify strategies for recruiting non-student samples into a research study.

3. Provide an example for when it may be more appropriate to use each of the following strategies:
   a. stratified random sample over a random sample
   b. convenience sample over a random sample
   c. online sample over an in-person sample

4. For each of the descriptions presented below, indicate which scale of measurement is being used.
   a. As part of a satisfaction survey for a fast-food chain, customers are asked to rate their satisfaction with the customer service they received on a 10-point scale from 1 (not at all satisfied) to 10 (extremely satisfied).

b. During a physical health screening, patients are asked how many glasses of alcohol they have consumed in the past week.

c. During a clinical interview, survivors of an earthquake are asked whether they have experienced specific symptoms of post-traumatic stress disorder in the past week. A value of 0 is assigned to "no" and a value of 1 is assigned to "yes."

d. A kindergarten teacher evaluates her incoming students and classifies them as non-readers (0), beginning readers (1), or advanced readers (2).

e. A school psychologist administers an intelligence test to a student. This is a standardized test with a mean of 100 and a standard deviation of 15.

5. The importance of formulating an analysis plan (and sticking to it) at the outset of research is widely debated. Some have argued that this is essential in reducing the temptation to "fish" for significant findings in one's data; others argue that the freedom to explore within a data set is important to the process of scientific inquiry. Where do you fall in this debate? Justify your position.

6. If you are conducting a research project as part of your course requirement, list and discuss some of the constraints that were identified in this chapter that may have an impact on your research study.

Key Terms

convenience sampling, p. 88

effect size, p. 94

interval scale, p. 91

Likert-type ratings, p. 92

measurement error, p. 89

nominal scale, p. 90

non-parametric test, p. 92

non-probability sample, p. 88

ordinal scale, p. 90

oversampling, p. 87

parametric test, p. 92

p-Hacking, p. 95

population, p. 82

probability sampling, p. 86

prospective power analysis, p. 94

random sampling, p. 86

ratio scale, p. 92

representative sample, p. 83

retrospective power analysis, p. 94

sample, p. 83

self-selection, p. 88

snowball sampling, p. 88

statistical power, p. 94

statistical significance, p. 95

stratified random sampling, p. 87

Survey and Interview Approaches

6

Chapter Contents

INSIDE RESEARCH: M. Gloria González-Morales

I started my career in psychology thinking that I would follow in my father's footsteps and take over his clinical practice once I finished my education. However, this didn't quite go as planned. After doing my practical in clinical psychology I realized that I did not want to work with clinical populations. I chose to redirect my interests into industrial and organizational psychology while maintaining my focus on mental health. Once I finished my Ph.D. I chose to stay in academia to continue my research.

Courtesy of M. Gloria González-Morales

Associate professor, psychology, and director of organization and management solutions, the consulting group of the I-O Psychology Program, University of Guelph

I became interested in understanding health in the context of work organizations. My main lines of research focus on work stress and gender and sexual diversity in the workplace. I also study respectful workplaces, with a particular interest in understanding incivility in the workplace. These research interests are all further tied together through my interest in emotional regulation and how this relates to being civil in the workplace, coping with stress, and managing gender relations.

continued

Doing research on incivility is hard. It is typically studied by asking people how frequently they have been harassed or disrespected in the workplace and how being victimized is related to their well-being, performance, and work attitudes. But with my research focus I am more interested in studying the antecedents of incivility in the workplace. I examine instances in which people behave uncivilly in the workplace and how this behaviour depends on individual, organizational, and cultural factors. This creates a particular set of challenges in studying this topic, because we are asking people about their likelihood of being rude or disrespectful to other people. In our debriefings, when describing the research study to participants, we need to be very careful in explaining that these behaviours are not uncommon and that engaging in them does not mean that they are bad people.

I employ multiple methods in my research. I have done experimental studies where we implement different interventions in the workplace with control groups. I have also conducted studies using vignettes representing different workplace scenarios involving incivility to identify antecedents of participants' perceptions or behaviours. The majority of my research makes use of survey methodology, often with complicated designs involving multilevel analyses. I am interested in looking at both group- and individual-level variables and how variables that emerge at a group level can affect individual-level attitudes and experiences. More recently, I've asked my participants to complete weekly or monthly diaries. This has been particularly effective in looking at how, for instance, mindfulness exercises can affect energy levels at the beginning and end of the working day.

M. Gloria González-Morales uses applied research methods to study stress, work–life and gender diversity, workplace mistreatment and victimization, workplace incivility and civility, emotion regulation, and how the implementation and evaluation of evidence-based interventions can enhance occupational well-being and performance. Her work has been published in outlets such as the *Journal of Applied Psychology*, *Journal of Occupational Health Psychology*, *Work & Stress*, and the *Journal of Organizational Behavior*.

Research Focus: Occupational health psychology and positive organizational psychology

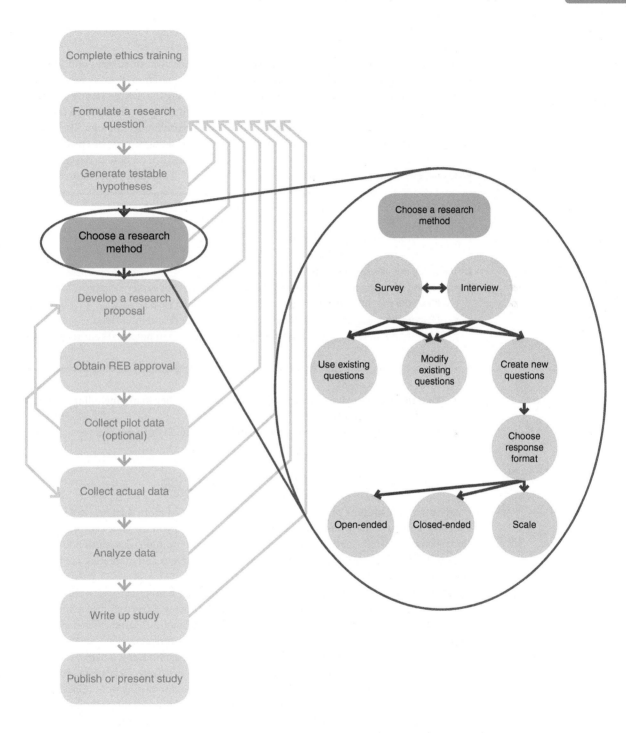

Chapter Abstract

This chapter focuses on the selection, design, and construction of surveys and interviews, highlighting key issues that you should consider in selecting an existing survey, creating a survey or interview, choosing a survey method, and obtaining the desired sample population. We first explain the factors you should consider when evaluating results reported for surveys, which have grown increasingly popular with the advent of online technology. Then, we help you decide whether to use an existing survey, modify an existing survey, or create your own survey from scratch. Finally, we provide you with some guidance on how to design and write your own questions and figure out which response types will best suit your research goals.

LEARNING OBJECTIVES

By the end of this chapter, you should be able to:
- Identify factors that contribute to the trustworthiness of survey results.
- Describe the difference between a survey and an interview.
- Discuss advantages and disadvantages to using surveys and interviews.
- Identify possible threats to the validity of survey data and potential solutions to these threats.
- Discuss when it is better to use an existing survey and when it is better to create a new one.
- Describe factors to consider in the construction of survey items, including question wording and response type.
- Identify strategies for assessing the reliability and validity of a new survey.

THE PERVASIVENESS OF SURVEYS

If you still have a landline phone, you have probably received more than one call from a telemarketer, and now many telemarketers know how to reach you on your cell phone. During election season, people may contact you asking about your opinion on various political issues and candidates. But even outside the realm of politics, surveys and marketing are part of the fabric of everyday life.

Survey results bombard us daily. They appear in all media—from print to television, from radio to Internet blogs—and report on an incredible range of topics. Survey studies reported in the media include the going rate of a tooth for the Tooth Fairy (Pisani, 2013), whether men or women cheat more on their partners (Schonfeld, 2013), and how much cannabis adult Canadians will consume in its first year of legalization (Miller, 2018). Topics range from the sublime, such as those listing travellers' recommendations for the best destinations (*Best Travel Destinations*, 2016), to the ridiculous, such as a survey examining the most absurd reasons for missing work (Gillie, 2012).

A central issue with all these surveys lies in the trustworthiness of the data. Should you believe the results of surveys that rank your school as one of the best colleges or universities in Canada ("Top Universities in Canada 2018," 2018) or as a party school (Schwartz, 2016)? Does the Tooth Fairy really shell out $20 a tooth? In other words, how can we tell whether the survey data are valid (that they measure what they are designed to measure) and reliable (provide consistent results across similar contexts or situations)?

The answer depends, in part, on knowing the questions asked in the survey, how the questions were asked, and who was asked the questions in the first place. For example, in the Tooth Fairy poll discussed in "Media Matters: The Profligate Tooth Fairy," what questions were parents asked and how were the parents recruited to complete the survey?

An earlier 2013 online version of this survey garnered mainstream media attention and appeared on a website titled *Practical Money Skills for Life* (Visa, 2013). Under the heading "Financial Literacy for Everyone" was listed a long series of questions about personal finances, three of which concerned the Tooth Fairy. The first was, "How much did the Tooth Fairy leave your kids in 2013?" Participants could choose from four responses:

A. More than $4
B. $2 to $3
C. $1 exactly
D. Less than $1

MEDIA MATTERS

The Profligate Tooth Fairy

The Tooth Fairy has gone on a spending spree, tucking as much as $20 or more for a tooth underneath children's pillows at night, according to a telephone survey by Visa Canada conducted in 2015 (Kozicka, 2015).

The survey reports that only about 5 per cent of all children receive that hefty sum, and children now receive an average of $3.44 per tooth. That figure is 23 per cent higher than in 2014. However, the Tooth Fairy appears to be more generous in some provinces than others, with kids in Quebec receiving just over $4 per tooth, on average. Kids in British Columbia were on the low end of the scale, with an average of $2.46 per tooth. Further, the Tooth Fairy pays more to Canadian kids than to kids in the States; American kids received an average of $2.19 per tooth.

Some reports use these results to urge parents to start financial discussions with their kids. Carla Hindman, director of financial education for Visa Canada (the company that conducted the study) says "The Tooth Fairy is paying a premium for Canadian baby teeth, which gives parents a great chance to start a conversation about money with their kids" ("Tooth Fairy Gives Canadian Kids a Raise This Year," 2015).

Other reports speculated on possible causes of the Tooth Fairy's extravagance. Neale Godfrey, author and chair of the Children's Financial Network, pointed to parental remorse. "I think the amounts have gone up because we feel guilty about our parenting. . . . We are not spending as much time with our children as we would like, and so we substitute money for time" ("Inflation Remains in Check," 2013).

Other sources explained the increase as a result of parents' age-old desire to keep up with the Joneses and spare their children's feelings. "A kid who got a quarter would wonder why their tooth was worth less than the kid who got $5," says Kit Yarrow, a consumer psychologist and professor at Golden Gate University (Pisani, 2013).

But parents (or the Tooth Fairy) can finally determine an appropriate amount to leave children. As part of the company's personal finance education program, Visa offers a downloadable Tooth Fairy Calculator app that tells users how much parents in their age group, income bracket, and education level are giving their kids, Alderman says. The newly updated app is available for iPhones and iPads on iTunes, and the calculator is available on the Facebook apps page (Pisani, 2013).

Although the reports ruminated on all the complexities, possible causes, and solutions to the Tooth Fairy's spendthrift ways, none of them examined the confusing, questionable survey methods that lay behind Visa's claims. Maybe the survey itself should have been the story.

If you checked the results in October 2013, you would find that there were only 643 votes; 28.8 per cent responded $1 exactly, 27.5 per cent responded more than $4, 23.2 per cent responded less than $1, and 20.5 per cent responded between $2 and $3.

It is not clear how these responses were averaged to obtain a single value, because the website includes no information about how averaging was done. For example, is the response "less than $1" coded as $1, 50 cents, or nothing? Are responses of "more than $4" coded as $4 or some other value? As you can see, it is difficult to understand how the sponsor of the study calculated an average of $3.70 per tooth from the responses given.

A subsequent question asked, "Parents, how much does the Tooth Fairy give your child for each lost tooth?" This time participants were given a different set of choices:

A. Nothing
B. Less than $2
C. $2 to $5
D. More than $5

The same problem of how to map these values onto the averages plagues this question. And how are the answers to this question combined with those from the previous question, especially given that this one attracted fewer respondents ($n = 624$)?

Another question later in the survey asked, "How much does the Tooth Fairy leave your kids?" Response choices were as follows:

A. Nothing
B. Less than $1
C. $1 exactly
D. $2
E. $5
F. More than $5

This question actually drew 1,130 respondents, with 40 per cent picking "C," or $1 exactly. Determining which data led to various media reports of children getting an average of $3.70 per tooth in 2013 (when 2013 had not even ended) is extremely difficult. What we *can* see is that these three questions result in different patterns of responses. As Figure 6.1 shows, the reliability and validity of this particular survey appear questionable. Different forms of the questions frame the issue in a variety of ways (a possible threat to validity), and different response categories clearly lead to a different pattern of responses (a possible threat to reliability). A repeat of this survey in 2015 changed its format from an online survey to a telephone interview involving 2,003 parents. However, it is not clear whether any changes were made to the specific questions asked of participants.

SURVEYS VERSUS INTERVIEWS

Although the terms "survey" and "interview" are often used interchangeably, they differ in format. With surveys, researchers present questions on paper or online for participants to complete on their own. With interviews, researchers ask participants questions orally—in person or on the phone.

Questionnaires are made up of a set of questions that let participants respond freely or choose from a preselected set of options. They can be presented in either a survey or an

survey A set of questions administered to a group of respondents, usually via paper or online, to learn about attitudes and behaviour.

interview A data collection technique in which researchers ask participants questions orally, either in person or over the phone.

questionnaire A set of questions that may be part of a survey or interview.

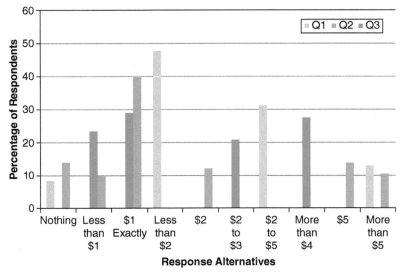

FIGURE 6.1   Percentage of respondents providing different responses to the Tooth Fairy question.

interview format. Questionnaires usually have a relatively narrow focus. Although the terms "questionnaire" and "survey" may be used interchangeably, the term "survey" is often reserved for measures that contain more than one questionnaire or that include interview methods. Individual questionnaires used in a survey will often have been developed by other researchers and have been shown to provide valid and reliable responses on some topic in past research.

In some cases, researchers copyright a particular survey or questionnaire and then charge researchers for use of the measure. In other cases, researchers will publish their measures in various academic journals. Some journals are open access, meaning that anyone can access the articles in the journal for free on the web. Other journals will require a paid subscription. College and university libraries will have access to some of these journals, so you should check with your library to see if you can access the articles, and measures, via your library for free.

Surveys and interviews are likely the most widely used methods in psychology and related fields. The use of surveys in particular has grown rapidly with the ease of conducting online research. Although both approaches possess a number of advantages, the research question—not just convenience—should always drive the choice of method.

THE PROS AND CONS OF SURVEYS

Surveys are a flexible and efficient means of collecting data, and because of their potential ability to engage participants surveys are popular, and they have a number of advantages compared with other research methods. Despite their popularity, there are a number of biases and threats to validity that are important to also consider.

Advantages of Surveys

Surveys are widely used by researchers because they are efficient, economical, and enable the collection of large samples in a relatively short time frame. They also allow for greater anonymity for participants and greater flexibility than some other methods.

Efficient and Economical.   Researchers can use surveys to collect a large amount of data in a relatively short time. For example, researchers can collect data from hundreds of students in an introductory psychology class within a single class period. With online surveys, researchers can contact thousands of potential participants in locations all over the world relatively quickly. We know of one online survey called the Personality Project that has collected information from 260,000 respondents to explore current personality theory and research (www.personality-project.org).

Large Sample Sizes.   When working with survey data, researchers can use more sophisticated statistical approaches for data analysis, often requiring large sample sizes that may be difficult (if not impossible) to collect using interviews or an experimental design. The cost in time and money of these other approaches often makes obtaining large samples impractical, whereas survey approaches offer a large sample, often readily within reach. If you collect a large sample, you can run statistical analyses on randomly selected portions of the data. This allows you to determine whether the statistical results can be reproduced within the same overall data set.

Anonymity.   Yet another advantage of survey methods is that researchers can use them to obtain information that a participant might not be willing to share in a face-to-face interview, especially if the information requested concerns sensitive or illegal behaviour. Questions about sexual behaviour, illicit drug or alcohol use, attitudes about ethnicity or gender issues or religious beliefs, or questions about immigration status are some of the many topics that individuals might be unwilling to discuss openly with an interviewer, but may be willing to answer on a survey as long as anonymity is ensured. Surprisingly, even telephone interviews provide a greater level of anonymity than face-to-face interviews. For example, there is evidence to suggest that surveys on the thorny topic of substance abuse, when conducted by telephone, can yield relatively accurate prevalence estimates (McAuliffe, Geller, LaBrie, Paletz, & Fournier, 1998).

Flexibility.   Surveys also have a number of other attributes that make them desirable. They can be used to investigate a large number of different research questions, they can be adapted to a participant's responses, and they can be completed at the convenience of the respondent.

With the use of computers and specialized software, surveys can be flexibly modified to present different sets of questions based on initial responses. This approach can provide a more efficient means of collecting the data because only those questions relevant to a participant will be asked. For example, a survey investigating sexual harassment in the workplace (see Erdreich, Slavet, & Amador, 1994) might provide a different set of questions to men and women. It is also easy to quickly modify your study if you discover a problem with some questions, realize you left out some important questions, or decide that an altogether different set of questions is needed.

A customized survey places less of a burden on participants because they need to respond only to questions that pertain to their circumstances. There is also evidence that, despite fears to the contrary, computer-based surveys that people complete independently provide data that are just as valid as that obtained from surveys given in a supervised location (Carlsmith & Chabot, 1997).

A related, substantial advantage is that participants may choose to complete the survey when they have the time and motivation to respond. This is not without its own risks, however, because we have been told that students sometimes complete surveys assessing the quality of an instructor or class late at night in a less-than-sober state of mind.

Disadvantages of Surveys

Despite the many advantages that surveys offer, they do have some downsides, including potential biases and fraud. Identifying and eliminating biases in a particular survey sample can be difficult, and researchers must acknowledge this as a potential limitation in their designs.

Selection Bias.   Participants may differ from non-participants because of issues with the sampling methodology or because they have different motivational issues or time constraints. The method for contacting potential respondents may induce a particular type of undesirable selection bias. As discussed in Chapter 5, phone surveys were historically completed over the phone by randomly selecting potential respondents from phone directories. This approach tended to miss relatively poor people (who could not afford to pay for a phone line), people who intentionally opted out of being listed in the phone directory, or people who moved repeatedly. See Figure 6.2 for an example of selection bias.

Today, researchers commonly collect data using online surveys, which are effective for recruiting participants who have an email address and online access. But again, this approach likely misses a large number of individuals who do not have regular online access (e.g., low-income people or older adults who may not be technologically savvy).

The description of the survey in the Tooth Fairy "Media Matters" feature does not provide information about who responded to the survey. All we know is that individuals who responded to the survey were telephoned by personnel from the Research House National Telephone Omnibus. We have no idea how representative the sample is.

selection bias Errors in sampling resulting from a selected sample not being representative of the population of interest. This may come about because of under- or oversampling of particular types of respondents, respondent self-selection, or respondent non-response.

FIGURE 6.2   An example of selection bias. The people participating in the poll are selected in such a way as to ensure they are not representative of the population of interest.

Non-response Bias. Non-response bias occurs when individuals who were contacted and chose to complete the survey differ in some ways from others who were contacted but chose not to take the survey. Individuals may have many reasons for not completing a survey, but a common reason is that they simply lack time. In some cases, this factor might skew or bias the sample in important ways. Suppose you are trying to conduct a survey of new parents. Those who are juggling work and family might not want to take the time to complete your survey. Thus, families who have more time to respond to surveys—for example, those with fewer children or those with one family member at home to care for the children—may be overrepresented in your sample. Depending on your research question, the sample of participants who choose to respond may bias your results in a particular direction. In the Tooth Fairy example, parents with fewer children may pay more per tooth than parents with more children. But without more information it is difficult to determine who has chosen to complete the survey.

Self-Selection Bias. The self-selection bias occurs when individuals are free to choose to complete a survey, which may be problematic when the choice to participate relates in some way to the research topic. For example, when people watching a television channel that has a particular political bias are asked to call in or complete an online survey to rate politicians or issues, the individuals who respond are likely to have views similar to those of the channel. Therefore, the results will likely show the same bias.

Researcher Bias. Yet another source of bias for survey design is the researcher. Researcher bias is not unique to survey methodology; it can occur in all aspects of the research process (design, analysis, interpretation). But the way it usually plays out is in the construction of the survey questions or items. The Pew Research Center for the People and the Press provides an excellent example of how subtle—and perhaps unintentional—differences in survey wording can dramatically affect results. In a 2005 Pew Research survey, 51 per cent of respondents favoured "making it legal for doctors to give terminally ill patients the means to end their lives," but only 44 per cent favoured "making it legal for doctors to assist terminally ill patients in committing suicide" (Pew Research Center, n.d.). You might imagine that researchers could unconsciously select one of these statements, depending on their own views. This is another example of a framing effect (see Chapter 1), which is also important to consider when constructing surveys.

Fatigue Effects and Attrition. Although surveys can be amazingly efficient in gathering information, they also risk fatiguing participants, so that the data that are eventually collected are not valid. Longer surveys are more susceptible to fatigue effects, so it is important to examine the data to see whether the pattern of responses indicates genuine participation. It is not uncommon in a longer survey for earlier responses to be valid (and appropriately variable), but then later answers to fall into a response set, which is the tendency to respond with a consistent pattern of responses regardless of the question being asked (e.g., answering "strongly agree" to a long string of questions).

A related problem to fatigue is attrition, in which participants begin the survey but decide to drop out after completing only a portion of it. Some participants may stop if they tire of your survey, whereas others may lose interest for various reasons (e.g., distractions). Procedures for dealing with missing data may involve the removal of cases with any missing values, application of special techniques for analyzing data with missing values, or using relationships among variables in the data set to provide best guesses as to what those missing values might be. How you deal with incomplete data, however, depends on a range of methodological and statistical issues beyond the scope of our discussion here. (For more information, see Enders, 2010.) As with survey responses that are compromised by fatigue, you will need to make decisions about what to do with partial responses.

Social Desirability Bias.   Another potential hazard in survey methodology is the issue of social desirability. Social desirability bias arises when you question participants about behaviours or attitudes that might not be viewed as acceptable in society. Although there is no easy fix for the problem of social desirability, some research instruments that ask about undesirable behaviours approach the topic with enough subtlety that participants may be more comfortable sharing otherwise stigmatized behaviours. For example, the Conflict Tactics Scale (Straus, 1979; Straus, Hamby, Boney-McCoy, & Sugarman, 1996) is a self-report measure widely used by researchers interested in domestic violence. The measure examines the use of reasoning, verbal aggression, and violence within the family. Because the survey asks about a full range of behaviours in a way that presents them all as normative ways of resolving conflict, participants may be more comfortable disclosing otherwise socially undesirable behaviours. For example, the negotiation scale items, presented in order of social acceptability, range from "Discussed an item calmly" at the low end of the scale to "Used a knife or gun" at the high end.

> social desirability bias The tendency of respondents to provide answers that will be viewed favourably by others.

Potential Threats to Validity and Possible Solutions.   You can never be sure that respondents are giving accurate, honest answers. Many of the factors that make surveys attractive to use (anonymity, ease of responding) potentially increase the rate of invalid responses and responders. There are at least three potential threats to validity: respondents who do not understand questions, respondents who answer fraudulently, and respondents with an agenda. Although it is not possible to completely protect your survey from all malicious behaviour, you can take a few steps to minimize the impact of potential invalidity.

Respondents Who Do Not Understand Questions

The first potential threat arises when an individual does not understand the questions; this may be a result of language or vocabulary issues or intellectual disabilities. In this case, the individual may produce invalid responses by answering in a random fashion. You may see response patterns that do not make sense (e.g., all of one type of response or a truly random pattern). Such a pattern would indicate that you should not use the data.

Respondents Who Answer Fraudulently

A second potential threat may arise when an individual fraudulently, or carelessly, completes a survey. Individuals may complete the survey as quickly as possible to receive compensation, such as when participants are required to complete a survey either for their job or for class credit (as is common in introductory psychology classes). This can be particularly problematic in Internet-based research, where there is no direct connection between the researcher and the participant (Ward, 2015). You can detect this through nonsensical or erroneous response patterns, such as the following:

1. Include "instructed response" questions such as, "Please select slightly disagree for this item," to ensure your participants are, in fact, reading the questions.
2. Look for even–odd consistency, where participants' responses to items measuring similar variables are checked for consistency. For example, if you strongly agree with the

statement "This textbook is riveting," then you should not slightly disagree with the statement, "This textbook has interesting content."

3. Use a strategy termed "LongString," which involves looking for response patterns where respondents repeatedly choose the same response option.

4. Include self-report items that directly ask participants whether their responses were accurate and of high quality (Ward, 2015).

This threat can also arise when participants attempt to complete the survey repeatedly to receive additional rewards. With online surveys it is possible to collect the IP addresses of the computers used to submit the survey responses and allow only a single submission from any one IP address. This restricts your sample to only one member of a household or to one participant from any public computer, such as those in university computer labs or public libraries, but it may be better than having multiple responses from a single respondent.

Another way researchers have reduced multiple responses is to prescreen participants. Researchers can collect certain demographic data in the prescreening (name, telephone number, address) that they can use later to double check against survey responses. For example, researchers may check to see whether the same identifying information appears in multiple surveys. If it does, one or both surveys are likely invalid. As long as the prescreening data are kept separate from the actual data, most research ethics boards will approve the approach. After individuals have completed the prescreening, they are usually given a separate link to the actual survey. This process ensures the confidentiality of the respondent.

Another way to detect fraudulent responses is to add similar (or even the same) questions in a long survey to see whether participants give similar responses. Divergent responses to similar items suggest that a participant is not taking the survey seriously and give you a reason for potentially dropping the data from that respondent. As a way of decreasing the incentive for fraud in the first place, it is important to consider the issue of compensation when deciding how you will select and recruit potential participants. By keeping the compensation level relatively low, or using a raffle, for example, where only 1 of 100 participants is compensated, you can minimize incentives for completing the survey multiple times.

Respondents with an Agenda

A third potential threat to the validity of your survey is posed by respondents who are motivated to deliberately bias the results or invalidate the study once they have already agreed to participate. In this case, participants who have a vested interest in a particular program might respond in a way that is likely to characterize the program positively (e.g., provide more extreme values than they really think are warranted). This type of threat can be addressed through the use of a "lie scale," a set of items that are written to check that participants are taking the task seriously and not just answering questions to present themselves in the best possible light. A typical lie scale item used by researchers is "I never get angry." Everyone gets angry sometimes, so participants who respond that they never get angry are likely not providing valid responses. If respondents answer too many items on the lie scale in a way that indicates they are not honestly engaging with the task, then you can consider their responses as invalid.

lie scale A set of survey items used to determine whether participants are taking the task seriously and not simply responding in such a way as to present themselves in the best possible light.

Although all of these challenges to ensuring valid data should not discourage you from capitalizing on survey methodology's many strengths, it is worth noting that, by themselves, surveys are only one method for reaching a conclusion. As with all the techniques we discuss, an approach that uses multiple methods will yield the most conclusive results.

THE PROS AND CONS OF INTERVIEWS

Interviews that involve the researcher talking with the respondent over the phone, in person, or through technologies such as FaceTime or Skype offer several advantages. Furthermore, they are common in qualitative research in which the researcher is seeking to explore a topic in depth and gain the respondents' understanding of the topic. However, although the issues related to threats to validity are often less likely to be a problem with interviews, they still exist.

Advantages of Interviews

Interviews can provide a rich source of data and enable the researcher to judge whether any threats to validity occur. In particular, researchers conducting interviews can often confirm that participants understand the questions and can also detect careless responding.

Rich Data. Interviews permit a researcher to collect much richer data than is possible with surveys alone. With the right kinds of questions and follow-up probes, a researcher can delve deeply into a participant's thoughts, attitudes, values, and behaviour. Interview responses can help explain the results of more limited questions posed in a survey because the interviewer can explicitly ask why a participant responded in a particular way. Interviewers can also develop a rapport with participants that may help the participants be more honest or provide more detailed responses. In these ways, interviews can provide compelling information that can be used in presentations and manuscripts to "bring the data to life."

Confirmation of Participant Understanding. Rich data are only useful if they accurately reflect participants' thoughts and feelings. To that end, it is important that participants understand what they are being asked. This is something that researchers must check for when they interview young children, individuals who may not understand the language, or individuals with cognitive impairments.

In the case of interviews with young children, researchers may provide a few pretest or warm-up questions designed to determine whether children understand the nature of the interview. In the case of individuals who might be cognitively impaired, researchers may provide a quick screening to assess cognitive function. One such instrument is the Mini-Mental State Examination, which provides a simple, quick assessment of cognitive functioning in older adults (Folstein, Folstein, & McHugh, 1975). If performance on this test falls below a certain score (typically 20 on the 30-point scale), then the respondent likely has some form of cognitive impairment. In general, if a respondent appears to have trouble understanding or has cognitive impairments, you must determine whether the main interview should proceed. Even if you continue with the interview, the data are likely to be invalid and should not be used in any subsequent analyses.

Detecting Careless Interview Responding. A clear advantage of interviews over surveys is that you can often detect careless responding (CR) as it occurs (rather than after data collection is complete, as is often the case in survey research) and take steps to remedy the situation. Signs of CR in interviews with young children include excessive laughing or a particular response set, for instance, a consistent "yes" to every question without regard to content. Sometimes merely asking children to provide their best answer can help them focus. In interviews with children under age 5, any indication of lack of understanding or CR is grounds for assuming the interview is not producing valid data. With adult interviewees, facial expressions (e.g., smirks) and a cavalier attitude may indicate CR. In these cases, you can politely ask the respondent to take the survey seriously, but again, these types of responses indicate that the data will likely be invalid.

Disadvantages of Interviews

Although interviews enable researchers to confirm that participants understand the questions and can ultimately provide rich data, they do have a number of drawbacks. These include lack of efficiency, potential interviewer effects, response biases, and issues of standardization.

Inefficient Use of Time and Resources.   Interviews can be very time consuming. Unlike online surveys that can reach hundreds or thousands of participants in a relatively short time and require little or no labour during the data collection phase, face-to-face interviews require an experimenter to meet in person with the participant. Even greater time and financial demands are required if the experimenter must travel to interview the participants. New technologies such as FaceTime and Skype enable researchers to conduct interviews without travelling and may be a viable alternative.

interviewer effects
Influences that the interviewer may have on responses, including the way in which they ask and respond to questions, tone of voice, or facial expressions. All of these may be interpreted by the interviewee as positive or negative evaluations of their responses and may lead the respondent to alter their answers.

Interviewer Effects.   Another disadvantage of interviews is the potential influence of the interviewer, known as interviewer effects. The way the interviewer asks questions and responds to the participant's answers may influence the way the respondent answers questions. Participants may interpret slight changes in the interviewer's tone, inflection, facial expressions (e.g., the raising of an eyebrow), or posture (e.g., a nod of the head or crossing of arms) as positive or negative evaluations of their responses. Over the course of the interview, these interpretations may lead participants to alter their answers. Interviewers should be trained to provide neutral responses, but even the most highly trained interviewer may inadvertently provide subtle cues that may influence the participant.

A famous example of this phenomenon is the case of "Clever Hans" (Pfungst, 1911). Hans was a horse who appeared to be able to do simple math. But on investigation, it was determined that the horse was responding to the subtle cues of his handler rather than performing any arithmetic. The handler was completely unaware that he was providing these cues and was convinced of the brilliance of Hans. A more recent case of this has been reported with drug-sniffing hounds that apparently respond to unintended signals from their handlers and produce many more false alarms in controlled tests than should occur if they were actually sniffing out the drugs (Lit, Schweitzer, & Oberbauer, 2011). Interviewers must be conscious that their own characteristics (e.g., age, gender, ethnicity) and behaviour, including the way they dress and present themselves, may influence participants in various, sometimes subtle ways.

response bias Errors in testing that are introduced into participants' responses to interview or survey questions because of such considerations as a desire to respond in a way the participant believes the researcher would want, an unwillingness to provide sensitive information, or a tendency to always respond positively when unsure about a question.

Response Bias.   Threats to validity, which are present in surveys, can also arise in face-to-face situations. Participants being interviewed in a face-to-face situation may exhibit a number of response biases. One common form of response bias occurs when individuals respond in a way they think the interviewer wants them to respond. Not usually done with malicious intent, response bias results from the participant consciously or unconsciously wanting to help or gain favour with the interviewer. Another type of response bias occurs when participants are unwilling to provide potentially sensitive or illegal information during face-to-face interviews.

A related problem is an **acquiescence bias**, where a respondent will respond affirmatively to any question when in doubt. These problems of response bias are not limited to interviews and may also arise with surveys.

Standardization.   To effectively quantify the responses of a group of participants, it is important to standardize interview questions. **Standardization** refers to the idea that all respondents answer the same set of questions. Complete standardization can be difficult with in-person interviews because participants often respond freely or an interviewer may ask follow-up questions to clarify a response. These free responses can be difficult to code and analyze using quantitative approaches because participants may each focus on different issues in their responses. Recall that the aim of quantitative research is to quantify participants' responses and generalize the results back to a larger population. If standardization is crucial to your research question, it may be better to use a standard questionnaire or survey rather than an interview.

Focus Groups

A special type of interview that is gaining in popularity is the **focus group**. Rather than interviewing a single person at a time, a focus group brings together a small group of about 6 to 10 individuals, who often share a common characteristic related to the topic of the discussion, and interviews them as a group. The focus group is conducted by a trained interviewer who is able to guide the session and promote participation among all members of the focus group. Focus groups share many of the same advantages and disadvantages of interviews. They allow for the collection of rich data, though not as rich as individual interviews, and can be influenced by interviewer effects and response biases. Additional advantages of focus groups are that they allow for the collection of data from a greater number of participants more efficiently (making them more cost effective) and they enable participants to hear and respond to the comments of others. An additional disadvantage of focus groups is that they are much more difficult to facilitate because of the greater number of individuals involved. This can be especially challenging when there are domineering participants who try to dominate the conversation or passive participants who do not speak up at all. This makes the ability of the interviewer to manage the discussion a critical element of an effective focus group.

USING AN EXISTING SURVEY VERSUS CREATING A NEW ONE

Before you come up with questions to include in your survey, it is important to revisit your research question or questions. What do you want to find out from the survey? Also, can you use questions or questionnaires constructed by other researchers to address your research question? It is always a good idea to start by looking for existing measures and only create your own if there are no valid or reliable measures in your research area. Sometimes you may not be able to find an instrument that exactly measures the variable you want, but if you can find one that is close, you can adapt the survey to your needs (e.g., change the items from a work focus to a school focus).

Researchers use pre-existing surveys or measures for a number of reasons. First, using an existing survey (or adapting one) is more efficient than constructing a new one. Creating a

acquiescence bias
Errors in testing where the participant responds affirmatively to every question or to every question where they are unsure of the correct response.

standardization The designing of interview questions such that they are used in a consistent manner by all interviewers.

focus group A small group of 6 to 10 individuals who are interviewed in a group setting.

survey from scratch can involve countless hours of writing, revising, and pretesting. Writing a good question is not easy, and even if you have a lot of expertise and practice, it may be challenging. For example, how should you assess social class? Should you ask about income? Only income? Should you ask the participants to report their yearly income (which many people are unwilling to do)? Or should you use some other measure of social standing? These are not simple issues, and many researchers have spent a lot of time thinking about and conducting research on this issue (e.g., Oakes & Rossi, 2003).

Second, researchers have determined the validity and reliability of the data provided by many existing survey instruments. That is, researchers have assessed how well the survey measures what it is designed to measure and how well it compares with other existing instruments, as well as how reliable the data provided by the measure is when used over repeated assessments (see Chapter 4). Unfortunately, some constructs, such as socio-economic status, have been measured using a variety of instruments, and widespread agreement on which measure is best to use for your own research is rare. Look for information on the validity and reliability of particular measures related to your research question and whether the existing studies were conducted on a population similar to the one you are planning to study. You might also choose a couple of different established measures to obtain converging information. Again, the choice of a particular instrument should be closely related to your overriding research question. If you have chosen to adapt an existing instrument, you do need to be cautious about what impact this may have had on the reliability and validity of the data provided by the adapted measure.

A final benefit of using an existing survey instrument is that it facilitates comparisons between studies that use the same measure. When researchers use established surveys—or adapt a series of items from existing instruments—they are better able to compare their results with other findings that have been previously reported. Making this kind of comparison can be especially valuable if you are doing research on a population that differs from those that have been already studied.

MacArthur Scale of Subjective Social Status A measure of subjective social standing, obtained by having respondents place themselves on a socio-economic "ladder."

For example, the **MacArthur Scale of Subjective Social Status** (Goodman et al., 2001) was developed to account for people's perceptions of how they fit within the social hierarchy. The assumption behind this measure is that people's *perceptions* of social standing may be a more valid measure of their social standing than their *actual* income, education, or occupation (Adler, Epel, Castellazzo, & Ickovics, 2000). One problem with objective measures of actual income is that many individuals are uncomfortable or unwilling to provide information about how much they earn. The MacArthur Scale asks respondents to place themselves on a ladder (see Figure 6.3) that represents people who have the most money, highest level of education, and highly respected jobs at the top and people who have the least money, little or no education, and no job or a job that is not respected at the bottom. This assessment tool uses a standard question format and includes published information about its reliability (Goodman et al., 2001) and validity (Cundiff, Smith, Uchino, & Berg, 2013).

As you decide whether to use an existing questionnaire/survey or write your own, spend some time examining the literature in your area of interest. If well-established survey instruments with information on their reliability and validity already exist, these should be considered first. However, if existing questionnaires do not really address the issue you are interested in, consider how you might modify some or all of the questions to be useful for your research.

Even established measures may require some modification if your study will include participants of different ages, groups, or cultures than were included in past research. For example, responses to the MacArthur Scale appear to vary by ethnicity (Wolff, Acevedo-Garcia, Subramanian, Weber, & Kawachi, 2010), so this measure may not capture the same

Imagine that this ladder shows how your society is set up.

- At the top of the ladder are the people who are the best off—they have the most money, the highest amount of schooling, and the jobs that bring the most respect.
- At the bottom are people who are the worst off—they have the least money, little or no education, no jobs or jobs that no one wants or respects.

Now think about your family. Please tell us where you think your family would be on this ladder. **Place an 'X' on the rung that best represents where your family would be on this ladder.**

FIGURE 6.3   The MacArthur ladder for measuring subjective social status.

information for different ethnic groups. That said, you should also be cautious about modifications. Once an instrument has been modified, the information on reliability and validity may no longer be valid, and you may need to pretest your questions or reassess the reliability/validity of the data provided by the modified instrument.

In some cases, it is entirely appropriate to develop your own survey or questionnaire. Obviously, if your topic has rarely or never been studied, then you will need to write your own questions. Also, if no surveys or questionnaires exist that provide sufficient reliability and validity evidence, then it is appropriate to design a new measure. Additionally, if your research involves a different sample than the original instrument was developed for, then you may need to modify an existing instrument or create a new one.

Finally, you may have empirical or theoretical reasons for creating a new measure. For example, researchers created the MacArthur Scale on both empirical and theoretical grounds. Empirically, some researchers found that the measure they used did not successfully predict outcomes of interest. Many people do not feel comfortable reporting their income; they may under- or over-report how much they earn. For this reason, measures of social status that take income into account are likely to be inaccurate. From a theoretical perspective, researchers argued that an individual's *perception* of social status, rather than social status measured by objective measures of income or education, was a more valid indicator of social status.

STEPS TO BUILDING YOUR OWN QUESTIONNAIRE

If you decide not to use an existing questionnaire, be aware that generating instruments that provide valid and reliable data require a number of steps and can take substantial time and resources. In fact, there is an entire field of psychology—called psychometrics—devoted to test construction and validation. If you do make the decision to create your own survey, this section includes some critical steps in the process.

Question Wording

Whether you create a new survey or modify an existing one, writing a *good* survey is challenging. The way you ask questions will strongly influence the responses you are likely to receive. If your questions are too complicated, you will probably confuse your participants and not obtain good data. Likewise, you must be careful about wording questions so as not to bias participants' responses. The overall goal of survey design is to create questions that will give you valid and reliable data. It is also important to remember what type of response you want from your participants (free response, multiple-choice, rating scale, etc.), which we will address after considering issues relevant to the form and content of the survey questions.

Simplicity Is Good!   Simple, straightforward questions are the best way to ask for information. Avoid long, complex questions or double-barrelled questions. You should also avoid terms or phrases that may not be understood by everyone (Fowler, 2002). Acronyms are abundant on university campuses, but unless students encounter them regularly, they may easily forget them. In one instance on our campus, two different committees had the same acronym (URGC). One stood for the *Undergraduate Research Grant Committee*, which funded undergraduate research proposals, and the other represented the *University Research Grant Committee*, which funded faculty research proposals. Asking questions about the URGC might lead to different responses depending on what contact a participant has had with these committees. In any case, avoid acronyms in your questions when possible, but if you must use them, make sure to spell them out at least once.

Write Questions at the Appropriate Reading Level.   Approximately 42 per cent of Canadians have a literacy level below the skill level typically needed to complete high school (Jamieson, 2006). The research ethics board may request that your survey be written at a reading level low enough to ensure that respondents clearly understand what they are being asked. Typically, it is recommended that survey questions should be written at a Grade 6 to Grade 8 level (Badarudeen & Sabharwal, 2010). Of course, if the grade level of your participants is lower than this (e.g., you have a sample comprising Grade 4 students), then you would need to adjust the reading level accordingly. Commonly used word processing programs enable you to check the "readability" or "reading level" of your questions.

double-barrelled question A question that refers to more than one issue but requires or expects only one response. Also known as a compound question.

Avoid Double-Barrelled Questions.   Double-barrelled questions (also called compound questions) refer to more than one issue but require or expect only one response. Consider the following examples:

- "Do you think your introductory psychology class was interesting, and was the instructor engaging?"
- "Do you like the prime minister of Canada, and do you think the prime minister is doing a good job?"
- "Do you agree or disagree with the following statement: 'Psychology majors are the most creative and interesting students'?"

In each of these examples, participants might have two different responses for the distinct parts of the question, but joining the issues in a single question does not enable the researcher to determine which part of the question is being answered. It is better to address each issue separately:

- "Was your introductory psychology class interesting?" and "Was the instructor for the class engaging?"
- "Do you like the prime minister of Canada?" and "Do you think the prime minister of Canada is doing a good job?"

- "Do you agree or disagree with the following statement: 'Psychology majors are the most creative students'?" and "Do you agree or disagree with the following statement: 'Psychology majors are the most interesting students'?"

Avoid Leading Questions.   A leading question is one that suggests a particular answer to the question because of the way it is phrased. An example would be: "Research methods is a difficult course because it requires a lot of reading, statistics, and papers. How difficult did you find the class?" This question assumes that the research methods course is difficult and potentially biases the respondent to answer in a particular way. A better approach would be to simply ask, "Did you find the research methods course to be difficult?" or to use some form of rating scale to assess the level of difficulty.

Some surveys may also be designed to skew responses in a particular direction (e.g., political polls), but good social science researchers understand that data obtained from such methods are neither reliable nor valid. Consider the following question: "Most people agree that the death penalty should be legal in Canada; do you agree that the death penalty should be brought back?" In this case, the statement "Most people agree that the death penalty should be legal in Canada" assumes that the respondent will share this view and likely advocate for the return of the death penalty. The way the question is constructed indicates a clear bias in favour of the death penalty. Although such a question may satisfy a particular political viewpoint, you would be hard-pressed to argue that it will yield objective, fair responses. A better question would be simply to ask, "Do you support the return of the death penalty?" (See Figure 6.4 for an example of a leading question.)

Avoid Loaded Questions.   A loaded question is one that contains an assumption about the respondent that might not be justified that can make the question difficult to answer. A classic example is the following question: "Have you stopped beating your spouse?" The question both assumes that you have a spouse *and* that you have been beating them. You cannot answer this question without implying that either you used to beat your spouse and have now stopped (the "yes" response) or that you are still beating your spouse (the "no" response). (See Figure 6.4 for an example of a loaded question.)

Be Positive!   In general, it is better to word questions in a positive or neutral manner than in a negative one. For example, "On a scale of 1 (not at all) to 5 (a lot), how much did you *like* your introductory psychology class?" is better than "On a scale of 1 (not at all) to 5 (a lot), how

leading question
A question that suggests a particular answer to the question because of the way it is phrased.

loaded question
A question that contains an assumption about the respondent that might not be justified and can make the question difficult to answer.

FIGURE 6.4   An example of a leading question. In the third panel, the question is worded in such a way as to suggest that a smart person would not be in favour of the current mayor.

much did you *dislike* your introductory psychology class?" That being said, there is some place for negatively worded questions as a way of ensuring that your participants are, in fact, paying attention as they answer questions. A participant who answers a positively worded and a negatively worded question in contradictory ways may not be providing you with valid responses.

Also, avoid double negatives, which are confusing and unlikely to yield valid, reliable data. Consider the question, "Which of the following is not an example of a method that you have not encountered in your research methods class: experiment, correlational study, or observational study?" The use of the word "not" twice may lead different participants to interpret the question in different ways. A better question would ask, "Which of the following methods have you encountered in your research methods class: experiment, correlational study, or observational study?"

Response Types

A key question in designing a survey is, How should the participant respond? We do not mean the actual content of the response, but the form the response will take. Surveys can present a large number of response types, including open-ended, closed-ended, true/false, Likert scales of various lengths, multiple-choice, fill in the blank, and many, many more. In picking your response type, it is important to consider how you will analyze the data collected from your survey. We present more detailed information about statistical analysis in Chapters 11 and 12.

closed-ended response item
A survey item/question that requires respondents to choose from a number of predetermined responses.

open-ended response item A survey item/question in which answers are not provided and respondents are able to answer the question in their own words.

Open-Ended versus Closed-Ended Responses.   Most surveys that you encounter in your everyday life likely involve closed-ended response items, which require you to choose among a variety of responses predetermined by the survey's author. Their popularity rests on the fact that they are simpler and easier than open-ended responses to quantify and analyze statistically, and they are more efficient for the participant to complete than questions that are open ended, making them more likely to be answered. An open-ended response item is one in which participants are not provided with answers to select from and are able to respond to the question in their own words. However, as we saw in the Tooth Fairy example earlier in the chapter, merely providing closed-ended responses will not guarantee a well-constructed question. Think carefully about your overarching research question and how you plan to use the responses to address that question when determining the most appropriate question type. If your goal is not to quantify but to conduct a more qualitative study (see Chapter 4), then open-ended responses may be most appropriate.

Many researchers avoid open-ended responses because of the potential problem of interpreting participants' answers, the difficulty in summarizing and quantifying responses across participants, and the constraints that open-ended responses place on potential statistical analyses. However, open-ended responses can be helpful in early stages of research and in providing a richer framework for interpreting responses to some closed-ended questions. Such responses can even be part of the strategy for developing and piloting survey items, which we discuss in the next section.

It is also possible to quantify open-ended responses, although it requires more steps in the analysis process. You must first reliably classify the responses into different types that can be quantified (i.e., develop a coding scheme). For example, in a study concerning parent–adolescent communication about sex, Jerman and Constantine (2010) included the open-ended question, "What is the most difficult part for you in talking to your child about sex and relationships?" Responses to this question were assigned to categories such as "difficulties related to embarrassment or discomfort" (e.g., "I think that it is just a comfort level that you feel, because it is a topic we are not in the habit of discussing"); "difficulties related to knowledge and self-efficacy" (e.g., "It is difficult for me to talk with her; I fear that I may explain something poorly to her or give her incorrect information"); and "cultural and social influences or issues" (e.g., "I think that sexual relations are a very delicate subject due to our culture"; p. 1169). Once responses were coded in this way, the researchers were able to assess which types of responses occurred most frequently and to evaluate how response frequencies differed with variables such as sex of the parent and age of the child.

Using open-ended questions during a pilot test of your ideas can also help you develop better, more-informed closed-ended questions for the actual survey. Open-ended questions can provide anecdotes that serve to highlight an interesting aspect of the results from closed-ended responses. For example, if you are surveying fathers about the ways in which they are involved in the lives of their young children, you could use a standard closed-ended measure that quantifies degrees of involvement. In addition, you could also ask men to describe what they most value about their parenting experience as a way of getting a deeper understanding of what drives their involvement. In this example, open-ended responses enrich and deepen the closed-ended responses (Gorvine, 2002), giving the best of both worlds.

Likert Scales and Response Format.   One of the most common survey item response types is the Likert response format, which was developed by Renis Likert in 1932 for his dissertation at Columbia University (Likert, 1932). A Likert response format includes an ordered range and is often used to measure particular attitudes or values. Response options usually include between three and seven choices that vary from "strongly agree" to "strongly disagree." Questions using a Likert response format generally start with a declarative statement (e.g., "I like rutabagas"), followed by an ordered continuum of response categories (e.g., "agree," "neither agree nor disagree," "disagree"). In this format it is important to balance the number of positive and negative options and provide descriptive labels for each category. A numeric value is usually provided for each category (Carifio & Perla, 2007).

Many researchers have modified the original Likert response format to assess frequency ("never," "once," "2–3 times," "4 or more times") or amount ("0," "$1," "$2," "$3+"), as in the Tooth Fairy example. You may more commonly see these scales referred to as "Likert-type scales." Others use a ruler on which respondents have to mark a continuous scale (as in the subjective social status ladder shown in Figure 6.3) or a "slider" for respondents to record their responses online (these are called "visual analogue" scales). The latter approaches yield interval data that are more appropriate for parametric statistical techniques (see Chapter 12 for a discussion of these issues).

If you decide to use a scale, you will need to consider several issues. First, how many different responses should you provide on your scale—3, 5, 7, or 21? Although there is no simple rule for deciding how many categories is appropriate, 5 is the norm. As you have probably guessed, this choice (as with all choices in research) should be driven by your research question. How many categories make sense with respect to your question? Are you able to provide a distinct label for each category? Are your participants likely to use the full range of responses given the question you are asking? The choice of how many response categories to use may also depend on whether the survey is administered online or via a paper survey, where it is easier to present more category options, or administered verbally, such as over the telephone, where presenting more response options may be cumbersome for the interviewer and taxing to the memory of the respondent.

Likert response format An ordered range of responses used to measure particular attitudes or values. Response options usually include three to seven options that vary from "strongly disagree" to "strongly agree."

midpoint The centre value of a scale with an odd number of response possibilities. An example of a midpoint on a scale of agreement is "neither agree nor disagree."

A second issue is whether you should provide a midpoint, the "neither agree nor disagree" option. Again, this depends on your research question, but using a **midpoint** and an odd number of categories ("agree"/"neither agree nor disagree"/"disagree") may yield different results than using an even number of responses with no midpoint ("agree"/"disagree"; Carifio & Perla, 2007). Some researchers, however, have found only negligible differences with particular measures when comparing the use of even and odd numbers of responses in Likert scales (Adelson & McCoach, 2010; Armstrong, 1987). If a midpoint makes sense for your measure and gives you useful information, then use a midpoint. If you want to force your respondents to indicate their view for one side or the other, then use an even number of responses.

A third issue involves labelling the response categories. This includes both which labels to use and whether to label all response options or just the extremes (e.g., only the first option is labelled as "strongly agree" and the last option as "strongly disagree"). First, there are many dimensions of ratings—agreement (e.g., agree/disagree), frequency (e.g., always/never), quality (e.g., excellent/poor), intensity (e.g., not/extremely)—and the choice of which labels to use should be based on the specific question you are asking. For instance, a fast-food restaurant may ask you to provide feedback on your recent visit. They are likely going to want to know your satisfaction with their service and may use an intensity scale (e.g., not at all satisfied to extremely satisfied). Second, labelling just the endpoints without intermediary labels makes it easier to construct a rating scale, as you only need to provide the two endpoints. However, labelling each response option helps facilitate a common interpretation for each and improves the reliability of the ratings (Weng, 2004). When designing your own Likert scales, we recommend that you look for examples of existing scales that have the same number of points as you intend to use and use their wording for the labels, as this will help strengthen the validity of your scale.

It is always a good idea to examine the distribution of your data to see whether respondents are avoiding the endpoints or clustering in the middle. If you discover either, in the next stage, your pilot test, you might consider rewording your questions to provide a more differentiated response pattern. You should also be sensitive to different participant populations (especially those from different cultures), who may view the scales and endpoints quite differently. A careful examination of the data, pilot testing, and sensitivity to group differences will help you determine an appropriate way to handle this particular issue.

A fourth issue regarding Likert and Likert-like response formats concerns data analysis. Many researchers treat the terms "Likert scale" and "Likert response formats" as equivalent (Carifio & Perla, 2007). However, the Likert response format refers *only* to how the responses are set up for a survey question. The sum of responses to multiple questions intended to measure the same variable form a **Likert scale** (Likert & Hayes, 1957).

Likert scale The sum of responses to multiple questions intended to measure the same variable using the Likert response format.

Although many researchers analyze the data from single questions that use a Likert response format, statisticians disapprove of this approach (Carifio & Perla, 2007; Gardner, Cummings, Dunham, & Pierce, 1998). As Carifio and Perla (2007) argue, would you ever try to use a single item on an IQ test to evaluate differences between groups? You should not! However, it is appropriate to examine responses to a single question as part of an item analysis or exploratory process as you develop your survey.

Evaluating Your Survey

Once you have completed a draft of your survey, it is crucial that you spend some time assessing its accuracy. Following are some tried-and-true ways of making sure your survey will accomplish what you want it to and ultimately address your research question.

Obtain Feedback.   Established researchers may run their questions by a panel of experts to garner feedback. These experts may consider whether the questions measure what they are supposed to measure (external validity) and whether subsets of questions sensibly group together to form coherent scales (internal validity). They may also make suggestions for modifying the items. Students or novice researchers working on their first research project may want to do their own version of this by running their questions by a group of peers.

Conduct Pilot Testing.   The next step involves conducting a pilot study to collect data to assess the instrument or try out a methodology. It is generally useful to obtain a relatively large sample for your pilot data. The exact number of participants you will need in your pilot study depends on a number of factors, including the number of items in your survey, the difficulty of obtaining samples from your target population (i.e., if you are studying a relatively hard to get group of participants, such as individuals with a rare disorder, you may not want to use members of this group in your pilot study), time and resources, and your overall goal. For some researchers, the piloting process may involve conducting interviews and asking open-ended questions to develop the more tightly worded items that will make up the final survey.

pilot study
A "prestudy" conducted before your actual study to assess your survey/ interview instrument or test a methodology.

Assess Instrument Reliability.   Recalling the concept of reliability from Chapter 4, a survey instrument provides reliable data to the extent that it yields similar results under similar conditions. There are three general types of reliability that may be relevant as you construct your survey: test–retest reliability, parallel forms reliability, and internal consistency.

Test–Retest Reliability
Test–retest reliability entails asking participants to complete your survey and then complete the same survey again at a later time. You then examine whether responses are consistent across the two surveys. You may do this for individual questions and for overall scores, if your survey is such that you combine items to arrive at a single score. Unfortunately, the test–retest approach suffers from the fact that participants may remember how they responded the first time, potentially leading to overestimates of reliability.

test–retest reliability
Correlation of the scores from the same measure that is taken by the same group of respondents at two different points in time.

Parallel Forms Reliability
Parallel forms reliability (also called alternate forms reliability) involves creating two differ- ent versions of the survey, with items in both surveys designed to probe the same variables. Standardized tests such as the GRE, TOEFL, and SAT use parallel forms: not everybody takes the exact same version of the test. As with test–retest reliability, participants' memories of their responses in one version of the survey may affect their responses on the second version, although the questions are not strictly identical. In addition, you may find a lack of consistency if the parallel items do not truly address the same variables.

parallel forms reliability A measure of survey reliability that examines the consistency of responses of respondents across two versions of a survey, with items in both surveys having been designed to probe the same variables. Also called alternate forms reliability.

Internal Consistency
If your survey uses multiple questions to measure a single variable, then you want to ensure that you have internal consistency in your instrument. A survey is internally consistent to the extent that items intended to measure the same variable yield similar responses. For example, suppose your survey has three Likert items that are meant to measure extraversion. If you find that partici- pants who agree with one item tend to also agree with the other two, whereas participants who disagree with one tend to disagree with the other two, then these items are internally consistent.

internal consistency
The degree to which the items within a measure assess various aspects of the same construct.

Cronbach's alpha (α)
A measure of the internal consistency of a set of scale items.

Cronbach's alpha (α) is a common statistical measure used to assess internal consistency, taking into account how well all of the items that relate to a single variable agree with one another (Cronbach, 1951). Alpha has an upper bound of 1.0, with higher scores indicating better internal consistency of the items. Many statistical packages allow you to examine the impact of deleting one or more items on the overall alpha. Depending on the outcome of this analysis, you may choose to remove or modify items to increase internal consistency. In general, it is recommended that a scale should ideally have an alpha coefficient of .80 or higher, and no lower than .70, to indicate acceptable reliability (Furr & Bacharach, 2014).

subscales Distinct parts of a larger instrument that measure different aspects of a variable.

factor analysis
A statistical technique that examines the relationships between items in a scale. This approach is useful for determining whether a scale measures a single variable or multiple ones.

Use Factor Analysis for Advanced Scale Construction. Distinct parts of a larger instrument that measure different aspects of a variable are referred to as subscales. These subscales may be derived in a similar way to the overall instrument, based on expert evaluation, conceptual groupings, or theoretical motivations. Researchers may use more sophisticated statistical approaches, such as factor analysis (Floyd & Widaman, 1995), a technique that examines the relation between items in a scale. Factor analysis is useful for determining whether your scale measures a single variable (or factor) or multiple ones. For example, in constructing a spirituality questionnaire, Parsian and Dunning (2009) used factor analysis to assign items such as "I am satisfied with who I am" and "I have a number of good qualities" to a self-awareness subscale, and items such as "I try to find answers to the mysteries of life" and "I am searching for a purpose in life" to a spiritual needs subscale.

PRACTICAL TIPS

Practical Tips for Survey and Interview Approaches

1. Understand the strengths and limitations of surveys and interviews.

2. Be aware of the various biases (selection, choice, researcher, social desirability) and, as much as possible, design your instruments to minimize these biases.

3. Minimize opportunities for careless responding, and inspect your data for signs of careless responding.

4. Consider using an already-existing survey instrument that has been subjected to tests of validity and reliability.

5. If you construct your own survey, be sure your questions are simple, written at the appropriate reading level, and, in general, expressed in positive terms. Avoid double-barrelled and loaded questions.

6. It is always a good idea to pilot your survey or interview before formally collecting data.

7. Carefully consider the purposes for which you might use closed-ended and open-ended items. You must consider the analyses that you will perform as you choose the items.

8. When constructing a new instrument, be sure to subject it to tests of validity and reliability. Pilot studies are a critical part of this process.

9. If you are conducting an interview, make sure your interviewers are trained and have practised the interview multiple times.

CHAPTER SUMMARY

Surveys and interviews provide powerful tools with which to conduct your research. Surveys in particular come with a host of advantages: They are economical and efficient, they provide the opportunity to conduct sophisticated statistical analyses because of their potentially large sample sizes, and they can ensure the anonymity of your participants. It is important to remember, however, that your surveys or interviews must serve your research question. You must also be vigilant of the range of potential biases that lurk in surveys and interviews, including response and sampling biases. And although online surveys enable greater speed, efficiency, and numbers of participants, they also open up a greater potential for careless responding and even fraud.

As you start to generate your survey, first look for an existing measurement instrument that has been shown to provide reliable and valid data for your proposed sample population. If one exists, consider using it. You may need to modify an existing instrument to address your particular research question or apply it to your specific population of interest. If no such instruments exist, start developing your own questions, simultaneously considering the response format you plan to use and the data analysis approach you plan to employ. Pilot test your questions. Check for readability, understanding, and meaningfulness to the potential participants.

End-of-Chapter Exercises

1. The ease of conducting surveys has increased with the ease of online methodologies for collecting data. The resulting proliferation of surveys and survey results has created many challenges for evaluating the quality of information that is "in the ether." What are the most important factors to consider in evaluating the utility of survey findings? What red flags may signal especially poor or potentially invalid survey results?

2. You are interested in conducting a study on the sexual practices of young adults in Canada. Discuss whether this should be done using a survey or an interview. Identify biases or threats to validity that may be a factor in collecting data for this survey. How could these be overcome?

3. For each of the survey items below, indicate whether the item is (1) too complex, (2) double-barrelled, (3) loaded, or (4) a good item.
   a. I agree with most students that the cost of textbooks is too high.
   b. I like to eat fruits and veggies.
   c. I think the voting age should be lowered.
   d. I am in favour of public inebriation on local beaches.
   e. I consider myself to be an empathic person.
   f. We should not reduce government cuts to education.

4. Select a topic for a survey. Write three open-ended and three closed-ended items. Which were easier to develop? Which set would be easier to collect data for and interpret?

5. Some experts assert that, because survey writing is such a complex and challenging task, novice researchers should be discouraged from designing their own survey instruments and should instead default to using existing measures. Given the difficulty of writing good survey questions, do you agree with this advice? Why or why not? Under what circumstances, if any, might a novice design a survey?

Key Terms

acquiescence bias, p. 115

attrition, p. 110

closed-ended response item, p. 120

Cronbach's alpha (α), p. 124

double-barrelled question, p. 118

factor analysis, p. 124

fatigue effects, p. 110

focus group, p. 115

internal consistency, p. 123

interview, p. 106

interviewer effects, p. 114

leading question, p. 119

lie scale, p. 112

Likert response format, p. 121

Likert scale, p. 122

loaded question, p. 119

MacArthur Scale of Subjective Social Status, p. 116

midpoint, p. 122

non-response bias, p. 110

open-ended response item, p. 120

parallel forms (or alternate forms) reliability, p. 123

pilot study, p. 123

questionnaire, p. 106

researcher bias, p. 110

response bias, p. 114

response set, p. 110

selection bias, p. 109

self-selection bias, p. 110

social desirability bias, p. 111

standardization, p. 115

subscales, p. 124

survey, p. 106

test–retest reliability, p. 123

Experimental Designs

7

Chapter Contents

INSIDE RESEARCH: Patrick McGrath

I never intended to become a scientist. I wanted to help people, and my goal was to become a clinician. My career as a researcher developed because of chance, repeated failure, my willingness to take risks, and both giving and receiving mentorship. My career has included periods of professional and personal difficulty as I shifted back and forth between academic health centres and universities in Canada. My research focuses on two areas: pain in child health and the use of technology to deliver care. Most of my research focuses on translating research into care. Researchers often talk about a "valley of death" that prevents research findings from becoming part of the health system.

Professor of psychiatry, pediatrics, community health and epidemiology at Dalhousie University and scientist at the IWK Health Centre in Halifax, Nova Scotia

Courtesy of Patrick McGrath

continued

This is partly caused by science and partly by politics. When I plan research, I try to think about how my research design will move my program into healthcare practice. I want to make sure that I am still using my work as a scientist to help others.

I develop new interventions based on research and use pragmatic randomized clinical trials to evaluate their success. These trials conform to the rules of randomization, blinding (when possible), and statistical rigour in analysis but differ from traditional trials in important ways. Where traditional trials ask, "Does intervention X work in ideal circumstances?" pragmatic trials ask, "Does intervention X work in a real-world environment?" Overall, pragmatic trials mimic the clinical situation by using regular staff for intervention, but they have a broad range of clients with few inclusion and exclusion criteria and often have more variation permitted in the protocol. These trials are sometimes called "effectiveness trials" (in contrast to "efficacy trials"). Although I have been amply recognized for my successes, my greatest learning has come from my failures. Success is nice, but failure is a much better teacher.

I currently lead major grants in developing and evaluating apps to allow family doctors to write prescriptions for their patients online (CIHR, Foundation Grant), a coached intervention for caregivers (Province of Nova Scotia, Major Grant), and a coached program for children with neurodevelopmental disorders and mental health problems (CIHR, Child Bright Network). In the near future, I hope to start another company focused on delivery of healthcare. The combination of intellectual stimulation mostly from my students and emotional gratification from making a difference for families has provided me with a rewarding career.

Patrick McGrath has published over 325 peer-reviewed papers, 50 book chapters, and 14 books and is senior editor of the *Oxford Textbook of Pediatric Pain*. His h-index (a metric used to assess author productivity and citation impact) is 91, and his work has been cited over 34,000 times (Google Scholar). He has received numerous national and international awards and recognitions for his research, mentoring, and advocacy, including being appointed an Officer of the Order of Canada and being elected as fellow of the Royal Society of Canada and the Canadian Academy of Health Sciences. He was co-winner of the Principal Award of the Manning Foundation in 2013 and the Governor General's Innovation Award in 2017 for the Strongest Families e-health system (www.strongestfamilies.com). He is the board chair of the not-for-profit Strongest Families Institute, which delivers mental healthcare to over 6,000 families each year across Canada and employs over 75 people. Recently, he was asked by the *Journal of Pediatric Psychology* to publish an academic biography (McGrath, 2018).

Research Focus: Pain in child health and the use of technology to deliver care

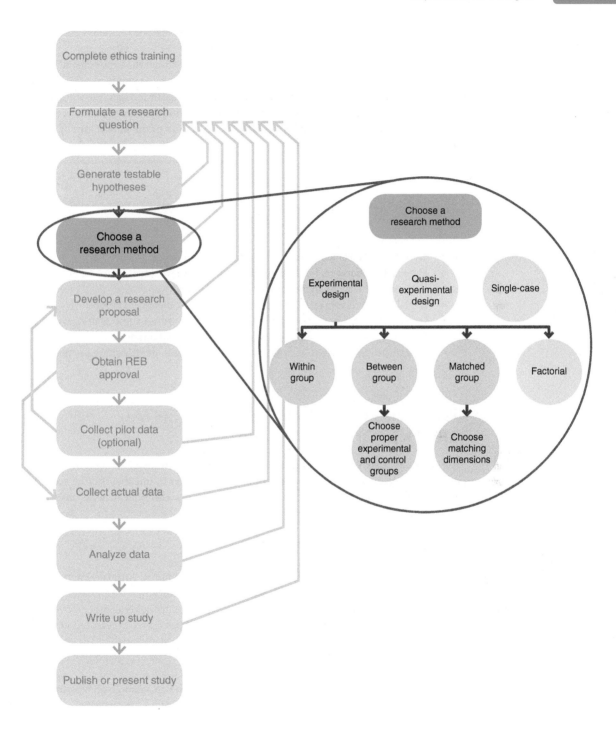

Chapter Abstract

In this chapter we turn to the gold standard for scientific study: the experimental design. We will consider why it has been championed as the optimal way to conduct research (and why that is not always the case), as well as its advantages and disadvantages. We will examine the key constructs that underlie experimental designs and introduce three different types of experimental designs. We finish the chapter with a discussion of the importance of controlling for confounding variables in such designs.

LEARNING OBJECTIVES

By the end of this chapter, you should be able to:

- Describe the essential features of an experimental design.
- Differentiate between internal validity and external validity.
- Distinguish between an independent and dependent variable.
- Explain why it is important to randomly assign participants to groups.
- Differentiate between a between-subjects design, a within-subjects design, and a matched-group design, and discuss the advantages and disadvantages of each.
- Describe different types of confounding variables and identify strategies to deal with them.

THE UNIQUENESS OF EXPERIMENTAL METHODOLOGY

Experimental designs offer two crucial and closely related advantages that set them apart from other available methods. The first is control over variables of interest, and the second is the ability to draw conclusions about causality. Experiments also offer benefits and drawbacks with respect to internal and external validity.

Experimental Control

independent variable A variable manipulated by the experimenter to observe its effect on a dependent variable.

The hallmark of experimental designs is experimental control. An experimenter exercises direct control over a variable (or variables) of interest. Specifically, the experimenter systematically manipulates an **independent variable**. The experimenter holds all other factors constant to see whether the **dependent variable**, the factor of interest being measured in the experiment, changes in response to manipulation of the independent variable. The goal is to construct a situation in which the independent variable is the only explanation for any observed change in the dependent variable.

dependent variable The factor of interest being measured in the experiment that changes in response to manipulation of the independent variable.

A study by Dwyer, Kushlev, and Dunn (2018) provides an example of experimental control. They wanted to examine the impact of smartphone use on the quality of social interactions with friends and family. They predicted that not having a smartphone present during a shared meal with three to five friends or family members at a local café would result in greater social and emotional benefits during the in-person social interaction. Like many published experimental studies, the full Dwyer and colleagues (2018) paper comprises multiple experiments, each of which examines a related aspect of their theory. Here, we focus on the first experiment only.

Dwyer and colleagues obtained their experimental control through a carefully manipulated independent variable, which consisted of two possible **conditions** (sometimes called "levels" of the experimental variable). In the "phone" condition, participants were told they would be asked to answer a questionnaire after ordering their food. They were instructed that they would receive a text message with the survey, so they needed to leave their phone on the table with the ringer or vibration on to ensure they received it. In the "phoneless" condition, participants were also told they would answer a questionnaire, but this would be given to them on a piece of paper. They were asked to turn their phones on silent and place them in a container that was on the table. The dependent variable was a questionnaire measuring a number of social and emotional variables (e.g., social connectedness, tense arousal, affect, and interest/enjoyment). The only key difference between the groups of participants was whether the participant had access to their smartphone. Dwyer and colleagues hypothesized that if the presence of the smartphone operated as expected, participants in the phone condition would report lower levels of social connectedness and interest/enjoyment, higher levels of tense arousal, and less pleasant affect.

condition The intervention or treatment in an experiment given to a particular group of participants.

Determination of Causality

The second hallmark of experimental design—and arguably its most important advantage—is that it enables experimenters to draw causal conclusions. Recall that a major constraint of observational and survey research is that they provide correlational data, meaning that however tempting it might be, you cannot draw cause-and-effect conclusions. The designs merely show that one variable is somehow related to another variable. In contrast, an experiment enables the experimenter to isolate the variables of interest and control the temporal ordering (ensuring that the independent variable occurs *prior* to the dependent variable), so that causal conclusions are justified. In addition, the ability to randomly assign your participants to different conditions (i.e., different levels of your independent variable) enables you to assume that the only difference between your groups is caused by that independent variable.

Christensen (2012) succinctly summarizes the key elements of an experimental design that allow you to assert causality. He notes that the experimental plan must control overall aspects of the experiment, including the assignment of participants to different groups, determination of who ends up receiving which treatment and in which order, and the amount of treatment that each individual receives. Choosing the amount or level of treatment is not an easy decision—arriving at the proper "dose" often requires considerable study, pretesting, and even some luck. Many experiments that were not effective because of the level of the dose or intervention languish in file drawers.

All of the participants in Dwyer and colleagues' (2018) experiment ate at the same café, completed the same survey questions after the meal, and were randomly assigned to the phone and phoneless conditions. The experimenters could then conclude that differences on the measures between the two groups were likely *caused* by the independent variable—the presence or absence of the smartphone. Of course, this would be true only if they could be sure that other uncontrolled variables were not also in play.

Internal versus External Validity

internal validity An assessment of whether a particular variable is the actual cause of a particular outcome.

Another advantage of a well-designed experimental method is its high level of internal validity. A design that has high internal validity allows you to conclude that the independent variable is the direct cause of a change in the dependent variable. In Chapter 4, we discussed how to evaluate whether *Baby Einstein* videos actually boost young children's intelligence. A well-designed experiment to evaluate this claim—that is, an experiment that is high in internal validity—would combine experimental control, temporal ordering of variables, and random assignment. It would enable you to determine whether the videos themselves cause an increase in intelligence or whether the parents who provide the videos for their children are doing other things that lead to the increase (e.g., reading to their children, engaging them intellectually in other ways).

external validity A measure of the degree to which the conclusions drawn from a particular set of results can be generalized to other samples or situations.

In contrast, external validity is the degree to which conclusions drawn from a particular set of results can be generalized to other samples and situations. The sample in a particular experiment may not represent the larger population of interest, and the experimental situation may not resemble the real-world context that it is designed to model because of its artificiality. The concern around artificiality is controversial and not shared by everyone who does psychological research. For example, Stanovich (2013) has argued "the artificiality of scientific experimentation is not a weakness but actually the very thing that gives the scientific method its unique power to yield explanations about the nature of the world" (p. 105). In essence, Stanovich insists that the very ability to isolate variables in the experimental paradigm is what makes it such a potent tool. He further notes the double standard for different sciences in this regard, pointing out that fields like physics are not criticized for using the experimental method, but psychological experimenters often are.

As with many of the debates in psychology today, we cannot tell you what to conclude about external validity. The truth is, it depends. External validity of experimental designs may matter more for some issues than others. On the one hand, if an experiment demonstrates effects of the independent variable even in an artificial setting, you could argue that the results (and the effect) are likely to be valid. On the other hand, because an experimental paradigm cannot truly replicate the reality of a situation, you could argue that any effects found in an experiment may not replicate in a real-life environment. In the Dwyer and colleagues (2018) experiment, for instance, the experiment was conducted at a local café rather than in a laboratory setting, which could be argued to increase the external validity of the results. However, this is offset by a loss in control over various extraneous variables, such as the day of the week the study was conducted on and other customers in the café, which could negatively impact the internal validity of the study. The interplay between internal and external validity serves to reinforce the advantage of using multiple methods to examine a research question. How better to demonstrate both the internal and the external validity of your work than to replicate your findings across different methodologies?

environmental manipulation A manipulation that alters the participants' physical or social context for each level of the independent variable.

instructional manipulation A manipulation that provides different directions for each level of the independent variable.

KEY CONSTRUCTS OF EXPERIMENTAL METHODS

Now that we have explored some of the unique features of experimental methods—experimental control, the ability to determine causality, and the trade-off between internal and external validity—we investigate the concepts that are crucial to understanding how experimental methods work, again using the experiment of Dwyer and colleagues (2018) as an example.

Manipulation of the Independent Variable

When an experimenter manipulates the independent variable, this manipulation can be classified according to its type: environmental, instructional, stimulus, or invasive. **Environmental manipulations** alter the participant's physical or social context. **Instructional manipulations** involve providing different instructions to participants in each level of the independent variable. **Stimulus manipulations** involve using different stimuli for each condition of the experiment (e.g., pictures versus words in a memory task to see which is remembered more easily). **Invasive manipulations** use the administration of drugs or surgery to create physical changes within the participant (see "Media Matters: The 'Sugar Pill' Knee Surgery" for an example of an invasive manipulation).

Experimenters will sometimes use a **manipulation check** to test whether the manipulation of the independent variable was effective and resulted in the expected differences between the experimental conditions. Manipulation checks can be conducted prior to and separate from the experiment, or as a check within the experiment itself. For example, if you are manipulating the body size of models used in magazine advertisements to study its effect on women's body image, a manipulation check done prior to the experiment will confirm that women do in fact perceive the models in the advertisements to be of different body sizes (e.g., extremely thin or average sized). The manipulation check might involve having a separate sample of women rate several advertisements of women of varying body sizes and then selecting those advertisements for use in the experiment that conform to the desired experimental conditions. As another example, if you are examining the impact of mood on participants' generosity and you are manipulating their mood via a short video clip, a self-report question assessing their mood after watching the video clip would test whether the intended mood was induced among the participants. This manipulation check could be easily carried out within the experiment itself. The disadvantage to conducting the manipulation check within the experiment is that if you find the manipulation did not work, then you have invalidated your experiment.

It is worth noting that experimenters do not always manipulate independent variables. For example, an independent variable might be a pre-existing characteristic of the participant that cannot be altered and to which one cannot be randomly assigned, such as sex, age, or ethnicity. We refer to such variables as **participant variables**.

Experimental and Control Groups

Another key characteristic of experimental design is the assignment of participants to different groups. The ability to compare outcomes across these groups is essential to the logic of the experimental method. In most classic experimental designs, experimenters compare at least two groups—an **experimental group** and a **control group**. The experimental group receives the intervention or treatment—that is, a dose of the independent variable. The control group serves as a direct comparison for the experimental group and receives either an inert version of the treatment or no treatment at all. The most familiar example of this design comes from drug studies in medical research, in which a treatment group receives the medication that is being tested and a control group receives a placebo ("sugar pill"). The belief is that, all other things being equal, if the treatment group does better than the control group on the relevant dependent variable (whatever the drug is designed to treat), there is evidence for the effectiveness of the medication.

stimulus manipulation
A manipulation that uses different stimuli for each level of the independent variable.

invasive manipulation
A manipulation that uses the administration of drugs or surgery to create physical changes within the participant for each level of the independent variable.

manipulation check
Assesses whether the manipulation of the independent variable was effective and elicited the expected differences between the experimental conditions.

participant variable
A pre-existing characteristic (e.g., sex, age, or ethnicity) to which a participant cannot be randomly assigned.

experimental group
In an experimental design, the set of participants that receives the intervention or treatment with the goal of determining whether the treatment impacts the outcome.

control group In an experimental design, the set of participants who do not receive the experimental treatment (or who receive an inert version). This group is compared with the experimental group.

This sort of design, however, does pose an obvious difficulty. To conclude that your treatment or intervention is responsible for any change that occurs, you must ensure that your control group receives everything that the experimental group receives, with the exception of the "active ingredient." Experimenters who are testing a pill can accomplish this fairly easily by having the control group simply receive an inert version of the pill. But most psychological research involves a more complex intervention. For example, imagine we are studying the effectiveness of a particular form of group therapy for reducing anxiety. What do we do with our control group? Do they simply sit at home while those in the experimental group receive the group therapy sessions?

A particular type of control group addresses this concern. Called an **attention control group**, it provides an experience as similar to that of the experimental group as possible (e.g., the attention control group receives the same amount of time and attention as the experimental group), with the only difference being the active ingredient of the experiment. In our experiment on group therapy for anxiety, an attention control group would also attend a weekly group meeting, but it might be a generic support group instead of one specifically for anxiety.

Dwyer and colleagues' (2018) work has clear experimental and control groups: Participants in the experimental group were assigned to the phone condition, whereas the control group was the phoneless condition. These two groups were otherwise identical and were given the same study instructions and questionnaire; by design, the only difference remaining between the groups was the experimental manipulation—the presence of the smartphone on the table.

Placebo Effect

An effect of treatment that can be attributed to participants' expectations from the treatment rather than any property of the treatment itself is called a **placebo effect**. In studies designed to test the beneficial effects of an intervention, the comparison between an experimental and placebo control group is essential, so that you can determine whether your treatment is more effective than a placebo alone. In drug trials, placebo control groups are given sugar pills, which should have no therapeutic effect. Even in such cases, participants often report beneficial effects, which is why experimenters must be able to show that the effects of their interventions exceed those of the placebo alone.

An example of a classic experimental/control group design that demonstrates the power of the placebo effect appeared in the *New England Journal of Medicine* (Sihvonen et al., 2013). The experiment was designed to evaluate the effects of surgery for a group of patients with degenerative wear and tear of the meniscus, which is part of the knee (see "Media Matters: The 'Sugar Pill' Knee Surgery"). The experiment compared a type of arthroscopic knee surgery with "sham" knee surgery. The sham knee surgery served as the placebo in this case, and individuals in this condition received an incision in the knee, but nothing was done to the meniscus. At a one-year follow up, there was no difference in reported knee pain between the two groups.

It is important to note that you should not think of placebo effects as fake effects. The benefits of placebos are real and measurable. Patients in both the arthroscopic meniscectomy and the sham groups reported reduced pain, thereby experiencing a real benefit.

In a high-profile meta-analysis, Kirsch and Sapirstein (1998) reported a similarly compelling power of the placebo in which they concluded that much of the benefit attributed to widely marketed antidepressant medications like Prozac could actually be the result of a placebo response. Again, the placebo response here was real—patients reported measurable improvement in their depressive symptoms, suggesting that such effects have true

attention control group A type of control group in which participants receive everything the experimental group receives (e.g., the same amount of time and attention), with the exception of the "active ingredient" of the intervention or treatment.

placebo effect A result of treatment that can be attributed to participants' expectations from the treatment rather than any property of the treatment itself.

The "Sugar Pill" Knee Surgery

Medical researchers have long recognized the strength of the placebo effect in studies on medical treatments. One recent groundbreaking experiment again confirmed its power and has led the medical community to question a common orthopedic procedure called arthroscopic meniscectomy intended to relieve knee pain. The experiment, published in the *New England Journal of Medicine* (Sihvonen et al., 2013) and conducted by researchers in Finland, tracked 146 patients between 35 and 65 years of age with symptoms of degenerative wear and tear of the meniscus, a piece of cartilage that cushions the shinbone and thighbone (Hellerman, 2013). They assigned patients to two groups: the first group underwent arthroscopic meniscectomy, a procedure in which a surgeon inserted a blade through an incision in the knee and trimmed the worn edges of the meniscus, whereas the second group received only a "sham" surgery, in which an incision was made in the knee, but nothing was done to the meniscus.

Neither the participants nor the experimenters who evaluated the results knew whether a particular patient had received the real or sham surgery. The surgeons clearly knew but did not communicate who received what treatment until the results were being analyzed. Both groups spent the same length of time in recovery and received the same walking aids, instructions for recovery, and directions for over-the-counter painkillers (Jaslow, 2013), making excellent use of an attention control group.

One year later, patients in both groups reported the same rate of recovery and pain relief. About two-thirds of each group said they were satisfied with the treatment and would undergo it again (Hellerman, 2013). "These results argue against the current practice of performing arthroscopic partial meniscectomy in patients with a degenerative meniscal tear," the experiment's authors concluded (Sihvonen et al., 2013).

Given the popularity of the surgery in the Canada, not to mention the $31 million in healthcare spending attributed to it, the experiment garnered considerable attention in the mainstream media as well as its share of controversy. Not surprisingly, some medical professionals were displeased with the findings. Dr. Frederick Azar, vice-president of the American Academy of Orthopaedic Surgeons, warned that the patients in the experiment were atypical because only 1 per cent of his patients have a degenerative meniscus tear and no evidence of arthritis. He also expressed concern that the experiment would scare away patients who could be helped. "This is a very useful low-cost intervention, with a short recovery time and good results in most patients" (Hellerman, 2013). Yet experiencing relief without the risks of surgery is an undeniably positive outcome.

Despite such intriguing results that attest to the potency of the placebo effect, exactly how and why it works remains unclear. One thing is for certain: Tapping into the mind's ability to cure disease and alleviate pain is an exciting, ongoing research opportunity.

neurobiological underpinnings. We do not mean to suggest that interventions should not seek to provide benefits beyond placebo, but rather propose that placebo effects in and of themselves can provide therapeutic benefits. Contemporary experimenters consider the placebo effect much more than inert physical content; rather, they recognize it as "the overall simulation of a therapeutic intervention" (Price, Finniss, & Benedetti, 2008, p. 565).

Random Assignment

Other than experimental control itself, the most notable hallmark of an experimental design is **random assignment**—the procedure by which experimenters place participants in different experimental groups (i.e., assign them to different levels of the independent variable) using

random assignment
The assignment of participants to different conditions in an experiment by methods that rely on chance and probability so that potential biases related to assignment to conditions are removed.

random selection The procedure by which experimenters recruit participants from the population into an experiment that involves each participant having a prespecified probability of being selected into the sample.

chance procedures. It is important to note that random assignment is different from **random selection**. Random selection refers to how participants are recruited from the population into your experiment (see Chapter 5), while random assignment refers to how they are then assigned into the conditions of your experiment. When random assignment is used, any given individual has an equal probability of being assigned to each group in the experiment. For example, in the knee surgery experiment, each patient had an equal probability of being assigned to the real surgery group or the sham surgery group. There are a number of ways to randomly assign participants into groups, such as flipping a coin, pulling a number out of a hat, or creating a randomized order list (http://random.org is a website that can be used to create such a list). While you may be tempted to just alternate participants into your experimental groups (control, experimental, control, experimental . . .), this is not random assignment. For instance, with this method, it would be possible for someone to figure out the ordering and then sign up for the experiment for the condition that they want; thus, they do not have equal probabilities of being assigned into the conditions.

Why bother with random assignment? The major benefit is that a random assignment procedure presumably balances out unwanted variation between the different groups (Dehue, 2001). This process helps ensure that the groups are similar prior to the manipulation of the independent variable. From a conceptual standpoint, if unwanted variation (resulting from individual differences and the randomness of the world) is eliminated, then what remains is the variation of interest caused by the experimental manipulation itself. Failure to use random assignment can lead to bias across the levels of your independent variable. This could then result in unwanted differences between your experimental groups that would act as an alternative explanation for any changes in your dependent variable.

Random assignment usually works effectively to equalize the many other extraneous variables that the experimental and control group might differ on besides the experimental assignment to groups. However, a truly random assignment is most likely to occur only when the groups are relatively large. In a relatively small experiment that comprises only a few participants per group, the likelihood of the experimental and control group differing on some dimension increases. For example, imagine you were running a small experiment with a pool of participants with equal numbers of men and women. You hoped to have 16 participants in the experimental group and 16 participants in an attention control group. You decide to flip a coin to randomly assign participants to groups: when the coin comes up "heads" you put a participant in the experimental group and when it comes up "tails" you place the participant in the control group. Just by chance, you might end up with a sample distribution of 11 women and 5 men in the experimental group and 5 women and 11 men in the control group. At the end of the experiment, it might be hard to rule out that any significant results were not caused by the unequal distribution of women and men. In a case such as this, with a smaller group of participants, you might choose to do a **quasi-random assignment** where you assign equal numbers of men and women across the experimental and control conditions.

quasi-random assignment The experimenter assigns equal numbers of participants with key characteristics (e.g., sex, age, or ethnicity) across the experimental and control conditions.

TYPES OF EXPERIMENTAL DESIGNS

In an experiment, experimenters can choose between two basic designs: between-subjects and within-subjects. They may also use a third design—matched group—which controls for individual differences by matching similar participants with each other. All three of these designs have advantages and disadvantages, which we discuss in the sections that follow.

Between-Subjects Designs

In a **between-subjects design** (also called between-groups design or independent-groups design), experimenters expose two (or more) groups of individuals to different conditions and then measure and compare differences between groups on the variable(s) of interest. In such a design, the experimenter is looking for differences *between* individual participants or groups of participants, with each group exposed to a separate condition. Both Dwyer and colleagues' (2018) smartphone experiment and Sihvonen and colleagues' (2013) sham knee surgery experiment are examples of between-subjects designs, with different groups being exposed to different conditions (phone versus phoneless, real surgery versus sham surgery). Figure 7.1 illustrates a between-subjects design. Note that the initial pool of participants is randomly assigned to different conditions and each group of participants is distinct from the others.

between-subjects design A type of experimental design in which the experimenter assigns individual participants or groups of participants to one of several conditions to detect differences *between* groups of participants, with each group exposed to a separate condition. Also called between-groups or independent-groups design.

Advantages of Between-Subjects Designs. Major advantages of between-subjects designs include simplicity of setup, their intuitive structure, and the relative ease of statistical analyses that they permit. As Keppel and Wickens (2004) note, the number of statistical assumptions required for a between-subjects design is smaller than that for other designs. Between-subjects designs are straightforward in their construction and interpretation.

Disadvantages of Between-Subjects Designs. Between-subjects designs have two notable disadvantages. One is cost. Because these designs require a separate set of participants for *each* condition, the resources required to gather a sample can be considerable depending on the numbers of conditions and participants.

The second disadvantage relates to variability. When looking at differences between groups, the individual differences that exist between your participants are a major source of variability. Dealing with this variability, in addition to the variability that really interests you (i.e., the variability caused by your treatment/experiment/intervention), makes for a less-powerful design in terms of successfully detecting treatment effects. With smaller samples, the between-subjects variability may be particularly problematic.

For example, suppose you are evaluating two different teaching methods. Method 1 is, in reality, more effective than method 2, raising test scores about 5 points on average. However, students vary greatly in their knowledge and testing abilities, so individual test scores can range from the 50s to the high 90s. Such a range of individual differences may swamp the 5-point advantage of method 1 over method 2, requiring quite a large number of participants to reveal this advantage with any statistical confidence.

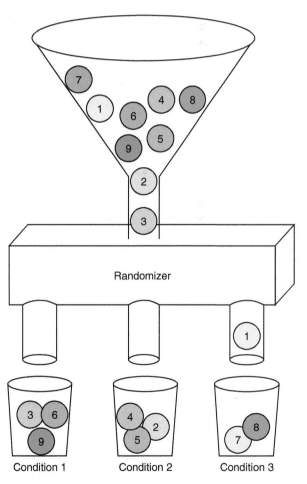

FIGURE 7.1   Randomization in a between-subjects research design.

Within-Subjects Designs

within-subjects design A type of experimental design in which the experimenter assigns each participant to all possible conditions. Also called a within-group or repeated-measures design.

A **within-subjects design** (also called within-group or repeated-measures design) assigns each participant to all possible conditions. For example, imagine you want to study the effects of caffeine on performance on a memory task. In your experiment you have three conditions: a "caffeine-free" condition in which participants are given a cup of decaffeinated herbal tea before performing the memory task, a "moderate-caffeine condition" in which participants are given a cup of green tea before the task, and a "high-caffeine condition" in which participants are given a triple shot of coffee before the task. In a within-subjects design, the same group of participants would take part in all three conditions (presumably on different days). In contrast, in a between-subjects design, separate groups of participants would take part in each condition. Figure 7.2 illustrates a within-subjects design, showing that the same group of participants repeats participation in each condition.

Another example of a well-designed within-subjects experiment comes from the work of Master and colleagues (2009). Prior research had shown that social support is associated with reduced pain. Master and colleagues were interested in the ways in which social support would impact the experience of pain in a group of participants. In particular, they wondered whether the simple presence of a romantic partner's photograph might provide the social support necessary to lessen pain.

To examine this hypothesis, the researchers recruited 28 women in long-term relationships (greater than six months). Participants received a series of "thermal stimulations" (applications of heat) that were tailored to their particular level of moderate discomfort based on a pretest. These thermal stimulations were given to each participant across seven different conditions:

- Holding her partner's hand (with the partner sitting behind a curtain)
- Holding the hand of a male stranger (also sitting behind a curtain)
- Holding a squeeze ball
- Viewing photographs of her partner
- Viewing photographs of a male stranger
- Viewing photographs of an object (a chair)
- Viewing a simple crosshair (i.e., no image)

During these conditions, participants rated their level of discomfort. As hypothesized, the experimenters found that holding a partner's hand lessened pain more than did holding an object or a stranger's hand. Similarly, viewing a partner's photograph lessened pain more than

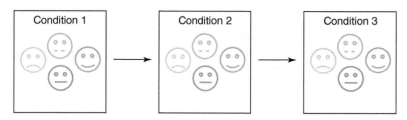

FIGURE 7.2 Example of a within-subjects design where the same four individuals are presented with three different conditions.

viewing photographs of an object or a stranger. This experiment was considered a within-subjects design because the women in the experiment participated in all seven conditions, rather than having seven separate groups of women participate in a single condition.

Advantages of Within-Subjects Designs. The major benefits of within-subjects designs are two-fold. First, relative cost—a disadvantage of between-subjects designs—is lower. You need fewer participants than in a between-subjects design because each individual participates in all the conditions. From the standpoint of recruiting your sample, this is a more economical option.

A second advantage is that you do not have to worry about variability resulting from unwanted individual differences among your participants. Because you use the same participants repeatedly, each participant serves as his or her own control, which lowers variability and helps to eliminate extraneous participant variables. This results in greater statistical power or, in other words, a greater probability of being able to detect an effect that is present, as discussed in Chapter 5.

Disadvantages of Within-Subjects Designs. Despite these advantages, the drawbacks of within-subjects designs are also substantial. First, if your experiment occurs across multiple days, you run the risk of participants not returning to subsequent sessions, a phenomenon referred to as drop out or **attrition**. This is problematic for two main reasons: (1) You are left with a smaller sample size, as you now having missing data for these participants and may not be able to include any of the data in your analyses; and (2) If those participants who drop out are different than those who remain in the experiment, it could potentially bias your final results.

Second, within-subjects designs have several potential side effects, called **order effects** (or carryover effects) because the order in which participants receive different experimental conditions may influence responses or behaviours in later conditions. There are several types of order effects: contrast, fatigue, and practice are the most common.

A **contrast effect** (or simple order effect) occurs when the particular order of the conditions influences the results. For example, if you were doing a taste test where participants had to try two different brands of coffee and rate which was better, the taste of the first brand of coffee may influence the taste of the second brand.

As a result of repeated exposure to experimental conditions in a within-subjects design, participants may show a fatigue effect (or **boredom effect**) and begin to perform more poorly as the experiment goes on. This may occur even if you vary the order systematically across participants. For example, in our caffeine–memory experiment described previously, it is easy to imagine that participants might grow weary of the memory task by the second or third session, even if the task were varied in some way. The resulting lowered motivation could skew the results.

An additional potential consequence of within-subjects designs is the **practice effect**. This occurs because a participant's performance under one experimental condition prepares them for a subsequent condition and results in increased performance. In our caffeine–memory experiment, a participant who becomes accustomed to the memory task and therefore more proficient at it exhibits a practice effect. This would complicate the ability of the experimenter to ensure that any differences between the conditions were caused by the true variable of interest, caffeine dosage.

In some cases, order or carryover effects will rule out the use of a within-subjects design. For example, you would be hard-pressed to conduct Dwyer and colleagues' (2018)

attrition The loss of research participants prior to completion of a study.

order effect When a participant's performance in a within-subjects experiment is affected by the order in which the participant receives the experimental conditions. Also called a carryover effect.

contrast effect When a participant's performance in a prior experimental condition influences the results of following experimental conditions. Also called a simple order effect.

boredom effect Participants begin to perform more poorly as the experiment goes on as a consequence of repeated exposure to experimental conditions in a within-subjects design. Also called a fatigue effect.

practice effect The result of a participant's performance in one experimental condition leading to improved performance on following experimental conditions due to increased familiarity and experience with the task.

smartphone experiment using a within-subjects design, because if a participant were exposed to both conditions it would likely reveal the purpose of the study, which could then skew participants' responses in the second scenario.

There is, however, a common way to reduce the chances of order effects having an adverse impact on the results in a within-subjects design: counterbalancing. **Counterbalancing** means that participants are tested in different orders. In complete counterbalancing, all possible orders of presenting the conditions of the independent variable are used in the experiment. When there are only two conditions this is straightforward; half of the participants start with condition 1 and then do condition 2, and the other half of the participants start with condition 2 and then do condition 1. When your experiment has three or more conditions, this quickly become more complicated. With three conditions there are six possible orders, and with four conditions there are 24 possible orders! If it is unfeasible to completely counterbalance, another alternative is to use a **Latin square** design, which is designed to balance the strengths of counterbalancing with a practical reality. Latin square designs allow you to control for order effects without implementing every possible order. For example, if you were conducting a driving simulation experiment under four different driving conditions (daylight and clear, daylight and rainy, dark and clear, dark and rainy), then you would have four order versions. In this example, the Latin square design would look like that shown in Table 7.1.

In a Latin square design, the number of possible orders will always equal the number of experimental conditions. This technique can be a good compromise for many research projects; however, it does still suffer from carryover effects. Drawing from the example above, the dark and clear driving condition always comes before the dark and rainy condition (except in order 2 when dark and rainy is the first condition). Therefore, the dark and clear condition can potentially affect the dark and rainy condition in three of the four possible orders.

Matched-Group Designs

An alternative approach to between-subjects or within-subjects designs is a matched-group design. A matched-group design has separate groups of participants in each condition and involves "twinning" a participant in each group with a participant in another group.

For example, imagine you want to conduct the sham knee surgery experiment as a matched-group rather than between-subjects design. Although you would still have two groups of patients—one that received the real surgery and another that received the sham surgery—you would also match each patient in one group with a patient in the other group *on dimensions*

---

counterbalancing
A strategy that ensures control for the order of experimental interventions. The experimenter calculates all the possible orders of interventions and confirms even distribution of the different order combinations across participants.

Latin square A type of counterbalancing technique in which participants receive different experimental conditions in a systematically different order.

matched-group design A type of experimental design in which experimenters assign separate groups of participants in each condition and "twin" a participant in each group with a participant in another group.

Table 7.1 Example of a Latin square design with four conditions and four possible orders.

	Condition			
	First	Second	Third	Fourth
Order 1	Daylight and clear	Daylight and rainy	Dark and clear	Dark and rainy
Order 2	Dark and rainy	Daylight and clear	Daylight and rainy	Dark and clear
Order 3	Dark and clear	Dark and rainy	Daylight and clear	Daylight and rainy
Order 4	Daylight and rainy	Dark and clear	Dark and rainy	Daylight and clear

that are critically related to the dependent variable. This point is crucial. Matched designs work only if the matching is on dimensions relevant to what is being measured. In the knee surgery experiment, matching would need to occur on the aspects of patients' medical history and background that relate to the nature of their injury (e.g., a background playing soccer) and their prognosis for recovery. If matching were done on some irrelevant aspect of the patient's background (such as eye colour or cholesterol level), then you would not be able to assert you had a true matched-group design. Once the matching has been done, then random assignment can be used to assign one of each pair to the experimental or the control condition.

Figure 7.3 illustrates a matched-group design. Imagine that the creatures in the figure are participants in an experiment comparing two different training programs designed to improve running speed. Suppose you know that two aspects of these creatures' anatomy most impact their innate running ability: foot shape and tail shape. In a matched-group design, you would pair each creature with another creature that has identical dimensions of foot and tail shape. Note that the creatures are not literal twins, that is, they still differ on many other dimensions (eye shape, ears, nose, etc.).

A matched-group design also offers you the option to conduct an experiment so that you match on more than one variable for the purpose of multiple analyses—especially if matching on different variables has different theoretical and practical implications. One area where matched designs are often used is in the study of individuals with various delays and disorders. Using a matching design allows you to examine whether any finding is caused by the disorder, delay, or some other factor such as mental age.

Joffe and Varlokosta (2007) studied the development of language syntax in a group of children with Down syndrome and another group with Williams syndrome (a genetic disorder that results in developmental delays that occur with relatively high verbal abilities). They decided to match their participants on three different dimensions: chronological age, mental age, and performance IQ (a subset of IQ test items that tap various aspects of non-verbal intelligence). Having a design that matched participants in three different ways for separate sets of analyses enabled the experimenters to tease out which dimensions (chronological age, mental age, or performance IQ) could provide the best basis of comparison for children with these differing disorders.

Although this example highlights how matching might be used, the study does not include a true experimental design because participants were not randomly assigned to different experimental conditions. An experimental design using a matched sample could be used to

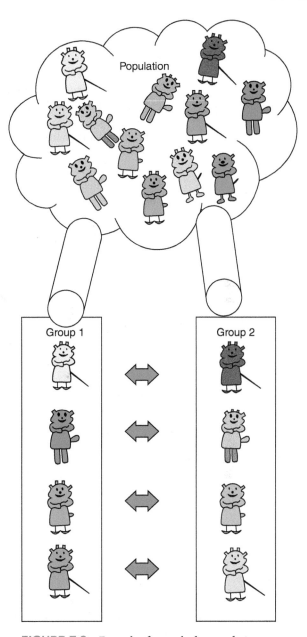

FIGURE 7.3   Example of a matched-group design.

investigate whether a new intervention might boost the acquisition of language skills in children with Down syndrome. The experimenter could use a matched sample to cancel out age and IQ differences as factors that might "interfere" with the intervention in this population. To do this, an experimenter would pair children with Down syndrome on chronological age and performance IQ and then randomly assign one member of the pair to an intervention group and the other to a control condition.

Advantages of Matched-Group Designs. Although you are using different participants across your conditions, as long as you have matched participants properly on dimensions of relevance to the dependent variable you will reduce a lot of the unwanted variability caused by individual differences. As was the case in the within-subjects design, participants in a matched-group design serve as their own controls. This results in greater statistical power or, in other words, a greater probability of being able to detect an effect that is present.

Additionally, order effects (a substantial limitation of a within-subjects design) are *not* a concern in a matched-group design. As we mentioned previously, the latter design involves separate participant samples that are only paired for the purpose of data analysis.

Disadvantages of Matched-Group Designs. As appealing as matched-group designs may be, they do have disadvantages. First, the process of matching can prove difficult. It can be hard to know on which dimensions you should match your participants, and if you cannot identify those dimensions correctly, your matching will be ineffective. Experimenters must be knowledgeable on the key variables. Matching in the knee surgery experiment required experimenters with expertise on the medical issues involved in this sort of knee injury. Participants were placed in different groups and were matched on age, sex, and the presence or absence of minor degenerative changes detected on a radiograph.

Second, recruiting matched samples may be difficult and expensive. Finding matches for a large set of participants with many matching dimensions poses challenges. Imagine that one type of creature in Figure 7.3 was relatively rare or that you lived in a community with a relatively small population. In these cases, you would have to devote considerable resources to finding the right match, such as travelling a long way to obtain your desired sample.

EXTRANEOUS AND CONFOUNDING VARIABLES

extraneous variable Any variable that is not part of your research study that could influence your results. These variables should be controlled to reduce variability in your data and to prevent confounds.

confounds Extraneous variables that change with the independent variable(s) in your experimental design and could account for effects that you find.

Any discussion of experimental methodology must include the important concepts of extraneous variables and confounding variables. An **extraneous variable** is any variable that you are not intentionally studying as part of your research. Extraneous variables could include participant variables, such as extraversion or age, or environmental variables, such as time of day or instructions. Typically, we try to control these extraneous variables so that they do not increase variability in our data (making it harder to find any effects of the independent variable) or become confounding variables, which are more commonly referred to as just **confounds**. Confounds are extraneous variables that correlate with your independent and dependent variables and create differences between your groups that are separate from the manipulation of the independent variable. This is problematic because confounds may affect the outcome of your experiment by introducing an alternative explanation for your findings. This could occur either in lieu of, or in addition to, an effect of the independent variable (i.e., your groups differ on just the confounding variable or both the independent variable and the confounding variable). When an experimenter fails to account for confounds, the validity of the findings comes into question.

For example, suppose you are comparing two different reading fluency training programs with a group of Grade 2 students. The teacher presenting technique A is more charismatic and engaging than the teacher presenting technique B, so the teacher's personal characteristics may be a confounding factor in your experiment. If you found that technique A was significantly more effective than technique B, you would be unable to conclude whether the difference was a result of the programs themselves or the greater effectiveness of the more appealing teacher. It could also be that technique A is more effective *and* the teacher's appeal is an additional variable influencing the results, but it would be impossible to separate out which of these variables accounts for what portion of the effect. Experimenters must account for several different types of potential confounds. First, we will discuss the different types of confounds; then we will discuss the various strategies for addressing confounds in your experimental design.

Participant Characteristics

The first potentially confounding variable that you must address concerns characteristics of participants in the experiment. The astonishing variability among human beings is what makes studying them equal parts fascinating and challenging. Because your goal is to isolate and measure the variability resulting from your design, you want to minimize or eliminate other variability that will confuse the issue, and variation in the characteristics of your participants may overshadow the variability that you are trying to investigate.

Of particular concern for experimenters is the possibility that experimental groups may differ systematically in their participant characteristics. What if the group assigned to the phoneless condition in Dywer and colleagues' (2018) experiment actually reported more social connectedness because they were more extraverted? That would call into question any interpretation of the findings around negative social and emotional effects of smartphones on social interactions.

Provided you have a large enough sample, randomization is likely to be effective in minimizing group differences. It is also an effective strategy when you do not know on which dimensions to match; in effect, randomization is the equivalent of matching on all possible dimensions.

The Hawthorne Effect

Another confounding factor relates to a potential effect of the experiment simply being an experiment. Aside from the various order effects we have discussed, you should also think about the impact of participants' awareness that they are in an experiment, which can change their actions. This is often referred to as the **Hawthorne effect** or observer effect, which acknowledges that the act of observation can alter the behaviour being observed.

The effect was first described by Landsberger (1958), who analyzed data from the Hawthorne Works factory, an electrical plant outside of Chicago. Landsberger intended to examine whether higher or lower levels of light would affect worker productivity, but his analyses revealed that worker productivity increased as a function of the interest shown by the experimenters and declined once the observation was over. Although controversy exists about what really drives the Hawthorne effect, the important lesson for experimenters is that participants' expectations, which are an unavoidable part of the research process, may sometimes drive effects in unanticipated ways.

Hawthorne effect
Participants in an experiment modify their behaviour as a result of knowing they are being observed. Also called the observer effect.

Demand Characteristics

demand
characteristics
Features of the
experimental design
itself that lead
participants to make
certain conclusions
about the purpose of the
experiment and then
adjust their behaviour
accordingly, either
consciously or
unconsciously.

Another major set of potential confounding factors in experimental design is referred to as demand characteristics. Demand characteristics are features of the experimental design itself that lead participants to make certain conclusions about the purpose of the experiment and then adjust their behaviour accordingly, either consciously or unconsciously. Demand characteristics can be a function of comments that participants have heard about the experiment before participating or may simply be based on what participants believe to be the goals of the research—even if you tell them otherwise.

An example of a demand characteristic familiar to virtually all experimenters who study cognitive development involves parental expectations. When parents bring their children into a laboratory setting for any study around cognitive developmental topics, experimenters have a hard time convincing them that they are *not* studying their child's intelligence, even when that is truly not the focus of their experiment. As a result, some parents try to influence their child's answers to make the child look as intelligent as possible. In grappling with the challenge posed by such characteristics, Orne (1962) argued that any participant must be recognized as an active participant in the experiment and, as such, the possibility of demand characteristics should always be considered.

Other Confounds

There are so many extraneous variables for any given experimental design that no experimenter can be expected to anticipate them all. As long as these variables are randomized across conditions, or properly controlled for, they will remain extraneous and will not become a confound. However, sometimes despite your best attempts to account for confounds, you may eventually uncover a confounding variable you had not initially considered.

Anderson and Revelle (1994) and Revelle, Humphreys, Simon, and Gilliland (1980) encountered an unanticipated confounding factor in their studies examining the complex interaction of personality (such as introversion–extraversion) with impulsivity, arousal level, and caffeine intake. For some time, Revelle and his colleagues were puzzled by difficulties in replicating a particular finding related to impulsivity and caffeine intake. After considerable discussion, they realized that their results varied depending on what time of day the data were collected. After further analysis, they found that the effects of impulsivity in conjunction with caffeine intake varied by time of day (Anderson & Revelle, 1994). For example, individuals low on impulsivity were more aroused in the morning and less aroused in the evening than were individuals with high impulsivity. By discovering this unforeseen confounding variable (time of day), the authors were able to explain some of their discrepant results. The point is, you should consider all dimensions that may affect an experimental design—even something that initially seems insignificant (like time of day).

Strategies for Dealing with Confounds

A carefully designed experiment anticipates possible confounds and ensures that the design either eliminates those confounds altogether or deals with them in other ways. The following four strategies will help you address confounds.

Hold Potential Confounding Variables Constant.   The first strategy works to minimize the influence of potential confounds. In the example of reading fluency training, a well-designed experiment would standardize the presentation of the two approaches as much as possible so that the only substantial difference between the technique A and technique B conditions would be the techniques themselves. Key characteristics of how the teachers administer the training would be held constant to reduce the impact of the teachers' personalities.

Vary Test Items and Tasks.   This strategy applies only to within-subjects designs. If practice effects are a concern, then the design should include a range of tests or tasks that vary enough such that practice alone would not lead to improvement. Participants might still benefit from repetition of testing in a broad sense (even if the details differ), but varying the items on the test would minimize this as a confound. For the related issue of fatigue effects, building rest into the design would be the best remedy. In our reading fluency example, for a within-subjects design you would need to employ different tests of fluency (with the same level of difficulty) across the different conditions. To reduce the effects of fatigue, you would need to ensure that the fluency tests are not overly long.

Use Single- and Double-Blind Designs.   In many experiments, either experimenters or participants are unaware of the experimental condition they are in. If only one of these groups is "blind" to the intervention, then the experiment is said to have a **single-blind design**. It is more common for experimenters to keep participants blind to the hypotheses than it is for experimenters to be blinded. Part of this reasoning is because of the pragmatics of conducting research; if all the experimenters are blind to the hypotheses, it becomes difficult to do the actual research.

In a **double-blind design**, which is often considered the gold standard because it most rigorously implements a blinded design, you would ensure that both the experimenter doing the rating *and* the participant receiving the intervention do not know to which condition they have been assigned. This was the case in the sham knee surgery example—neither the experimenters nor the patients knew which surgery the participants had received.

Statistically Control for Variables That Cannot Be Experimentally Controlled.   A fourth strategy for dealing with confounds is through **statistical control**. In analyzing your experiment's results, you can make a statistical adjustment that will account for the influence of a specified third variable and allow you to analyze the results with the influence of that third variable eliminated. Statistical control requires you to know what your confound is, to measure it systematically, and to include these measurements in your statistical analysis.

In our reading experiment example, say that you suspect that students' reading fluency prior to the interventions will have a substantial impact on their response to the different techniques. (Perhaps the students who were better readers to start with will reap larger benefits from the techniques.) As long as you measure reading fluency at the beginning of the experiment, you would be able to statistically control for the pre-study fluency and ensure that you were only measuring change resulting from the independent variable of interest, the interventions themselves.

Ceiling and Floor Effects

Although they are not considered confounding factors per se, ceiling and floor effects have the potential to derail your experimental design. Both occur when your instrument for data measurement (the measure of your dependent variable) has a constraint such that you end up with a cluster of scores at either end of the instrument's measurement scale. The former, called

---

single-blind design
Either the participants or the experimenters collecting the data are unaware of the condition to which participants have been assigned.

double-blind design Both the participants and the experimenters collecting the data are unaware of the condition to which participants have been assigned.

statistical control In analyzing experiment results, the experimenter makes a statistical adjustment that accounts for the influence of a specified third variable and allows for the analysis of results with the influence of that third variable eliminated.

ceiling effect Occurs when scores on a measure cluster at the upper end (the "ceiling") of the measure.

floor effect Occurs when scores on a measure cluster at the lower end (the "floor") of the measure.

a *ceiling effect*, occurs when the scores cluster at the upper end of the measurement scale, whereas the latter, a *floor effect*, occurs when the scores cluster at the lower end.

Although ceiling and floor effects are of concern in many areas of research, they frequently occur when developmental experimenters use measures that are not appropriate for the given population. Consider the following pair of examples: Gorvine, who teaches college-level statistics, gives his final exam to his daughter's Grade 4 class. What is likely to happen? Conversely, what would happen if he gave his college students the elementary math exam from his daughter's class? In the first example, the likely result would be a floor effect (see Figure 7.4), whereas in the second example, the likely result would be a ceiling effect (see Figure 7.5).

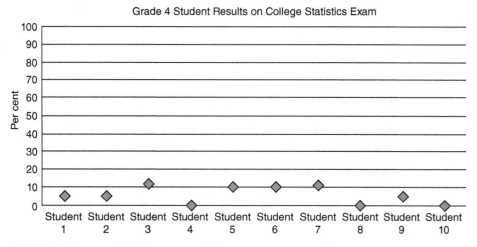

FIGURE 7.4   Example of a floor effect. All participants perform relatively poorly on the exam, suggesting that the exam was too hard for the students.

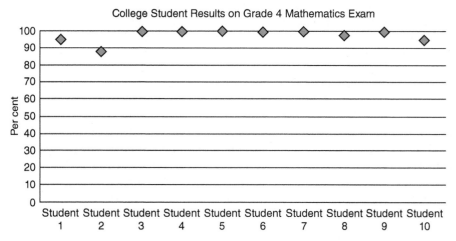

FIGURE 7.5   Example of a ceiling effect. In this example, all participants performed well, suggesting that the exam was too easy.

Ceiling and floor effects remind experimenters that, as much as you need to carefully construct your design to minimize confounds, your measurement tools also must be appropriately sensitive for the purposes for which you will use them.

WHAT DWYER, KUSHLEV, AND DUNN FOUND

Throughout this chapter, we have used the work of Dwyer, Kushlev, and Dunn (2018) on the impact of smartphone use on face-to-face social interactions to demonstrate various aspects of experimental design. We would be remiss in using this example without telling you what the research found.

Dwyer and colleagues (2018) hypothesized that having a smartphone present during a social interaction (having dinner out with friends or family) would compromise the benefits of face-to-face social interactions. By having a smartphone present it was believed that it may orient people away from their immediate social environment and remind them of other things they may need or want to do. They predicted that those participants in the smartphone condition would experience lower levels of social connectedness and interest/enjoyment, would report higher levels of tense arousal, and would report less pleasant affect.

Some of these hypotheses were supported. They found that participants in the phone condition did, in fact, report lower levels of interest and enjoyment in the social interaction. Participants also reported feeling more distracted, and even more bored, in the phone condition. Overall, they concluded that people enjoyed a meal out more when their phones were put away than when their phones were present. Given that much of our understanding of how phone use benefits or limits people during social interactions is in its infancy, this study provides some initial evidence that smartphone use can negatively impact face-to-face social interactions.

ETHICAL CONSIDERATIONS IN EXPERIMENTAL DESIGN

Although we offer a much more extended discussion of ethics in Chapter 2, it is worth noting that experimental designs evoke two specific ethical issues. One involves the placebo/control group and denial of treatment; the other entails the use of confederates and deception in experimental design.

Placebo/Control Group and Denial of Treatment

Use of a placebo or control group in an experiment becomes problematic when there is reason to believe that your treatment group will receive some therapeutic benefit. The experimenter must grapple with the ethical concerns of denying treatment to the placebo/control group. This is an obvious challenge in research on medications for serious illnesses (e.g., a new cancer drug), but it can also arise in other contexts more directly relevant to psychological research, such as an experiment focusing on a particular educational technique or a new psychotherapy approach.

In some cases, the ethical challenge of denying the control group the therapeutic benefit can be met by a waitlist approach. Once the initial evaluation has been made, the control group receives the treatment on a delayed schedule, if the intervention proves to be effective. However, in other cases—especially if time is short (i.e., if a patient may not survive the delay)—a waitlist approach may not be sufficient. This concern arose in an experiment by Zannad and colleagues (2012), which investigated the development of therapeutic approaches for heart failure. One controversial option is for experimenters to stop a clinical trial early for therapeutic benefit. In the example of the heart failure treatment, an investigation of the medication eplerenone for patients with mild heart failure symptoms was halted early after several interim data analyses revealed substantial clinical benefits for those in the treatment group over those in the placebo group (lower incidence of cardiovascular death or hospitalization for heart failure).

There is no singular answer as to how to proceed in such situations, and there is a tension between scientific rigour (which may suggest completing the experiment on the designated timeline) and the rights of trial participants to receive potentially beneficial treatments, as well as the broader public good of sharing information about therapeutic benefits as quickly as possible. This tension is succinctly summarized by Zannad and colleagues (2012): "Maintaining the integrity of the trial and obtaining precise final results must be balanced against the risks for patients who are randomly assigned to an apparently inferior treatment and the need to rapidly disseminate evidence supporting a treatment benefit to the broader community" (p. 300).

Confederates and Deception

The second ethical issue, the use of confederates in experimental studies, relates more broadly to questions around deception of research participants. A confederate refers to an actor who is part of an experiment (i.e., they are "in on it") and plays a specific role in setting up the experimental situation. Participants are generally unaware of the role of the confederate, believing the individual to be another participant in the experiment.

confederate A person (accomplice) who is part of an experiment or study (but unknown to the participants) and plays a specific role in setting up the experimental situation.

Studies by Stanley Milgram and Solomon Asch provide two classic examples of the use of confederates. In the Milgram (1963) study, discussed in more detail in Chapter 2, the confederate pretended to be shocked when the participant flipped switches on a shock generator, going so far as to scream in pain and beg the participant to stop the shocks. In the Asch (1951) experiment, the participant was the only real participant in a room full of confederates (seven confederates took part in the original experiment). Asch was interested in whether an individual would conform to the opinion of the majority, even when the majority was clearly wrong. In the original experiment, the participant was presented with a card showing three lines of different lengths and asked to choose one that matched a line on another card. After a warm-up period during which the confederates responded accurately, Asch had all of the confederates make a clearly wrong choice prior to the participant's turn to choose. The participant was then asked to state their choice. Seventy-five per cent of participants provided the inaccurate, conforming response.

Marion and Burke (2017) conducted an experiment that participants believed was on dyadic problem solving. During one of these sessions, a mock theft was staged and participants had to either corroborate or refute a false alibi that a confederate was with the participant when the theft occurred. The experimenters were interested in how likely the participants were to lie for the confederate. They found that participants were more likely to lie when asked by the confederate to lie on their behalf and when the confederate was a friend rather than a stranger.

This study highlights the risk of such experiments. Participants may be upset or angry about having been deceived and may even behave aggressively toward the confederate and experimenter. It is important to consider not only the safety of the participant and research team, but also the impact of deception on the participant's self-worth. For example, tricking participants into acting in a shameful way may have a negative impact on their self-image. When you engage in deception, you are ethically obligated to consider the benefits and risks of the deception and to properly debrief the participant subsequent to the experiment to ensure that they are left physically and emotionally intact. Most research ethics boards require that you demonstrate that your experiment cannot be completed without the use of deception.

PRACTICAL TIPS

Practical Tips for Experimental Designs

1. Carefully consider the different conditions for your experimental design and choose the levels of your independent variable with experimental control in mind.

2. In designing your experiment, consider the temporal ordering of your variables (i.e., the hypothesized cause must precede the hypothesized effect).

3. To simplify your analyses and interpretation, consider designing a few discrete experiments that build on one another, rather than conducting a single large experiment with many factors.

4. Ensure the internal validity of your design through random assignment of participants to your different experimental conditions. If you have a small sample size, quasi-random assignment to guarantee distribution of participants across key characteristics may be necessary.

5. Ensure that any control group in your design is equivalent to the intervention group on all possible dimensions other than the intervention itself.

6. Assess whether your topic can be best examined through a between-subjects or within-subjects design. Make your decision based on both practical considerations and what is likely to give you the most accurate results.

7. Consider the confounds that may be present in your design. When you can, use strategies to control for these confounds as part of the design or account for them in analyzing your results.

CHAPTER SUMMARY

Experimental designs offer a potent tool for testing your hypothesis, giving you control over your variables of interest, and enabling you to draw conclusions concerning causality. Although experimental designs rate high in internal validity, they sometimes do not fare as well in external validity and, therefore, may not generalize to populations beyond your specific sample of participants. Whether you choose a within-subjects, between-subjects, or matched-group design, it is better to design a few discrete experiments that build on one another than to conduct a large experiment with many factors. Increasing the number of factors that you include in an experiment increases the complexity of the statistical analyses and can make the interpretation of your results more difficult. In our next chapter, we discuss more complicated experimental designs, including factorial designs.

End-of-Chapter Exercises

1. It is often said that experimental methodology is the "gold standard" approach in psychological research. Why are experimental methods often given such a prized status? Is this status deserved? Are there any circumstances under which you might argue that experimental methods are not the gold standard?

2. For each of the scenarios below, identify (1) the independent variable, (2) the dependent variable, and (3) the confounding variable (if any).

   a. A group of experimenters is interested in comparing a mindfulness-based cognitive therapy (MBCT) approach and a cognitive-behavioural therapy (CBT) approach for treating depression. Participants were randomly assigned to a six-week session of MBCT lead by Dr. Hui or a six-week session of CBT lead by Dr. Weltens. Both groups were assessed for depression before and after the six-week session.

   b. Dr. Justus teaches two sections of an introductory research methods course. One section is done in a traditional face-to-face format, and the second section is done in an online format. Dr. Justus administers the same final exam to both sections and compares their scores to see if there are any differences in performance between these two classes.

   c. Emmons and McCullough (2013) hypothesized that being grateful will increase well-being. They randomly assigned participants to one of three conditions: gratitude, hassle, or neutral life events. Every week for 10 weeks participants would record five things they were grateful for, five hassles they experienced, or five events that occurred in the previous week (depending on which condition they were assigned to). Each week they also completed a global appraisal on how they felt about their life as a whole during the week.

3. Describe at least two different ways you could randomly assign participants into the conditions of an experiment.

4. Imagine that you are interested in studying whether eating breakfast has an effect on academic performance. Describe how you could design this experiment using (1) a between-subjects design, (2) a within-subjects design, and (3) a matched-group design.

5. In experimental research in psychology, between-subjects designs are much more common than within-subjects or matched-group designs. Given some of the substantial methodological and statistical advantages of within-subjects and matched-group designs, why do you think such designs are less frequently used? What are the major barriers to setting up a within-subjects or matched-group experiment? Do you think the extra effort needed to use these methodological approaches is worth it, given the advantages?

Key Terms

attention control group, p. 134

attrition, p. 139

between-subjects design, p. 137

boredom effect, p. 139

ceiling effect, p. 146

condition, p. 131

confederate, p. 148

confounds, p. 142

contrast effect, p. 139

control group, p. 133

counterbalancing, p. 140

demand characteristics, p. 144

dependent variable, p. 130

double-blind design, p. 145

environmental manipulation, p. 132

experimental group, p. 133

external validity, p. 132

extraneous variable, p. 142

floor effect, p. 146

Hawthorne effect, p. 143

independent variable, p. 130

instructional manipulation, p. 132

internal validity, p. 132

invasive manipulation, p. 133

Latin square, p. 140

manipulation check, p. 133

matched-group design, p. 140

order effect, p. 139

participant variable, p. 133

placebo effect, p. 134

practice effect, p. 139

quasi-random assignment, p. 136

random assignment, p. 135

random selection, p. 136

single-blind design, p. 145

statistical control, p. 145

stimulus manipulation, p. 133

within-subjects design, p. 138

Variations on Experimental Designs

8

Chapter Contents

INSIDE RESEARCH: Colleen MacQuarrie

I am curious about how we make our world a better place. I am motivated to work within communities to address questions that will enhance social justice. Early in my career, I explored and was trained in research methods that sought to find truth through experimentation. I loved the fun of designing experiments to test specific hypotheses and the challenge of collecting quantitative data to calculate descriptive and inferential statistical tests to interpret the findings. However, it did not satisfy my need to ask more complex questions about the contexts in which we navigate sometimes unequal power relationships fraught with tension. I began to question the philosophy of science as a hypothesis-driven and deductive enterprise that was best conducted in a controlled environment like a laboratory. Through qualitative inquiry, I adopted an approach to research that embraces the intersecting, political contexts of how people live their lives and that asks different kinds of questions to explore phenomenal human existence, discourse, and systemic issues.

Courtesy of Colleen MacQuarrie

Professor of psychology, University of Prince Edward Island

continued

My Ph.D. research in British Columbia enabled me to work with couples who were grappling with the impacts of dementia, specifically early stage Alzheimer's disease. I was interested in how individuals change over time, so I invited couples to help me learn with them over a six-month longitudinal project. We met them in their homes, and I spoke with each couple together and separately. In speaking with people over the course of six months, I learned about the dance of insight and awareness that people living with Alzheimer-type dementia experience. I better understood the couple's struggles while facing daily challenges to sustain a relationship together and apart—how they attempted to maintain their lives and to conserve the dignity of the person whose cognitive abilities were shifting dramatically.

I have spent my career thinking about how to do relevant work and how to create learning experiences for participants as well as myself. Of particular note, my work on health policies concerning abortion access in PEI and reproductive justice resulted in historic policy changes in 2016. We implemented a collaborative community action research project to document the health impacts of PEI's abortion restrictions, using the process and the results to successfully challenge and change abortion access in the province. It is not all about research—it is also about what you plan to do with your research. To accomplish local policy change, I helped organize the PEI Abortion Rights Network and was a founding member of PEI Abortion Access Now; I initiated the first international conference on abortion and reproductive justice scholarship and activism in Charlottetown in 2014—naming it "The Unfinished Revolution," with the vision that it would continue every two years in places where abortion access was fettered to inspire networking for ongoing academic activism to improve women's lives.

Colleen MacQuarrie explores how aspects of wellness and inequality are used to address policy and practice issues, with a particular focus on abortion access. Arising out of The Unfinished Revolution conference, she co-founded the Reproductive Activism and Abortion Research Network (RAARN) and initiated a co-edited book, *Crossing Troubled Waters: Abortion Access in the Republic of Ireland, Northern Ireland, and Prince Edward Island*, published in 2018. She is currently establishing the foundation for a new research and advocacy journal: *Abortion and Reproductive Justice: International Community Research*, which will continue the project of sharing knowledge for feminist academic activism with communities to continue the unfinished revolution for empowered embodiment.

Research Focus: Creating opportunities for social, economic, and reproductive justice through community-based collaborative action research

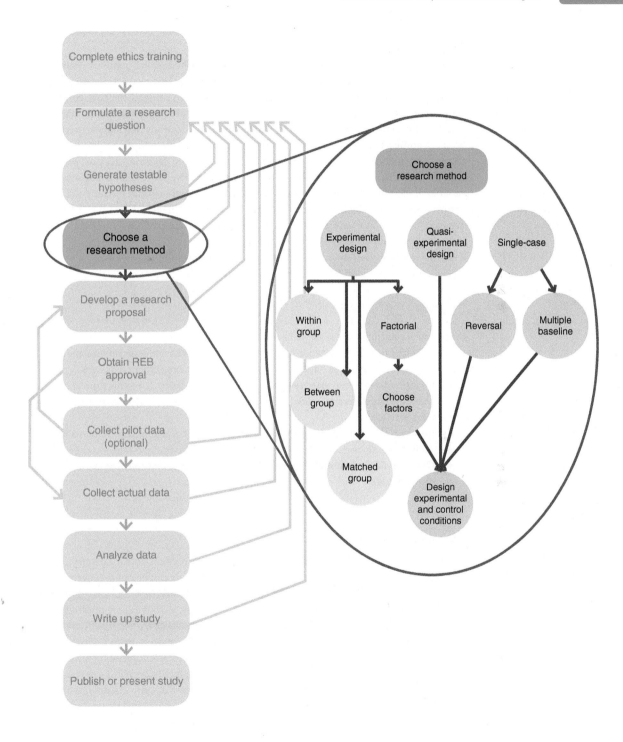

Chapter Abstract

Although the classic experimental design that we described in the previous chapter is often seen as the gold standard in research methodology, a number of variations on such designs also merit attention and discussion. These variations retain some of the core components of experimental methodology but differ in important ways. We begin the chapter with an investigation of quasi-experimental designs, which have modifications that allow experimenters to preserve some of the benefits of full experimental design while dealing with practical issues around the manipulation of variables. Next, we examine factorial designs, which enable experimenters to consider complex effects that may involve more than a single independent variable. Following this, we move on to a discussion of higher-order factorial designs, which permit experimenters to consider three or more factors. Finally, we end the chapter with an introduction to single-case experimental designs, which are experimental designs investigating a single participant or small cluster of participants.

LEARNING OBJECTIVES

By the end of this chapter, you should be able to:

- Describe how a quasi-experimental design differs from an experimental design.
- Discuss the advantages and disadvantages of quasi-experimental designs.
- Describe what a factorial design is and the advantages to using this type of design.
- Describe the difference between an experimental independent variable and a participant variable.
- Interpret the information provided by a main effect and an interaction in a factorial design.
- Describe single-case experimental designs and discuss their advantages and disadvantages.

QUASI-EXPERIMENTAL DESIGNS

quasi-experimental design A design that is similar to a true experiment but does not randomly assign participants to conditions or randomly assign the order of the conditions.

A **quasi-experimental design** is partially experimental; in effect, it is a category for a design that does not fit neatly into any other single category. A study can be quasi-experimental when it manipulates an independent variable but perhaps does not have a full set of other experimental controls (such as random assignment). Conversely, a study can be quasi-experimental if it has some experimental controls but does not fully manipulate an independent variable.

A good example of a quasi-experimental design can be found in research from DeLoache, Uttal, and Rosengren (2004), who studied a group of 18- to 30-month-old children to examine a behaviour they labelled "scale errors"—that is, the failure to correctly use visual information about size when interacting with objects (see Figure 8.1). An example of a scale error would be a child trying to sit in a dollhouse-size chair. They speculated that such errors were a result of the combination of failing to correctly use visual information to identify objects and a lack of ability to suppress an action that is inappropriate for a given situation.

Experimenters brought children into a laboratory playroom with large versions of objects (an indoor slide, a child-size chair, and a toy car). The children were allowed to play freely in

FIGURE 8.1   Examples of young children performing scale errors. (a) A 21 month old attempting to slide down a miniature slide. (b) A 24 month old attempting to get in a miniature car. (c) A 28 month old attempting to sit on a miniature chair.

the room, although the experimenter made sure they interacted with the large toys at least a couple of times. Children were then taken to an adjacent room to complete a different task. Once the child left the room, the experimenter replaced the large toys with miniature versions, and then the child was returned to the original room and allowed to play. In the second round of play, children were not compelled to play with the miniature objects, but the experimenter did draw the children's attention to the toys if they did not spontaneously interact with them. Experimenters then analyzed video data of the play sessions for scale errors to identify when children tried to interact with the miniature toys in the same way they had interacted with the larger versions. Twenty-five of the 54 children committed scale errors on the miniature objects, attempting to slide down the miniature slide, sit in the miniature chair, or climb in the miniature car.

Note that some elements of the study are clearly experimental. For example, children came to a laboratory environment with a standardized collection of toys and objects, and they played in the laboratory playroom for a standardized amount of time. Experimenters interacted with children in a minimal and standardized manner. There was a fair amount of control over the situation, as is typical of an experimental design. Yet the study lacked other elements of a classic experimental design. For example, there was no random assignment of participants to different conditions (rather, the design was within-subjects, with children exposed to both full-size and miniature furniture conditions) and no explicit manipulation of the independent variable. Instead, children were exposed to different stimuli in a loose sort of fashion. The study was a hybrid of a full-fledged experimental design and an observational design.

Two of the most common categories of quasi-experiments are the non-equivalent groups design and the pretest–posttest design. Recall that in a between-subjects experiment (Chapter 7), participants are randomly assigned to the conditions of the experiment. This process helps to ensure that the resulting groups are likely to be quite similar to one another on various extraneous variables (e.g., intelligence, extraversion) and can be considered equivalent. If random assignment is not used, the resulting groups are likely to be dissimilar in some ways and, thus, considered non-equivalent. Further, for some variables, it is not feasible to randomly assign participants into conditions (e.g., smoker/non-smoker; online/lecture-based classroom). Therefore, a **non-equivalent groups design** is a between-subjects design in which participants have not been randomly assigned to conditions.

An example of a non-equivalent groups design comes from the research by Jhangiani, Dastur, Le Grand, and Penner (2018), who compared textbook preferences and academic performance between students in seven sections of an introductory psychology course

non-equivalent groups design A between-groups quasi-experimental design in which participants are not randomly assigned to conditions.

who were assigned one of three versions of a textbook: commercial print, open print, or open digital. An open textbook is one that is available freely to students in an online version, or in a print version for a very low cost compared to a traditional commercial textbook when purchased as a print version. Some of the key findings from this quasi-experiment were that students using an open textbook performed as well as or better than those using the commercial textbook, and the students tended to prefer the print version (of both textbooks) to the digital version. What makes this an example of a non-equivalent groups design is that the students were not randomly assigned to a textbook condition; they were required to use the textbook that been assigned to the section of the psychology course they had registered in.

pretest–posttest design A within-subjects quasi-experimental design in which participants are tested before and after an experimental treatment or condition is introduced.

In a **pretest–posttest design**, the independent variable is measured on two occasions: before the treatment or experimental condition is implemented and again after it has been implemented. This design is similar to the within-subjects design described in Chapter 7, but differs in that the order of conditions is not counterbalanced. The order of presentation in a pretest–posttest design is fixed: The pretest measurement must always come first, and the posttest measurement must come after the experimental condition has been implemented. The study on scale errors described above would be considered a pretest–posttest design since all the children played with the large objects first, followed by the second condition, which contained the miniature objects.

Advantages of Quasi-experimental Designs

The primary advantage of a quasi-experimental design is flexibility. Because quasi-experimental methodology does not have as many requirements as a full experimental design, experimenters have greater freedom, both in how they set up their methods and in the topics they choose to study. In fact, quasi-experimental research designs offer good options for studying a number of topics that pose practical or ethical constraints that would prevent them from being studied using full-fledged experimental studies. For example, we may be interested in studying the effects of teacher:student ratio on cognitive gains in elementary school classrooms. Although we would probably not have the opportunity to randomly assign students to classrooms or schools with differing teacher:student ratios (and it would be unscrupulous to do so), we can take advantage of naturally occurring groups to study the effects of the differing ratios. In such a study we might still be able to exercise some elements of experimental control (e.g., standardizing the curriculum or the approach of the classroom teachers), while living with the practical constraint of not being able to use true random assignment.

Disadvantages of Quasi-experimental Designs

Although flexibility is a benefit, the trade-off in using a quasi-experimental design, rather than a true experimental design, is clear: Quasi-experimental designs will not provide as much clarity about cause-and-effect relationships as full experimental designs. In fact, the line between a quasi-experimental study and a correlational study can be fuzzy. In the case where a quasi-experimental design has a naturally occurring independent variable, it may even be indistinguishable from a correlational design. However, when quasi-experimental designs involve at least some experimental control, they still allow experimenters to reach powerful conclusions.

FACTORIAL DESIGNS

Another set of research designs examines issues that are so complex they require more than a single independent variable. A factorial design refers to any experimental design that has more than one independent variable (also known as a factor, i.e., an independent variable manipulated by the experimenter).

Before we delve into the particulars, it is worth asking, Why would anyone want to examine more than one independent variable in a single design? A factorial approach offers some major benefits. First, because a factorial design examines multiple independent variables together, it gives you the ability to look not only at the effects of single variables in isolation, but also at the effects of combinations of variables (i.e., different variables working in tandem). The second, perhaps more compelling, reason is the way factorial designs allow us to examine the complexity of the real world in an experimental paradigm. Many of the most interesting questions and hypotheses may involve different variables influencing one another, and if we are really interested in designing experiments with good external validity (i.e., that represent the reality of the outside world), then factorial designs may give us the best chance of representing this complexity.

As an example, we might be interested in the extent to which a therapist is directive (provides specific prompts and guidance) versus non-directive, and whether one of these therapeutic styles is more likely to generate positive change for clients. In a single-factor design, the independent variable would be therapeutic style (whether the therapist is directive or non-directive) and the dependent variable would be a measure of client change. This could undoubtedly yield interesting findings. Suppose you had reason to believe that the question of when a therapeutic style is most effective depends on certain characteristics of the client, such as openness to the therapeutic process. To examine that question, you would need a factorial design, where one factor would be the therapeutic style and the second factor would be client openness to therapy (which is a participant variable). In this example, we would want clients who were low or high on openness to therapy. Participants would be randomly assigned to the therapeutic styles in a manner that balanced the number of participants who were high or low on openness to therapy in each of the therapeutic conditions. We will return to this example when we discuss the types of results factorial designs can yield.

Basic Factorial Designs: The 2 × 2

The most basic example of a factorial design is the 2 × 2. But what do we mean when we say "2 × 2"? First, each number refers to a factor, or independent variable. In a 2 × 2 design, we would examine two factors. In a 2 × 2 × 2 design, we would examine three factors (see "Media Matters: Almighty Avatars" for an example of a study that includes a 3 × 2 design).

Second, each number tells you how many levels each factor has. A level refers to a condition within the factor, so that a two-level factor has two possible conditions. In our therapy example, the two levels of the therapeutic style factor would be directive versus non-directive.

To make referencing the factors more convenient, we often assign a letter to each factor. In the 2 × 2 design, we would refer to the first factor (therapeutic style) as factor A and to the second factor (openness to therapy) as factor B.

The number of conditions in a factorial design—or all the possible combinations of your independent variables—can be easily computed by multiplying the numbers of levels of your different factors. A 2 × 2 design has four possible conditions, computed by multiplying

factorial design An experimental design that has more than one independent variable.

factor A variable manipulated by the experimenter.

levels The values taken on by an independent variable or factor. For example, in a drug effectiveness study, you may have a factor of "treatment," which has levels of "placebo" and "drug."

Almighty Avatars

If you had to choose between the fearsome villain Lord Voldemort and the legendary hero Superman as your avatar in a video game, which would you pick? What if someone told you that your choice could potentially affect your behaviour in the real world? You might think, "How could that be true? It's just a game!"

Yet experimenters found that participants who took on the persona of a villain in a video game were more likely to make questionable moral decisions in real life. Those who chose the role of hero were more likely to act in an altruistic way when they were not playing the game (Yoon & Vargas, 2014).

Gunwoo Yoon and Patrick Vargas used factorial design in a study titled "Know Thy Avatar: The Unintended Effect of Virtual-Self Representation on Behavior," which comprised two experiments. In the first experiment, which was a 3 × 2 design, participants were told they would take two unrelated tests, the first on game usability and the second a blind taste test. The experimenters did not tell them the true nature of the study. They randomly assigned each participant to one of the three avatars of Superman, Voldemort, and a neutral circle. Participants played the video game for five minutes and then answered questions designed to measure their identification with their avatar (Yoon & Vargas, 2014). This is the first factor with three levels.

Next, participants were asked to taste either (delicious) chocolate or (scorching) hot chili sauce and then determine how much of the food they tasted would be given to another, unknown volunteer (Yoon & Vargas, 2014). This is the second factor with two conditions. The experimenters anticipated that participants who played the video game as Superman would be more likely to pick chocolate to give to others, and the Voldemorts would tend to pick hot chili for the unsuspecting volunteers. They were right—heroes were twice as likely to act heroically and the villains villainously (Herbert, 2014). This was after *only five minutes* of playing the game.

In the second experiment, Yoon and Vargas wanted to rule out alternative interpretations of the results (Herbert, 2014). They compared the tendency among those who actually played the game (players) to act like their avatars with those who were asked merely to put themselves in the shoes of Superman or Voldemort, but did not play the game (observers). They found again that playing the game caused participants to act in ways consistent with their avatars and that these effects were stronger in players than in observers (Yoon & Vargas, 2014).

Yoon and Vargas theorized that playing video games results in an "arousal" that incites action in real life and that violent video games could lead players to behave violently in real life. Yoon said he was surprised that participants continued to act in the real world in ways consistent with their avatars' characters even if they said they did not closely identify with them ("Channelling Superman," 2014). Yoon and Vargas suggested that creating more heroic avatars for gamers could promote prosocial behaviour in general (Vincent, 2014).

The avatar study received a sizable amount of media attention from outlets such as *The Economist*, the *Harvard Business Review*, Reuters, *Huffington Post*, and *The Independent*, as well as mentions in several psychology blogs (Herbert, 2014; Raven, 2014; Vincent, 2014). The coverage the study received was good; every story correctly cited the experimenters' names, the institution where the research took place, and the facts. In addition, reporters refrained from overstating the study's implications, such as proclaiming that people who play violent video games are likely to commit crimes. *The Independent* went the extra step of placing the study in the context of previous research on gamers (Vincent, 2014), which showed that people who play a lot of video games report game images appearing offscreen. The line between "virtual" and "real" grows more blurry by the study.

the number of levels of factor A (two) by the number of levels of factor B (two). A 2 × 3 design would have six possible conditions, whereas a 2 × 2 × 2 would have eight. Each condition (often referred to as a cell) represents a unique combination of the levels of the independent variables. In the therapeutic style (directive/non-directive) and openness of the client (high/low) example, there are four possible combinations: directive therapy with a high-openness client, directive therapy with a low-openness client, non-directive therapy with a high-openness client, and non-directive therapy with a low-openness client (see Table 8.1).

Experimental Independent Variables versus Participant Variables. It is important to note that each factor can be either a traditional independent variable (i.e., an experimental condition that is systematically varied across participants) or a participant variable (i.e., a characteristic that varies across participants but is not manipulated by the experimenters).

For example, we might have a 2 × 2 design where one independent variable is the therapeutic style (directive versus non-directive) and the second independent variable is the participant's gender. Our first variable (therapeutic style) is a traditional independent variable in the sense that the experimenter manipulates it, whereas the second variable (gender) cannot be assigned experimentally but is a set characteristic of your participants. Likewise, the openness of the client to therapy is considered a participant variable (i.e., it is a pre-existing characteristic that is not subject to experimental manipulation). Table 8.1 presents a factorial design that contains both an experimental independent variable as one factor (therapeutic style: directive versus non-directive) and a participant variable (openness to therapy: high or low) as a second factor.

Main Effects and Interactions. A factorial design allows you to look for two different types of effects. The first, called a main effect, refers to the effect of a single independent variable—acting alone—on a dependent variable. (This can also be examined in a single-factor experimental design.) If we want to see whether directive or non-directive therapy is more effective in terms of eventual client outcome, we will look at the main effect of therapy style (and essentially ignore whether the individual has high or low openness). If we want to see whether high-openness or low-openness individuals do better in therapy, then we will look at the main effect of client openness (ignoring the style of therapy individuals received).

> **cell** A combination of one level from each factor in the experiment. The number of cells in a factorial design equals the number of levels of the different factors multiplied by each other. For example, a 2 × 2 design would have 4 cells, whereas a 3 × 4 design would have 12 cells.

> **main effect** The overall effect of a single factor on the dependent variable, averaging over the levels of all other factors.

Table 8.1 Example of a 2 × 2 factorial design with an independent variable and a participant variable.

Factor A	Factor B	
Therapeutic style (independent variable)	Openness to therapy (participant variable)	
	Low openness	High openness
Non-directive	Low openness Clients receive non-directive therapy	High openness Clients receive non-directive therapy
Directive	Low openness Clients receive directive therapy	High openness Clients receive directive therapy

interaction Occurs when the differences on one factor depend on the levels of at least one other factor.

The other type of effect that you can examine is the interaction—arguably the main reason to use factorial methodology. An interaction refers to the joint effect of multiple independent variables considered in combination. Another way of thinking about an interaction is that it creates an "it depends" situation in terms of how the factors relate to the dependent variable. If there is an interaction, then whether or not there is a difference, or the size of the difference, between the levels of one factor will *depend* on the levels of the second factor. There may not be a difference at all levels of the second factor, or the difference may be larger or smaller on the other level(s) of the factor.

In our 2 × 2 therapy study, the interaction question would be whether the effectiveness of therapy type depends on the level of openness of the client. It is not simply that therapy type matters and client openness matters as two separate effects. Although such an interaction might play out in several different ways, one possibility is that a particular style of therapy works better for one type of client than for another. The combination of directive therapy and low openness, or non-directive therapy and high openness, might yield the best therapeutic outcomes. Examining only main effects in this example would miss the important way in which these two factors operate jointly.

Figure 8.2 illustrates an interaction effect for our hypothetical therapy study. When using directive therapy, there is no difference in the effectiveness of the therapy between high-openness and low-openness individuals. In contrast, when using non-directive therapy, the therapy is considerably more effective for high-openness individuals. Because the effectiveness of the therapies depends on the openness of the client, we say that there is an interaction between therapy and openness with respect to therapeutic effectiveness.

Main effects and interactions can occur in a number of combinations. You can have multiple main effects *and* an interaction; you can have only main effects (or a single main effect) and no interaction; or you can have no main effects but still have an interaction. Consider the five interaction charts displayed in Figure 8.3. They represent different combinations of the presence or absence of main and interaction effects, and they are just a sampling of the types of patterns you might see with a 2 × 2 design. The key takeaway point, however, is that when interactions are graphed, they will lead to non-parallel lines.

interaction chart A diagram that represents different combinations of the presence or absence of main and interaction effects.

When significant interactions are present, they substantially modify how one might frame (or think about) the importance of the main effect. In our therapy example, a finding

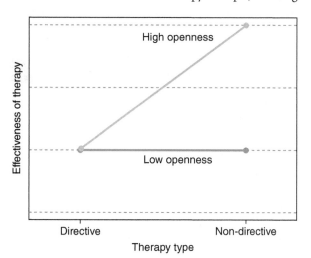

FIGURE 8.2   Illustration of an interaction between therapy and openness.

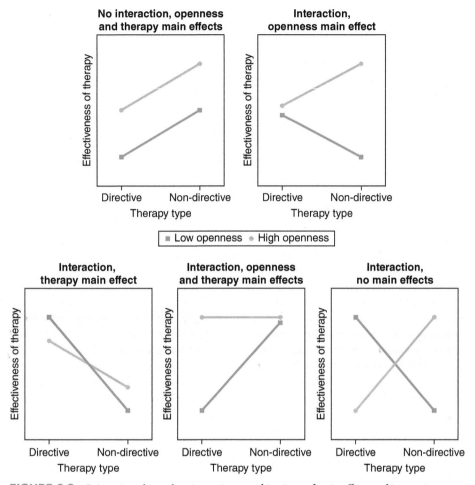

FIGURE 8.3   Interaction charts showing various combinations of main effects and interactions.

of a main effect for client openness would not be particularly meaningful by itself if there were a significant interaction between type of therapy and client openness. An interaction effect (e.g., that clients who are more open would do better in non-directive therapy) would tell the more important story. In the next sections, we provide examples of between-subjects, within-subjects, and mixed factorial designs, ending with a brief discussion of higher-order factorial analyses.

An Example of a Between-Subjects Factorial Design.   You might recall the classic work of Michelene Chi (1978), originally introduced in Chapter 3. Chi's work serves as an excellent illustration of a between-subjects factorial design. Chi was interested in determining whether age or knowledge (expertise) was the central driving force for cognitive development in the area of memory recall. To determine which was more important, she pitted child chess experts against college-age novices in a task to recall either pieces on a chessboard or a list of numbers. Her study is an example of a 2 × 2 between-subjects factorial design: The first factor, memory task, had two levels—either chess pieces or the number list. The second factor, maturation/expertise (a participant variable), also had two levels—either child expert or adult novice. (You might argue that the second factor is two different factors—age and expertise combined into one.)

Chi's findings indicated that child experts performed at a superior level to adult novices when completing the chessboard task, but adult novices outperformed child experts on the number list task. The findings serve as an elegant example of an interaction, in this case, between type of memory task and age/expertise, such that performance on the memory task that evoked expertise (the chessboard) was higher when participants had greater expert knowledge (the young chess experts), whereas performance on the memory task that evoked pure retention (the number list) was higher for the older (novice) participants who had more advanced cognitive development (see Figure 8.4). Chi's work also illustrates both types of independent variables defined previously: an experimental variable (memory task) and a participant variable (maturation/expertise). It is important here to remember that because the maturation/expertise variable is a participant variable, this study is a quasi-experimental factorial design, and while we can speak to differences seen between the two levels of the maturation/experience variable, we cannot make direct cause-and-effect conclusions about the role of maturation/expertise on memory performance.

An Example of a Within-Subjects Factorial Design.   In contrast to the between-subjects factorial design, within-subjects factorial designs involve conditions where the groups for each level of a factor are not independent of each other, but rather each group is exposed to each level of the factor. The term "repeated measures" reflects the idea that groups are repeatedly exposed to the different levels of the factor(s). Imagine that you are interested in the effects of caffeine dosage (high or low) on two different memory tasks—a visual recall task (where participants are shown a list of words and then asked to recall as many of them as possible after a set increment

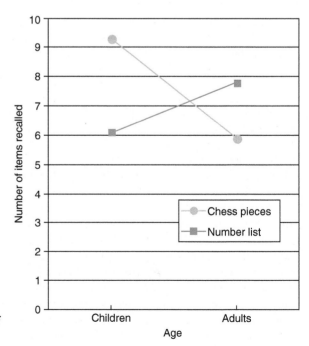

FIGURE 8.4   Interaction plot of data adapted from Chi (1978).

of time) and an auditory recall task (where participants are read a list of words and are then asked to recall as many as possible). This could be set up as a 2 (high versus low caffeine dosage) × 2 (visual versus auditory memory task) within-subjects design, so that your research participants participate in both the auditory and the visual recall tasks (probably on different days) and are given both high and low dosages of caffeine in combination with the recall tasks.

An Example of a Mixed Factorial Design.   Given the range of advantages and disadvantages for between-subjects and within-subjects designs, some experimenters opt to maximize the benefits of both approaches in a mixed factorial design (also called a mixed design), an intentional hybrid. In the most basic version of a mixed design, one independent variable is set up as between-subjects and another is set up as within-subjects. In the simplest mixed design (a 2 × 2), participants would be randomly assigned to one of the two conditions of the first independent variable (the between-subjects independent variable), and each participant would then be exposed to both conditions of the second independent variable (the within-subjects independent variable).

Suppose you were interested in studying exposure therapy versus traditional supportive therapy (the "aspirin" of psychotherapy) to treat coulrophobia, the fear of clowns. Exposure therapy is a popular technique for treating phobias; it operates on the premise that exposing someone to a feared stimulus, coupled with techniques for relaxation (deep breathing, imagery, progressive muscle relaxation), can break the association between the stimulus and the fear response (Nowakowski, Rogojanski, & Antony, 2014).

In a mixed design, you would recruit a group of coulrophobic participants and then, as a pretest, measure their level of anxiety during exposure to a clown. After completing the pretest, you would randomly assign your participants to one of two groups: the exposure therapy condition or the supportive psychotherapy condition. Participants would undergo therapy for a predetermined period of time and then would again be measured in a posttest for their level of anxiety during exposure to a clown.

How exactly is this a mixed design? When you look at your two factors, you will note that one (anxiety pre- and posttest) is a within-subjects factor because the participants take part in all levels (the pre- and posttest levels of anxiety). The other (type of therapy) is a between-subjects factor because the participants are assigned either to exposure therapy or to supportive psychotherapy. As an experimenter, you get the benefits of a "within" comparison (being able to look at the change in anxiety within particular individuals) and the benefits of a "between" comparison (being able to compare two different therapies without worrying about the problems of carryover effects). In some ways these designs give you the best of both worlds: They allow for generalization because they are repeated over the randomized groups levels, and they also reduce errors resulting from individual differences.

Higher-Order Factorial Designs

Complexity is an issue that permeates all factorial research designs. In addition to the two-factor designs we have reviewed, experimenters may also choose higher-order factorial designs (i.e., designs with three or more factors that are considered simultaneously).

Imagine that you are a memory researcher looking at the most effective strategies for short-term retention of a list of nouns. A higher-order factorial design with three independent variables could involve one experimental variable (one of two different memory strategies that

mixed factorial design A design that includes both within- and between-subjects factors.

higher-order factorial design A design that includes more than two independent variables. For example, a 2 × 2 × 2 design, with three factors, two levels for each factor, and eight cells or conditions.

participants are asked to use, say either rote rehearsal or imagery) and two different participant variables, gender (male or female) and age (high school, postsecondary, middle age).

In this 2 (strategy) × 2 (gender) × 3 (age) design, you would be able to examine a number of research questions, including whether one memory strategy works better than the other, whether one gender has superior memory to the other, and whether one age group does better than the others in terms of memory. Although they all would be valuable main effect questions, the real benefit of the higher-level design is that you could also look at the complex interplay between two, or even all three, of your factors.

For example, a possible two-way interaction between gender and strategy might reveal that imagery is an effective strategy for both men and women, but it gives women in particular a large boost in performance. A possible three-way interaction (gender × strategy × age) could be the enhanced effectiveness of the imagery strategy when used with women, but only for high school and postsecondary-age women, with middle-aged women showing no benefit of imagery beyond the benefits for men.

Many of the most interesting questions that we want to ask in social science are not univariate sorts of questions—they are not about single causes and single effects. A higher-order factorial design is best suited to capture the complexity of the world we live in. As you might recall from Chapter 4, external validity depends on ensuring that your research design captures the reality of your topic. Higher-order factorial designs may be used to increase the external validity of your study.

The downside of such complexity often appears at the level of interpretation. Consider the description of the three-way interaction between strategy, gender, and age as just described—and then imagine adding a fourth or fifth factor into the mix. Conceptualizing a two- or three-factor interaction is challenging enough, and the more complexity you add, the greater the challenge becomes.

SINGLE-CASE EXPERIMENTAL DESIGNS

single-case experimental design A design in which experimental methodology (e.g., manipulation of a variable and experimental control) is typically applied to a single participant or small group of participants using repeated measurements.

The final modification of experimental design that we will discuss in this chapter is a **single-case experimental design**. This design is a variation of a within-subjects design (see Chapter 7) but is based on a different research paradigm. The experimental designs discussed thus far have been based on group designs, where data are collected for a large sample of participants and conclusions are drawn from the means, or averages, of these samples using inferential statistical analyses (see Chapters 11 and 12). Alternatively, single-case experimental designs study participants at the individual level using repeated measurements and experimental control. The data are then graphed and visually inspected for patterns and trends so that conclusions about the effects of the manipulation of a variable can be made. These designs typically study a single participant, or small cluster of participants, but could also include large numbers of participants; the key is that the unit of analysis is at the individual, rather than group, level. This design is also distinct from case study methodology, which also focuses on one individual, because it uses the same systematic procedures as other experimental designs. Case studies, although they yield rich, useful information that can guide subsequent research, do not have the benefits of experimental control and often do not lead to generalizable information (see Chapter 9).

There are four essential features of a single-case experimental design: (1) A baseline measure is identified, (2) the dependent variable is repeatedly measured over the course of the experiment, (3) the independent variable is manipulated, and (4) there is replication of the effects of the independent variable within the same participant over time, which enables the participant to serve as their own control. It is the manipulation of the independent variable and the ability of the participant to act as their own control by participating in all of the conditions that ensure this design is, in fact, an experiment. Although single-case experimental designs are not widely used in many areas of psychology, they are often used in research in clinical psychology and in medicine. Understanding how these designs work provides a good analogue for research design more generally. In this final section, we will introduce some of the more common single-case experimental designs.

Building on the authors' well-established obsession with caffeine, imagine that your roommate has struggled with insomnia for the past several months. Observant and considerate roomie that you are, you notice that she often drinks a cup of coffee with dinner at the dining hall. (Assume you and your roommate always eat dinner around the same time each day, 6:00 p.m.) It occurs to you that her late-day dose of caffeine may be driving her insomnia. You decide to devise an experiment to gather evidence about whether caffeine is, in fact, the cause of her sleep difficulties.

A single-case design gives you a couple of options to examine this situation. The most basic would be a **reversal design**, in which you start by measuring the individual's behaviour of interest (the dependent variable) at baseline—that is, before implementing any intervention. You then implement your intervention (the independent variable) and measure the behaviour of interest again. Finally, you withdraw the intervention and measure the behaviour of interest again.

In the case of your roommate, the dependent variable (the variable you hope to change) is sleep. Although there are several ways to operationalize your friend's insomnia, we will settle on how long it takes her to fall asleep at night. Imagine that the intervention is to have your friend switch from caffeinated to decaf coffee for several weeks. It would be a good idea to not tell your friend when she is drinking caffeinated versus decaf so that she would be blind to the experimental condition (and less likely to have her expectations shape the results, as with a placebo effect).

If the amount of time your friend requires to fall asleep decreases from baseline A, when she drinks regular coffee, to intervention B, when she drinks decaf, and then reverts back to baseline A after she resumes drinking regular coffee, then you have evidence that the intervention worked (see Figure 8.5).

reversal design (ABA design) A type of single-case experimental design in which baseline measurements are initially taken (A), a treatment/intervention is then implemented and measurements are taken (B), and finally the treatment/intervention is removed and measurements are taken one last time (A).

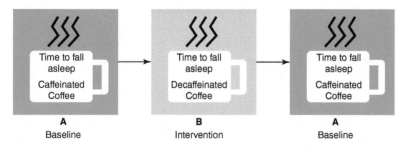

FIGURE 8.5 Example of a reversal design to examine the influence of caffeine consumption on time to fall asleep.

This sort of reversal design is sometimes referred to as an ABA design, which underscores the importance of the particular order of baseline–intervention–baseline. Knowing the baseline *first* is crucial for identifying meaningful change. Returning to baseline A is just as critical. Without it, determining the efficacy of the intervention would be impossible. In a sense, the final A of the ABA design serves as a placebo group in a traditional experimental design. If the behaviour of interest differs in the final A condition from the initial A condition it may suggest there is some carryover effect from the intervention.

Figure 8.6 shows hypothetical results of an ABA design for our caffeine study. Following baseline measurements for five days (first A), we see a drop in the amount of time to fall asleep when we remove caffeine (B), and then a rise when we once again have the participant drink caffeinated coffee (second A).

ABAB design A type of single-case experimental design that involves a baseline measurement (A), a treatment/intervention measurement (B), a measurement following removal of the treatment/intervention (A), and finally a second treatment/intervention measurement (B).

A second, superior option for the insomnia study would be an ABAB design. This design offers the same benefits as a reversal design but involves more than one iteration of the intervention. Instead, you have at least two rounds of baseline and intervention (hence, ABAB), or as many repetitions as you want. Going beyond a single reversal provides more data (and consequently greater certainty) to establish a difference between the baseline and intervention state—and it ensures that the change from baseline to intervention is not just part of a normal pattern of variation. If your friend takes less time to fall asleep during the intervention phase of the experiment (decaf coffee) the first time around, then you can feel pretty good about the effectiveness of your approach. If your friend takes less time to fall asleep during the decaf coffee intervention for several rounds, then you have even stronger evidence to support your hypothesis that coffee is the culprit (see Figure 8.7).

Figure 8.8 shows what happens when the intervention of decaffeinated coffee is applied a second time (the final B phase). We once again see a drop in the amount of time it takes our participant to fall asleep. These results provide further evidence for the effect of our intervention of administering decaffeinated rather than caffeinated coffee.

Given possible ethical concerns regarding the removal of an intervention that is shown to be effective and the inability to reverse some treatment effects (e.g., individuals who receive therapy cannot undo the effects of the therapy given), the reversal design is not always a

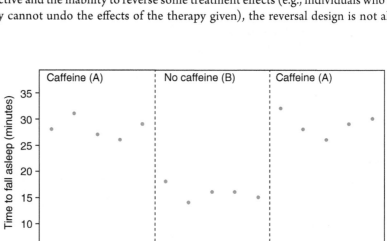

FIGURE 8.6   Hypothetical results for a caffeine study with an ABA design.

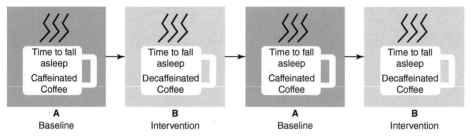

FIGURE 8.7   Example of an ABAB design to examine the influence of caffeine on time to fall asleep.

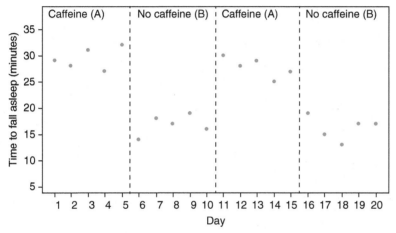

FIGURE 8.8   Hypothetical results for a caffeine study with an ABAB design.

feasible option. An alternative option to either a reversal design or an ABAB design is a **multiple baseline design**. In this design, a series of AB designs are implemented that are systematically staggered over time (to help control for the influence of extraneous variables). There are three variations of the multiple baseline design: across participants, across behaviours, or across settings. In a multiple baseline design across participants, the same behaviour is observed in each of several participants. First, a baseline measurement is established for each participant. Then, the intervention is introduced for one of the participants while the baseline in maintained for the others. This staggering of the intervention is continued for the remaining participants so that any effects of the intervention can be more clearly attributed to the intervention itself. For instance, if gains were found for all participants at the same time even though one or more were still in baseline, the changes could not be attributed to the intervention.

In a multiple baseline design across settings, a single behaviour would be examined to see if the intervention could replicate across different situations or conditions. For example, the effectiveness of an intervention for a child could be established in a classroom, at a playground, and in the home environment.

An example of a multiple baseline design across behaviours comes from research by Witt, Stokes, Parsonson, and Dudding (2018) who sought to test the effects of caregiver behaviour

multiple baseline design A series of AB designs that are systematically staggered over time to examine the effect of the intervention or treatment across participants, settings, or behaviours.

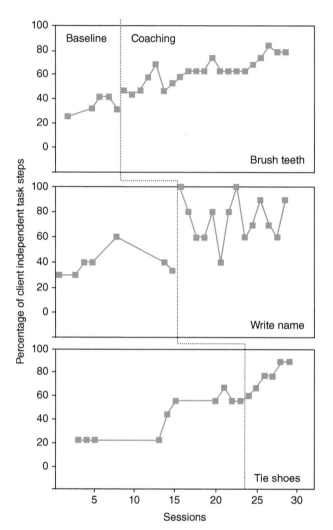

FIGURE 8.9   Results for a skill acquisition intervention using a multiple baseline design across behaviours (taken from Witt et al., 2018).

Source: From Witt, M. R., Stokes, T. F., Parsonson, B. S., & Dudding, C. C. (2018). Effect of distance caregiver coaching on functional skills of a child with traumatic brain injury. *Brain Injury*, 32(7), 894–899. https://doi.org/10.1080/02699052.2018 .1466365. Courtesy Taylor & Francis Ltd, http://www.tandfonline.com

on the skill acquisition (i.e., brushing teeth, writing name, and tying shoes) of a child with a brain injury. During baseline, no positive prompts (the intervention) to complete the targeted behaviours were provided by the caregiver to the child. Then, the intervention was introduced for brushing teeth, followed by name writing, then finally shoe tying. Measurements were taken as to whether the child was able to independently complete these tasks. Figure 8.9 shows the results from Witt and colleagues' (2018) study. All three skills showed improvement after the intervention was implemented, suggesting that the positive prompting provided by the caregiver was effective in the skill acquisition.

Advantages of Single-Case Experimental Designs

Single-case designs have a number of benefits. First, a single-case design can be conducted with only one individual, which is obviously easier and more convenient than assembling a large group of participants. However, if an experimenter wishes to go beyond a single individual but still use this type of design, replicating the impact of an experimental manipulation over a number of participants with repeated single-case designs enhances the validity of the research (Dallery, Cassidy, & Raiff, 2013).

This type of design also retains the powerful advantage of experimental control, allowing you to collect evidence to determine causal relationships. For instance, being able to determine the cause of your friend's insomnia (or at least rule out the non-causes) would be enormously useful. Single-case designs are also useful for establishing the preliminary efficacy of specific interventions. Experimenters have used these designs to evaluate new technology-based health interventions on the Internet (Dallery et al., 2013) and to provide relatively low-cost, efficient alternatives to randomized clinical trials that evaluate treatments for behaviours such as suicide and self-injury (Rizvi & Nock, 2008).

Disadvantages of Single-Case Experimental Designs

Although it is often assumed that single-case experimental designs have limited utility in terms of the generalizability of their findings, this is not necessarily the case. If an effect can be replicated repeatedly within an individual or over a number of participants, it is possible to produce generalizable research (Raiff & Dallery, 2010). Generalizability is often not the goal of a single-case design, however. As with your insomniac roommate, you would be less interested in broad data supporting the hypothesis that caffeinated coffee contributes to sleep difficulties than in solving your individual friend's sleep problems.

A second disadvantage of single-case experimental designs is that multiple observations and exposures to the intervention itself may affect the responses of your participant, similar to the effect of within-subjects designs. How much you should be concerned about it depends on what you are studying. Returning to our caffeine example, you probably would not be especially concerned with carryover effects (because it is unlikely that repeated exposure and withdrawal from caffeine itself would create a problem for your findings). But if you were conducting a single-case design on the effects of an antidepressant medication for a single patient, you would be much more concerned. There is the potential for real-life consequences (and some ethical challenges) in having an individual alternate between taking a potentially efficacious medication and then withdrawing from that medication for some increment of time.

Relatedly, a final drawback to these designs relates to ethics. In particular, what are the ethics of withdrawing treatment, which is required to measure the benefits of the treatment approach? If your friend is able to fall asleep more readily after the introduction of decaf coffee, is it problematic to reintroduce caffeinated coffee, knowing that this will likely lead your friend's insomnia to return? Ultimately, the justification for the design is the certainty of the answers that it can provide. In other words, although your friend may temporarily return to her unhappy sleepless state, the benefit of being sure that caffeinated coffee is the culprit exceeds the risk posed by the discomfort.

Practical Tips for Variations on Experimental Designs

1. Remember that your research design and methods should be determined by your research question and not the fancy, high-tech equipment you might have access to.

2. Carefully consider whether a traditional experimental design can be used to conduct your study or whether a variation from the traditional design is necessary.

3. Learn to recognize and evaluate main effects and interactions in factorial designs.

4. Be wary of using complex factorial designs that result in numerous main effects and interactions. Evaluating more than a three-way interaction effect can be quite difficult.

5. Consider the other tips we provided in Chapter 7 for experimental designs in general.

CHAPTER SUMMARY

After reading this chapter you should understand the range of variations of experimental designs available to experimenters today. Quasi-experimental designs contain some elements of experimental control but are not completely experimental; often they make use of independent variables that cannot be manipulated. Factorial designs require more than a single independent variable. They permit experimenters to study the effects of combinations of variables and examine the complexity of the real world in an experimental model. Examples of factorial designs include the basic 2×2, mixed, between-subjects, and within-subjects designs. All of these enable experimenters to look for a main effect and an interaction among multiple independent variables. In higher-order factorial designs, experimenters can simultaneously consider three or more factors.

Single-case experimental designs are often used to evaluate interventions typically focused on one participant and measure how a dependent variable responds to changes in the independent variable. The most basic single-case design is a reversal design, which measures a baseline of behaviour before the implementation of any intervention and follows an ABA pattern. An ABAB pattern is an extension of the reversal design because it repeats the intervention, whereas a multiple baseline design examines interventions across participants, settings, or behaviours.

End-of-Chapter Exercises

1. An experimenter hypothesizes that students who study with peers learn better than students who study individually. Describe how you could design a quasi-experimental study to test this hypothesis. If you find support for your hypothesis, can you conclude that studying with peers causes more learning? Why or why not?

2. Suppose you are interested in the effectiveness of a particular teaching method on algebra test scores. You select two algebra classes in which average test scores

and the distributions of test scores have been about the same across several tests. You implement the new teaching method in one of these classes and keep the old method in the other class (the control group). You then look at scores for the next two tests to see whether the teaching method leads to increases in scores relative to the control group. This is a quasi-experimental design. What characteristic(s) does it share with a true experimental design? What characteristic(s) keep it from being experimental? What challenges would you face in interpreting the results?

3. An experimenter was interested in the effect of hair length on judgments of attractiveness. Male participants were shown photographs of women whose hair was either very short, shoulder length, or very long, and female participants were shown photographs of men whose hair was either very short, shoulder length, or very long. Participants were asked to rate the attractiveness of each of the photographs.
   a. Identify the design (e.g., 2 × 2).
   b. Identify whether the independent variables are experimental or participant variables.
   c. Is this a between-subjects, within-subjects, or mixed factorial design?
   d. Identify the dependent variable.

4. A researcher was interested in the effects of alcohol consumption on the ability to concentrate, and also wondered whether gender and age were important factors. The participants included both males and females who were divided into three age categories (18–29, 30–44, 45–60). The researcher had participants drink

"cocktails" containing either no alcohol, 3 ounces of alcohol, or 6 ounces of alcohol. After 30 minutes, participants read a short story followed by a test of comprehension. The researcher collected the reading time and number of correct items on the comprehension test for each participant.
   a. Identify the design (e.g., 2 × 2).
   b. Identify whether the independent variables are experimental or participant variables.
   c. Is this a between-subjects, within-subjects, or mixed factorial design?
   d. Identify the dependent variable.

5. Look back at the interaction charts in Figure 8.3. How would you describe the results presented in each of the charts? For example, we described Figure 8.2 as follows:

> When using directive therapy, there is no difference in the effectiveness of the therapy between high-openness and low-openness individuals. In contrast, when using non-directive therapy, the therapy is considerably more effective for high-openness individuals.

6. Your best friend complains that his dog constantly barks and growls at the door every time the mail carrier comes to the house with the mail. Come up with a strategy that may deter your friend's dog from barking and devise a single-case experimental design to test your hypothesis. What would you expect to find if your hypothesis is correct?

Key Terms

ABAB design, p. 166

cell, p. 159

factor, p. 157

factorial design, p. 157

higher-order factorial design, p. 163

interaction, p. 160

interaction chart, p. 160

levels, p. 157

main effect, p. 159

mixed factorial design, p. 163

multiple baseline design, pp. 167

non-equivalent groups design, p. 155

pretest–posttest design, p. 156

quasi-experimental design, p. 154

reversal design (ABA design), p. 165

single-case experimental design, p. 164

Observation, Case Studies, Archival Research, and Meta-Analysis

9

Chapter Contents

INSIDE RESEARCH: Martin Daly

As an undergraduate at the University of Toronto, I initially enrolled in "MPC" (math, physics, and chemistry), because math had been my strength in high school. Alas, I was too immature to be self-motivated. I played cards, skipped classes, and flunked out. Had I chosen the wrong program? I started over in social and philosophical studies, where I discovered that an inspiring professor can change the trajectory of a student's life: George Mandler's superb introductory course drew me into psychology,

Courtesy of Martin Daly

Professor emeritus, psychology, McMaster University

and Jerry Hogan's upper-level seminar made me want to pursue research on animal behaviour.

   The U of T psychology program provided excellent training in statistics and experimental design, but after my Ph.D. I crossed over to the "dark side," pursuing topics where controlled experiments were seldom possible. As a postdoctoral fellow, I joined a research group whose goal was to understand why closely related animal species often have radically different social behaviour: Why are some antelope species monogamous and others polygamous, or why do some monkeys live in territorial family units while others move about in large mixed-sex troops? We weren't going to get anywhere with such

continued

questions unless we followed the animals around in their own world and tried to get a handle on their feeding ecology and their predators.

For one study, colleagues and I implanted tiny radio-transmitters in desert-dwelling kangaroo rats to track their movements. Once in a while, a radio would suddenly be found to be transmitting from a coyote or an owl or a rattlesnake. It took years, but we were eventually able to show that predation wasn't selectively removing the young, the old, and the feeble, as had been widely supposed, but was selectively removing healthy dominant males in their prime. Those were the animals who were taking the greatest risks—such as running across open spaces, even under a full moon—in pursuit of mating opportunities. You couldn't have found that out by running experiments.

In 1977, my late wife, Margo Wilson, and I began a program of research on human violence. This was another topic that couldn't be pursued experimentally, and it couldn't be pursued observationally either. Our approach was to get the best data we could find on confirmed assaults (which often meant focusing on homicides) and to combine those data with population-at-large data from the census and other sources to pinpoint risk markers and patterns. One of our most striking findings was that stepchildren were assaulted and killed by parents at vastly higher rates than children living with both birth parents. But was being a stepchild itself relevant, or might it be "confounded" with other risk factors, such as poverty? Addressing such questions requires lots of careful analysis, and you can never be sure that you've disposed of all plausible confound hypotheses; thus, we still don't have any firm conclusions. These are the same obstacles that sociologists, economists, and epidemiologists face today as they try to discover causal links in a world where everything seems to be correlated with everything else. It's messy, yes, but that's the world we live in, and the one we want to understand.

Martin Daly is professor emeritus at McMaster University, where he combined fieldwork in animal behaviour with epidemiological studies of homicide, always in collaboration with the late Margo Wilson, with whom he co-authored four books and dozens of research reports. In 1998, he and Wilson were elected fellows of the Royal Society of Canada.

Research Focus: Since retiring from McMaster, Martin has produced a research monograph on the links between economic inequality and homicide (*Killing the Competition*, 2016) and, in collaboration with his wife, Gretchen Perry, he now studies when and why grandmothers are caregivers for their grandchildren.

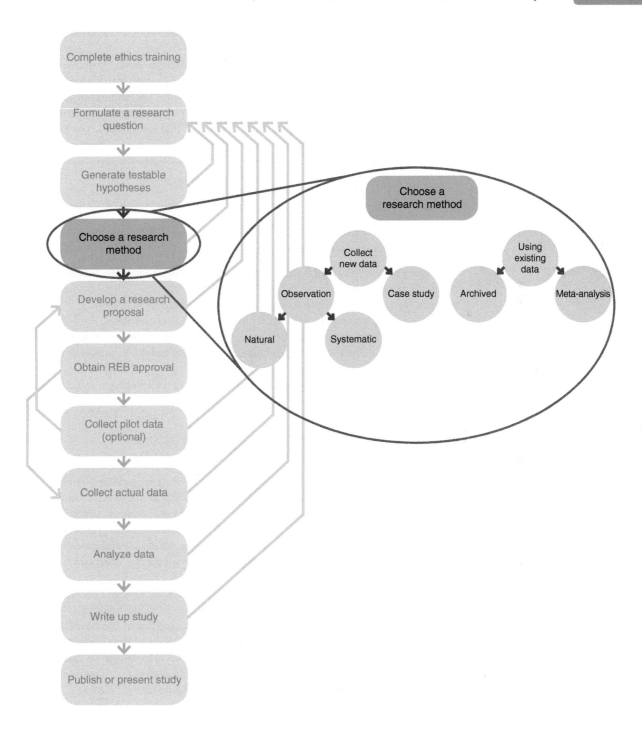

Chapter Abstract

In this chapter, we delve into how to select and use particular methods by examining the strengths and limitations of each one. The designs discussed in this chapter go beyond the pure experimental method. On the one hand, observational methods—including naturalistic and systematic observation—and case studies involve observing phenomena as they occur. Often, researchers using these two methods systematically record that information. On the other hand, archival research and meta-analysis—two additional designs—use existing data sources.

LEARNING OBJECTIVES

By the end of this chapter, you should be able to:

- Compare naturalistic and structured observational methods, including the advantages and disadvantages of each.
- Define reactivity and identify strategies to deal with reactivity.
- Discuss advantages and disadvantages to video recording observations.
- Describe the three types of sampling strategies used when coding observational data.
- Describe what a case study is and discuss the advantages and disadvantages of this methodology.
- Compare archival research and meta-analyses, including the advantages and disadvantages of each.

OBSERVATIONAL METHODS

observational methods A class of research techniques that involve gathering information by observing phenomena as they occur.

As the name suggests, observational methods involve gathering information by observing phenomena as they occur. But what distinguishes observation as a research methodology from just "looking around"? Observational methods, as used by researchers in psychology and other social sciences, are more formal than most people's casual understanding of observation. Observational research methods focus on a specific issue or set of issues and are organized around a specific goal. Particular rules and structures shape how the observation is constructed, depending on the type of technique.

Observational methods can be described in a number of ways, but we think the most useful distinction involves two broad categories: naturalistic and structured. The boundaries between these categories may seem blurry, but they are primarily distinguished by the extent to which the researcher manipulates the setting. Each comes with its own set of advantages and disadvantages, and choosing one over the other involves a complex set of trade-offs. To illustrate the strengths and challenges of each technique, we present several studies that serve as excellent examples of how researchers can examine the same question with different methods.

Naturalistic Observation

naturalistic observation Looking at phenomena as they occur (naturally) in the environment.

Considered the most basic type of observational method, naturalistic observation involves watching and studying phenomena as they naturally occur in the environment. Although the researcher may be interested in specific behaviours, in naturalistic observation the researcher does little to control the setting. A researcher seeks to describe phenomena by recording them through a variety of techniques, most commonly through some form of note-taking or transcribing. This method has its roots in the anthropological tradition in which an impartial observer or, in those cases where an outsider does not have access to the setting, someone who participates in the setting ("participant observation") takes field notes.

Although it is clearly associated with anthropology, naturalistic observations also have their place within psychological research. For example, Piaget's theory of cognitive development (1926, 1952) was based in part on natural observations of his own and other children. He watched his infant son, Laurent, as he moved his body and interacted with the environment, leading Piaget to the concept of the sensorimotor stage of development. "At 0:1 Laurent in his crib with hunger. He is lifted to an almost vertical position. His behavior goes through four sequential phases quite distinct from one another. He begins by calming himself and tries to suck while turning his head from left to right and back again while his hands flourish without direction. Then (second phase) the arms, instead of describing movements of maximum breadth, seem to approach his mouth. Several times each hand brushes his lips; the right hand presses against the child's cheek and clamps it for a few seconds" (Piaget, 1952, pp. 51–2).

Many people assume that researchers conduct naturalistic observation by going into a setting of interest and waiting for something to emerge. There is some merit to this approach because it takes time to become a good observer of behaviour. Indeed, William Charlesworth, an ethologist (ethology is the study of animal behaviour) who studied child behaviour, argued that a new investigator should devote at least 1,000 hours to merely observing children in their natural environments before conducting any formal research. This type of naturalistic observation, if done thoughtfully and carefully, may help researchers better understand how a behaviour is influenced by a particular context and more effectively generate ideas for future research. Yet, outside of a few researchers interested in human behaviour (Blurton Jones, 1972; Charlesworth, 1986; Eibl-Eibesfeldt, 1967), most current researchers do not devote this much time to developing the skills of broad observation because of constraints on time and resources.

Most naturalistic observations start with a relatively focused area of interest. The researcher's background and theoretical orientation often constrain the focus of the research. For example, a developmental psychologist interested in gender differences may look generally at the activity levels of boys and girls in a playground setting. In contrast, a researcher interested in aggression might focus only on aggressive acts between boys on a playground.

It is important to note that naturalistic observation may involve ethical considerations. For example, if you observe parenting behaviour in a grocery store that is verging on abusive, do you maintain your status as impartial observer, or do you have obligations to report the behaviour or intervene for the protection of the child? There are no simple formulas for answering this question, but as with other areas of research, ethical dilemmas can arise.

Advantages of Naturalistic Observation.   The benefits of a naturalistic approach are perhaps obvious—and significant. First, naturalistic observation may be the only practical way to study certain topics. Second, by its very definition, naturalistic observation is high in external validity. You may recall from our discussion of validity in Chapter 4 that external validity reflects the extent to which your findings can be generalized to other settings. Because naturalistic observation involves gathering data directly in the settings of interest, we can assume that its external validity is high. This means it may be especially useful for complex, novel settings that would be hard to simulate in a laboratory.

Imagine, for example, that you were interested in observing parenting practices in a grocery store (Fortner-Wood & Henderson, 1997; O'Dougherty, Story, & Stang, 2006), the behaviour of parent spectators at youth sport events (Arthur-Banning, Wells, Baker, & Hegreness, 2009; Shields, Bredemeier, LaVoi, & Power, 2005), or family interactions at the dinner table (Messer & Gross, 1995; Moens, Braet, & Soetens, 2007). It is hard to envision any methodology other than direct observation for understanding behaviour in these contexts. Similarly, many studies in environmental psychology rely heavily on naturalistic research because they seek to answer questions about how people use physical spaces such as parks or plazas (Kaczynski, Potwarka, & Saelens, 2008; Shores & West, 2010).

Disadvantages of Naturalistic Observation.

As powerful as naturalistic observation can be in complicated, unique settings, clearly defined research questions and hypotheses may justify a structured or even experimental approach. In particular, the lack of control in naturalistic observation that is an asset when you are still developing your questions becomes more problematic if you have already defined them. In such cases, something that started as a naturalistic observation may become more structured as definitions become clearer.

A second limitation of naturalistic observation has to do with the timing and frequency of the event(s) that you examine. In the example of prosocial behaviour on the playground, you can imagine that you will witness several examples of children helping each other during a single recess if you are patient. In contrast, if you want to observe accidents on the playground and how children react, you may have to spend a lot of time gathering enough data. Naturalistic observation, then, may not be the best choice for studying relatively infrequent behaviours.

A third limitation of naturalistic observation is the problem of bias. When you ask participants to observe within their own context (e.g., parents to observe their own children), you may imagine they would find being objective difficult. For example, parents may interpret a babbling sound made by a young infant as an actual word that a trained observer would conclude has no meaning. Because this lack of objectivity has no absolute remedy, the best way to address participant observation is to acknowledge this inherent limitation and to provide training and as many guidelines as possible for observers to minimize bias. Depending on your research question, the participant observer may still be the best source of information.

The final challenge with naturalistic observation is embedded in the methodology itself. Reactivity occurs when the individuals being observed know they are being watched and, as a result, change their behaviour. Although researchers who use observational methods seem to worry more about this problem than those who use experimental methods, in reality reactivity is *always* a concern when people in any setting know their behaviour is being studied.

There are two imperfect strategies for dealing with reactivity. The first, concealment, means exactly what the word suggests: The observer finds some credible way to prevent participants from knowing they are being watched. Some situations are less challenging than others. For example, if you conduct an observation at a laboratory childcare centre (found at many universities) in which classrooms have observation rooms behind one-way mirrors, concealment is a non-issue. But if you are in the open classroom, the challenge to be non-intrusive is much greater. The observer must also contend with the ethics of concealment and gain the consent of the observed. Generally speaking, researchers may observe only public behaviour unless they have the consent of participants.

The second strategy for dealing with reactivity is waiting it out. Researchers who regularly conduct naturalistic observations often spend a lot of time in the environment before beginning the formal observation, so that those being observed become used to their presence.

reactivity A shift in an observed individual's normal behaviour as a result of the knowledge that they are being observed.

concealment A strategy for handling participant reactivity by keeping observers or recording equipment hidden from participants.

This strategy takes advantage of habituation, meaning that individuals become accustomed to a novel stimulus in the environment (see Chapter 3), in this case, the researcher.

Although we can never be certain that observing behaviour in a natural setting does not at least subtly change behaviour, some research over the years has concluded that reactivity does not always pose a significant threat to the validity of observational research (Christensen & Hazzard, 1983; Jacob, Tennenbaum, Seilhamer, Bargiel, & Sharon, 1994). In fact, recording behaviour with technology alone (i.e., a video recording device) or with a live observer using technology may not affect the level of reactivity (Johnson & Bolstad, 1975). Ultimately, we may have to live with the uncertainty suggested by Craig Gilbert, the producer of the 1973 PBS series *An American Family*, the first true reality show (see "Media Matters: *An American Family*"). In summing up the effect of filming on the family, Gilbert states "There is no question that the presence of our camera crews and equipment had an effect on the Louds, one which is impossible to evaluate" (PBS Video, 2013). Although we still have no conclusive answers about how being observed affects human behaviour, it is interesting to consider how contemporary reality television culture has shifted our expectations and perceptions of the scrutiny of others.

habituation Diminished response to a stimulus that comes about through repeated exposure to that stimulus.

MEDIA MATTERS

An American Family

Before Snookie, before the *Real Housewives of Vancouver*, before the Kardashians, there was *An American Family*, the first-ever reality television show. Although most people today have never heard of it, the series debuted more than 40 years ago on PBS and drew more than 10 million viewers (Maerz, 2011).

The show broke new ground by televising the daily lives of the Louds, an upper-middle-class family in Santa Barbara, California. Camera crews followed Bill and Pat Loud and their children—Lance, Delilah, Grant, Kevin, and Michele—for seven months, filming 300 hours from May 30 to December 31, 1971. Conceived and directed by the television producer Craig Gilbert, the series debuted in 1973 and consisted of 12 one-hour episodes. The show was shot in cinema vérité, a naturalistic style of filmmaking that has no host, no interviews, and very little voiceover narration. In fact, by today's standards, *An American Family* resembles an exercise in naturalistic observation with its slow pacing, long takes, and lack of background music. As Lance put it later, the footage could be "draggy" (Heffernan, 2011).

This is not to say that the Louds were free of drama. Although early episodes depicted self-conscious

Photo by John Dominis/The LIFE Images Collection via Getty Images/Getty Images

conversations around the breakfast table, later episodes eventually revealed—and perhaps exacerbated—painful tensions that ripped the family apart. After 20 years of marriage, Pat asked for a separation from Bill, who had been unfaithful for years. Lance, the eldest, was the first person to announce that he was gay on national television, and the show included scenes from his life in New York. When the show concluded, Bill and Pat divorced, although they reunited in 2001 after Lance died from AIDS-related complications (Galanes, 2013).

Immediately after the series had aired, the Loud children appeared on the Dick Cavett show and discussed the issue of their reactivity to the cameras. "I felt that I was pressed for something to say when there was no action or anything, and we'd just be sitting there talking to friends," Delilah said. "Viewing yourself, you think, 'Oh God, say something intelligent, don't just sit there.' Because if you're just sitting there and they're filming you, there's nothing you can say, except try to strike up anything, like 'Hey, how was school?'"

Cavett responded, "So you said a lot of stuff just because you need to say something?"

"Yes, you felt pressed for something to say," Delilah agreed.

The Louds and Gilbert were shocked by viewer reaction to the show. Critics attacked the Loud family as "affluent zombies," and many viewers blamed Bill and Pat for seeking publicity and failing to keep their family together. The family has largely kept out of the public eye since, although they did allow the filmmakers of the original series to record Lance's last days, at his insistence.

After *An American Family* aired and Gilbert saw what happened to the Louds, he became deeply depressed for many years. He recalled receiving phone calls from Pat, who was hysterical over the attacks on her family. "That, right there, was the beginning of my own confusion. What have I done? What do I do? I've never resolved it. I didn't know what I had wrought. I still don't" (Winer, 2011).

Gilbert never produced another television show, but reality television has lived on.

Example of Naturalistic Observation: Parent and Child Sportsmanship Behaviour.

In a study using naturalistic observation, Arthur-Banning and colleagues (2009) examined the relationship between adult behaviours and the behaviours of athletes in Grades 3 through 6 in a community basketball league. Trained observers recorded all examples of positive and negative sportsmanship behaviours of parents, coaches, and athletes during 142 games. They worked with a list of examples of positive sportsmanship (e.g., cheering on opponents, checking on an injured player) and negative sportsmanship (e.g., taunting opponents, yelling at referees, acts of excessive aggression). Prior to data collection, observers received training that involved viewing video examples of sportsmanship behaviours, rating those behaviours, and reaching agreement with other trained observers.

Using this methodology, the researchers found some expected associations: Positive spectator and coach behaviours served as predictors of positive athlete behaviour, whereas negative spectator behaviours predicted negative athlete behaviour. Being able to directly link adult behaviour to child athlete behaviour has obvious implications for how youth leagues might set policies to maximize sportsmanlike conduct among athletes.

Example of Naturalistic Observation: Childcare Quality.

One major hurdle in naturalistic observation is that for your data to be meaningful and valid, you must develop a comprehensive coding system to narrow the questions and variables *beforehand*. Benjamin Gorvine's experience with naturalistic observation as part of the National Institute of Child Health and Human Development (NICHD) Study of Early Child Care in the mid-1990s illustrates this challenge.

The NICHD study was an ambitious project designed to examine short- and long-term outcomes for young children in different care arrangements (home daycare, centre daycare, parental care, etc.). A major task for this study was to figure out ways to use observation to systematically measure the characteristics of care being received by children. This was accomplished through a carefully constructed checklist called the Observational Record of

Classroom Environment (ORCE). The ORCE listed caregivers' behaviours that had been identified in the research literature as facilitating positive cognitive or socio-emotional development in infants and young children (NICHD Early Child Care Research Network, 2003).

Gorvine, who worked as a research assistant on the study, and the other observers received training in both live settings and via video recordings and had to demonstrate a high level of reliability before engaging in actual data collection. This means they had to accurately identify and record behaviours based on the ORCE, and the observations had to match a set of "master codes" with a high level of consistency. Observers were retested every three to four months to ensure that their observations had not drifted from the original system. The NICHD observers conducted **time sampling**, alternating observation and recording (in 30-second intervals) for a specific time period (in this case 44-minute segments), with the goal of capturing as many caregiving behaviours on the lengthy checklist as possible. ORCE training carefully operationalized and exhaustively illustrated all of the behaviours on the checklist. For example, positive categories of caregiver behaviour included "positive physical contact," "responds to vocalization," "asks questions," and "shared positive affect," whereas negative categories included items such as "restricts infant's activities," "uses negative physical actions," and "restricts in physical container" (NICHD Early Child Care Research Network, 1996).

In Gorvine's experience, reaching adequate proficiency and accuracy in completing observations with this measure involved many months of difficult, often tedious training. As shown in Figure 9.1, observations were focused exclusively on specific, carefully defined caregiver behaviours. In addition, the behaviours of interest were clearly informed by both previous research and theory about what behaviours facilitated (or discouraged) successful development. Although thoughtfully designed naturalistic observations can yield useful data, creating a workable observational scheme and training researchers to use that scheme reliably require a substantial investment of time and effort.

time sampling
Observing and recording behaviours during predetermined units of time; for instance, one minute at the start of every five-minute period.

Example of Naturalistic Observation: Scale Errors.

The work of Rosengren, Gutiérrez, Anderson, and Schein (2009) on scale errors provides a final example of the naturalistic observational approach. Recall from Chapter 8 that scale errors are behaviours where children attempt to act on objects that are much too small to accommodate their actions. In their 2009 study, Rosengren and colleagues recruited a group of mothers of 13- to 21-month-old children and asked the mothers to record scale errors they observed in their children over a six-month period.

This project involved a data collection method called **event sampling**, where researchers count each occurrence of a particular behaviour or event. Event sampling is effective when behaviour can be easily categorized and when the researcher wishes to record a relatively small number of events.

The design used by Rosengren and colleagues (2009) is best described as **participant observation**, where an individual who is part of the environment (in this case, a parent) observes the behaviour of interest (in this case, scale errors by their children). To address potential observer bias, parents attended a 40-minute training session where experimenters gave a clear definition of scale errors and showed videos of different types of scale errors. Parents were also asked to rate the occurrences on a scale from "Definitely pretending" to "Definitely serious" and to record details of the child's reactions to their unsuccessful actions. Experimenters discussed the ratings and observations with parents during training to make sure they understood what was being asked of them and then provided forms and a notebook so parents could record their children's behaviours. Experimenters checked in with parents monthly to ensure they were continuing their observations and to see whether they had any questions.

event sampling
Observing and recording each occurrence of a targeted behaviour or event; shows how frequently a behaviour or event occurs.

participant observation An individual who is part of the environment observes and records a behaviour of interest (e.g., a parent making observations of a child during their normal interactions).

Form ☐ of ☐	CHILD-CAREGIVER OBSERVATION SYSTEM	EXHIBIT 1
ID# ☐☐☐☐☐☐☐☐	CHILD-FOCUSED	
Interviewer ID # ☐☐☐☐☐	OBSERVATION FORM	

CODING PERIOD: *START:* ☐☐:☐☐ AM/PM END: ☐☐:☐☐ AM/PM   CHILD'S AGE: ___ Years ___ Months

CHECK ALL THAT APPLY	1	2	3	4	5	6	7	8	9	10
A. TYPE OF CAREGIVER TALK (ALL CODES IN "A" ARE FC/FC GROUP EXCEPT RESPONDS)										
Responds to FOCUS CHILD (FC) Talk (CODE TYPE BELOW)										
Language or Communication Requested										
Action Requested										
Reading										
Other Talk/Singing										
B. FC TALKS TO. . .										
Self or Unknown										
Other Child(ren)										
Direct Provider										
Other Caregivers										
C. FC INTERACTION WITH OR ATTENDING TO. . .										
Other Child(ren) or Group										
Caregiver										
Material (played with or explored)										
Television or Video										
None: Wandering/Unoccupied										
D. FC WAS. . .										
Smiling/Laughing										
Upset/Crying										
Being Hit/Bit/Bothered by Other Child										
Hitting/Biting/Bothering Other Child										
E. THE MAIN CAREGIVER INTERACTING OR ATTEMPTING TO INTERACT WITH FC WAS. . . CHECK ONE ONLY										
Direct Provider of Care										
Other Caregiver										
All Caregivers Roughly Equal										
No Interaction										

FIGURE 9.1   Example of time sampling coding form from Boller, Sprachman, and the Early Head Start Research Consortium (1998).

Source: Boller, K., S. Sprachman, and the Early Head Start Research Consortium. "The Child-Caregiver Observation System Instructor's Manual." Princeton, NJ: Mathematica Policy Research, Inc., January 1998.

The study yielded useful observational data indicating that children did, in fact, commit scale errors in their everyday lives, with parents reporting an average of 3.2 scale errors per child over the six-month period. Parents reported that their children tried to sit in tiny chairs, slide down tiny slides, and lie down on tiny beds. Keep this finding in mind, because we will return to another example of scale error research that shows the value of using converging evidence across observational methods to study an issue.

Structured Observation

In contrast to the open-ended context of naturalistic observations, researchers use more structured observation when they are ready to exert greater control over the setting in which the observation occurs. In the example of parent and child sportsmanship discussed previously, there was no attempt to control the setting (youth basketball games) in which the behaviour was observed. A study of sportsmanship that observed youth behaviour in two different leagues with systemically different rules and policies about parent and athlete behaviours could be called a structured observation since an element of control over the setting (the rules and norms of the leagues) has now been introduced.

Structured observations are often more useful when you have already identified and carefully defined the phenomenon of interest based on theory, prior research, or some combination of the two and you have some particular ideas about how the phenomenon might vary based on specific factors in the environment. Contrast this with a naturalistic observation approach where a researcher might take notes or otherwise code all occurrences of the behaviour(s) of interest without exerting any control over the environment.

> **structured observation** An observational approach where researchers exert greater control over the setting in which the observation is occurring.

Advantages of Structured Observation.   The structured approach can allow for discoveries that would not be possible in naturalistic studies. For example, structured observations can reveal the ways in which specific factors influence the context of interest in your research. If more stringent policies and norms for how parents must behave in a youth league relate to higher levels of athlete sportsmanship, then there is practical information that can be useful for commissioners of youth leagues going forward.

Because well-designed structured observations involve a process of carefully defining the variables of interest and controlling the environment in which these variables occur, they have the potential for *both* high external and construct validity. Construct validity, which refers to the degree to which a variable captures the behaviour it is intended to measure, is often a strength of good observational research generally. Structured observations also offer the benefit of high external validity, which refers to the extent to which findings can be generalized to other settings.

Disadvantages of Structured Observation.   The primary disadvantage of structured observation lies within the idea of the structure itself. To effectively use and benefit from the structured observational approach, you must be able to specify the dimensions where the structure will be applied. In the youth sport example, the idea of creating different rule structures is an obvious approach, but depending on what you are observing, it may not be obvious where control should be applied.

Example of Structured Observation: Scale Errors.   We previously described a naturalistic observational study of scale errors in young children. Rosengren and his colleagues used a more structured observational approach in a different study of the same phenomenon. Rosengren, Schein, and Gutiérrez (2010) observed 24 children between 18 and 29 months of age who attended a laboratory preschool. In contrast to the naturalistic design, in which parents recorded scale errors as they occurred over a period of months, this structured observational design was intended to increase the likelihood of observing scale errors by placing miniature replica toys in the preschool classroom during predetermined observational periods.

Although the findings showed that most young children do, in fact, perform scale errors, the systematic approach in this study revealed substantial individual differences in frequency and persistence of committing scale errors. This study also found that the frequency of such errors decreased during the 10-week observation period. These discoveries would not have been possible in the naturalistic parent report method used previously. This demonstrates that multiple approaches can provide converging evidence, different perspectives, and complementary data on the same issue.

Video Recording

Many observational approaches involve video recordings. Video recording has been used for several decades, and recent technological advances have made it easier and less expensive than ever before. Still, you should consider a number of issues when you record participants as part of an observational approach.

The first obvious issue is reactivity. The visible presence of recording equipment may increase the artificiality of the observational situation (e.g., participants "acting" for the camera). As we have mentioned, there is no "magic bullet" solution for reactivity. Concealment of the observer or recording device and habituation by the participant to the observational situation are often the best solutions available. Ultimately, as researchers we must wrestle with the uncomfortable truth that we can never truly know the impact of our observation on those being observed.

A second issue relates to the ethics of research. Advances in technology have made concealment easier and more convenient, but privacy concerns are a serious issue (see Figure 9.2). As a general principle, you can record without the consent of those being recorded only if you are observing in a public setting; other types of recording require the explicit consent of those being observed (ruling out concealment as an option).

coding The process whereby data are categorized to facilitate analysis.

Despite the challenges posed by ethics and reactivity, recording equipment offers researchers substantial advantages, including more narrow, focused, and tightly operationalized constructs and variables. In addition, recorded video data can be viewed repeatedly, which reduces the possibility of missing a key event or behaviour. Recording data also allows for the use of multiple raters to assess levels of agreement on the coding of behaviours. If you code an observation for a child's aggressive act on the playground, you can check that multiple observers also noted and recorded it.

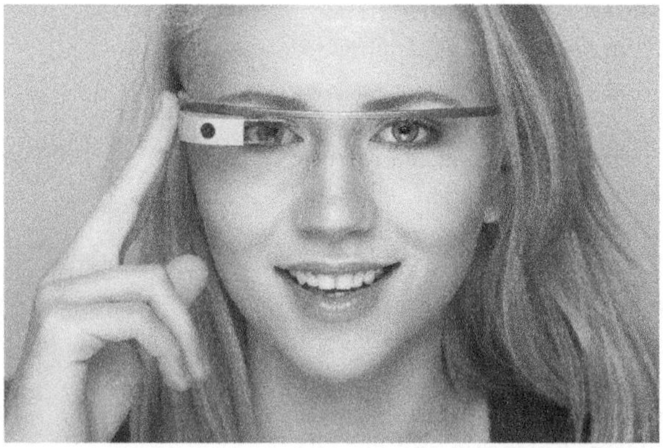

Peppinuzzo/Shutterstock

FIGURE 9.2 Google Glass enables users to covertly film anywhere without other people knowing. However, a number of businesses banned them from their premises because of privacy concerns (Stenovec, 2013), leading Google to scale back on their marketing of this device. Although the privacy issue is serious, tools such as these glasses may someday be useful, allowing observational researchers to effectively capture a wide range of behaviour while simultaneously inputting coded data.

Coding of Observational Data

As previously mentioned, video recording offers the possibility of capturing large amounts of information, which can then be coded and examined quantitatively. **Coding** is a broad term referring to the process whereby data are categorized to facilitate analysis. In the context of observations, coding typically refers to taking the rich, qualitative information that is gathered and distilling it into a form that is more readily amenable to statistical examination. Although coding is often discussed in the context of video recording (especially since such recording has become virtually ubiquitous in modern social science research), it is worth noting here that coding more generally refers to a process, which can be applied to any form of observational data.

There are three broad types of sampling that relate to the process of coding: specimen record, event sampling, and time sampling. In a specimen record approach, all instances of a targeted behaviour in a given time period are recorded and described in detail. In this approach, it is essential to have access to technology such as video recording to ensure that nothing of importance gets missed. A specimen record approach when observing children on a playground would mean recording and describing all of the predetermined targeted behaviours that were observed. A somewhat more focused type of approach is reflected in event sampling, where a count of all instances of a specific behaviour in a given time period are recorded (previously described in Rosengren et al., 2009). An event sampling approach on that same playground might involve recording all the instances of aggressive behaviour between children that occur during a recess period. In a final approach, time sampling (previously described with the ORCE and the NICHD Child Care study), the observer records whether certain behaviours occur during a sample of short, predetermined time intervals. So, returning to our playground, you might record all instances of aggressive behaviour that occur within a predetermined series of 30-second intervals (or note if no such behaviours occur during those intervals).

Regardless of the type of sampling implemented to gather your data, developing a good coding system to deal with those data involves creating a careful set of categories that will provide both valid and reliable data. They must be valid in the sense that they should reflect the concept you are trying to capture, and they must be reliable in that different observers seeing the same thing would agree on the category to use within your coding system. In our playground aggression example, it would be important to develop a clear list of behaviours that would be coded as aggressive (e.g., pushing, hitting, biting), while also making decisions about how coders should define an aggressive act. This can include a complex—but arguably important—set of decisions. For example, should an "accidental" act of aggression still be counted as aggression (e.g., one child absent-mindedly bumps another child), or does the child's behaviour need to be intentional? How will verbal aggression be coded? What counts as a discrete act of aggression? If a child punches another child three times in rapid succession, is that three acts of aggression or just one? There are many possible "right" ways to answer these questions in a coding system, but the most important thing for any system is that the answers are clear and well reasoned so that, in the end, you can make the case that your coding system really did capture the behaviour(s) of interest and that it did so in a way that was clear and reliable.

specimen record
Observing and making a detailed record of a targeted behaviour during a given time period.

CASE STUDIES

Although observational methods make up a substantial proportion of non-experimental research, another major category for non-experimental design is the case study, a detailed examination of a single individual over a period of time (not to be confused with single-case experimental designs, discussed in Chapter 8). Case studies are most useful for studying rare phenomena and are often the only way to do so. Because they are limited to one person, their primary strength is also their weakness: A case study can provide rich data about that unique circumstance, but it cannot provide information that can necessarily be generalized to other situations or individuals.

case study A detailed examination of a single individual over a period of time.

Although this lack of generalizability constrains the broad application of findings from case studies, it does not mean that the case study methodology cannot yield useful information. Indeed, case studies can suggest themes and directions for future systematic study. One area in which case studies have been used frequently is in the field of neuropsychology. Case studies in this field have been used to provide new insights into the working of the brain and how particular brain injuries yield changes in specific psychological functions and behaviours (Martin & Allen, 2012). We now turn to two case studies—Nadia and H.M.—that provide excellent examples of how remarkable individuals or idiosyncratic events can yield amazingly rich, useful case study information.

Drawing Insight from the Exceptional Drawing of Nadia

A well-known case study involves Nadia, a young girl with autism, who at the age of three and a half began to create highly realistic drawings well beyond the ability of most children her age (Selfe, 1977). Lorna Selfe studied Nadia extensively over several years and published her drawings in *Nadia: A Case of Extraordinary Drawing Ability in an Autistic Child*.

What was so intriguing about Nadia was her ability to capture motion and perspective on par with that of gifted artists (see Figure 9.3). Yet, in terms of language and cognitive function, Nadia was severely impaired. At six and a half years of age, Nadia could produce two-word utterances (e.g., "good girl," "bed time"), but not longer ones. Because many cognitive evaluations rely heavily on verbal abilities, assessments of her cognitive function are difficult to interpret; however, based on her performance on the Wechsler Intelligence Scale for Children, Nadia was considered below average (Selfe, 1977).

Many researchers have used the case of Nadia and others like hers to examine the relation between autism and giftedness (Drake & Winner, 2011; Henley, 1989; Mottron, Limoges, & Jelenic, 2003; Pariser & Zimmerman, 2004; Selfe, 1977, 2011) and even the neuropsychology of artistic production (Chatterjee, 2004; Ramachandran, 2002). When evaluating case reports such as these, you should consider whether the inferences are based on actual studies of the individual or drawn from reports of the original case study. As in the old game of telephone, data can be transformed in secondary reports.

By permission of Dr. Lorna Selfe

FIGURE 9.3   Drawing of a horse by Nadia at age 5 (Henley, 1989).

The Memorable Case of H.M.

One of the most famous (if not *the* most famous) case studies in psychology and neuroscience is that of the patient H.M. (Ogden & Corkin, 1991). At age 10, this individual began suffering minor seizures, which developed into major seizures by the time he was 16. The seizures became so severe that he had difficulty with daily functioning and was unable to work. When H.M. was 27, he and his family agreed to an experimental surgery that they hoped would reduce or eliminate the debilitating seizures. The effects of the surgery were much more dramatic than expected. In addition to effectively reducing the frequency and severity of the seizures, the surgery had the side effect of rendering him unable to remember any recent events (Scoville & Milner, 1957).

Until his death in 2008, when his name was finally revealed, Henry Molaison had likely been studied by every prominent memory researcher and neuroscientist in the world. The many case studies of H.M. were instrumental in determining the hippocampus's role in memory (Scoville & Milner, 1957); the impact of amnesia on everyday functioning (Corkin, 1984, 2002); and the relationship between memory and language processing (MacKay, James, Taylor, & Marian, 2007).

A number of films have captured the challenges faced by H.M. *Memento* (2001) is a psychological thriller involving a killer with anterograde amnesia (similar to that of H.M.) that makes it difficult for him to remember new events. The romantic comedy *50 First Dates* (2004) portrays the difficulty of having a relationship with an individual who has a form of anterograde amnesia. As was the case with H.M., the main character has great trouble remembering new information. Unlike H.M., the movie has a Hollywood ending.

Advantages of Case Studies

If case studies are detailed and extensive, they provide incredibly rich data sets that can address interesting theoretical or applied research questions. Many neuropsychologists have used case studies of individuals with particular lesions or intriguing characteristics to explore different theories of brain function and brain–behaviour linkages. In many circumstances, insights obtained from case studies (such as those of Nadia and H.M.) would not likely have been obtained using other types of research methods.

Disadvantages of Case Studies

Although case studies can provide a wealth of data, you must be careful about generalizing too far from any one case study. For example, any brain injury is unique to that individual. Because of the plasticity of the brain and changes in brain structure and function over development, the diversity of experiences pre- and postinjury and any subsequent recovery are also likely unique to that individual (Von Hofsten, 1993). In fact, individuals with brain injuries are a more diverse group than individuals without brain injuries. Drawing inferences from a case study to the more general population may not be valid.

Case studies can also include both accurate and inaccurate information, and it may not be easy to determine what information is the most accurate. In the case of Nadia, reports differ greatly on when and why she apparently stopped drawing (at age 8, Pariser & Zimmerman, 2004; or at age 12, Carter, 1999) and whether she lost her exceptional ability or merely the desire to express herself in drawings. Some imply that as she gained language skills, she lost her ability to create the highly realistic drawings that led her to be labelled gifted (Selfe, 2011). Others posit that Nadia lost her ability to produce remarkable drawings because of a combination of therapy, loss of her mother, and aging (Henley, 1989). However, over a number of sessions, Henley (1989) was able to coax more skilled drawings from an older Nadia, who no longer spontaneously produced extraordinary art.

In historical cases or cases studied by only a few researchers, such as Nadia, you should consider both the validity and the reliability of the reports, because they may be incomplete or biased by the researcher's expertise. Although this is arguably the case for all research reports, it is of particular concern for case studies where there is only one observer reporting at a time and only one participant of observation. In the case of Nadia, a cognitive psychologist (Selfe, 2011) drew different conclusions than an art therapist (Henley, 1989).

ARCHIVAL RESEARCH

archival research The study of data that have been previously collected.

Archival research refers to studies of data that have been previously collected. Although some research ethics boards will require approval to analyze these records, many place this type of research in the exempt category, meaning you do not need to obtain research ethics board approval.

Many archival databases are available for use by any researcher interested in analyzing the data. Probably the best-known archival database in Canada is Statistics Canada, which provides online tools that enable researchers (or anyone) to examine data from a variety of social, economic, and environmental categories. For example, the Canadian General Social Survey (GSS) provides access to data collected on a number of variables related to people's views about work, home, leisure, and well-being. One study that published data from the GSS explored various risk factors for online victimization (Reyns, 2015). The researcher found that online exposure (e.g., booking/making online reservations, social networking) and target suitability (e.g., posting personal information, visiting risky websites) increased one's risk of being victimized through phishing, hacking, or malware infections.

Researchers interested in using Statistics Canada data for a research project must submit an online application form and a project proposal. More information regarding this process, and the types of data that can be requested, can be found at www.statcan.gc.ca/eng/rdc/index.

Advantages of Archival Research

Using archival or existing data offers several clear advantages. First, researchers do not need to collect the data themselves, which saves substantial time and money. Second, many archives include a large amount of data on a large number of respondents. The nature of the data, if collected and analyzed appropriately, enables the researcher to obtain a relatively large, representative sample. The previously mentioned study by Reyns (2015) reported data from over 10,000 respondents. Large samples such as this enable investigators to use complex, sophisticated statistical approaches to test different models or theories against one another.

Disadvantages of Archival Research

The biggest problem with using existing databases is that they limit your research questions to the specific data that have been collected. The database might not include variables that you want, may include items worded differently than you like (see Chapter 6 on survey construction), or may have been collected on populations that differ from those you wish to study. Databases do add or subtract questions and generally improve the quality of the data they contain over time. However, databases that were established some time ago may contain questions that are no longer viewed as valid assessments of the constructs you are most interested in.

META-ANALYSIS

Meta-analysis is a statistical technique that permits researchers to compare results across a number of studies (Cooper, 2010; Valentine, 2012). Imagine that you were interested in determining whether various personality traits, such as introversion and extraversion, remain relatively stable across the lifespan. Although you could conduct a longitudinal study that examines this issue in a group of adults, many studies have already examined this topic. For example, Roberts, Walton, and Viechtbauer (2006) report on 92 studies that examined whether personality traits changed with age. Rather than using precious resources to replicate the existing work, a more efficient and effective approach might be to summarize and synthesize this past research. But how would you go about this?

> **meta-analysis** A statistical technique that combines results across a number of previous studies.

You could evaluate the past research in a number of ways. First, you could read the entire body of research and write a review paper that captures the overall conclusions from the individual reports. This type of review paper is common and can be useful for uncovering gaps in our knowledge and providing directions for new research. However, these reviews often represent the particular bias of the writer and may lack systematic comparison across different studies. For example, the author may emphasize certain results or articles more than others if they fit better with the proposed theory or model.

Second, you could count the studies that show one outcome, the studies that show the opposite outcome, and the studies that are inconclusive. By comparing counts across these three categories, you could argue that past research supports a particular outcome. However, this approach could treat a study examining the stability of the Big 5 personality traits (openness, conscientiousness, extraversion, agreeableness, and neuroticism) among 25 participants as having the same evidentiary power as a study of one or two of these traits among 500 participants.

Finally, you could opt for a third and more effective method by conducting a meta-analysis that compares the effect sizes across different studies. The term effect size most often refers to the strength of the relationship between or magnitude of the difference of two variables. You can assess effect sizes (Borenstein, 2012) based on a single study or single measure (non-standardized) or based on converted measures that can be used to compare results across studies or measures (standardized).

> **effect size** The magnitude of an effect (such as a difference of means or a relationship between two variables).

The correlation coefficient (r) is one type of standardized measure of effect size. Another common measure of effect size used in meta-analyses is the standardized mean difference, which is often labelled as Cohen's d (Valentine, 2012). The nature of the research question and the data will determine your choice. (We discuss effect size, the correlation coefficient, and Cohen's d in greater detail in Chapter 11.)

Conducting a meta-analysis requires several key steps. Researchers first must devise a method for locating studies, ideally by casting as wide a net as possible. This search approach is logical, extensive, and reported fully in the method section of the paper (Roberts et al., 2006). Depending on your research question and your expertise in a particular field, you may find other methods appropriate. For example, you may want to search more medically oriented articles for some topics by using PubMED rather than PsycINFO to find relevant studies.

Finding articles is only the beginning. Next, you must establish some criteria for including particular studies in your meta-analysis. Some articles may be too tangential to your main research question, or the research may not be of sufficiently high quality to include in the analysis. Roberts and colleagues (2006), in their study of whether personality traits change with age, required that studies meet the following five criteria for inclusion in their meta-analysis:

1. Include dispositional or trait variables, which are relatively consistent across different situations.
2. Measure variables more than once using test–retest intervals of one year or longer.
3. Report information on mean-level change, sample size, and age of participants.
4. Focus on non-clinical samples.
5. Focus on fairly narrow age ranges because one of the study questions addressed the impact of age on personality development.

The approach described here yielded 92 studies; however, some of the articles reported on more than one sample. Thus, the researchers included 113 different samples with a total of more than 50,000 participants. It is important to note that these five criteria were based on the research question. Different research questions will warrant different selection criteria and will yield different numbers of studies.

The next step, which can be done simultaneously with the development of the selection criteria, is selection of the variables to be examined. Because Roberts and colleagues (2006) were interested in the stability of personality traits over the lifespan, participant age was one of their key variables. Again, they used established criteria to focus their sample, only including studies of participants over the age of 10. They also made decisions regarding how to group ages into different categories.

Because the research mainly focused on the stability of personality across the lifespan, the variables of interest were the Big 5 personality traits. Roberts and colleagues (2006) also identified a number of moderators. **Moderating variables** influence the direction or strength of the relationship between independent and dependent variables. For example, Roberts and colleagues (2006) identified the sex of the sample (all male, all female, or both) as one moderating variable, because they expected that the stability of personality might vary in these different samples as a function of having only male participants, only female participants, or both. Other potential moderators include ethnicity, education, and socio-economic status.

In most cases, researchers conducting a meta-analysis will need to make a number of choices about the variables they are examining. For example, researchers must determine how to classify and combine data from different scales that assess either similar or somewhat different variables, how to code data into meaningful categories that can be used in the analysis, and what to do with low-quality or missing data.

Once researchers have coded all the studies, they compute a standardized effect size for each study, which can be done in a variety of ways. Roberts and colleagues (2006) calculated a standardized effect size by subtracting the mean of the trait scores at the second time point (Time 2) from those obtained at the initial time point (Time 1). They divided the mean value by the standard deviation of the raw scores at the first time point to create a standardized effect size for each study. Then they used the values in a variety of statistical analyses to examine the main research question and explore the influence of various moderating variables. Overall, Roberts and colleagues (2006) found that as people age, they show an increase in measures of social dominance (an aspect of extraversion), conscientiousness, and emotional stability.

moderating variable
A variable that influences (but does not causally explain) the direction or strength of relationship between two other variables.

They did not find that sex had much effect on the relationship between personality traits and development, so there was minimal moderating influence.

Advantages of Meta-Analysis

As with archival research, you do not need to collect data to conduct a meta-analysis. Depending on the area of study, you can also obtain a relatively large sample of studies (and participants) in a relatively short period of time. Likely the greatest advantage of meta-analysis is that it provides an objective way to compare findings across many studies, even those that have very different sample sizes or use different types of scales or measures. Also, meta-analysis assigns more weight to studies with larger samples, so they have a greater influence on the overall analysis than studies with relatively small samples. By standardizing effect sizes across different scales or assessments, they provide a measure of the overall effect.

Meta-analysis also enables researchers to examine particular claims to determine whether the overall evidence supports the effectiveness of an intervention or whether personality traits or behaviours change over the life course. Researchers can sift through a large number of studies to determine an overall effect that, without the use of meta-analysis, might have remained unknown because of the variety of results reported in multiple studies.

Disadvantages of Meta-Analysis

The quality of a meta-analysis depends on finding high-quality research reports, which may simply be lacking in some areas of interest. In addition, only studies that find statistically significant effects tend to be published. This is known as the **file-drawer problem**, because studies with non-significant findings are often tossed into a file and never published. An example of how this problem has led to biased reports in the scientific literature comes from work on bilingualism.

De Bruin, Treccani, and Della Sala (2015) document such a publication bias favouring studies with positive results over those with null results, showing that bilingual individuals have an advantage over monolingual individuals in cognitive "executive control tasks"—those involving memory, attention, planning, monitoring, and so on. Through a systematic examination of the research literature, particularly conference presentations (where data are often presented before being submitted for publication), they were able to document that studies showing a bilingual advantage, followed by studies showing mixed results, were more likely to be published than those with null findings (i.e., no differences between bilinguals versus monolinguals). This systematic bias means that if you were conducting research on whether bilingual individuals possessed this cognitive advantage, you would be likely to conclude more of a scientific consensus than actually exists.

One example of a remedy to this problem is a research registry, such as the Open Science Framework maintained in the United States, at https://osf.io, where a comprehensive record of research conducted around the world is registered. While it is not mandatory to register your study with this registry, it is recommended. The goal of such a registry is to ensure that all results—not just the positive ones—become part of the public scientific record.

Another disadvantage of meta-analysis is that it is time consuming to search for studies, code each study, and conduct the analysis. Each of these steps requires some expertise and experience with the content area and methods used in meta-analysis, which can make this approach relatively challenging for the beginning researcher.

file-drawer problem Bias in published research resulting from the issue that studies that do not exhibit statistical significance are less likely to be published (or even submitted for publication) than findings that do exhibit statistical significance.

Practical Tips for Observation, Case Studies, Archival Research, and Meta-Analysis

1. Be aware of participant reactivity and techniques for managing it, such as concealment and habituation.

2. Carefully choose a system for coding observational data, taking into account the need for both reliability and validity.

3. Consider using a case study if you come across an individual with an interesting set of behavioural characteristics.

4. Consider archival research if you are looking for a more efficient and economical approach to answering your research question.

5. Be aware of the file-drawer problem: Null findings on a particular phenomenon may be underreported.

6. As part of a literature review, consider using meta-analysis to combine and analyze results across multiple studies.

CHAPTER SUMMARY

Depending on your research question, it may be appropriate to use a non-experimental design, which does not involve experimental controls. You may choose from one of four types: observational, case study, archival research, or meta-analysis. An observational study, whether naturalistic or systematic, offers the widest range of methods. Naturalistic observation will be optimal if you plan to delve into a new area of research, whereas systematic observation will be more effective if you have already operationalized key variables of interest. A case study focuses on an unusual individual and is most common in neuropsychology.

Archival research involves studies of data that have already been collected, particularly large databases such as Statistics Canada. This method provides a ready-made, relatively large representative sample, but it may limit the scope of your question. Meta-analysis also uses pre-existing data and allows you to compare results across studies. It requires locating studies, determining criteria for inclusion into your study, selecting variables, and finding the standardized effect size.

End-of-Chapter Exercises

1. Suppose you want to study the ways in which people at different job levels interact within a company. How might you use naturalistic observation in your research? How might you use systematic observation? What are the advantages and disadvantages of each observational method?

2. You are interested in studying preschoolers' interactions with their peers and plan to conduct daily observations at a preschool centre for a month. Discuss why reactivity may be a concern and what you could do to lessen its impact.

3. Go to a public place, such as your school's cafeteria or a local park, and conduct a naturalistic observation for 30 minutes. Keep a record of your observations.

4. Imagine that you are interested in observing how the public interacts with homeless people. Develop a coding system that you would use to make your observations. In your coding system you should identify the types of behaviours you would observe and provide operational definitions of these behaviours.

5. If you are interested in the effects of caffeine on short-term memory, how might you use naturalistic observation, systematic observation, case studies, archival research, and meta-analysis to research these effects?

Key Terms

archival research, p. 188

case study, p. 185

coding, p. 184

concealment, p. 178

effect size, p. 189

event sampling, p. 181

file-drawer problem, p. 191

habituation, p. 179

meta-analysis, p. 189

moderating variable, p. 190

naturalistic observation, p. 176

observational methods, p. 176

participant observation, p. 181

reactivity, p. 178

specimen record, p. 185

structured observation, p. 183

time sampling, p. 181

Research over Age and Time

10

Chapter Contents

INSIDE RESEARCH: Erin Barker

I wrote my very first university term paper in introductory psychology on the topic of stress. Fast forward to today, and I'm still learning and writing about stress. There are several research method paradigms used to study how people respond when they encounter a stressor. For example, experimental designs are often used in stress research. In those studies, different types or different levels of a stressor are administered to different groups of participants, typically in a controlled laboratory setting where random assignment to conditions has been employed. Then, physiological and psychological responses to the stressors may be measured and compared, for example.

Associate professor of developmental psychology, Department of Psychology, Concordia University

My research on stress follows a different paradigm. My graduate and postdoctoral training followed a lifespan development perspective, where the focus is on describing and explaining patterns of change—how people grow or decline—across different phases or stages of the life course. The lifespan development perspective intersects with other subfields of psychology to examine the development of neurological, cognitive, psychological, and social processes and psychopathology over time.

In my research I use developmental designs and methods to study stress. The life course is marked by tasks, transitions, and turning points that can be challenging, stressful, and can compromise well-being if

continued

coping resources are not adequate. To understand how developmental experiences contribute to stress, I use repeated measures survey designs (e.g., longitudinal designs, daily diary designs) to assess the stressors people experience and their psychological reactions to those experiences during developmental transitions. In my surveys I often assess subjective reports of stress and emotional states, the coping strategies the people use to manage their emotions and stress, social support network size and quality, personality and character strengths, and well-being and mental health. When we ask people to report on their stressors and their responses on multiple occasions over time we can start to map out different patterns of experience during particular periods of the life course that may be more or less adaptive.

My main line of research focuses on stress experienced during the transition from adolescence to young adulthood, in particular for university students. Canadian youth have been enrolling in university programs at increasing rates; for many it has become a central part of the transition to adulthood. University students, as a group, experience high levels of stress, but large proportions of students also report moderate to high levels of life satisfaction and happiness. Emotional well-being tends to improve across the transition to adulthood, but prevalence rates of mental health problems, like depression, also peak during this life course stage. My research program uses repeated survey measurements of stress, coping, and emotional well-being to better understand who, when, and why young people experience stress during this transition and the implications of these experiences for well-being and mental health. I conduct much of this work in collaboration with Dr. Andrea Howard, who works in the Department of Psychology at Carleton University in Ottawa.

The lifespan development approach provides a naturalistic complement to laboratory-based research on stress. It is important to employ different types of research frameworks to the same general topic because each approach has its strengths and limitations with respect to conclusions that can be drawn. For example, when using survey designs it can be challenging—and sometimes impossible—to disentangle cause-and-effect relationships, but you can identify temporal ordering or cascading patterns that can lend insight into when and why different people experience different levels of stress.

Erin Barker is a developmental psychologist who uses longitudinal and daily diary repeated measures survey data to differentiate patterns of well-being in the context of stressful life course experiences.

Research Focus: Stress, coping, well-being, and mental health during the transition to adulthood and within the university context

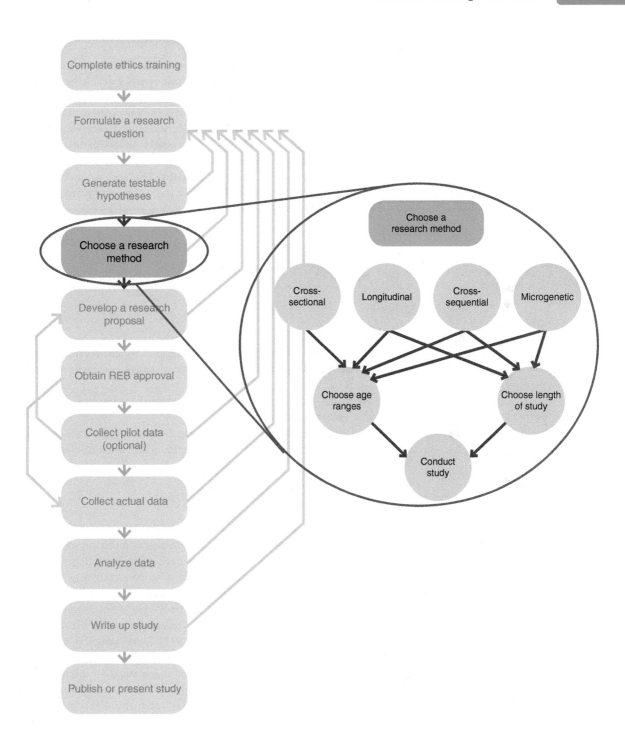

Chapter Abstract

In this chapter, we discuss a variety of designs to study the behaviours and psychological processes of human beings over time and throughout the lifespan. First, we define the terms commonly used in this type of psychological research: development, maturation, aging, and change over time. Then, we present and explore the methods most commonly used to examine these phenomena: cross-sectional, longitudinal, cross-sequential, and microgenetic studies. We include a discussion of issues and problems that must be addressed with each of these designs, as well as their strengths and weaknesses. Last, we examine large, well-known longitudinal studies, such as the Canadian Longitudinal Study on Aging and the CHILD project, and the controversial yet undeniably important study of Lewis Terman on the outcomes of gifted children.

LEARNING OBJECTIVES

By the end of this chapter, you should be able to:

- Distinguish between development, maturation, aging, and change over time.
- Compare cross-sectional, longitudinal, cross-sequential, and microgenetic research designs.
- Discuss the advantages and disadvantages of cross-sectional, longitudinal, cross-sequential, and microgenetic research designs.
- Discuss challenges of longitudinal designs related to determining the cause of change, finding equivalent measures across ages, and determining the sampling interval.

DEFINING DEVELOPMENTAL TERMS

development
Multidirectional changes that occur over the lifespan (e.g., from conception through old age).

Although many scientists use the word **development** as an umbrella term to describe any research that studies humans over time, it is only one of several relevant terms, which also include aging, change over time, maturation, and learning. Each differs in subtle yet important ways and applies to specific research designs. Because these terms actually signify different concepts, it is important to move past use of the term "development" as a catch-all.

Development refers to changes that occur over the entire lifespan, from conception to old age. These developmental changes are multidirectional, meaning they can occur in both a positive (gains) and negative (losses) direction (Berger, 2011). Development is often used to describe changes in such areas as motor skills, language, and cognition.

maturation Growth and other changes in the body and brain that are associated with underlying genetic information.

Although some scientists use the terms development and maturation interchangeably, **maturation** refers to growth and other changes in the body and brain that are associated with underlying genetic information. In this sense, maturation is "automatic" and related to genes. In contrast, development encompasses both maturation *and* an individual's life experiences. As we have gained increasingly sophisticated knowledge of the interaction of genes and experiences (Caspi, Hariri, Holmes, Uher, & Moffitt, 2010; Champagne & Mashoodh, 2009; Manuck & McCaffery, 2014; Taylor & Kim-Cohen, 2007), researchers have come to realize that maturation and experience interact in complex ways, influencing one another and leading to psychological and behavioural changes. Indeed, Champagne and Mashoodh (2009) argue that a critical feature of development is the dynamic interaction between genes and environments.

Aging refers specifically to changes, both positive and negative, associated with the latter part of the lifespan (e.g., from adulthood to death). For example, researchers have studied declines in language function in older adults (e.g., Burke & Shafto, 2004). However, an increasing number of researchers are studying the potential benefits of aging, with considerable work being done on "resilient aging" (Aldwin & Igarashi, 2015; see "Media Matters: An Aging and Able Workforce"), as well as variables that may ameliorate some of the negative impacts of aging. Considerable research has shown that speaking more than one language may improve cognition and delay the onset of dementia in older adults (Bak, Nissan, Allerhand, & Deary, 2014; Bialystok, Craik, & Freedman, 2007). Other researchers have examined the positive impact of activity and exercise on the cognitive function of older adults (e.g., Colcombe & Kramer, 2003).

aging Changes, both positive and negative, associated with the latter part of the lifespan (e.g., from adulthood to death).

MEDIA MATTERS

An Aging and Able Workforce

Although millions of baby boomers turned 65 in 2011—the first members of that iconic generation to move into retirement age—many of them have no intention of stopping work anytime soon. For one thing, the recession of 2008–9 disproportionately affected older individuals who were in their prime earning years, plunging many of them into long-term unemployment and damaging their financial prospects for retirement, although the impact on Canadians was less than that of their American counterparts (Crowley, Clemens, & Veldhuis, 2010; Tugend, 2013; Winerip, 2013). For another, many boomers are healthier and more active than previous generations, and they want to continue working through their sixties and beyond. One survey found that 62 per cent of Canadians between the ages of 50 and 64 plan to continue working after "retirement" age (Gatehouse, 2010).

Negative stereotypes about aging workers in a youth-oriented culture certainly do not help their chances as they vie for coveted jobs in a global marketplace. Television shows, movies, and advertising are full of jokes and messages about older workers as cognitively and physically slower, technophobic, and resistant to change (Scheve & Venzon, 2015). According to David Foot, a professor at the University of Toronto, and Rosemary Venne, a professor at the university of Saskatchewan, older workers "often desire transitional or partial retirement." Even though the economy could benefit from these workers, employers are not as accepting of these older workers, and "age discrimination is the most socially accepted form of prejudice" (Crawley, 2019).

New developmental research, however, is upending some of those assumptions and revealing the benefits of aging to the workplace. It turns out that some traits actually improve with age. According to Susan Fiske, a psychology professor at Princeton University, older workers tend to be more knowledgeable, reliable, and emotionally stable than younger employees and can "stand back and see the big picture" (Sleek, 2013).

People in middle age and beyond also show higher levels of "crystallized" intelligence (as opposed to "fluid" intelligence, which peaks in a person's twenties). People acquire crystallized intelligence through experience and education and improve in areas such as verbal ability, inductive reasoning, and judgment. Rather than a direct product of genetics, crystallized intelligence depends more on factors such as personality, motivation, opportunity, and culture (Cohen, 2012).

change over time
A general way to capture temporal changes, particularly changes brought about by learning and experience.

Change over time is a more general way to capture temporal changes, particularly changes brought about by learning and experience. Although psychologists have long debated how to distinguish development from **learning** (Piaget, 1964/1997; Vygotsky, 1978; and many more), the term learning is often restricted to changes tied to specific instruction or experiences over relatively short periods of time. Development, in contrast, is thought to be a universal process impacting all members of a species.

learning Changes tied to specific instruction or experiences over relatively short periods of time.

DESIGNS TO STUDY CHANGE OVER AGE AND TIME

Determining the causes of underlying differences between individuals of different ages, or in the same individuals assessed at different points over their lifespans, makes developmental research both interesting and challenging. These challenges have led to the creation of a number of specific research designs: cross-sectional, longitudinal, cross-sequential, and microgenetic.

Cross-Sectional Designs

cross-sectional research designs The most common types of studies across age and time, involving simultaneously comparing a number of different age groups.

Cross-sectional research designs are the most common types of studies across age and time and involve simultaneously comparing two or more different age groups. Suppose you wanted to conduct an educational research study to assess Grade 3 and Grade 9 students in reading and mathematics (see Figure 10.1). Before determining which age groups to study and the spacing between the ages, you should consider results from past research, theoretical arguments about the timing and process of developmental change, and your specific research question. In other words, you should choose the ages for your design based on specific questions that you are trying to address about those particular ages. In any written report of your research you will need to justify your choice of age groups.

Advantages of Cross-Sectional Designs.   Cross-sectional designs enable researchers to gather information about different age groups in a short period of time. For instance, researchers conducting cross-sectional studies in schools may be able to collect all the data in

FIGURE 10.1   An example of a cross-sectional design. In this example, researchers might compare the performance of children in two separate classrooms, studied at the same point in time, on reading and math skills.

a single day by having participants from different grades complete a survey. This approach uses fewer resources and results in lower overall costs.

Cross-sectional research also offers an excellent way to discover and document the age-related differences associated with certain behaviours. In a relatively short period of time, you can potentially identify ages at which an important change in behaviour occurs (e.g., a toddler saying her first word) or document the increase or decrease in a behaviour of interest (e.g., an improvement or decline in a cognitive skill). For this reason, cross-sectional designs are often useful for determining transition points in development, identifying standard behaviour at certain ages, and tracking trends in development or aging. Determining standard or normative levels of behaviours is also essential for developing assessments that can help to determine how a child performs compared with peers of the same age.

Disadvantages of Cross-Sectional Designs.   Although cross-sectional designs are excellent for revealing differences among different age groups, in general they do not identify the underlying causes of differences. For example, imagine we find that Grade 5 students perform significantly higher than Grade 3 students on a mathematics test. We cannot tell what is causing this difference: age, maturation, specific learning experiences, or a combination of all of these. It could also be a cohort effect, the result of experiences that impact an entire group of individuals. An example of a cohort effect is the start of compulsory education or the invention of smartphones. Individuals who lived through these events will think or behave differently than those who were born at some other time. In the mathematics test example, we might expect a cohort difference for Grade 1 and 4 students growing up in the age of smartphones, all of which have built-in calculators, when compared to Grade 1 and 4 students from an earlier generation who did not have access to smartphones with embedded calculators.

Another difficulty posed by cross-sectional designs is verifying that the methods are equally good at measuring the behaviour of interest for the different age groups in the sample, also known as equivalent measures (to be discussed at greater length later in this chapter). For many standardized measures of cognitive or language behaviour, the assessments are pretested (normed) to be appropriate for use with individuals in a particular age range. Use of the assessment outside of that range is likely to lead to floor or ceiling effects (see Chapter 7).

Finally, cross-sectional designs tend to underestimate variability within an age group, which can be quite large, to characterize differences between groups. By focusing on differences between age groups, achievements obtained at specific ages gain greater status than they likely deserve. Examples are motor milestones such as crawling and walking, which are often displayed in developmental textbooks as happening at 9 months and 12 months, respectively. This leads the reader to assume that this is the normal pattern of development, but it ignores or obscures the large amount of variability found among children of the same age in both the timing and the pattern of crawling or walking.

Longitudinal Research Designs

Longitudinal research designs track groups of participants over a period of time with two or more assessments of the same individuals at different times. Figure 10.2 shows an example of five different individuals studied at three different time points. Longitudinal studies can be of any length. Researchers often use short-term longitudinal studies to study young infants, who undergo rapid changes in a short time (e.g., weeks or months). However, most longitudinal studies cover longer time periods, often several years or, in rare cases, even decades. Although

cohort effect
Differences that emerge between different age groups resulting from shared characteristics or experiences that impact an entire group of individuals (e.g., the invention of smartphones).

equivalent measures
Methods that are equally good at measuring a behaviour of interest for different age groups in a sample.

longitudinal research designs Designs that track groups of participants over a period of time with two or more assessments of the same individuals at different times.

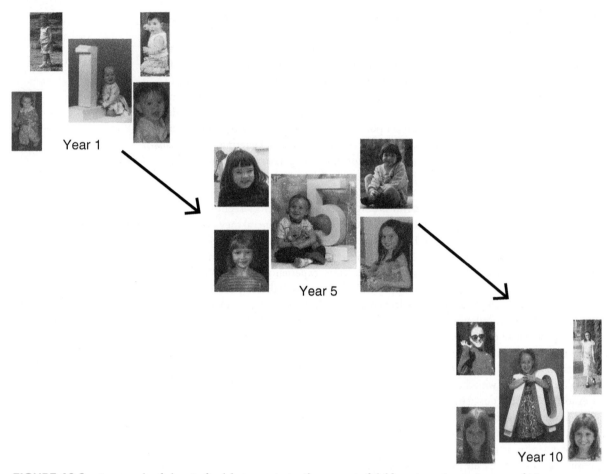

FIGURE 10.2   An example of a longitudinal design capturing the same set of children at ages 1 year, 5 years, and 10 years.

it was not a formal academic study, the highly acclaimed 2014 film *Boyhood* took this longitudinal approach in telling the story of Mason. Filming began when the actor was 6 years old and continued at intervals over the next 12 years.

The longest-running longitudinal study was started in 1922 by Lewis Terman (Terman, 1925, 1930, 1947). Terman advocated eugenics, which was a movement in the early part of the tewntieth century that claimed certain people were genetically superior to others. Eugenics sought to improve humans through selective breeding and refinement of the gene pool. For this reason, Terman's work is highly controversial, although the longitudinal nature of his data still has great value.

Terman's goal was to examine the development of highly gifted individuals over their entire lifespans in the hope of dispelling a belief that was common at the time—namely, that gifted children were less healthy than their non-gifted counterparts. He collected data from more than 1,500 children between the ages of 8 and 16 living in California who scored 135 or higher on his intelligence test (the Stanford–Binet intelligence test). Every 5 to 10 years, Terman collected a massive amount of data from participants, including surveys completed by parents, teachers, the participants, and their spouses; one-on-one interviews; a battery of IQ tests;

assessments of health and physical and emotional development; and home, family, school, and employment histories.

Although Terman's study helped convince the general public that intelligent children could be healthy and happy, it did not find that high intelligence leads directly to success (Leslie, 2000). Two-thirds of the participants (whom he affectionately called "Termites") earned bachelor's degrees, which was 10 times the national average at the time. They were also more likely to complete graduate degrees than the general population: 97 earned Ph.D.s, 57 earned MDs, and 92 became attorneys. But in other aspects, participants appeared vulnerable to the same troubles afflicting their peers. They died by suicide, developed alcohol use disorders, and got divorced at the same rates as non-Termites. One participant went to prison, and a few were arrested (Leslie, 2000).

Notable Canadian longitudinal studies include the Canadian Longitudinal Study on Aging (Raina et al., 2013) and the Canadian Healthy Infant Longitudinal Development (CHILD) Study (www.childstudy.ca). The Canadian Longitudinal Study on Aging recruited over 50,000 men and women between 2010 and 2015 who ranged in age from 45 to 85 when recruited. The goal is to follow these participants until 2033, or death, and track their patterns of aging. Data collection occurs every three years and includes measures of health and aging, with 30,000 participants also undergoing additional in-depth examinations, including blood and urine samples. Key questions being addressed in this study are (1) identifying determinants of change (biological, physical, psychological, and social) across time and ages, (2) identifying the importance of genetic and epigenetic factors in the process of aging, (3) exploring why some people experience healthy aging and others do not, and (4) identifying patterns in mid-life cognitive function that may predict dementia (Raina et al., 2013). As of 2018, over 100 projects have been approved using this data set (www.clsa-elcv.ca).

The CHILD project is a prospective longitudinal birth cohort study that was started in 2008. The study recruited over 3,500 pregnant women who gave birth between 2009 and 2012 in Vancouver, Edmonton, Winnipeg, and Toronto. These children and their parents were followed until the child was at least five years of age, and many continue to participate in the study. The primary goal of the project is to investigate how genes and the environment interact to cause atopic diseases, including asthma, allergies, allergic rhinitis, and eczema. The study involves collecting a series of environmental and health questionnaires, clinical measures, and biological samples. Key findings from this study have included demonstrating that infants who are breastfed longer are at a lower risk for asthma (Azad et al., 2017) and exposure to cats and dogs during early life can reduce the risk of allergies and obesity (Tun et al., 2017).

Advantages of Longitudinal Designs.   Researchers studying change over time often argue that more longitudinal research should be done. They say that longitudinal research provides the only way to truly understand the process of change in individuals, because they track change within the same individuals over a period of time. Cross-sectional designs, although they are convenient, can only infer such change based on comparisons of different groups of individuals.

Another advantage of this method is that it can yield a considerable amount of data that enable researchers to explore a wide variety of different research questions—even ones that were not part of the original study. For example, the Terman study, mentioned previously, led to more than 100 journal articles and many books on numerous topics.

Disadvantages of Longitudinal Designs.   Longitudinal designs pose a number of challenges. Probably the biggest obstacle for using a longitudinal design is the cost in time and

series of repeated assessments. Figure 10.3 provides a simplified version of this design. The original cross-section comprises four groups (2, 4, 6, and 8 year olds); each of these groups is measured three times, with a two-year interval between assessments, which are labelled Time 2 and Time 3. Sometimes researchers add samples during later assessment to (1) increase their sample size and (2) study the effects of time on the same-age children—to see, for example, whether children of a particular age (e.g., preschoolers) look similar to one another even if they were born a few years apart. In Figure 10.3, additional groups of 2 year olds are brought in at Time 2 and Time 3 (Groups 1A and 1B). These repeated periods of data collec-tion are often referred to as **waves**. At Time 3, the original 2 year olds are now 6, and the 8 year olds are now 12. Over four years (Time 1 to Time 3), the researchers collected data on chil-dren from ages 2 to 12.

waves Repeated periods of data collection in a cross-sequential design.

Advantages of Cross-Sequential Designs.

Mixing cross-sectional and longitudi-nal designs in a single study enables the researcher to study a wider age range in a shorter time period than traditional longitudinal designs. The additional groups of children enable re-searchers to examine whether children of the same age provide similar data even when the data are collected at different time points. If you trace up the grey diagonal lines in Figure 10.3, you will see that at each wave of data there is a group of 2 year olds, as well as groups of 4, 6,

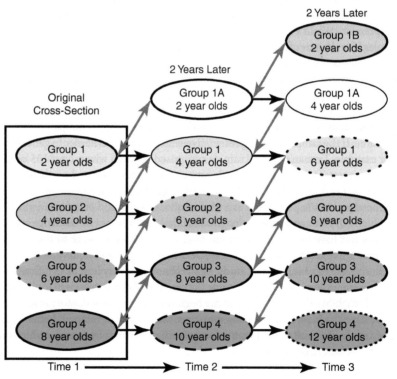

FIGURE 10.3   Example of a cross-sequential design. Black lines and shapes indicate the same groups of children over time. Grey double-sided arrows and similar outlines around the ovals indicate comparisons of same-age children at two or more different time periods to explore possible cohort effects. Columns represent cross-sections collected at a single time point.

and 8 year olds. If the data collected from one age group differ from that collected for the same age group at a different wave, it suggests there is a cohort effect and the different cohorts of the same age are distinctive. Ideally, researchers hope that measurements from the same age group collected at different points in time are similar, so they can be potentially combined in some of the data analyses. In this way, researchers can explicitly test for cohort effects, something that is not possible in a traditional longitudinal design.

Disadvantages of Cross-Sequential Designs.   Cross-sequential designs share many of the same disadvantages as longitudinal designs with respect to issues of repeated testing, equivalent measures, and susceptibility to attrition. They are also costly to conduct in terms of time and resources. Yet they usually cost less than a longitudinal study covering the same age range. In addition, most researchers would argue that, when they are possible to implement, the advantages of cross-sequential designs far outweigh the disadvantages.

Microgenetic Designs

The final research design pertinent to change over time is referred to as the **microgenetic design** (Siegler, 2006; Siegler & Crowley, 1991). The overall goal of this design is to observe changes as they occur and attempt to understand the process involved in any observed changes. This focus on the specific process of change is what makes this design different from longitudinal and cross-sectional designs, which focus on the product of change. The major aspects of the microgenetic design include focusing on a key **transition point** or dramatic shift in the behaviour of interest (Granott & Parziale, 2002). In developmental research, transition points could focus on behaviours such as the shift from crawling to walking (Karasik, Tamis-LeMonda, & Adolph, 2011), acquisition of the first few words (MacWhinney, 1987), or attainment of new strategies for adding or subtracting numbers (Siegler & Jenkins, 1989).

Researchers employing a microgenetic design conduct a large number of closely spaced observations that begin prior to the transition point and then continue until the behaviour has stabilized after the transition point. For example, a researcher interested in the transition from crawling to walking would start with determining the possible transition point. In this case, because past researchers have documented the timing of key motor milestones, the researcher could merely consult an earlier study of this transition. The World Health Organization has been collecting these data as part of a Multicentre Growth Reference Study (WHO Multicentre Growth Reference Study Group, 2006). This particular transition point occurs at approximately one year of age. The researchers then define a time window around this point, starting at an age where no child being observed is yet walking and ending at an age where all the children being observed are walking. The Multicentre Growth Reference Study suggests that the window of walking independently occurs between 8 and 18 months. In this time window, the researcher would conduct frequent observations of motor behaviour that might be related to the start of independent walking. Adolph and Robinson (2011) advocate for a sampling frequency as often as once a day, although this is rarely feasible for any study involving a relatively large time window.

Seigler and Crowley (1991) suggest that three characteristics define the microgenetic approach: (1) a focus on a key transition in behaviour; (2) densely packed observations that follow the behaviour before, during, and after the period of developmental change; and (3) a focused analysis of the behaviour that documents the processes involved in the change.

microgenetic design
An approach that attempts to observe changes as they occur and to understand the process involved in any observed changes by focusing on a key transition point or dramatic shift in the behaviour of interest.

transition point The point in development where key changes occur; often the focus of microgenetic designs.

Advantages of Microgenetic Methods. A key advantage of the microgenetic approach is that it can provide new and important insights about the processes that lead to change. This in turn can provide information that may be used to accelerate transitions (e.g., the acquisition of new addition strategies), identify behaviours that indicate the transition is imminent, and specify places where interventions can be implemented for individuals having difficulty making the transition. A growing number of researchers (Adolph & Robinson, 2011; Siegler, 2006) suggest that the microgenetic approach offers the best way of capturing both quantitative and qualitative aspects of behavioural change.

A second advantage of this approach is that it enables researchers to examine transitions that occur infrequently in detail. For example, children make the transition to walking only once, acquire their first word once, and learn to ride a bicycle once. Over the normal life course, these behaviours are not forgotten. Capturing these transitions can only really be done using microgenetic methods.

Disadvantages of Microgenetic Methods. Microgenetic studies share some of the same disadvantages as longitudinal and cross-sequential designs with respect to the issues of repeated testing and susceptibility to attrition. In addition, microgenetic methods are difficult and time consuming to conduct (Siegler & Crowley, 1991). Determining precise transition points in many behaviours is also challenging. Even with the transition to walking, the age range during which children achieve independent walking is quite large, and this and most other behaviours exhibit considerable variability in onset (Rosengren, 2002; Siegler, 2007). Thus, a researcher wanting to be sure that they capture the transition point and stable periods before the transition might need to start collecting data around 6 months of age and continue to as long as 19 or 20 months of age.

Most microgenetic studies involve a relatively small number of participants. This is primarily because of the limitations of making a larger number of observations in a relatively small time period. However, using relatively small samples means that the sample may not be representative of the larger population of children. Thus, another disadvantage is that microgenetic research may not be generalizable. Researchers using this approach generally focus on behaviours that are more or less universal (e.g., transition to walking, acquisition of first words) so that their findings are likely to be relevant and meaningful. The relatively small sample size also affects how the data can be analyzed. In particular, the small sample and densely packed observations can make it difficult to use traditional statistical approaches.

ADDITIONAL CHALLENGES TO CONSIDER IN DEVELOPMENTAL DESIGNS

The research designs used to study change over time are more challenging than some of the other designs discussed in this book, in part because of the problems that researchers must consider as they design their research study. Although we have discussed a number of issues related to specific designs, several other issues are relevant for all of the designs discussed in this chapter. These include (1) determining the cause of any observed changes, (2) determining whether measures used at different times or for different ages are equivalent, and (3) determining the appropriate sample interval.

Determining the Underlying Cause of Changes

One of the main reasons researchers examine changes in behaviour over time is to uncover what factors play the most important role in causing observed changes. Unfortunately, this is not an easy task, because changes can be a result of age, maturation, learning, specific experiences, and cohort effects. Many of these factors also interact in a complex manner, as discussed previously with respect to interactions between genes and the environment.

Developmental changes are thought to be driven by underlying genetic factors that operate at both the species and the individual levels. For example, genes guide the universal emergence of crawling, walking, and running in developing humans, but individual factors and the specific environments in which the child grows up influence when and how these changes happen (Berger & Adolph, 2007). For example, in some cultures infants walk at earlier or later ages because of differences in parenting practices (Dennis, 1940; Hess, Kashigawa, Price, & Dickinson, 1980). Other researchers have shown that infants learn through specific experiences exploring the environment, such as finding the most efficient manner of getting from one place to another (Adolph, Robinson, Young, & Gill-Alvarez, 2008). It can be highly challenging to tease apart age, maturation, or learning as the causes of change. Researchers who succeed in separating these influences do so using complex (cross-sequential) designs and sophisticated statistics and by collecting the right kinds of data.

One additional factor that may lead to differences between individuals of different ages is the cohort effect. Experiencing the first generation of smartphones (or, in the case of your authors, the very first video game) is a different and more striking event than growing up in a generation that has never experienced life without them. Cohort differences are also associated with different generations such as baby boomers, generation Xers, or millennials. Again, the idea is that members of these different cohorts have shared a set of universal experiences that make them think and behave differently from members of other generations.

Finding Equivalent Measures

It would be ideal if developmental researchers could use a single assessment to measure a behaviour of individuals of different ages. But a particular assessment that works best for toddlers may not work so well for teenagers. Young children cannot perform well on tasks that require language skills, whereas older children find tasks designed for younger children too easy. This problem resembles the floor and ceiling effects discussed in Chapter 7. Tasks that are at the correct level for one age group are often too easy (ceiling effect) or too difficult (floor effect) for another age group. One solution for this challenge is to test measures across different ages to find those that provide a reasonable assessment across all different ages. The National Institutes of Health have created a set of assessments or toolboxes that can be used to study various behaviours over the age range of 3 to 85 years (Zelazo & Bauer, 2013).

A tangible example of creating developmentally appropriate assessments can be found in the work of Rovee-Collier (1999). In her work on memory in young children, she begins with a task for three-month-old infants involving a mobile in a crib; the task makes use of classical conditioning to measure memory at this very young age. However, to trace the development of memory from infancy to toddlerhood, Rovee-Collier develops a parallel but different memory task to acknowledge the limitation that toddlers are no longer stimulated by mobiles. Her older (toddler) participants instead learn how to operate a train by pressing a button.

The mobile and train tasks are equivalent measures of memory, but they are attuned to the developmental skills and interests of the participants at different ages.

Determining the Appropriate Sampling Interval

sampling interval The amount of time elapsed between different data collection points in a developmental study.

A final issue confronting researchers examining change over time is choosing an appropriate sampling interval. By its very nature, research on development and aging requires that sampling occur at different ages or different time points, but how frequent should these sampling periods be? As Adolph and Robinson (2011) discuss, most researchers opt for relatively large spacing between ages or repeated assessments.

The risk of inadequate sampling is that the pattern of change over time may be mischaracterized, leading to theories built on faulty data (Adolph & Robinson, 2011). As Adolph and Robinson point out, large sampling intervals can make uncovering important relationships difficult (Boker & Nesselroade, 2002), can lead researchers to miss important events or transitions (Collins & Graham, 2002), and can lead researchers to underestimate variability in the behaviour of interest (Siegler, 2006). Large gaps in sampled participants' ages can also make modelling the pattern of change or distinguishing between a variety of different potential trajectories of change difficult (Adolph et al., 2008). For example, if you are studying the development of theory of mind (how children come to understand that other people have thoughts and feelings that differ from their own) and you wait an entire year between measurements, you might be left with the impression that children's theory of mind dramatically emerges, like flipping on a light switch. Theory of mind actually seems to emerge for most children sometime between the ages of three and four. A longitudinal study that involves multiple measurements between the ages of three and four is more likely to reveal a pattern of change that shows subtle, incremental shifts, rather than a single dramatic jump.

Adolph and Robinson (2011) advocate frequent longitudinal sampling, arguing for a default sampling rate involving daily summaries for each 24-hour period. The appropriateness of this technique depends on the particular age of the participant (it may be most useful for studying periods of rapid change, such as those found in infancy) and the particular behaviour of interest.

They base this decision on a study (Adolph et al., 2008) that collected summaries of 32 motor skills—including rolling, crawling, sitting, and walking—in young infants. They tracked 11 infants from birth until 17 months of age. They were able to use the data to examine how patterns of development would look if they had used different sampling rates (daily, every other day, every third day, etc.). They found that the patterns across and within children were highly variable, and that the daily summary approach yielded the best characterization of the data. Frequent sampling is expensive, but it yields a lot of data.

SUMMARY OF RESEARCH INVESTIGATING CHANGE OVER TIME

Although research studying change over time can be difficult to conduct, the designs discussed in this chapter can be useful for addressing research questions that focus on changes over the lifespan and processes that may cause these changes. Table 10.1 highlights the four designs discussed in this chapter—cross-sectional, longitudinal, cross-sequential, and microgenetic—providing a summary of some of the advantages and disadvantages of each approach.

Table 10.1   Advantages, disadvantages, and relative cost in time and money of different designs to measure change.

Design	Advantages			Disadvantages				Cost
	Good for documenting normative differences	Good for documenting factors influencing change	Problem of determining underlying cause of differences between Time 1 and Time 2	Problem of repeated testing	Problem of equivalent measures	Problem of attrition	Time/$
Cross-Sectional	X		XX				Fast/ Low $
Longitudinal		X		X	X	X	Slow/ High $
Cross-Sequential	X	X		X	X	X	Slow/ High $
Microgenetic		X		XX		X	Fast/ High $

PRACTICAL TIPS

Practical Tips for Doing Research over Age and Time

1. In the study of change over age and time, be clear on whether you are studying development, maturation, aging, or some combination of the three.

2. Weigh the benefits and drawbacks of different research designs: cross-sectional, longitudinal, cross-sequential, and microgenetic. When time and resources allow, consider combinations of these different methods.

3. When assessing underlying causes of change, be sure to consider all possible sources: age, maturation, learning, specific experiences, and cohort effects.

4. Explicitly test for order effects and use different versions of your assessment to combat the negative impact of repeated testing.

5. Be attentive to the problem of finding equivalent measures for different ages. Test measures across different ages.

6. Consider strategies to reduce attrition in longitudinal studies by devoting a substantial amount of research resources to recruitment and retention of participants.

7. Be thoughtful in choosing an appropriate sample interval in your study of change over age and time. The choice of spacing between ages or repeated assessments should be dictated by the research question and appropriate use of theory.

CHAPTER SUMMARY

Psychological research over age and time is a far richer, more rewarding, and more challenging area than its more commonly used name—developmental psychology—suggests. Research over age and time encompasses the study of the complex processes of maturation, learning, change over time, and aging. Researchers can choose from four methods to investigate questions in this area: cross-sectional, longitudinal, cross-sequential, and microgenetic designs.

Cross-sectional studies are the most popular because they enable researchers to simultaneously assess several different age groups and, in doing so, discover and document age-related differences in behaviour. Longitudinal studies track participants over a period of time, assessing individuals at least twice at different times. Data from previous longitudinal studies, such as the Canadian Longitudinal Study on Aging, can serve as a tremendous resource for researchers trying to answer new questions. Cross-sequential designs combine aspects of cross-sectional and longitudinal designs. They enable researchers to study a wider age range in a shorter amount of time than traditional longitudinal designs. Researchers using microgenetic studies capture changes as they occur by conducting many closely spaced observations on key transition points, for example, as infants shift from crawling to walking.

Because of its complexity, research over age and time presents some challenges, most notably determining the underlying cause of observed changes, assessing the impact of repeated testing on participants' responses, determining equivalent measures, controlling attrition, and choosing an appropriate sample interval. In Chapter 11, we will turn our attention to statistics, specifically, how to transform raw data into understandable conclusions.

End-of-Chapter Exercises

1. Developmental researchers can select from a range of methodologies: cross-sectional, longitudinal, cross-sequential, and microgenetic. What sorts of factors should be considered when choosing from these different broad approaches in a developmental research design? Of these approaches, do you think some produce more valid and reliable findings than others? Considering Table 10.1, which set of advantages or disadvantages would you most heavily weigh in your decision about what methodology to use?

2. Dr. Rutherford studied skills in digital literacy among samples of 20, 40, and 60 year olds. The 20 year olds were found to be the most advanced in these skills, and the 60 year olds were the least advanced.
   a. What type of research design is this?
   b. Can you conclude that people become less digitally literate as they get older? Why or why not?
   c. Propose one of the other study designs discussed in this chapter as an alternative way to study this topic.

3. You are interested in studying the decline of functional fitness among older adults. Propose a longitudinal study to address this topic; include the duration and frequency of measurements in your answer. Discuss what problems you might face regarding attrition and how you could deal with these problems.

4. You are interested in studying moral development among children. Propose a cross-sectional and a cross-sequential study design to address this question. What are the advantages of each design? Which design would you use and why?

5. Do you agree with the argument put forth in this chapter that developmental research designs may face special challenges that go beyond other research designs (e.g., determining underlying causes of change, finding equivalent measures, determining the appropriate sampling interval)? What sort of impact do you think these unique challenges have on researchers interested in studying development?

Key Terms

aging, p. 199

attrition, p. 204

change over time, p. 200

cohort effect, p. 201

cross-sectional research designs, p. 200

cross-sequential research design, p. 205

development, p. 198

equivalent measures, p. 201

learning, p. 200

longitudinal research designs, p. 201

maturation, p. 198

microgenetic design, p. 207

sampling interval, p. 210

selective attrition, p. 204

transition point, p. 207

waves, p. 206

Analyzing Your Data I: An Overview

11

Chapter Contents

INSIDE RESEARCH: Kyle Matsuba

When I started graduate school, I really wasn't that interested in research. I was more interested in clinical-type work. My graduate supervisor at UBC thought I had research potential, and I took a risk that I would grow to like it. As it turned out, I love research! I love the theoretical and conceptual thinking that goes into research. I like the methodological design and statistical analyses that go with research, too. I find the statistical findings are often the rewards you get after all the work you put in at the front end.

Currently, I am involved in two main research projects. The first project is focused on children's development in northern Uganda. The area is a postwar, impoverished region, and this research focuses on understanding and fostering the social and emotional development of at-risk children, and the changes in well-being

Courtesy of Kyle Matsuba

Psychology instructor, Kwantlen Polytechnic University

continued

associated with participating in intervention programs. I have been working with the Goldie Hawn Foundation and the Mind and Life Institute to help children to develop mindfulness practices that allow them to better regulate their emotional state, gain social skills to navigate difficult situations, and improve their academic performance over time.

The second project focuses on environmental attitudes and behaviour. In light of the effects of global warming and increases in pollution, the question my colleagues and students are asking is, How do we get people to change their attitudes and behaviour so their actions are less harmful to the environment? Part of our approach has been to study environmental activists to gain enlightenment from them and how their personality and past experiences interact to influence their behaviours. Currently, we are considering how adolescent factors, such as personality, religion, and political ideology, predict environmental attitudes and behaviours in adulthood among a more normative sample. Finally, my honours student and I are also developing and evaluating a 30-day environmental campaign on our campus to raise awareness and change attitudes and behaviours regarding environmentally sustainable behaviours.

Kyle Matsuba is a developmental psychologist whose research focuses on the moral personality and identity of individuals engaged in extraordinary endeavours. His recent work has considered personality factors associated with prosocial behaviours, and he has co-authored a book on personality development in emerging adulthood. Kyle also spends part of his year in northern Uganda, training teachers to implement a mindfulness/social–emotional program in schools and assessing student outcomes on well-being measures.

Research Focus: Identifying the personality predictors associated with changes in prosocial behaviour and psychological well-being over time

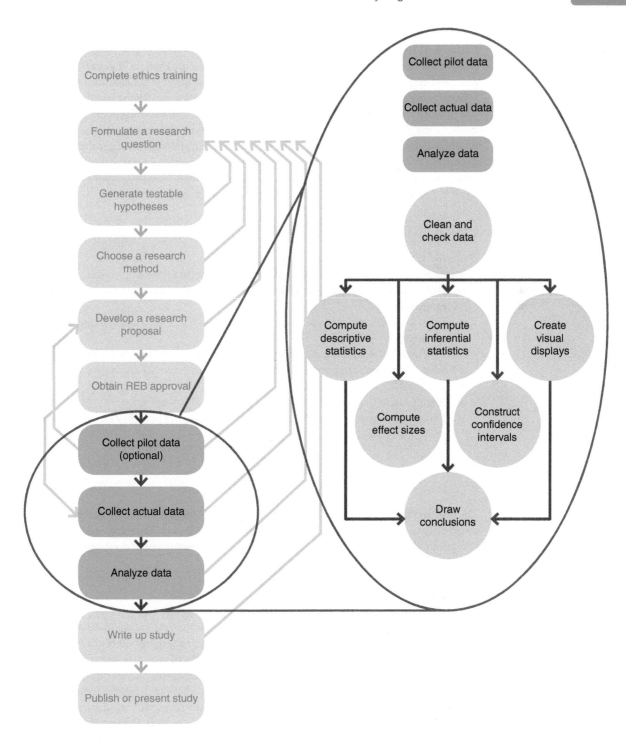

Chapter Abstract

In this chapter, we provide an overview of data analysis, discuss a variety of descriptive statistics and visual displays that will help you understand your data, describe the rationale for traditional inferential statistics, and examine issues related to performing analyses. With a well-designed study, you should know before you begin collecting data how your analysis will proceed. Your research question, the characteristics of your study design, and the type of data you collect will inform the type of analysis you will perform. This chapter is not meant to replace a more formal statistics class, but instead to serve as a review of statistical issues that are important for researchers to consider.

LEARNING OBJECTIVES

By the end of this chapter, you should be able to:

- Explain the purpose of checking and cleaning your data prior to analysis.
- Describe the difference between univariate and bivariate descriptive statistics, and give examples of each.
- Describe various ways to create graphical displays of your data and the kind of information each provides.
- Briefly describe the steps of null hypothesis significance testing (NHST) and indicate what conclusions can be made through NHST.
- Distinguish between a type I and a type II error.
- Identify and discuss some criticisms of NHST.
- Discuss what effect sizes and confidence intervals are and how they are more advantageous than *p* values.

THE STEPS OF DATA ANALYSIS

The process of transforming raw, unprocessed data into conclusions consists of the following steps: checking and cleaning your data; computing scale means; checking scale reliabilities; computing descriptive statistics, including effect sizes; creating visual displays; constructing confidence intervals; and computing inferential statistics.

Checking and Cleaning Data

data cleaning The process of checking that your measurements are complete and accurate prior to any analysis.

Data cleaning is the process of checking that your measurements are complete and accurate prior to any analysis. Although it is not the most exciting or engaging part of analyzing data, it is a critical step. If your data values are inaccurate, the results of your data analysis will be inaccurate and potentially misleading. As the saying goes, "Garbage in, garbage out."

Incorrect calculations and the failure to check data can have catastrophic results. In 1999, rocket scientists failed to convert data from English units to the metric system, leading them to overestimate the distance to Mars, and the $125 million Mars Orbiter crashed (Lloyd, 1999). In another example, known as the "London Whale" venture, financial analysts at JPMorgan Chase & Co. mistakenly divided by a sum instead of an average when modelling data. This mistake led to wildly wrong predictions (Kwak, 2013) and ultimately trading losses of more than $2 billion for JPMorgan Chase & Co. The lesson is that although it is boring, *check your data and your calculations and have someone else check them too!*

If responses are entered manually, it is *always* a good idea to have more than one person review the entered data for accuracy. One strategy is to have two different people enter the values and then have each check the other's work or have other people check the values. Data entry, particularly for larger data sets, can be tedious and mistakes are common.

When checking data, look for values that fall outside the allowed responses. For example, suppose you asked participants to respond to a series of questions using scale responses ranging from 1 to 7. Values less than 1 or greater than 7 would be invalid. And if only whole numbers are allowed, you should not see entries with decimal points.

Visual displays, such as graphs and other figures that show numerical data, can help in identifying unusual data points. Extreme values or values that do not match the pattern of the rest of your data are known as **outliers**. Outliers may be valid, but they may also arise as a result of data entry errors.

outliers Extreme values that do not match the pattern of the rest of the data.

Calculating Scale Means and Reliabilities

Any time that you are working with established multi-item scales or measures, you have to calculate the scale totals or means and check their reliability prior to their use in further analyses. Multi-item scales consist of a number of individual items, and they are generally intended to be combined into a single score or a set of smaller scores called subscales. For instance, the Health Education Learning Environment Survey (Rusticus, Wilson, Casiro, & Lovato, 2019) is a 35-item measure that assesses six dimensions of the learning environment. These six subscales represent the means of their associated items. One subscale, the Work–Life Balance subscale, consists of seven items (e.g., "I am able to maintain a healthy work–life balance") that are averaged to a single score representing overall perceptions of workload and stress.

Prior to calculating the subscales, it is important to determine whether any of the items need to be reverse scored. For the Work–Life Balance subscale mentioned above, the items are responded to on a five-point scale ranging from 1 (strongly disagree) to 5 (strongly agree). A higher score represents a more positive work–life balance. One of the items on this scale, "My workload is often overwhelming," needs to be reverse scored. If a respondent were to indicate a 2 for this item, indicating that they disagree that their workload is overwhelming, this indicates they have a positive perception of their work–life balance. Therefore, this item needs to be reversed so that it is contributing 4 points, and not 2 points, to the subscale total. For a five-point response format, for example, items should be reverse in the following way: 1 = 5, 2 = 4, 3 = 3, 4 = 2, and 5 = 1. All necessary items need to be reverse scored prior to calculating the subscale total or mean or checking the scale reliability.

Once all scales or subscales have been calculated, you should next check their internal consistency reliability (i.e., Cronbach's α; see Chapter 6). Most statistical packages will be able to calculate this for you. In general, it is recommended that a scale should have an alpha coefficient of .80 or higher, and no lower than .70, to indicate acceptable reliability (Furr & Bacharach, 2014). If you find that any of your scales have reliabilities lower than .70, you should be very cautious in using the scale in your analyses; a low reliability indicates there is substantial measurement error in your scale, which could invalidate the results of your analyses. One alternative option would be to consider removing some of the items to see if you can bring the reliability up, but you must also be mindful that if you change the original scale, this could impact the validity of the data as well.

Computing Descriptive Statistics

Descriptive statistics tell us about our samples. They are numerical values that summarize the data, whether it is a single item or a scale mean, and give a sense of the shape and spread of the data or the extent to which two variables are related to one another. We distinguish between **univariate statistics**, which are computed for one variable at a time, and **bivariate statistics**, which characterize the relationship between two variables.

Univariate descriptive statistics fall into the categories of central tendency, variability, or shape. Measures of **central tendency**—including **mean**, **median**, and **mode**—let us know the typical or average values of our data. **Variability** refers to how spread out, or variable, data values are in our sample. **Shape** refers to whether the data values are normally distributed, have a flat or sharp peak, or are **skewed** to one end or the other of the data **range**. Bivariate statistics measure the degree to which two variables vary with one another, for example, whether higher verbal GRE scores tend to be accompanied by higher quantitative GRE scores. Table 11.1 presents a summary of the most common descriptive statistics.

descriptive statistics Numerical values that summarize the data and give a sense of the shape and spread of the data or the extent to which two variables are related to one another.

univariate statistics Numerical values that summarize one variable at a time.

bivariate statistics Numerical values that characterize the relationship between two variables.

central tendency A description of the typical or average values of the data.

mean A measure of central tendency that is calculated by summing all of the values in a data set and then dividing by the number of values in the data set. Also called the arithmetic average.

median A measure of central tendency that is the middle value of all the data points; 50 per cent of the values are below the median and 50 per cent are above.

mode A measure of central tendency that is the most common value in the data set.

variability Refers to how spread out data values are in a sample.

Table 11.1   Common univariate and bivariate descriptive statistics.
UNIVARIATE DESCRIPTIVE STATISTICS
Central tendency
Mean—arithmetic average—sum of values divided by the number of values
Median—the middle value (or average of the two middle values for an even number of values)—50 per cent of the values are below the median and 50 per cent are above
Mode—the most common value
Variability
Range—the maximum value minus the minimum value
Variance—the average squared deviation of values from the mean value
Standard deviation—the average deviation of values from the mean; it is the square root of the variance
Shape
Skewness—a measure of how asymmetric a distribution of values is
Kurtosis—a measure of how flat or peaked a distribution is relative to the normal distribution
BIVARIATE DESCRIPTIVE STATISTICS
Association
Pearson correlation—measure of the strength of *linear* relationship between two interval or ratio variables
Spearman correlation—measure of the strength of relationship between two sets of ranks (ordinal data)
Phi (φ) coefficient and Cramer's V—correlation-like measures for the relationship between two categorical (nominal) variables

The three hypothetical data sets displayed in Table 11.2 will be used to illustrate the common univariate descriptive statistics and their associated visual displays. You also need to keep in mind which descriptive statistics are appropriate to calculate for the type of data that you have. For example, a mean and standard deviation can be calculated for an interval or ratio level variable, but not for a nominal or ordinal level variable. See Table 5.1 in Chapter 5 to review the four measurement scales.

The first two sets of data show hours of television watched per week for 30 students at each of two different schools. The third shows response times in a timed task for 20 individuals.

Table 11.3 presents descriptive statistics for the three sets of data. The means and medians give us a sense of the "centres" of the data sets—about 20 hours for both television-watching samples and 1,000 milliseconds for the response-time data. The **standard deviations** tell us how much, on average, the sample values tend to deviate from the mean values. We also see that the samples from the two schools have identical means and standard deviations, but diverge somewhat with respect to the median and its shape (skewness and **kurtosis**). These summary values start to give us a feel for the data, but it is difficult to get a full understanding from these numbers alone.

Creating Visual Displays for Univariate Descriptive Statistics

Presenting your data graphically can be extremely useful in helping you understand your data set and the story it tells. Commonly used graphical displays include histograms and box-and-whisker plots. These displays are particularly useful for helping you understand any interval or ratio level variables in your data set.

shape Refers to whether the data values are normally distributed, have a flat or sharp peak, or are skewed to one end or the other of the data range.

skewness A measure of how asymmetric a distribution of values is.

range The maximum value minus the minimum value in a data set.

standard deviation A measure of the variability of a data set that indicates how far, on average, data points deviate from the mean.

kurtosis A measure of the shape of a distribution that assesses how flat or peaked the distribution is relative to the normal distribution.

Table 11.2 Sample data sets to illustrate descriptive statistics and visual displays.

HOURS OF TELEVISION WATCHED PER WEEK						RESPONSE TIMES (MILLISECONDS)	
School 1			School 2				
21	35	24	16	30	15	763	861
31	19	25	14	15	29	690	881
12	29	33	10	13	17	2,511	1,100
17	16	11	28	12	22	1,813	833
30	6	26	7	11	29	541	632
21	22	27	29	24	0	1,045	891
18	22	21	13	26	30	1,039	1,133
3	0	22	28	8	35	999	941
10	27	13	14	19	14	772	750
19	17	8	20	26	31	962	1,197

Table 11.3   Descriptive statistics for the three data sets in Table 11.2.

	HOURS OF TELEVISION WATCHED PER WEEK		RESPONSE TIME (MILLISECONDS)
	School 1	School 2	
Number of participants	30	30	20
Mean	19.5	19.5	1,017.7
Median	21	18	916
Minimum	0	0	541
Maximum	35	35	2,511
Range	35	35	1,970
Variance	77.3	77.3	194,679
Standard deviation	8.8	8.8	441.2
Skewness	−0.38	−0.11	2.4
Kurtosis	−0.31	−0.86	6.9

histogram A visual display that uses bars to show the frequency of responses in the data set.

unimodal A data set with a single peak in the distribution of data.

bimodal A data set with two distinct peaks in the distribution of data.

box-and-whisker plots A visual display that uses a box to represent the interquartile range and whiskers to represent the minimum and maximum values of the data set. Often simply called box plots.

interquartile range The range of values from the 25th percentile to the 75th percentile; the middle 50 per cent of values.

Histograms.   Histograms show how many responses on a variable fall within predefined ranges of values, with these counts being represented by bars in a chart. Figure 11.1 presents histograms for the two television-watching samples. We learned from the descriptive statistics in Table 11.3 that the mean, range, and standard deviations for these two school data sets are identical. The histograms, however, reveal that the shapes of the two samples are quite different. The sample for school 1 shows a single peak—that is, it is unimodal—with more values in the lower 20s than anywhere else. In contrast, the school 2 values show two distinct peaks—bimodal—one in the lower teens and the other in the upper 20s. This relatively simple method of displaying data clearly tells us something about the samples we could not immediately see from the descriptive statistics alone.

Box-and-Whisker Plot.   Box-and-whisker plots (often simply called box plots) display a number of descriptive statistics in graphical form. Two slightly different variations of box-and-whisker plots are shown in Figure 11.2 for the response-time data of Table 11.2.

In the plot on the left, the minimum and maximum values are represented by the shorter horizontal bars (the "whiskers"), the median is represented by the heavy horizontal bar inside the box, and the box itself represents the interquartile range, meaning the range of values from the 25th percentile (the bottom of the box) to the 75th percentile (the top of the box). Although it is not always included, it is also instructive to include the mean, represented by the small filled squares in the plots.

The box-and-whisker plot on the left of Figure 11.2 reveals that the most extreme response times are not distributed symmetrically around the mean or median, with the maximum value being much farther than the minimum from the centre. A slightly different version of this

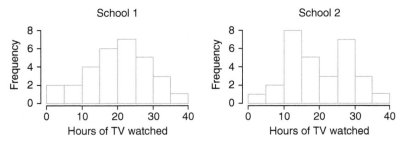

FIGURE 11.1   Histograms for television-watching data.

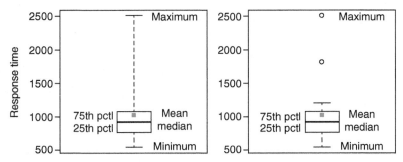

FIGURE 11.2   Box-and-whisker plots for response-time data.

box-and-whisker plot is shown on the right side of Figure 11.2. This version illustrates that the large spread of values above the central box in the plot on the left is caused by just two outliers. Rather than representing the absolute minimum and maximum values in this figure, the whiskers represent the most extreme values that fall within 1.5 times the interquartile range from the top and bottom of the box. Any values outside those limits are plotted as small circles and indicate outliers in your data.

The box-and-whisker plot allows you to see whether the data set is symmetric about the mean, in what direction non-symmetric data are skewed, how spread out the values are, how close the median and mean are to each other, and whether there are potential outliers in your data. Because of the amount of information conveyed in these plots, it is always a good idea to construct box-and-whisker plots for interval or ratio level variables.

Computing Bivariate Descriptive Statistics and Creating Visual Displays

Often, we are interested not only in describing single variables, but also in understanding how two variables are associated with one another. For example, if we collect high school and university grade point averages (GPAs) for a sample of undergraduate students, we might be interested in knowing whether high school GPA is a strong predictor of university GPA or whether university GPA is only weakly related to high school GPA. Similarly, we might want to know how responses to different attitudinal questions on a survey about social and political issues are related to one another.

Pearson's r A bivariate statistic that measures the extent of the linear relationship between two interval or ratio level variables and ranges from −1 to +1. The full name is the Pearson product-moment correlation coefficient.

A common bivariate statistic for interval/ratio data is the Pearson product-moment correlation coefficient (often simply called **Pearson's r**). Pearson's r measures the extent of the linear relationship between two interval or ratio level variables and ranges from −1 to +1; it provides information about both the direction and strength of the relationship. A positive correlation indicates that values change in the same direction; larger values on one variable tend to be associated with larger values on the other (similarly for smaller values). A negative correlation indicates that values change in opposite directions; larger values on one variable tend to be associated with smaller values on the other variable. The closer the value is to 1, the stronger the relationship between the two variables, or the more closely a change in one variable corresponds to a specific change in the other variable. A zero correlation indicates no linear relationship between the two variables.

scatterplot A method for simultaneously displaying the values for two or more variables that is useful for investigating the relationship between those variables.

Scatterplots.   A **scatterplot** simultaneously displays the values for two variables and is useful for investigating the relationship(s) between those variables. The values for hypothetical pairs of variables are displayed in the scatterplots in Figure 11.3, along with Pearson's r. Figure 11.3a presents two variables that are positively correlated with one another, with a Pearson's r of .80, indicating a relatively strong positive relationship. Figure 11.3b illustrates a negative relationship between the two variables, with a Pearson's r of −.80. Note that for both a and b, the relationships appear to be relatively linear.

Figure 11.3c displays two variables with a correlation of 0, indicating no relationship between them. In such a case, knowing whether X takes on a large or small value tells you nothing about whether the Y value is likely to be large or small.

Finally, the two variables represented in Figure 11.3d also exhibit a Pearson correlation of .0. There is clearly a relationship between the variables, although not a linear one; rather, it is an inverted-U relationship. A finding such as this underscores the importance of examining scatterplots to determine whether a relationship might exist between two variables that the

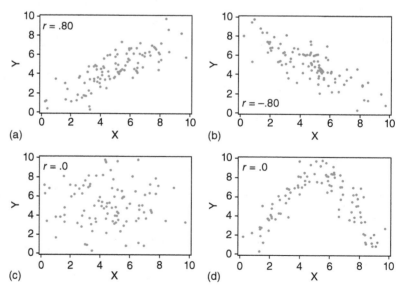

FIGURE 11.3   Scatterplots showing (a) positive, (b) negative, (c) no, and (d) non-linear relationships between pairs of variables.

Pearson correlation (a measure of linear association) might not reveal. Such non-linear relationships may be modelled with more sophisticated techniques.

Contingency Tables.   When we have measurements on each of two categorical/nominal level variables for a set of respondents, we can construct what is known as a contingency table or cross-tabulation. Suppose you sample 200 registered voters from city 1 and 150 from city 2 and ask them who they are likely to vote for in an upcoming political election. You might construct something like Table 11.4, in which each value in the table indicates the number of respondents who fall into the corresponding table cell. Of the 200 respondents in city 1, 75 intend to vote for candidate A and 105 for candidate B. Similarly, 75 of the city 2 respondents intend to vote for candidate A, but only 50 for candidate B. In addition to the actual counts, it is also instructive to include percentages in the table. This is especially true when the row (or column) totals are unequal. In this example, we have included row percentages (the percentage of respondents in each row who fall into the given cell). However, depending on your design and purpose, column percentages may also be appropriate.

The correlation-like measures **phi** (φ) and **Cramer's *V*** are used to summarize data in contingency tables. For 2 × 2 contingency tables (e.g., if we had two groups of participants and only two possible responses, such as "yes"/"no," the φ coefficient may be computed as a measure of association between group membership and response. For contingency tables with more than two categories for either variable, Cramer's *V* may be used. Like Pearson's *r*, φ ranges from −1 to +1, whereas Cramer's *V* ranges from 0 to 1.

Computing Effect Sizes

An important category of descriptive statistics is effect size, which we introduced in the section on power analysis in Chapter 5. According to Cohen (1990), "Effect-size measures include mean differences (raw or standardized), correlations and squared correlation of all kinds, odds ratios, kappas—whatever conveys the magnitude of the phenomenon of interest appropriate to the research context" (p. 1310). Cumming (2012) pithily describes an effect size as "simply the amount of something that might be of interest" (p. 34). An effect, then, is a primary measurement that you use to test your hypothesis, and the effect size is simply the magnitude of that effect. There are three general classes of effect size: raw effects, standardized effects, and correlation-like effects.

contingency table
A tabular display for representing categorical or nominal level data. Also called a cross-tabulation table.

phi (φ) A correlation-like measure used to summarize data in 2 × 2 contingency tables.

Cramer's *V* A correlation-like measure used to summarize data in contingency tables.

Table 11.4   Contingency table for hypothetical voter study.

NUMBER AND PERCENTAGE OF VOTERS PREFERRING EACH CANDIDATE					
	Candidate A	Candidate B	Someone Else	Undecided	Total
City 1	75	105	5	15	200
	37.5%	52.5%	2.5%	7.5%	100%
City 2	75	50	13	12	150
	50%	33.3%	8.7%	8%	100%

raw effects
Straightforward measures of effect size, such as the difference in the means for two samples. Also called unstandardized effects.

standardized effect
Adjusts the raw effect based on the amount of variability in the data.

Cohen's *d*
A standardized effect size that is defined as the raw effect divided by its standard deviation.

Raw Effects.   Raw effects (also called unstandardized effects) include common, straightforward measures such as the difference in the means for two samples. For example, if you observed the mean IQ scores for two different groups of respondents to be 101 and 113, the size of the raw effect of the difference of means would be 12.

Standardized Effects.   Standardized effects adjust the raw effect based on the amount of variability in your data. For example, a common measure of effect size for the independent-samples *t* test is Cohen's *d*, which is defined as the difference in the means for the two samples divided by a combined standard deviation for both samples. If we continue with the IQ example and find that the standard deviation for our data values is 15, then Cohen's *d* would be the raw effect of 12 divided by the standard deviation of 15 to give a standardized effect size of 0.8.

Standardized effects have two main advantages over raw effects. The first is that they can readily be compared across studies even when the specific measures used are on different scales. For example, Cohen's *d* computed on data using a measurement scale ranging from 0 to 20 can be meaningfully compared with Cohen's *d* computed on data from a 0 to 100 scale. This comparison would not make sense using raw effects. The second advantage of standardized effects is that they can be interpreted with respect to the standard deviation. For example, the effect size of 0.8 for our IQ example tells us that the two groups differ in mean IQ scores by a little less than one standard deviation.

Table 11.5 illustrates the difference between raw and standardized effect sizes. The mean scores for groups A and B are identical in the two scenarios, but the standard deviations are twice as large in scenario 2. The raw effect size of the difference between mean scores is 12 in both scenarios, but the standardized effect, which we compute by dividing the raw effect by the standard deviation, is twice as large in scenario 1 as in scenario 2.

Correlation-Like Effects.   These effects measure the association between two variables. Pearson's *r* falls into this category. We can also compute a point-biserial correlation—the correlation between a binary variable (one that takes on only two values such as "yes" or "no") and a continuous variable—as an effect size when comparing the means of two independent samples. To continue with our IQ example, if we assign a numerical value of 0 to all respondents in the first of our two groups and a 1 to all respondents in the second group, then the Pearson correlation of this 0/1 group variable with the continuous IQ score variable is a point-biserial correlation.

point-biserial correlation A measure that describes the degree to which a binary variable (e.g., yes/no) relates to a continuous variable.

Table 11.5   Illustration of the difference between raw and standardized effects.

	SCENARIO 1		SCENARIO 2	
	Group A	Group B	Group A	Group B
Mean IQ score	101	113	101	113
Standard deviation	15	15	30	30
Raw effect	12		12	
Standardized effect (Cohen's *d*)	0.80		0.40	

Correlation-like measures such as eta squared (η^2) and omega squared (ω^2) may be computed with analysis of variance designs, where we have multiple factors or more than two levels on a single factor. Although showing how these effect sizes are computed is beyond the scope of this chapter, they are part of the standard output of many statistical packages. The relationships between pairs of variables in contingency tables are often quantified using phi (φ) for 2×2 tables and Cramer's V for tables with more than two categories on either variable. We will present several of these effect sizes for the examples discussed in Chapter 12 with specific inferential tests.

Confidence Intervals

Whereas effect size indicates the magnitude of a finding, **confidence intervals** give a sense of the precision of your estimate of the effect. A confidence interval is a range of values around the effect size obtained in your sample that is likely to contain the true population effect size with a given level of plausibility or confidence.

Most commonly, we use 95 per cent confidence intervals in behavioural research. A 95 per cent confidence interval is constructed so that if we were able to identify the true population value of our measure of interest (e.g., a difference of two group means), there is a 95 per cent chance that our confidence interval would contain that true value. The size of a confidence interval depends on both the variability in your data and your sample size.

Figure 11.4 presents confidence intervals for a hypothetical study examining the effects of alcohol on speed of response in a timed task. The plot on the left shows 95 per cent confidence intervals for the means for each of the two experimental conditions (alcohol versus no alcohol). The plot on the right shows the 95 per cent confidence interval for the difference of the two means.

confidence interval
A range of values around the effect size obtained in a sample that is likely to contain the true population effect size with a given level of plausibility or confidence.

INFERENTIAL STATISTICS AND NULL HYPOTHESIS SIGNIFICANCE TESTING

To this point we have presented methods for describing and displaying collected data. Depending on the details of your study, you have computed such statistics as means, medians, standard deviations, correlations, frequencies, and proportions, and you have displayed your

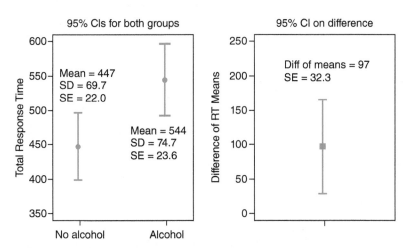

FIGURE 11.4   Confidence intervals for means and difference of means.

inferential statistical tests Statistical methods such as t tests or χ^2 tests that enable researchers to use sample data to draw conclusions about the population of interest.

null hypothesis significance testing (NHST) A traditional approach to inferential statistical tests that attempts to determine whether a specific hypothesis (the null hypothesis) can be rejected at a given probability level.

null hypothesis Typically, a statement of "no effect" in your results. For example, a null hypothesis might suggest no difference in mean responses for different experimental conditions or zero correlation between two variables.

statistical significance level A conventional probability value, usually .05 or .01, used to assess whether the null hypothesis in NHST should be rejected.

test statistics Computed values associated with particular inferential tests designed to test hypotheses.

probability value (p value) Indicates how likely it would be to see results at least as extreme as those observed under the assumption that the null hypothesis is true.

data or summary statistics using box-and-whisker plots, histograms, scatterplots, or contingency tables. Where appropriate, you have also computed effect sizes and confidence intervals.

One might argue that once all of these steps have been completed, you have done all you need to in terms of analysis and all that remains is interpretation. Most behavioural researchers, however, have traditionally followed one additional step: applying **inferential statistical tests**—that is, statistical methods such as t tests or chi-square (χ^2) tests that enable you to use sample data to draw conclusions about your population of interest. Furthermore, they typically apply these tests in the context of what has become known as **null hypothesis significance testing** (NHST).

NHST generally comprises the following steps:

1. Specify a **null hypothesis** (usually denoted H_0). This is typically (but not necessarily) a hypothesis of "no effect," meaning, for example, no difference between mean responses for different experimental conditions or zero statistical correlation between two variables. An alternative hypothesis (denoted H_1 or H_A) of "there is an effect" is usually implied. For example, there *is* a difference in mean responses or there *is* a linear relationship between two variables.
2. Choose a **statistical significance level**, denoted by the Greek letter alpha (α), typically .05 or .01.
3. Compute your **test statistics** (e.g., t, F, χ^2) and their associated **probability (p) values**. This p value indicates how likely you were to see results at least as extreme as those you observed under the assumption that the null hypothesis is true.
4. If the computed value of p is smaller than the significance level chosen in step 2, then H_0 is rejected. Small values for p (i.e., values less than your significance level) indicate it is very unlikely that you would have gotten the results you did if the null hypothesis were true. Instead, we then interpret these results as suggesting it is much more likely that the null hypothesis is not correct and the alternative hypothesis is more likely to be true. If $p > \alpha$, then we fail to reject the null hypothesis and treat the test results as statistically non-significant. In this case you must conclude that there is insufficient evidence to support an effect, or difference, among your conditions or variables. You might be tempted to use the less convoluted phrase of "accept the null hypothesis" rather than "fail to reject the null hypothesis," but the former implies that we have proven that the null hypothesis is, in fact, true, and the NHST process does not allow you to actually make that kind of conclusion.

Example 1: Assessing the Fairness of a Coin

To illustrate the steps and logic of NHST, we present a simple example of determining whether a coin is fair by flipping it 20 times. If the coin is fair, we would expect to get somewhere in the neighbourhood of 10 heads and 10 tails. How far from an equal split of heads and tails, however, would lead us to conclude the coin is unfair?

We know that we cannot necessarily expect to get exactly 10 heads and 10 tails in 20 flips. In any process that involves uncertainty, we anticipate fluctuations from the expected value just by chance. This chance deviation is known as **sampling error**. Note that the term "error" in this context does not indicate any kind of mistake, but a difference between what we observe in the sample and what we would expect from the population.

Referring back to step 1 of NHST, we will specify a null hypothesis (H_0). In this case, our null hypothesis is that the coin is fair—in other words, the probability of getting a head on any given flip is exactly .5, as is the probability of getting a tail, that is, prob(H) = prob(T) = .5. The alternative hypothesis (H_A) is that the coin is not fair, that is, prob(H) ≠ .5.

With these two hypotheses, consider the possibilities outlined in Table 11.6 regarding the true state of the coin and what we might conclude about it after we conduct our experiment of flipping the coin 20 times.

Two of the cells represent a correct decision and two represent errors. If the coin is fair and we do not reject the null hypothesis of a fair coin, then we have made a correct decision. Similarly, if the coin is unfair and we reject the null hypothesis of a fair coin, this is also a correct decision. A **type I error** occurs if you conclude the coin is unfair—that is, you reject the null hypothesis—when, in fact, the null hypothesis is true. In this example, a type I error would occur if we conclude that the coin is unfair when it is actually fair. The probability of a type I error is the same as the value of α noted in step 2 above.

A **type II error** occurs when you fail to reject a null hypothesis when it is, in fact, false. Here we would fail to reject the null hypothesis of a fair coin when the coin is actually unfair. In this example, a type II error would occur if we conclude that the coin is a fair coin, when actually it is unfair. The probability of a type II error is typically denoted by the Greek letter beta (β). Another way to say this is that β represents the probability of failing to identify an experimental effect when such an effect actually does exist. Recall that in Chapter 5 we discussed the concept of the power of your experimental design. The quantity $1 - \beta$ is known as the power of the test and tells you, in essence, how likely you are to detect a real effect of a certain magnitude given your sample size. A power of .80 has traditionally been considered a reasonable level to shoot for, although the powers of studies frequently fall well below this mark (Cohen, 1962; Maxwell, 2004; Mone, Mueller, & Mauland, 1996; Rossi, 1990; Sedlmeier & Gigerenzer, 1989).

For step 2 of NHST, the traditional approach is to set the probability of a type I error sufficiently low, so that if you performed your experiment over and over, you would commit a type I error, on average, only 1 time in 20. In other words, the probability of a type I error, α, is 1/20 = .05. Another often-used α level is .01 (or 1/100), but for our coin-flipping experiment, we will use an α level of .05.

The key to using NHST to draw conclusions about our data comes in step 3, in which we compute test statistics and p values based on certain assumptions about the data. With our

sampling error Differences in the measurements observed in a data set and what would be expected from the population values.

type I error Occurs if a researcher rejects the null hypothesis when, in fact, the null hypothesis is true.

type II error Occurs if a researcher fails to reject the null hypothesis when, in fact, it is false.

Table 11.6 Illustration of type I and type II error in a coin-flipping example.

What is the true state of the coin?	WHAT DO WE CONCLUDE AFTER FLIPPING THE COIN 20 TIMES?	
	Fail to reject null hypothesis that coin is fair	Reject null hypothesis that coin is fair
Coin is fair (H_0) Prob(H) = Prob(T) = .5	Correct decision	Type I error
Coin is unfair (H_A) Prob(H) ≠ .5; Prob(T) ≠ .5	Type II error	Correct decision

Table 11.7   Probabilities of obtaining the given number of heads in 20 flips of a fair coin.

No. of heads	Probability	No. of heads	Probability
0	.00000095	20	.00000095
1	.00001907	19	.00001907
2	.00018120	18	.00018120
3	.00108719	17	.00108719
4	.00462055	16	.00462055
5	.01478577	15	.01478577
6	.03696442	14	.03696442
7	.07392883	13	.07392883
8	.12013435	12	.12013435
9	.16017914	11	.16017914
10	.17619705		
		Total	1.00

Sum = .0207 (for heads 0 through 5)

Sum = .0207 (for heads 15 through 20)

coin-flipping example, we do not need to compute a test statistic but can directly compute a p value using rules of probability theory. Suppose we flip the coin 20 times and obtain 15 heads and 5 tails. For a fair coin, the probabilities of obtaining 0 through 20 heads on 20 flips are presented in Table 11.7.

When we compute a p value for an inferential test, what we are computing is the probability of obtaining a result *at least as extreme* as the one we obtained *given that the null hypothesis is true*. With 15 heads on 20 flips, we would add up the probabilities of obtaining 15 heads, 16 heads, and so on up to 20 heads. This gives a total probability of .0207. We are not done computing the p value of interest, however, because we also need to consider that the coin might be biased toward tails. A result of 15, 16, . . ., or 20 tails would be just as extreme a result as 15, 16, . . ., or 20 heads, so when we add up all the values, we obtain a p value of .0207 + .0207 $\approx$ .041.

Finally, we apply step 4 of NHST. We had set an α level of .05 and we computed a p value of .041. Because .041 is less than .05, we reject the null hypothesis of a fair coin in favour of the hypothesis of an unfair coin. The logic demonstrated here applies similarly for situations more complex than flipping coins.

Example 2: Comparison of Two Means

To understand the logic of statistical inference for situations more complex than coin-flipping, such as comparing the mean responses across different experimental conditions, we need to review four statistical concepts: the normal distribution, sampling distributions, standard error, and the central limit theorem.

The Normal Distribution.

The normal distribution is central to the traditional approach to statistical inference, and a number of statistical tests for means include an assumption of normally distributed populations. Figure 11.5a displays the histogram for a hypothetical population of normally distributed values with a mean of 100 and standard deviation of 15. The smooth curve overlay takes the shape of the classic bell curve of the normal distribution.

Many natural phenomena, such as height, weight, and IQ scores, follow a normal distribution. This distribution is the most important probability distribution in statistics and has several important features. It is symmetric about its mean, median, and mode, all of which are equivalent. When you have normally distributed data, the standard deviation has a meaningful interpretation. As shown in Figure 11.5b, 68 per cent of the values fall within one standard deviation on either side of the mean, and 95 per cent of the values fall within 1.96 standard deviations on either side of the mean.

We can use the properties of the normal distribution to determine the likelihood of obtaining any particular value from the distribution. For instance, imagine that you randomly selected a value from the distribution shown in Figure 11.5b. If you selected a value of 95, this value is very close to the mean of 100 and would be a very representative value for the distribution. If you selected a value of 135, this value is more than two standard deviations away from the mean and is an unlikely value to select; there is only a 2 per cent chance of selecting a value this large from this distribution.

normal distribution A unimodal pattern of data, with the mode occurring in the centre of the distribution and values dropping off sharply in a symmetrical pattern on both sides of the mean.

Sampling Distributions.

When we collect data and compare the responses for different groups or experimental conditions, we generally do not compare individual responses across the groups, but instead compare summary statistics—such as means or proportions—from each sample. Sampling distributions describe the distributions of values for these summary statistics.

Suppose we take a random sample of 20 men from a large population of men, measure their heights, and compute the mean of those 20 heights. Then we take a second random sample of 20 men and compute their mean height. We continue to do this many times, computing mean heights for each sample of 20 men. Now, in addition to the original distribution of individual heights in the population, we have a distribution of means based on these many samples of size 20. This distribution of means is the sampling distribution of the mean for a sample size of 20. If we had used repeated samples of, say, 30, we would have a different sampling distribution.

Sampling distributions are not limited to means. In theory, they may be constructed for any summary statistic such as medians, standard deviations, ranges, and even differences in means for pairs of samples (this latter is the sampling distribution used for the independent-groups

sampling distribution of the mean The pattern of mean values obtained when drawing many random samples of a given size from a population and computing the mean for each sample.

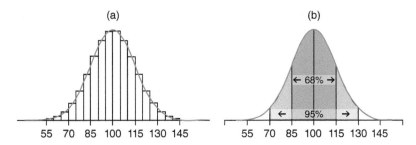

FIGURE 11.5   Histograms for a hypothetical population of normally distributed values.

t test). In practice, we are rarely able to draw large numbers of samples from our population of interest, so we are not able to construct a sampling distribution based on repeated sampling from that population. Instead we *estimate* the sampling distribution based on the relatively few samples we do collect.

The top row of Figure 11.6 displays sampling distributions of the mean for sample sizes of 1, 5, and 10. The bottom row displays sampling distributions for the difference obtained by repeatedly drawing pairs of samples, each of the given sample size, and computing the difference between each pair of means. These are all based on an original "population" of values that are normally distributed with a mean of 100 and standard deviation of 15. Note that a sampling distribution for a sample size of 1 simply reflects the original distribution of values.

To see how the sampling distribution informs inferences about our data, we will focus on the plot in Figure 11.6f. Suppose we collect information for two groups of 10 participants and we find that the mean score for group 2 is 10 points higher than that for group 1. Suppose we make the simplifying assumption that the standard deviation of the population is 15. Then we have the situation illustrated in Figure 11.6f. The two shaded regions represent differences in pairs of means of 10 or more. We see that these two regions account for 13.6 per cent of all values. Given the assumptions of a normally distributed population with a standard deviation of 15, if both samples were drawn from this same population we would expect a difference in means of 10 or more 13.6 per cent of the time, or with a probability of .136. In reality, we rarely, if ever, know the true standard deviations of the populations we are studying, so we must estimate them from our samples. In such cases, we use the *t* distribution, rather than the normal distribution, to compute the probabilities, but the same logic holds true.

As illustrated in Figure 11.6, an important property of sampling distributions is that as sample size increases, the variability (**variance**, standard deviation) of the sampling distribution decreases. This leads us to the concept of standard error.

variance A measure of the dispersion of a data set; the average squared deviation of values from the mean value.

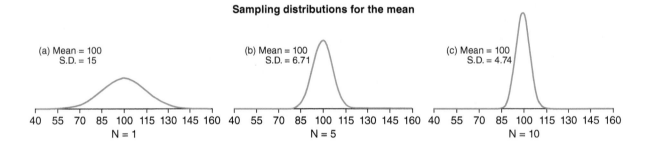

Sampling distributions for the mean

(a) Mean = 100   S.D. = 15

(b) Mean = 100   S.D. = 6.71

(c) Mean = 100   S.D. = 4.74

40 55 70 85 100 115 130 145 160   40 55 70 85 100 115 130 145 160   40 55 70 85 100 115 130 145 160
N = 1   N = 5   N = 10

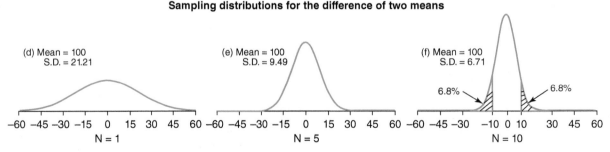

Sampling distributions for the difference of two means

(d) Mean = 100   S.D. = 21.21

(e) Mean = 100   S.D. = 9.49

(f) Mean = 100   S.D. = 6.71

6.8%   6.8%

−60 −45 −30 −15   0   15 30 45 60 −60 −45 −30 −15   0   15 30 45 60 −60 −45 −30 −10 0 10   30 45 60
N = 1   N = 5   N = 10

FIGURE 11.6   Sampling distributions of the mean and difference of pairs of means for sample sizes of 1, 5, and 10.

Standard Error.   A standard error is the standard deviation of a sampling distribution. In Figures 11.6a–c, the variability in the distributions reflects the standard errors of the mean for sample sizes of 1, 5, and 10. In Figures 11.6d–f, the variability reflects the standard error of the *difference* of pairs of sample means for sample sizes of 1, 5, and 10. The standard error decreases as sample size increases in a regular way: The standard error of the sampling distribution equals the standard deviation of the original distribution divided by the square root of the sample size, that is:

$$\text{Standard error} = \text{Standard deviation}/\sqrt{n}.$$

As a result, the larger the sample size, the greater precision in our estimates and the smaller our *p* value will be. The standard error of the mean plays an important role in the computation of both confidence intervals and test statistics, such as the *t* value for a *t* test.

standard error The standard deviation of a sampling distribution. This value is calculated by dividing the standard deviation by the square root of the sample size.

central limit theorem A theorem that says with a large sample size, the sampling distribution of the mean will be normal or nearly normal in shape.

Central Limit Theorem.   In Figure 11.6, we can see that the sampling distributions of both means and differences of means when sampling from a normal distribution appear to be normally distributed themselves, and this is, in fact, true. Figure 11.7 displays two distributions that deviate substantially from a normal distribution, one being bimodal and the other being heavily skewed. Also presented are sampling distributions of means and differences of pairs of means for sample sizes of 2, 10, and 30. Remarkably, despite the marked non-normality in the populations, the sampling distributions appear to take on the familiar normal curve shape with increasing sample size.

The **central limit theorem** confirms this observation and tells us that even with populations having dramatically non-normal distributions, the sampling distribution of the mean will be increasingly normal in shape as sample sizes increase. This allows us to make use of the many attractive properties of the normal distribution, even when underlying distributions may not themselves be normal.

Although NHST has been the dominant approach for drawing inferences about data for a long time, criticisms of this approach have increased over the past several decades. In this next section we explore these criticisms to emphasize that researchers should always be thoughtful about the decisions they make in the design and analysis of their research.

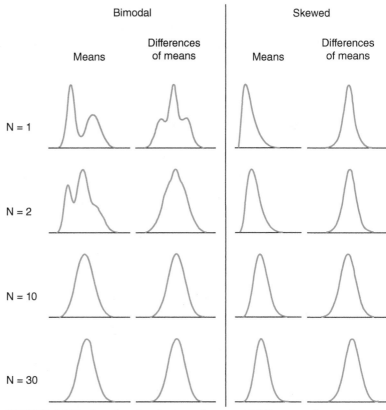

FIGURE 11.7 Sampling distributions of means and differences of means for two non-normal distributions.

CRITICISMS OF NHST

Although behavioural researchers have relied heavily on NHST to analyze and interpret data, criticisms of NHST have appeared regularly (Carver, 1978, 1993; Gigerenzer, 2004; Hubbard & Lindsay, 2008; Krueger, 2001; Loftus, 1996; Rozeboom, 1960). Although some support of NHST continues (Hagen, 1997; Harris, 1997; Wainer, 1999), many arguments in its favour have been refuted (Schmidt & Hunter, 1997), leading to demands for modifications to or the outright abandonment of NHST in a variety of fields. As criticisms mount, it is clear that the traditional NHST approach has serious limitations, some of which are based on misunderstanding and misapplication of the process and others on NHST's inherent weaknesses as a tool in the scientific effort. Three of these common issues surrounding the use of NHST are (1) the misuse of p as an indicator of effect size or importance, (2) the arbitrary nature of a reject/fail-to-reject decisions based on p, and (3) the overemphasis on α and type I errors, leading to underpowered research studies.

Misuse of p as an Indicator of Importance

Unfortunately, some researchers misinterpret statistical significance as a measure of the size of an effect or as a measure of the meaningfulness of a result. The word "significance" in NHST refers only to *statistical* significance and to neither the magnitude of the effect (e.g., the value of a correlation or the difference between two means) nor the importance of the result (i.e., how meaningful the result is). The p value only represents the probability of obtaining a specific result from the population distribution that is specified by the null hypothesis, and whether this represents a typical or extreme result. The use of the p value to evaluate statistical significance depends on three things: the size of the experimental effect, the sample size, and the variability in sample values. We will focus on sample size to show why p is a poor indicator of effect size or importance.

Consider Table 11.8, which presents the results of six hypothetical studies evaluating the effectiveness of two teaching methods. Each study includes two independent groups of students, one experiencing method 1 and the other experiencing method 2, with the measurement being student scores on an exam of 100 possible points. Both study 1 and study 2 show method 2 having an eight-point advantage over method 1; that is, the magnitude of the raw effect in both studies is identical. Yet, because of the difference in sample size, the p value resulting from an independent-samples t test for study 2 is .016 (statistically significant by the $\alpha = .05$ criterion), whereas the p value for study 1 is .090 (not statistically significant). Although we have the same raw effect in both studies, NHST leads us to reject the null hypothesis of no difference for study 1, but fail to reject the null hypothesis for study 2.

Now consider studies 3 and 4. For both studies, method 2 enjoys a two-point advantage over method 1. Again, however, a difference in sample sizes leads to different p values (in this case, substantially different) and conflicting decisions on whether to reject or fail to reject the null hypothesis.

The other piece of information the p value does not carry is the theoretical importance of the result. Study 4 yields a statistically significant p, but to what extent is a two-point increase on test scores an important finding? In contrast, study 1 yields a larger p value than study 4, but the eight-point advantage (nearly a whole letter grade) of method 2 over method 1 in study 1 might well be considered a meaningful result.

Table 11.8 Results of six hypothetical studies to illustrate problems with the *p* value.

	N of each group	MEAN TEST SCORES		Difference of means	Std. dev. in each group	p
		Method 1	Method 2			
Study 1	10	70	78	8	10	.090
Study 2	20	70	78	8	10	.016
Study 3	30	70	72	2	10	.440
Study 4	200	70	72	2	10	.046
Study 5	13	70	78	8	10	.053
Study 6	14	70	78	8	10	.044

It is clear from these examples that *p* is a poor surrogate for effect size, yet effect size is one of the findings we should most care about. It is, therefore, recommended that effect sizes be included in the presentation of any research results (see Wilkinson et al., 1999), and many journal editors now require this information to be included in any publication. The practical importance of a finding can only be determined in the context of the particular phenomenon under investigation (e.g., a small effect may be quite important in medicine), but it should be clear that gauging importance should not rely so heavily on the magnitude of *p*.

Arbitrary Nature of Reject/Fail-to-Reject Decisions

As we saw in the steps outlining the NHST process, once we have computed our test statistic and *p* value, we either reject the null hypothesis if our computed *p* is below our pre-specified cutoff value of (usually) .05 or .01, or we fail to reject the null hypothesis if *p* is too large. Does such a dichotomous decision to either reject or fail to reject the null hypothesis make sense?

Consider studies 5 and 6 in the final two rows of Table 11.8. A strict adherence to NHST and a critical *p* value of .05 would lead us to reject the null hypothesis of no difference between the two methods for study 6. However, we would fail to reject the same null hypothesis in study 5, although the mean difference in both studies is identical and the sample sizes differ only by one case. It seems preferable to use a process in which we treat the evidence for or against our experimental hypothesis in a more continuous rather than all-or-none manner, for example, through the use of effect sizes and confidence intervals.

A Culture of Low-Power Studies

Earlier in this chapter we described type I and type II errors and revisited the concept of statistical power from Chapter 5. Recall that a test is powerful to the extent that it is able to detect an effect of a certain size. If, for example, we consistently designed studies to achieve statistical power of .8 for medium-size effects, then over the course of many such experiments, we would expect to detect an effect 80 per cent of the time.

Figure 11.8 demonstrates how statistical power increases with sample size when comparing means from two independent samples (where the independent-samples t test is typically applied). This relationship is shown for three different values of Cohen's d, a commonly used measure of effect size. The values of .2, .5, and .8 for small, medium, and large effect sizes were suggested by Cohen (1988) and can be used as a guideline for the interpretation of an effect. However, it is important to also keep in mind that the relative importance of an effect of a given size can also depend on the specific context.

The dashed horizontal line in Figure 11.8 corresponds to the widely accepted benchmark of .8 at which a study is deemed to have adequate power. To achieve such power in the presence of a large effect, 25 participants (the leftmost dotted vertical line) would be required for each of the two groups. For a study with a medium effect size, sample sizes of 63 (the rightmost dotted vertical line) are required to achieve a power of .8. Finally, the point at which the "small effect" curve meets the .8 power line reaches well beyond the extent of the chart and, in fact, 393 participants would be required in each of the two samples.

A number of researchers have examined statistical power across many published studies and found that the average power to detect small or even medium effects is often below .5 (Cohen, 1962; Fraley & Vazire, 2014; Rossi, 1990; Sedlmeier & Gigerenzer, 1989). A power of .5 means that in half the studies in which a real, medium effect exists, the null hypothesis will *not* be rejected. Low power can lead to an increase in type II error, leading a researcher to potentially equate failure to reject H_0 with no effect. In turn, this may lead to the researcher deciding not to submit the statistically non-significant findings to a journal, contributing to the file-drawer problem described in Chapter 9 (i.e., the research report is not accepted for publication, contributing to a bias in published studies; see "Media Matters: Publication Bias and a Possible Solution").

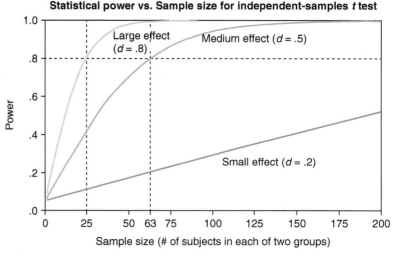

FIGURE 11.8   Statistical power as a function of sample size when comparing the means from two independent groups.

MEDIA MATTERS

Publication Bias and a Possible Solution

Editors at top scientific journals have traditionally shown bias when selecting from the hundreds of new research papers coming out every year. They tend to look for studies that have produced positive and innovative results, the kind that make readers (and reporters) sit up and take notice and help launch younger researchers' careers. They also tend to shun so-called negative findings—those that declare a theory is unsupported or discount a relationship between two things.

As a result, the editorial process motivates some researchers to manipulate their methods or comb through their data until they come upon a positive finding. This practice has come to be known as "*p*-Hacking," because it stems from a desire to the make statistical significance stronger and hence the findings more believable.

This environment has also discouraged researchers from attempting replication of previous studies, which, as a *Slate* article put it, "is science's most basic way of verifying correctness" (Meyer & Chabris, 2014). This has led many to declare a "replication crisis" in scientific research, including psychology. A 2012 survey of the top 100 psychology journals discovered that a scant 1 per cent of papers published since 1990 were true attempts at reproducing previous findings (Meyer & Chabris, 2014).

These problems have prompted distress in the scientific community for years. A blog post by Michael Inzlicht (2016), a professor at the University of Toronto, stated that "as a field, we tend only to publish significant results. This could be because as authors we choose to focus on these; or, more likely, because reviewers, editors, and journals force us to focus on these and to ignore nulls. This creates the infamous file drawer that altogether warps the research landscape." He goes on to say that this file-drawer problem, in combination with *p*-Hacking and unconscious data analysis decision biases, may "explain why so many of our cherished results can't replicate."

Recently, mainstream media have begun to weigh in on the matter. *The Conversation Canada* ran a story about Registered Replication Reports, where researchers attempt to replicate the results of previous studies (Leyser, Kingsley, & Grange, 2017). These are then published in the associated journal *Perspectives on Psychological Science*, with the papers analyzing the replication studies to establish their level of reproducibility.

So how can we address the replication crisis? Nyhan (2014) suggests that journal editors and peer reviewers study designs and analysis plans and pledge to publish the results if the researchers conduct and report the study in a professional manner. That approach, Nyhan argues, will motivate authors and reviewers to develop the strongest possible designs and discourage them from finding or emphasizing significant results after the fact. Nyhan ends his article optimistically, noting that several journals across the social and natural sciences have adopted a new scientific format titled Registered Reports, which uses this approach. If federal funding rewarded publications that used Registered Reports, top scientists would respond accordingly, and publication bias would decrease (Nyhan, 2014).

GOING BEYOND NHST: EFFECT SIZE AND CONFIDENCE INTERVALS

Given the limitations of NHST, how can we improve on the analysis and interpretation of data? We recommend using effect sizes, confidence intervals, replication, and meta-analysis as tools to augment (and perhaps replace) NHST in the investigation and analysis of data. NHST can speak to whether or not your study has statistical significance, whereas effect sizes and confidence intervals can speak to whether your study has practical significance.

statistical significance
An indicator of the probability of obtaining an effect size as large as (or larger than) the one you obtained; also indicates that the differences between groups are not due to sampling error.

practical significance
The differences between groups are large enough that they represent a meaningful difference in a real-world context.

- Perform a power analysis as part of the design of your study. In doing so, you will be forced to think about effect size (see step 3) and will have a much better sense of what your sample size should be.
- After checking data and performing any necessary cleaning, compute descriptive statistics, compute scale scores, and construct visual displays.
- Compute—and place more focus on—effect sizes.
- Construct and visually present confidence intervals around effect size measures such as means, differences in means, and correlations.
- Carry out your inferential tests and compute *p* values, but do not let *p* be the main driver for the presentation and interpretation of results.
- As part of any continuing research program (in contrast to a single experiment or two), incorporate replication and meta-analysis as part of the cumulative scientific endeavour.

Focus on Effect Size

There are a number of reasons to emphasize practical significance, and effect size, rather than simply using the *p* value as the only decision-making criterion:

- In nearly all cases, we are (or should be) interested in the actual size of the effect and not simply whether we have enough evidence to reject the null hypothesis of no effect.
- Effect sizes are not dependent on sample size in the way that *p* is. As we increase our sample size, the effect size will start to converge to the actual population value. In contrast, the *p* value approaches 0 with increasing sample size.
- Computations of power require the specification of an effect size (albeit prior to collecting your data).
- Effect sizes (particularly of the *d* and *r* types) can be meaningfully compared with one another. This can be useful when performing a meta-analysis (see Chapter 9).
- We can place confidence intervals around effect sizes to get a sense of the precision of our findings.

Use Confidence Intervals

Like *p* values, confidence intervals depend on the variability in your sample values and on the sample size. All other things being equal, confidence intervals narrow as your sample size increases. Like *p* values, confidence intervals may be used to draw the types of inferences (e.g., reject/fail to reject) common with NHST. In fact, confidence intervals on a single mean or on a difference of two means may be used to reject/fail to reject the null hypothesis of no difference with precisely the same results as the *p* value.

Similar to *p* values, confidence intervals are subject to misinterpretation. When we construct a 95 per cent confidence interval, this does *not* mean that there is a 95 per cent chance that the population mean falls within the boundaries of that interval. The population mean has a specific value and it either does or does not fall within our interval range. The correct interpretation is that if we knew the population mean, there is a 95 per cent chance that our interval would include that mean (Savory, 2008). Said differently, in the long run, we would expect 19 of 20 of the 95 per cent confidence intervals we construct to contain the true population mean (Savory, 2008).

Given the many shared characteristics of *p* values and confidence intervals, why would we recommend confidence intervals in addition to or even in lieu of *p* values? Confidence intervals give you a sense of the precision of your results; that is, they provide a range of values for our effect that might be considered reasonable given your data. By doing so, they also lead you to focus on effect size as opposed to only the *p* value, which, as described previously, tells you nothing of substance about your effect.

PRACTICAL TIPS

Practical Tips for Analyzing Your Data

1. Plan your data analysis before you collect your data.

2. Be sure to check and double-check your data.

3. As the first part of your analysis, always compute descriptive statistics, compute scale means, and create visual displays of your data.

4. Be sure your statistical tests are appropriate for your data.

5. Be sure to check all calculations.

CHAPTER SUMMARY

All data analysis should begin with a thorough checking of your data, ideally with the help of someone else, so that you know your analysis will be accurate. Once you have completed that task, using descriptive statistics and visual displays will give you a deeper understanding of the numerical values in your data and the story they tell about your samples.

Data for individual variables may be displayed in histograms and box-and-whisker plots. For examining the relationship between two variables, data may be displayed in scatterplots or contingency tables. The Pearson product-moment correlation (Pearson's *r*) measures the strength of the relationship between two variables.

An effect size communicates the magnitude of your phenomenon of interest. Effect size comprises three general classes: raw effects, standardized effects, and correlation-like effects.

Whereas effect size indicates the magnitude of a finding, confidence intervals give a sense of the precision of your estimate of the effect. Confidence intervals are computed for either traditional statistics, such as means and differences of means, or standardized effect sizes.

NHST is a traditional data analysis tool used by behavioural researchers that has come under heavy criticism over the past few decades. Researchers who rely solely on NHST commonly misinterpret the *p* value and tend to produce low-power studies. Effect sizes, confidence intervals, replication, and meta-analysis can all be used to augment or even replace NHST in the investigation and analysis of data.

End-of-Chapter Exercises

1. Suppose you are interested in the impact of different types of background noise on performance in a memory task. You randomly assign participants to one of three groups, which differ in the type of noise presented. Once you have collected your data, the first thing you do is compute the mean scores on the memory task for each group and find that they are nearly identical. At this point, should you simply conclude there were no differences among the three groups and move on to another study? If not, what are some things you might want to do with the data?

2. You are conducting a study investigating how sleep and caffeine consumption affect performance on a memory task. For each of these variables, indicate the scale of measurement and which of the following descriptive statistics would be appropriate to calculate for that variable.

   a. Hours of sleep (less than 4 hours; 4–6 hours; more than 6 hours)

      Scale of measurement: _____

      Mean: _____ Yes   _____ No

      Median: _____ Yes   _____ No

      Mode: _____ Yes   _____ No

      Standard Deviation: _____ Yes   _____ No

   b. Caffeine consumption (2 cups of regular coffee or 2 cups of decaf coffee)

      Scale of measurement: _____

      Mean: _____ Yes   _____ No

      Median: _____ Yes   _____ No

      Mode: _____ Yes   _____ No

      Standard Deviation: _____ Yes   _____ No

   c. Academic performance (GPA)

      Scale of measurement: _____

      Mean: _____ Yes   _____ No

      Median: _____ Yes   _____ No

      Mode: _____ Yes   _____ No

      Standard Deviation: _____ Yes   _____ No

3. You are interested in exploring whether there is a relationship between self-esteem and body dissatisfaction. After having participants complete measures of both of these variables, you create histograms, box-and-whisker plots, and a scatterplot to visually examine your data. Interpret what you see in each of the figures below.

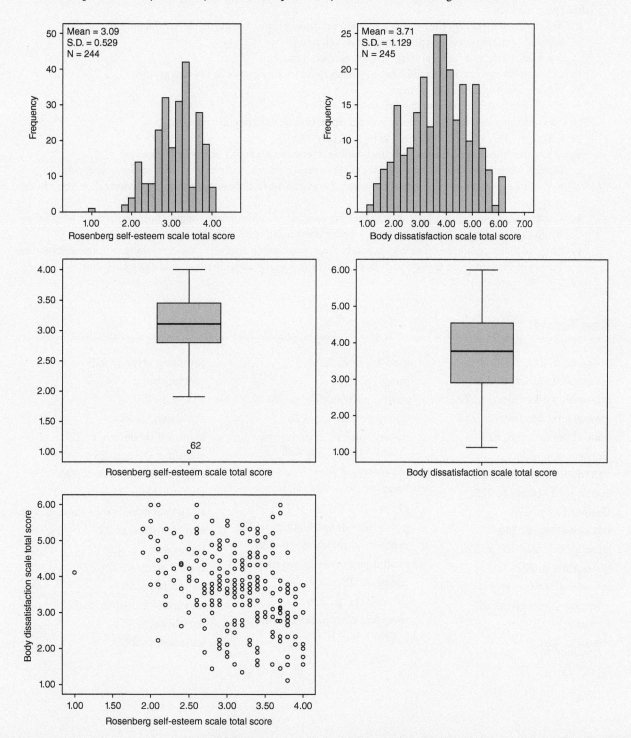

4. Suppose you run an experiment to examine the effects of alcohol consumption on speed of response in a timed task. Participants in one group consume no alcohol, whereas those in the second group consume a moderate amount of alcohol. What types of information do each of the following give you to help you understand your data or draw conclusions about your results?
   a. descriptive statistics for the response times in each group (mean, standard deviation, etc.)
   b. box-and-whisker plots of response times for each group
   c. confidence intervals for mean response times in each group
   d. a confidence interval for the difference in mean response time between the two groups
   e. cohen's d for the difference of means
   f. the p value from the t test on the difference of means
5. Place the following Pearson correlations in order from weakest to strongest relationship:
   $r = .81; r = -.25; r = .03; r = .47; r = .72; r = -.91; r = -.11$
6. For each of the following scenarios, indicate whether it represents a type I or a type II error.
   a. Riane has concluded there is no difference in performance on a memory task between students who were listening to rock music versus country music. However, there really was a difference in memory performance between the groups.
   b. Calvin reports that individuals who follow his exercise plan lose more weight those individuals who follow Rashid's exercise plan. In actuality, both exercise plans result in no weight loss.
   c. Imagine that a computer repair technician looks at your laptop and says that everything is running smoothly. However, next time you turn on your laptop to work on a class assignment, it won't turn on properly.

Key Terms

bimodal, p. 222

bivariate statistics, p. 220

box-and-whisker plots, p. 222

central limit theorem, p. 233

central tendency, p. 220

Cohen's d, p. 226

confidence interval, p. 227

contingency table, p. 225

Cramer's V, p. 225

data cleaning, p. 218

descriptive statistics, p. 220

histogram, p. 222

inferential statistical tests, p. 228

interquartile range, p. 222

kurtosis, p. 221

mean, p. 220

median, p. 220

mode, p. 220

normal distribution, p. 231

null hypothesis, p. 228

null hypothesis significance testing (NHST), p. 228

outliers, p. 219

Pearson's r, p. 224

phi (φ), p. 225

point-biserial correlation, p. 226

practical significance, p. 238

probability value (p value), p. 228

range, p. 221

raw effects, p. 226

sampling distribution of the mean, p. 231

sampling error, p. 229

scatterplot, p. 224

shape, p. 221

skewness, p. 221

standard deviation, p. 221

standard error, p. 233

standardized effect, p. 226

statistical significance, p. 237

statistical significance level, p. 228

test statistics, p. 228

type I error, p. 229

type II error, p. 229

unimodal, p. 222

univariate statistics, p. 220

variability, p. 220

variance, p. 232

Analyzing Your Data II: Specific Approaches

12

Chapter Contents

INSIDE RESEARCH: Scott Ronis

While at home on holiday break during my second year of my undergraduate work at Brandeis University, I took a nap and had a dream. When I woke up, I told my sister, without any apparent reason, I was going to be a psychologist. When I returned to school, I became involved in various research labs and volunteer experiences while I worked on my dual majors, psychology and Spanish. I also spent a lot of time talking to faculty about my graduate school and career choices, and they offered me advice on a variety of issues, such as choosing between developmental psychology and clinical psychology. I didn't have the best grades when I finished, so I decided to work in paid research for a couple of years to give myself time to bolster my CV and study for the GRE exam.

Associate professor of psychology and director of graduate studies, University of New Brunswick

continued

When I applied to graduate school in clinical psychology, I was advised to seek out potential mentors and be open to working on their projects. I applied widely. For me, grad school was an adventure, and I didn't want to place geographic limitations on my choices. I found a real connection at the University of Missouri with Dr. Charles Borduin, co-founder of a community-based intervention (multisystemic therapy) for treating youth with serious behavioural problems. At the time, he was working on a project on juvenile sexual offending. This was not something I had planned on researching, but I went with it because it allowed me to work with Dr. Borduin, and I liked that it focused on an underrepresented population in need of further understanding. I also took every possible research methods and statistics course or training I could take, even ones located outside my home institution. I found that many of the trainings were subsidized for graduate students, so this was a great opportunity to develop a niche.

As the years rolled along and I became knowledgeable about the field of sexual offending from my work with Dr. Borduin, I was often asked to collaborate with others in that area of research. After finishing my predoctoral internship at the Virginia Treatment Center for Children, I completed my one-year post-doctoral clinical training at adult and youth correctional facilities in Virginia. From there, I applied for academic positions—again, widely—and found a home in Canada. At the end of it all, I look back and realize that I could have never predicted this path. I found it by being willing to take chances on various opportunities and persevere despite countless challenges.

Scott Ronis has taught a graduate statistics course for doctoral students at the University of New Brunswick along with undergraduate and graduate courses in psychotherapy and forensic psychology. His work has spanned various research topics and designs and has used quantitative statistical methods as well as qualitative approaches. By using mixed methods, he has been able to examine phenomena from a variety of perspectives and consider effective knowledge mobilization practices.

Research Focus: Emotional and behavioural difficulties of adolescents, with an emphasis on problem sexual behaviour; barriers and facilitators of youth access to mental health services; family communication and relationship patterns

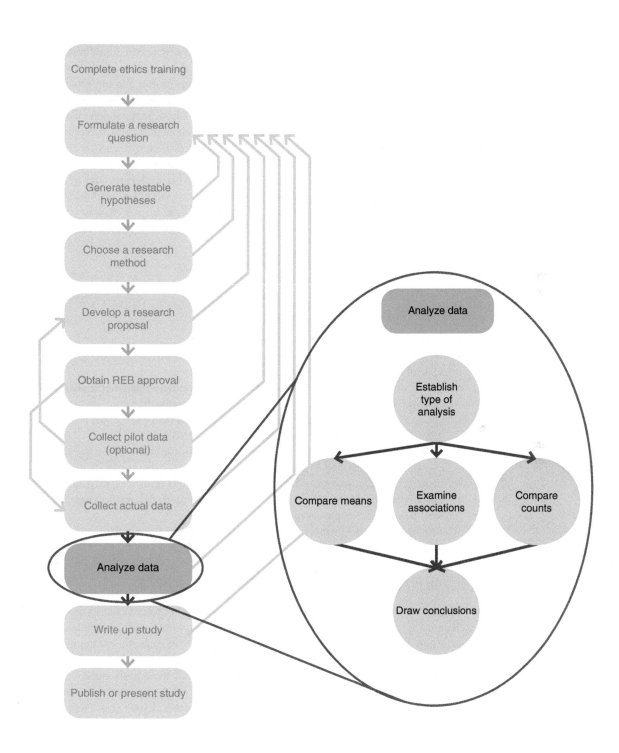

Chapter Abstract

In this chapter, we present analysis techniques for the types of data commonly encountered in behavioural research. At the core of your analysis plan you should consider how best to answer the research question you have designed your study to address. It is also important to realize that few, if any, research studies turn out exactly as planned. To understand your results, you will probably have to do some investigative data sleuthing. We begin the chapter with a general approach to data analysis, providing flowcharts to help you choose your path of analysis depending on your experimental design, the scales of your measures, and whether you are comparing means, analyzing count data, or investigating associations among variables. We also emphasize the use of visual displays to help you understand and interpret your results. Moreover, we describe how to use effect sizes and confidence intervals as you work with your data. We end with a brief introduction to robust statistical methods.

LEARNING OBJECTIVES

By the end of this chapter, you should be able to:

- Determine what type of analysis to conduct based on your research design and the scale of measurement of your variables.
- Briefly explain the difference between a parametric and non-parametric statistical test, and indicate when you would use a non-parametric statistical test.
- Compare and contrast methods for comparing means (i.e., one-sample *t* test, independent-samples *t* test, matched-pairs *t* test, ANOVA).
- Compare and contrast methods for investigating associations between variables (i.e., chi-square, correlations).
- Identify the effect size measures appropriate for various statistical analyses.
- Discuss the importance of checking assumptions prior to data analysis and identify methods for assessing assumptions.
- Briefly describe the purpose of robust statistical methods.

GENERAL APPROACH TO DATA ANALYSIS

In Chapter 11, we identified a number of steps to take as part of your data analysis. These steps include computing descriptive statistics and effect sizes, creating visual displays, and constructing confidence intervals. In this chapter, we will describe each of these steps in detail for a variety of different types of data analyses.

Although we presented a number of criticisms of null hypothesis significance testing (NHST) in Chapter 11 and recommend de-emphasizing inferential tests in drawing conclusions from your data, we do include such tests throughout this chapter (e.g., *t* test, analysis of variance [ANOVA], χ^2 test). At present, NHST still represents the dominant approach in psychology and related disciplines and remains the approach expected by many academic journals. Although effect sizes and confidence intervals are increasingly required to be reported in journal articles, the emphasis remains on test statistics and their associated p values (see "Media Matters: The Power of the p Value"). In addition, many decades' worth of published studies have used NHST to analyze data, and you must be familiar with inferential tests to understand the interpretation of results in these studies.

The Power of the *p* Value

Many researchers have questioned the soundness of the traditional NHST approach for decades. The continued power of p values in current research, however, cannot be denied. No one knows this better than W. Scott Harkonen, a physician who was prosecuted and sentenced to six months of home confinement in 2013 for his interpretation of p values in medical research. Specifically, what landed Harkonen in hot water was a two-sentence press release based on that interpretation.

Harkonen had been the chief executive officer of InterMune, a publicly traded biotechnology company that manufactured a drug called interferon-γ-1b (marketed as Actimmune) to help patients suffering from idiopathic pulmonary fibrosis (IPF), a terminal lung disease (Brown, 2013). In hopes of gaining US Food and Drug Administration approval for Actimmune in the treatment of IPF, InterMune launched a clinical trial in 2000 that randomly assigned 330 patients in 58 hospitals around the world to receive either interferon-γ-1b or placebo injections (Brown, 2013). Of the patients receiving the placebo, 52 per cent worsened or died, whereas only 46 per cent of those receiving Actimmune had the same outcomes. The trial's results had a p value of .08, which is larger than .05, the conventionally accepted level of significance (Brown, 2013). Within the traditional NHST approach to statistical hypothesis testing, this $p = .08$ value would not allow the researcher to conclude the drug was effective.

Yet Harkonen remained hopeful about proving the drug's efficacy. After examining the data more closely, Harkonen found that more patients with mild to moderate cases of IPF survived than the original participant group as a whole (Briggs, 2013). When InterMune's statisticians ran the numbers again within that subset, they found that only 5 per cent of those patients died, as opposed to 16 per cent of the original group. These percentages yielded a p value of .04, a value that suggests the drug was effective. Excited by the new interpretation,

Harkonen issued the following press release: "InterMune Announces Phase III Data Demonstrating Survival Benefit of Actimmune in IPF. Reduces Mortality by 70% in Patients with Mild to Moderate Disease" (Brown, 2013).

Harkonen's statement was technically true, which is what makes this case so strange. But someone (in fact, another statistician by the name of Thomas Fleming) took issue with Harkonen's methodology (Briggs, 2013). The US government agreed and filed a lawsuit, alleging that Harkonen drew "improper conclusions" from the data and that he did so for financial gain (Brown, 2013). He was convicted of fraud, a decision that was upheld by the 9th Circuit Court of Appeals.

According to Allan Gordus, a lawyer in the Justice Department's office of consumer litigation, "The government has always agreed that there was no falsification of data here. Whether there was falsification of the conclusions that could be drawn from the data—that was what the trial was all about" (Brown, 2013).

Steven N. Goodman, a pediatrician and biostatistician at Stanford University, put Harkonen's conviction in another context in an article that appeared in *Nature*: "This would be a lot like throwing weathermen in jail if they predicted a 40% chance of rain, and it rained" (Callaway, 2013).

Although this case did not draw much media attention, it alarmed the drug industry and countless researchers who rely on p values to establish statistical significance. "If you applied this rule to scientists, a sizable proportion of them might be in jail today," said Goodman, who submitted a statement supporting Harkonen's appeal (Brown, 2013).

Harkonen served his home incarceration and paid a fine of $20,000. In addition, he was banned by the US Department of Health and Human Services from working for virtually all medical institutions until 2016 and barred by the US Food and Drug Administration from employment by any company seeking the agency's approval for a product (Brown, 2013).

As we have emphasized throughout this book, you should choose a statistical approach *as you develop your research question and plan your study*. You should know whether you will be comparing mean responses across various experimental conditions, whether you will compute measures of association between pairs of variables, or whether you are interested in differences in the frequencies of certain types of responses. Figures 12.1 and 12.2 are meant to help you determine the steps that should be part of your data analysis.

Figure 12.1 outlines the decisions you must make to compare means. To the left in Figure 12.1 is the decision tree to consider if your comparisons involve a between-subjects design, and to the right is the decision tree for determining what kind of analysis to conduct for within-subjects or mixed designs. The second row from the bottom lists particular statistical tests that can be done (e.g., *t* test, one-way ANOVA, factorial ANOVA). At the top, middle, and bottom of Figure 12.1 are reminders to calculate descriptive statistics, visually display your means and confidence intervals, and compute effect sizes. The decision trees in the figure address questions about whether you have a between- or within-subjects design and whether you are examining one or more factors or one or more groups of participants.

Not all research questions, however, require comparisons of means. Many research studies explore the relationships between two or more variables. Figure 12.2 provides a data analysis flowchart for deciding what type of analysis to use to explore a research question involving such relationships. The top row of Figure 12.2 presents different types of data (e.g., interval/ratio,

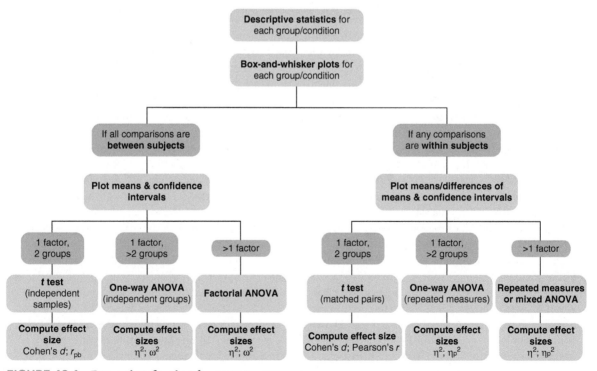

FIGURE 12.1   Data analysis flowchart for comparing means.

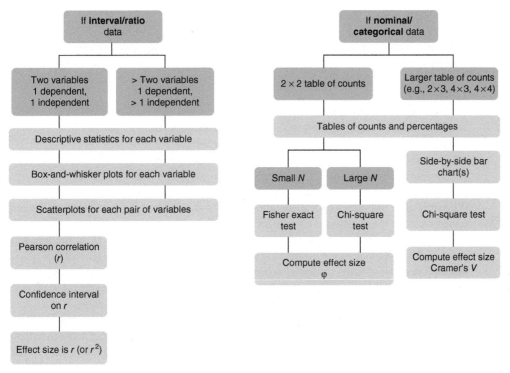

FIGURE 12.2   Data analysis flowchart for examining relationships among variables.

nominal/categorical) and the second row displays the steps or decisions that must be made depending on the number of variables and the size of your sample. As with the comparison of means, the bottom row advocates for the calculation of effect sizes.

In the next section, we provide a review of the methods for comparing two or more means. We then review statistical approaches to examining the association between variables.

COMPARING MEANS

Behavioural researchers are commonly interested in looking at patterns of means across conditions. The standard approach to the mean for a single sample or comparing the means for two samples is to use *t* tests. The approach for comparing means for more than two samples or for more than one factor is called an **analysis of variance (ANOVA)**. Both of these approaches include variations depending on whether the researcher has used a between- or within-subjects design.

A *t* test or an ANOVA test is an example of a **parametric test** that assumes data are interval or ratio level and the data values are normally distributed. **Non-parametric tests** do not make such strong assumptions and can be used to analyze ordinal and nominal data and data sets that deviate substantially from normality. With each parametric test below, we also list a non-parametric alternative.

analysis of variance (ANOVA) A statistical technique to test for differences among means. (See also one-way ANOVA, repeated-measures one-way ANOVA, two-way ANOVA.)

parametric test A statistical test that requires that the measurement scale of your data be interval or ratio and makes strong assumptions about the distribution of measurements in your population.

non-parametric test A statistical test that makes few assumptions about the population distribution and may be applied to nominal and ordinal measurements.

One-Sample *t* Test

t test, one sample
A statistical test for comparing the mean of a single sample to a specified value.

The one-sample *t* test is used to compare the mean of a single sample with some criterion or "standard." The assumptions of this test are as follows:

***Assumptions*:**
1. Interval or ratio level data
2. Observations/cases are *randomly sampled* from the population of interest
3. Observations/cases are *independent* of one another
4. The values in the population from which we are sampling are *normally distributed*
   Non-parametric alternative: One-sample Wilcoxon signed-rank test

Wilcoxon signed-rank test A non-parametric alternative to the one-sample or matched-pairs *t* tests.

When the data are either ordinal or non-normally distributed, the one-sample Wilcoxon signed-rank test may be used as a non-parametric alternative.

As an example, we revisit the school 1 data set introduced in Table 11.2. The box-and-whisker plot and frequency histogram for these data are reproduced in Figure 12.3. Suppose you want to know whether students in school 1 watch more hours of television per week than a reported national average of 22 hours. Hence, 22 is the value that we will compare our sample mean against. These 30 values have a mean of 19.5, a median of 21, a range of 35, and a standard deviation of 8.79. From Figure 12.3, the data look to be relatively symmetric about the mean, perhaps with a slight *negative skew* (there is a longer tail to the left than to the right), but none of these displays suggests that the data values deviate seriously from normality or that there are problematic outliers (see the section on assumption violations later in this chapter for more formal methods of assessing normality).

Our raw effect size is simply the sample mean of 19.5 minus the hypothesized value of 22, which gives –2.5. We can also compute a standardized effect size such as Cohen's *d*, which is simply the difference of –2.5 divided by the sample standard deviation of 8.79, giving a *d* value of –0.28 (which would be considered a "small" effect). Cohen (1992) recommends the following guidelines for interpreting Cohen's *d* effect sizes: 0–0.19 = very small effect; 0.20–0.49 = small effect; 0.50–0.79 = medium effect; ≥0.80 = large effect.

Confidence intervals calculated for the mean would range from 16.22 to 22.78. This confidence interval includes the national average of 22 hours, so we are unlikely to conclude that students of school 1 watch statistically fewer hours of television than the national average. We can also construct the confidence interval around the difference of –2.5, which would give us the range of –5.78 to 0.78. Here, we see that a difference of 0 is included within the confidence interval, so again we are unlikely to conclude that the students of school 1 watch statistically fewer hours of television than the national average.

When reporting the results from the statistical tests we conduct, students and researchers in psychology will typically conform to the guidelines put forth by the American Psychological Association (known as APA format). For the one-sample *t* test, we would get the following results (in proper APA format): $t(29) = -1.56$, $p = .130$. Since our *p* value

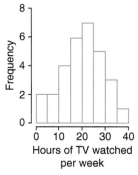

FIGURE 12.3   Box-and-whisker plot and histogram for the school 1 data in Table 11.2.

of .130 is greater than our α value of .05, we fail to reject H_0 and conclude that the average number of hours of television watched in this classroom does not differ from the national average.

Independent-Samples t Test

An independent-samples *t* test is used to compare the means of two independent samples. Assumptions of the test and alternative tests follow. Regarding the fourth assumption, the impact of unequal variances is less when your two samples are the same size, so it is a good practice to try to obtain the same number of participants per group (Mewhort, Kelly, & Johns, 2009).

Assumptions:
1. Interval or ratio level data
2. Random sampling and independence of observations/cases
3. The values in the two populations from which the samples are drawn are normally distributed
4. The two populations from which the samples were drawn have equal variances
   Alternative test when variances cannot be assumed to be equal: Welch's *t* test
   Non-parametric alternative: Mann–Whitney *U* test/Wilcoxon rank-sum test

The values in Table 12.1 represent total response times across 10 trials for 20 hypothetical participants participating in a Stroop interference task. In the interference condition, respondents had to name the colour of the ink for colour words where the ink colour disagreed with the colour named by the word, for example, the word "red" printed in blue ink. In the no-interference condition, colour-neutral words were used with the same colour-naming task, for example, the word "cat" printed in blue ink. Each participant took part in only one of the conditions.

t test, independent samples A statistical test for comparing the means of two independent samples.

Welch's t test A version of the independent-samples *t* test that takes into account unequal variances between the two groups.

Mann–Whitney U test (Wilcoxon rank-sum test) A non-parametric alternative to the independent-samples *t* test.

Table 12.1 Total response times across 10 trials for 20 participants, half assigned to each of two conditions in a Stroop task.

Total Response Time (Sec) for 10 Trials	
No Interference	Interference
3.27	4.08
3.35	5.46
2.07	3.89
2.62	5.13
2.51	2.58
3.63	3.12
3.45	3.51
4.28	4.37
3.91	6.11
2.64	4.87

Table 12.2 Descriptive statistics for Stroop data of Table 12.1.		
	No Interference	Interference
Mean	3.17	4.31
Median	3.31	4.23
Standard deviation	0.69	1.10
Variance	0.48	1.20
N	10	10

Table 12.2 presents descriptive statistics for these two samples, and Figure 12.4 displays box-and-whisker plots and histograms. The visual displays do not reveal any severe outliers or obvious deviations from normality. The variance for the interference group is larger than that for the no-interference group by a factor of about 2.5, but this is still within a reasonable range. We also see a good degree of separation between the two groups, both in the box-and-whisker plot and in the histogram, suggesting a fairly strong effect.

Effect sizes can be calculated a number of ways. For this data set, we could calculate the effect size using the difference of means (effect size = 1.14) or Cohen's d (effect size = 1.24), which suggests a large effect.

Confidence intervals may also be constructed for each of the two groups, which would give us 95 per cent confidence intervals ranging from 2.68 to 3.67 and 3.53 to 5.10 for the no-interference and interference groups, respectively. These are plotted in Figure 12.5. Note that the confidence intervals for the two conditions overlap just a little. The overlap in confidence intervals does not necessarily suggest that the difference is statistically non-significant, so it is useful to construct the 95 per cent confidence interval for the difference of the two means. Doing so would give us a range from 0.28 to 2.00. This confidence interval does not span 0, so we are on solid ground in concluding that the means for the two groups are not equal to one another. The confidence interval for the difference of the means is displayed in Figure 12.5b.

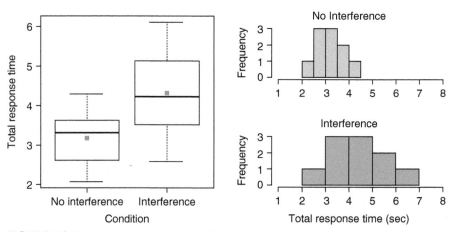

FIGURE 12.4   Box-and-whisker plots and histograms for data in Table 12.1.

Applying the independent-samples t test gives us $t(18) = 2.77, p = .013$. Our p value is less than .05, so we reject the null hypothesis of no difference between the means and conclude that the means are statistically different from one another. Note that for the independent-samples t test, $df = n - 2$, where n is the total count for both samples. When reporting the results of the t test in APA style, the effect size measure can be included at the end: $t(18) = 2.77, p = .013, d = 1.24$.

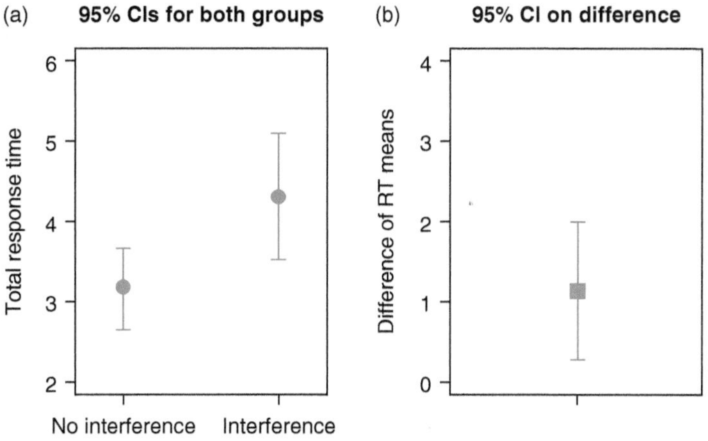

Matched-Pairs t Test

A matched-pairs t test compares means of the same participants on two different measures. Test assumptions and an alternative test are shown here.

FIGURE 12.5   The 95 per cent confidence intervals (a) around the two means and (b) around the difference in the means.

Assumptions:
1. Interval or ratio level data
2. Random sampling
3. Independence of observations (between cases, not within)
4. Difference scores are normally distributed
   Non-parametric alternative: Wilcoxon signed-rank test

t test, matched pairs
A statistical test for comparing the means of two matched samples. The samples may represent two different measurements from the same participants or different participants matched on some criteria (e.g., academic achievement).

Suppose you want to determine whether Grade 12 students at a particular high school score higher on the math portion of a standardized test than on the verbal portion. You randomly select 10 students, administer the tests, and collect the test scores as shown in Table 12.3.

Since the same individuals are participating in both conditions, our two conditions are not independent of one another, and we should not use the independent-samples t test. The matched-pairs t test operates on the differences of the matched scores (i.e., the differences between the math scores and verbal scores) computed for each individual. The mean difference between the math and verbal scores is 8.1, and the 95 per cent confidence interval for this mean ranges from 1.30 to 14.90. Since the confidence interval does not include 0, we would conclude that the students in the school do score differently on the two portions of the standardized test. To determine the size of the effect, we could calculate the effect size using the difference of means (effect size = 8.1), Cohen's d ($d = 0.85$), or a Pearson correlation ($r = .72$), all of which indicate a large effect. Cohen (1992) recommends the following guidelines for interpreting the effect size for r correlations: 0–.09 = very small; .10–.29 = small; .30–.49 = medium; ≥.50 = large.

Application of the matched-pairs t test gives $t(9) = 2.70, p = .025, d = 0.85$, and we would reject the null hypothesis of no difference between the two sets of test scores. Note again how the p value leads to the same conclusion of rejecting the null hypothesis as the 95 per cent confidence interval did, but the confidence interval combined with the mean value gives us important information about the size of the difference and the precision of our estimate.

Table 12.3   Verbal and math test scores for 10 students.

Student	Verbal Score	Math Score	Difference (Math – Verbal)
1	43	52	9
2	54	76	22
3	56	70	14
4	65	75	10
5	72	69	–3
6	72	71	–1
7	73	80	7
8	79	71	–8
9	79	96	17
10	81	95	14
Mean	67.4	75.5	8.1
Standard deviation	12.6	12.9	9.5

COMPARISONS OF MORE THAN TWO MEANS: ANOVA

one-way analysis of variance (ANOVA)
A statistical technique to test for differences of means on a single factor.

Often we want to consider the means from more than just two groups, samples, or conditions. If we wish to compare the means for three or more samples on a single factor, then we employ **one-way analysis of variance (ANOVA)**. Just as with *t* tests in the two-group case, the analysis proceeds differently depending on whether we have used a between-subjects design (independent groups) or a within-subjects design (repeated measures).

Independent-Groups One-Way ANOVA (Between Subjects)

A one-way ANOVA is used to compare two or more independent samples. The assumptions for independent-groups one-way ANOVA are identical to those of the independent-samples *t* test:

Kruskal–Wallis test
A non-parametric alternative to one-way analysis of variance.

Assumptions:
1. Interval or ratio level data
2. Random sampling and independence of observations
3. The values in the *k* populations from which the samples are drawn are normally distributed (k = # of groups or factor levels)
4. The *k* populations have equal variances (homogeneity of variance)
    Non-parametric alternative: **Kruskal–Wallis test**

Table 12.4 Data and descriptive statistics for memory task for 30 participants, each assigned to one of three conditions.

	No Caffeine	Moderate Caffeine	High Caffeine
	88	78	85
	82	82	84
	79	93	64
	90	91	66
	68	94	87
	70	69	74
	61	90	82
	65	76	77
	91	96	59
	75	88	69
Mean	76.9	85.7	74.7
Median	77.0	89.0	75.5
Standard deviation	10.8	9.0	9.8
Standard error	3.4	2.8	3.1

Consider a specific example using the hypothetical caffeine experiment described in Chapter 7, where we tested the effects of caffeine on performance in a memory task. We will first start with a between-subjects version of this experiment and later consider a within-subjects version when we discuss repeated-measures ANOVA.

Each of 30 participants is randomly assigned to one of three conditions: a "caffeine-free" condition, where participants are given a cup of herbal tea before performing the memory task; a "moderate-caffeine condition," where participants are given a cup of green tea before the task; and a "high-caffeine condition," where participants are given three shots of strong coffee before the task. The memory task scores for each participant, along with means, medians, standard deviations, and standard errors, are shown in Table 12.4. Box-and-whisker plots and 95 per cent confidence interval plots are shown in Figure 12.6.

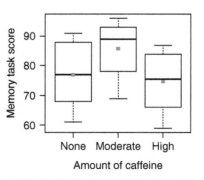
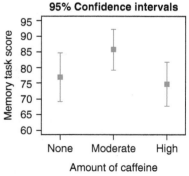

FIGURE 12.6 Box-and-whisker and confidence interval plots for the caffeine study data.

ANOVA table A table
used to organize and
display the results of
analysis of variance.

sums of squares
Mathematical quantities
that measure the amount
of variability in data.
These include between-
subjects, within-subjects,
and total sums of
squares.

omnibus null
hypothesis In analysis
of variance, the null
hypothesis that all group
means are equal.

eta squared (η^2) An
effect size measure for
one-way analysis of
variance.

The plots in Figure 12.6 strongly suggest a difference between the moderate-caffeine group and the other two groups. On the one hand, there is a small amount of overlap between the moderate- and high-caffeine confidence intervals and somewhat more overlap for the moderate- and no-caffeine groups. The high- and no-caffeine groups, on the other hand, have similar means and nearly completely overlapping confidence intervals.

The ANOVA table for these data is presented in Table 12.5. Three types of sums of squares, all of which measure the amount of variability in the data, are displayed. The between-subjects sum of squares shows the extent to which the group means deviate from the overall mean. The within-subjects sum of squares indicates the extent to which each data point deviates from its group mean. Adding the between- and within-subjects values gives the total sum of squares that indicates the extent to which the data values deviate from the overall mean. Each mean square value, which is computed by dividing the corresponding sum of squares by its associated degrees of freedom, is an estimate of the population variance. If the between-subjects mean square is considerably larger than the within-subjects mean square, it suggests that differences between the groups are greater than differences within the groups and provides evidence that the group population means differ from one another.

The omnibus null hypothesis tested by one-way ANOVA is that the population means for all the groups are equal. According to the ANOVA table, the p value is smaller than our standard α level of .05, so we would reject the null hypothesis and conclude that the three population means are not equal.

A common effect size for a one-way ANOVA is eta squared (η^2), which is defined as

$$\eta^2 = \frac{SS_{between}}{SS_{total}}$$

The value of η^2 ranges from 0 to 1. For the caffeine data, $\eta^2 = .20$. According to Cohen (1988), an effect size of .01 is considered small, .06 medium, and .14 or higher, large. For this example, we have obtained a large effect. Overall, the results for the ANOVA would be reported as follows: $F(2,27) = 3.46$, $p = .046$, $\eta^2 = .20$.

Multiple Comparisons

As described above, the F test and its associated p value for the caffeine experiment led us to conclude that the means for the three populations under consideration are not identical. Beyond that, we concluded nothing else about where the differences lie. In this example, there are three pairwise comparisons we could make: no caffeine versus moderate caffeine, no

Table 12.5   One-way analysis of variance table for between-subjects caffeine study.

	Sum of Squares	df	Mean Square	F	p
Between subjects	677.61	2	338.81	3.46	.046
Within subjects (error)	2,647.13	27	98.04		
Total	3,324.74	29			

caffeine versus high caffeine, and moderate caffeine versus high caffeine. We do not know, for example, whether the moderate-caffeine mean differs from the other two while the other two means may not statistically differ from one another. We need something to go beyond the omnibus test. We need to do some follow-up tests to determine which means are actually statistically different from one another.

A number of tests have been developed to make these follow-up comparisons. We will not cover them or their differences here, but which test to use depends on a number of factors, including whether your comparisons were planned prior to collecting your data or whether they were unplanned (post hoc), concerns around risks of type I and type II errors, whether equal variances can be assumed, and the types of comparisons being made (simple pairwise or complex). Some of the more common multiple comparison tests include Tukey's HSD, Games–Howell, and the Bonferroni–Dunn test.

Repeated-Measures One-Way ANOVA (Within Subjects)

Recall from our discussion of the *t* test that when respondents provide measures for both variables under study, we are able to apply the matched-pairs *t* test. The advantage of a matched-pairs design is that it helps control for the variability across participants. In a similar way, **repeated-measures one-way ANOVA** incorporates the same kind of control when we are investigating more than two conditions. Assumptions for this test are as follows:

repeated-measures one-way ANOVA A statistical technique for testing differences of means across a single factor in which the same participants provide measurements for each level of the factor.

Assumptions:
1. Interval or ratio level data
2. Random sampling and independence of participants (but not the *k* observations within a participant)
3. The values in the *k* populations from which the samples are drawn are normally distributed
4. The *k* populations exhibit sphericity, which is an extension of the homogeneity of variance assumption

   Non-parametric alternative: **Friedman test**

Friedman test A non-parametric alternative to repeated-measures one-way analysis of variance.

Sphericity means that if you compute differences between all pairs of experimental groups, the variances of those differences should be approximately equal. Many statistical packages include diagnostic tests for sphericity, and violations of the sphericity assumption may call into question the results of your ANOVA.

Consider a repeated-measures (or within-subjects) variation of our caffeine experiment as displayed in Table 12.6. In this case, rather than having each of 30 participants take part in only one of the three caffeine conditions, each of 10 participants took part in all three conditions (presumably with enough intervening time and in different orders to control for some of the potential hazards of within-subjects designs described in Chapter 7).

sphericity An assumption for repeated-measures analysis of variance that requires the variances of the differences between all pairs of groups be approximately equal.

The values in Table 12.6 have been ordered in such a way that you can easily see that respondents who scored relatively low on one of the memory tests also tended to score relatively low on the others, whereas those who scored high on one tended to score relatively high on all tests. This might reflect the fact that some people tend to have better memories, in general, than others. By controlling for this variation across participants, we can increase the power of our ANOVA test.

The ANOVA table for this analysis is shown in Table 12.7. Now we see that the test for condition (between groups) gives $F(2,18) = 4.94$, $p = .020$. In this case, we reject the null

Table 12.6   Data for repeated-measures version of caffeine study.

Participant	No Caffeine	Moderate Caffeine	High Caffeine
1	72	73	67
2	69	81	67
3	66	68	71
4	88	91	73
5	67	79	74
6	78	87	75
7	80	88	78
8	81	92	88
9	91	82	88
10	90	93	89
Mean	78.2	83.4	77.0

hypothesis of equal means across the three conditions. For a one-way repeated-measures design, effect size is commonly measured by partial η^2, defined as SS condition$/(SS$ total $- SS$ participant). For our example, partial $\eta^2 = .35$.

Two-Way ANOVA (Factorial ANOVA)

two-way ANOVA (factorial ANOVA)
A statistical technique for comparing means when the experimental design includes two factors.

Researchers frequently collect information on more than one factor, as we discussed in Chapter 8. For example, in our hypothetical caffeine study, suppose we want to investigate not only the effects of caffeine, but also the effects of amount of sleep. In this case, we might use a **two-way ANOVA** to analyze our results. As with one-way ANOVA, we can have between-subjects and within-subjects measurements. We will focus here on a two-way between-subjects example. The assumptions are the same as those for the independent-samples t test and between-subjects

Table 12.7   Analysis of variance table for repeated-measures analysis of data in Table 12.6.

	Sum of Squares	df	Mean Square	F	p
Caffeine condition	231.53	2	115.77	4.94	.020
Participant	1,668.12	9	185.35		
Error	421.90	18	23.44		
Total	2,321.55	29			

Table 12.8 Memory task scores for 30 participants with two between-subject factors.

Amount of Sleep	No Caffeine	Moderate Caffeine	High Caffeine
4–5 hours	61	74	59
4–5 hours	67	83	53
4–5 hours	71	75	63
4–5 hours	78	89	71
4–5 hours	83	89	64
7–8 hours	72	80	85
7–8 hours	79	92	76
7–8 hours	82	87	93
7–8 hours	86	95	89
7–8 hours	91	96	87

one-way ANOVA, with the addition of the assumption that all cells have the same number of observations.

Consider the data in Table 12.8. We have added a second factor to our study examining the effects of caffeine on performance in the memory task, namely the amount of sleep (4–5 hours or 7–8 hours) the previous night. Each of 30 participants took part in a single combination of the two factors. The combination of three caffeine levels and two sleep levels gives a total of six experimental cells with five participants per cell.

Means and standard deviations for each of the six groups are shown in Table 12.9, and the 95 per cent confidence intervals around the means are shown in Figure 12.7.

Table 12.9 Means and standard deviations for each of the six groups in the 2 × 3 caffeine study.

| Amount of Sleep | Amount of Caffeine | | | |
	None	Moderate	High	Overall
Low (4–5 hours)	Mean = 72 (SD = 8.72)	82 (7.28)	62 (6.63)	72 (10.99)
High (7–8 hours)	82 (7.18)	90 (6.60)	86 (6.32)	86 (7.07)
Overall	77 (9.19)	86 (7.79)	74 (14.05)	79 (11.54)

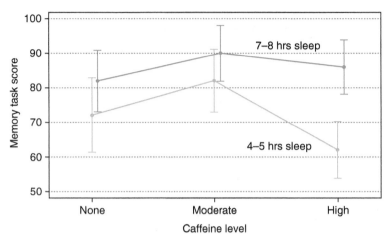

FIGURE 12.7 95 per cent confidence intervals for each of the six groups in the 2 × 3 memory task study.

main effect The overall effect of a single factor on the dependent variable, averaging over the levels of all other factors.

We note several things from the descriptive statistics and the confidence intervals. The low-sleep means (4–5 hours) all fall below the high-sleep means (7–8 hours), although there is significant overlap in confidence intervals for the no- and moderate-caffeine levels. There is a large difference in the means for the two sleep levels at the high-caffeine level. Moreover, the mean scores for the moderate-caffeine groups are consistently larger than those for the no-caffeine and high-caffeine groups. The ANOVA table for this data set is shown in Table 12.10.

Look at the rows labelled Caffeine and Sleep. The results represented in these rows are for **main effects**, and they tell us the effect (the pattern of responses across the different levels) of each factor separately. We observe values of $p < .05$ for both main effects. Within the NHST framework, then, we would reject the null hypotheses of (1) no difference in means for the three levels of caffeine and (2) no difference in means for the two levels of sleep, and conclude that there are statistical differences among the levels for both of these factors. We see from Table 12.9 and Figure 12.7 that the overall mean memory score for the moderate-caffeine group (86) is notably larger than the scores for the no-caffeine (77) and high-caffeine (74) groups. We also see that the mean score for the high-sleep group (86) is higher than that for the low-sleep group (72).

interaction effect A measure of the extent to which the effect of one factor depends on the levels of the other factor.

The third row of the ANOVA table shows us the caffeine × sleep **interaction effect**. As we discussed in Chapter 8, the interaction effect tells us the extent to which the effect of one factor depends on the levels of the other factor. An examination of Figure 12.7 should make this clear. We see that the difference, or the gap between means, for the low-sleep participants and the high-sleep participants is considerably larger for the high-caffeine group than for either of the no-caffeine or the moderate-caffeine groups. In Table 12.10, the p value of .040 for the caffeine × sleep interaction leads us to reject the null hypothesis of no interaction and conclude that there is a statistically significant interaction between caffeine and sleep.

Table 12.10 Analysis of variance table for memory task experiment with between-subjects sleep and caffeine factors.

	Sum of Squares	df	Mean Square	F	p
Caffeine	780	2	390.00	7.60	.003
Sleep	1,470	1	1,470.00	28.64	<.001
Caffeine × sleep	380	2	190.00	3.70	.040
Residual (error)	1,232	24	51.33		
Total	3,862	29			

Table 12.11   Effect sizes for the caffeine and sleep example.

	η^2	Partial η^2	ω^2
Caffeine	.20	.39	.17
Sleep	.38	.54	.36
Caffeine × sleep	.10	.24	.07

Since we are investigating three different effects (two main effects and one interaction effect), we compute an effect size for each. As with between-subjects one-way ANOVA, we may use η^2 as a measure of effect size, although we may also use partial η^2 and ω^2. These effect sizes are shown in Table 12.11 and suggest moderate to large effects (Cohen, 1988).

Interactions.   Because the concept of interactions can be difficult to grasp, we want to say just a little more about them here. As we noted earlier, we observe an interaction when the strength of the effect of one of our factors (e.g., amount of caffeine) depends on the level of the other factor (e.g., amount of sleep). As we saw in Figure 12.7, the difference between the low-sleep and high-sleep groups is much greater in the high-caffeine condition than in the other two conditions. This suggests an interaction between caffeine level and sleep level. Figure 12.7, in which we plotted the means for all six groups and then connected the means within each of the sleep levels, gives an example of an interaction chart. The non-parallel lines suggest the presence of an interaction effect.

As part of the interpretation of an interaction chart, you should consider confidence intervals in conjunction with the patterns of means. In Figure 12.8a, the large separation of the confidence intervals strongly suggests an interaction effect. In contrast, the large overlaps in Figure 12.8b do not provide support for an interaction effect.

Multiple Comparisons.   As with one-way ANOVA, various methods for investigating the multiple comparisons can be made among the different groups/cells in the experimental design. Typically, these comparisons will not be examined unless at least one of your effects is statistically significant and your factor has more than two levels.

COMPARING COUNTS/ FREQUENCIES

So far in this chapter, we have focused on statistical tests for data that are on interval or ratio scales. But suppose you are interested in whether men and women differ in their preferences for two political candidates. This yields a different type of data and requires different statistical

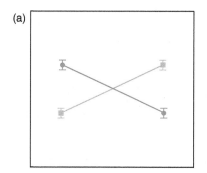
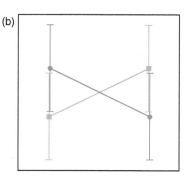

FIGURE 12.8   Interaction charts with confidence intervals: (a) large separation of confidence intervals and (b) large overlap of confidence intervals.

approaches. For example, imagine that you randomly sample 90 men and 100 women and ask them to choose between candidate A and candidate B (for this example, assume that no one is un-decided). Consider the hypothetical results in Table 12.12 showing the number of men and women who prefer each candidate. Rather than examining differences among mean responses as we did when considering t tests and ANOVA, we are now interested in whether there is a difference in the patterns of counts or frequencies between men and women with respect to their candidate preferences. The two variables (sex and preferred candidate) are both nominal/categorical, and we are interested in whether there is an *association* between the two variables.

We will first consider a 2×2 table as in Table 12.12. Then we will move on to tables with more than two levels on at least one of the variables/factors.

2 × 2 Tables

To better understand what the data tell us, we will first transform the counts to percentages. In this case, we are more interested in the percentage of each sex who prefer each candidate (rather than the percentage of those who prefer each candidate who are men or women), so we will compute row percentages as shown in Table 12.13.

The results suggest an association between sex and preferred candidate, with men more likely than women to prefer candidate A over candidate B. For 2×2 contingency tables, the most common measure of effect size is the coefficient phi (φ). Like a correlation, φ ranges from -1 to 1. For the data in Table 12.12, $\varphi = .15$. Cohen (1992) provides the following guidelines for interpreting φ: $0-<.10 =$ very small effect, $.10-<.30 =$ small effect, $.30-<.50 =$ medium effect, and $\geq.50 =$ large effect. Another measure of effect size for 2×2 contingency tables is

Table 12.12 Number of men and women preferring each of two candidates.

| | Preferred Candidate | | |
	A	B	Total count
Men	57	33	90
Women	48	52	100
Total	105	85	190

Table 12.13 Row percentages for candidate preference data.

| | Preferred Candidate | | |
	A	B	Total
Men (%)	63	37	100
Women (%)	48	52	100

simply the difference in proportions. If we focus on preference for candidate A, then the proportion of respondents who prefer candidate A is .63 for men and .48 for women. The difference in these proportions, then, is .63 − .48 = .15.

The chi-square (χ^2) test for independence is commonly applied to contingency tables. Assumptions for this test are shown here:

Assumptions:
1. Random sampling and independence of observations
2. For 2 × 2 tables, all expected frequencies should be at least 5
3. For larger tables, 80 per cent of expected cell frequencies should be at least 5, and none should be 0 (Yates, Moore, & McCabe, 1999, p. 734)

For the current example, the result of the χ^2 test, in APA style, is χ^2 (1, n = 190) = 4.50, p = .034, φ = .15.

χ^2 Test of Independence for $R \times C$ Contingency Tables

When we have more than two levels on either of the factors, we still use a χ^2 test for independence to determine whether the distribution of responses on one variable is independent of the distribution of responses on the second variable. Table 12.14 shows the number of men and women who prefer each of four candidates.

Table 12.15 allows us to more easily detect potential differences between men and women with respect to their voting preferences. For example, we see that the differences between the percentages is largest for candidate A and smallest for candidate C.

Table 12.14 Number of men and women preferring each of four candidates.

	Preferred Candidate				
	A	B	C	D	Total
Men	54	26	30	10	120
Women	38	39	29	24	130
Total	92	65	59	34	250

Table 12.15 Row percentages for candidate preference data of Table 12.14.

	Preferred Candidate				
	A	B	C	D	Total
Men (%)	45.0	21.7	25.0	8.3	100
Women (%)	29.2	30.0	22.3	18.5	100

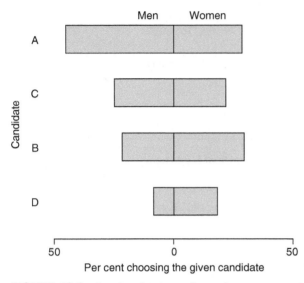

FIGURE 12.9 Bar plot of voting preference by sex.

When we have more than two categories for either variable, it can be instructive to graph the data, as in Figure 12.9. In addition to the absolute differences that we were able to observe in Table 12.15, the bar plot highlights the relative differences; for example, the percentage of women preferring candidate D is more than double the percentage for men.

The disparities between the bars on the left (for men) and the bars on the right (for women) certainly suggest a difference in candidate preferences between men and women. A common effect size measure for $R \times C$ contingency tables is Cramer's V, which ranges from 0 to 1. For the current example, Cramer's V is .21, a small effect; specific guidelines for interpreting Cramer's V depend on the size of the contingency table (Cohen, 1988).

Finally, the χ^2 test gives us $\chi^2(3, n = 250) = 10.78, p = .013$. With an α of .05, we would reject the null hypothesis that the proportions of respondents who prefer each candidate are the same for men and women. As with ANOVA, it is possible (and usually desirable) to perform additional tests to determine where the differences lie (see Pallant, 2016).

Tests of Association: Correlation

As we discussed in the section on bivariate descriptive statistics in Chapter 11, the most common measure of the association between two interval or ratio level variables is the Pearson product-moment correlation (Pearson's r). Next, we provide an example with confidence intervals.

Pearson's r. Pearson correlations are used when you want to determine the degree of linear association between two interval or ratio level variables. This approach assumes that the two populations are normally distributed and that the relationship between the variables is linear.

Hypothetical math and verbal standardized test scores for 12 students are shown in Table 12.16, and a scatterplot of these scores is shown in Figure 12.10. The plot suggests that, on average, higher math scores are associated with higher verbal scores. In addition, there does not seem to be an obvious non-linear relationship that we need to be aware of.

The Pearson's r is .60 (this is also the effect size), and the 95 per cent confidence interval is from 0.04 to 0.87. The p value for testing the null hypothesis of $r = 0$ is .039, so we would reject this null hypothesis of zero correlation. In APA style, these results would be reported as $r = .60$, $p = .039$, 95% CI [0.04, 0.87]. The wide confidence interval (which is not unexpected with such a small n), however, provides a sense of just how imprecise our estimate of the population correlation really is.

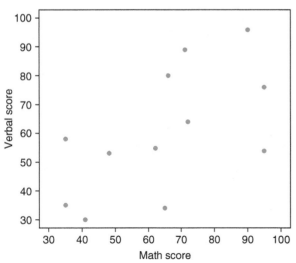

FIGURE 12.10 Scatterplot of math and verbal test scores.

Table 12.16   Math and verbal test scores for 12 students.

Student	Math Score	Verbal Score
1	62	55
2	41	30
3	65	34
4	95	54
5	66	80
6	35	35
7	90	96
8	72	64
9	35	58
10	48	53
11	71	89
12	95	76

ASSUMPTION VIOLATIONS

Throughout this chapter, we have provided lists of assumptions for the various statistical tests, because performing a statistical test when its assumptions are violated may affect the accuracy of confidence intervals, p values, and your estimates of quantities such as means and standard deviations, as well as increasing the probabilities of type I or type II errors. Early in the analysis phase, you should examine your data for obvious assumption violations. Unfortunately, there is considerable disagreement about which violations are the most potentially damaging and how to assess and address these violations (Hoekstra, Kiers, & Johnson, 2012; Norman, 2010). Despite this lack of agreement, however, it is still important to be familiar with the main concerns and possible solutions. In the remainder of this section, we briefly review a number of potential assumption violations and point to diagnostic tools and potential aids for analyzing data in the presence of those violations.

Random Sampling and Independence of Observations

Random sampling and independence of observations are key assumptions for nearly any common statistical test. We discussed random sampling in detail in Chapter 5 and how deviations from random sampling affect your ability to generalize your results. Independence of observations means that a measurement you obtain, say, from one participant in your experiment, does not depend on the measurements you obtained from other participants: Their

independence of observations
A measurement obtained on an observation (e.g., from a participant) in the experiment does not depend on the measurements obtained on other observations (e.g., from other participants). The responses are *independent* of one another.

responses are *independent* of one another. In general, random sampling and independence of observations are elements of the experimental design process as opposed to assumptions you evaluate after collecting your data.

Non-normal Distributions

A number of statistical methods include the assumption of normally distributed population values. Since we rarely, if ever, are able to determine the actual distribution of values in the population, we rely on inspection of the values in our samples and evaluate the extent to which the sample data may violate normality. Here, we will consider two of the more worrisome deviations from normality: distributions with outliers and strongly skewed distributions.

Outliers.   Outliers (extreme value or values that deviate dramatically from the overall pattern of your data) represent one of the more serious problems you may encounter with your data. They can dramatically affect your estimates of means, standard deviations, and effect size measures, as well as confidence intervals, test statistics, *p* values, and the probabilities of type I and type II errors, particularly when sample sizes are small. Because of their potential effects on your results, you should always check your data for outliers.

Histograms and box-and-whisker plots are helpful for identifying outliers for individual variables, whereas scatterplots can help identify outliers when you examine bivariate relationships. It is important to understand that if you drop outliers from your analysis, you must explicitly state that you have done so, offer a rationale for dropping the value(s), and show how your analysis differs with and without the outliers.

Skewed Distributions.   You may have a data set that does not have values that would be considered outliers but is still non-normal by being skewed either to the left or right (see Figure 11.7). Histograms are useful for rough visual assessments of normality—for example, you look for a pattern similar to the bell shape of the normal curve. Another visual tool is the QQ plot (or **normal quantile–quantile plot**), two examples of which are displayed in Figure 12.11. Our school 1 data are reproduced in the histogram in the top left of Figure 12.11. In a QQ plot, normality is indicated by points falling along a relatively straight line. This certainly seems to be the case in the school 1 QQ plot at the bottom left of Figure 12.11. In contrast, the histogram in the upper right of Figure 12.11 represents an obviously skewed, quite asymmetric data set. The S-shape distribution of the points in the corresponding QQ plot strongly suggests a non-normal distribution of data values. A third technique that can be used to assess normality is to examine the skewness and kurtosis values for the data (see Chapter 11). In a normal distribution, both of these values would be 0. The further they are from 0, the more the data deviate from normality. Although differences exist in what values of skewness and kurtosis indicate problems with normality, a common rule of thumb is that both need to be between –2 and +2 (Tabachnick & Fidell, 2013).

QQ plot A graphical technique to identify deviations from normality in a data set. Also called a normal quantile–quantile plot.

Unequal Variances

Statistical tests like the independent-samples *t* test and ANOVA tests have the assumption of equal variances across the different groups. With equal group sizes, the impact of unequal variances may be minor, but you should always inspect your data to look for large

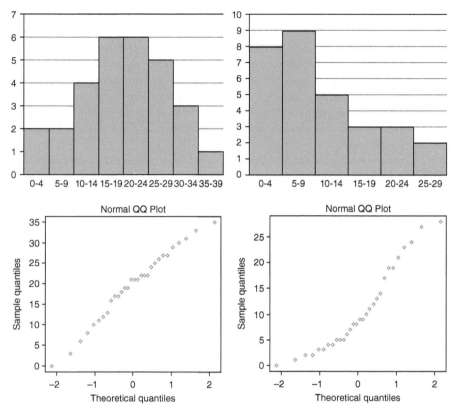

FIGURE 12.11 Histograms and normal QQ plots for an approximately normally distributed data set and a skewed data set.

differences in group variances. Examining descriptive statistics and side-by-side graphical displays such as box-and-whisker plots and histograms for each group will give you a good sense of how variances differ across groups. Statistical tests of equality of variances such as **Levene's test** may also be applied. The Levene's test is a hypothesis test in the same sense that a *t* test or ANOVA is a hypothesis test. In looking at the results of the Levene's test, a *p* value that is less than .05 indicates that the null hypothesis of no difference across the groups must be rejected (and thus the assumption of equal variances has been violated). A *p* value greater than .05 for the Levene's test indicates that the assumption has been met.

Levene's test A test of the equality of two variances.

Unequal Cell Sizes in Factorial ANOVA Designs

To the extent that it is possible, you should strive for equal numbers of respondents across all groups in factorial ANOVA designs. Unequal group counts are problematic because they can lead to confounding of experimental effects—that is, one cannot completely separate the effects of the different experimental factors. Analyzing such data requires the computation of a different type of sum of squares than appears in the standard ANOVA table and can complicate the interpretation and presentation of your results.

Lack of Sphericity with Repeated Measures

Mauchly's test of sphericity A test of the sphericity assumption in repeated-measures analysis of variance.

Greenhouse–Geisser correction A statistical adjustment to account for violation of sphericity in repeated-measures analysis of variance.

Recall that the condition of sphericity in a repeated-measures ANOVA design means that if you compute the differences between all pairs of groups on a within-subjects factor, the variances of those differences should be approximately equal. Violations of sphericity may increase the probability of a type I error. You can look for sphericity violations by examining the variances of the differences between groups or by applying a test such as Mauchly's test of sphericity. In the face of sphericity violations, you may analyze your data by applying statistical adjustments such as the Greenhouse–Geisser correction.

With the use of descriptive statistics, visual displays, and various diagnostics offered by statistical programs, you should have a good sense of whether your data exhibit worrisome violations of assumptions. With this information, you can determine whether to proceed with the originally planned tests, perhaps after removing outliers, or whether a different approach is required, such as a non-parametric alternative or robust statistical methods.

Before we end this chapter, we will introduce you to robust statistical methods, which involves the application of techniques that may provide more accurate test statistics, p values, and estimates of effect sizes and confidence intervals when assumptions are violated. Although such methods may still fall within the domain of NHST, they are often more appropriate than traditional tests.

ROBUST STATISTICAL METHODS

robust statistical methods Statistical tests that are not greatly affected by conditions that violate the assumptions of standard parametric tests, for example, the assumption that population values are normally distributed.

We have already alluded to robust statistical methods by listing non-parametric versions of statistical tests. Given the increasing availability of robust techniques available in statistical packages such as SPSS, SAS, and R, as well as criticisms regularly levelled against the blind application of classic parametric statistical tests (e.g., t tests and ANOVA), it is worth saying just a few more words about robust statistics.

Statistics (such as means, standard deviations, or medians) and statistical tests are robust to the extent that they are not greatly affected by conditions that violate the assumptions of standard parametric tests, for example, the presence of outliers, skewed distributions, or unequal variances. Robust statistical tests may be either non-parametric or parametric. Classic non-parametric tests include those we listed earlier as alternatives to parametric tests, such as the Wilcoxon signed-rank test, the Wilcoxon rank-sum test, the Mann–Whitney U test, and the Kruskal–Wallis test. These methods are applicable to relatively simple experimental designs, such as those that might otherwise be analyzed using simple t tests or one-way ANOVA.

trimmed mean A mean computed after removing some fixed percentage (often 10 or 20 per cent) of the largest and smallest values in a data set.

Robust tests may also be parametric. Welch's t test is a parametric test that is robust under violations of the equal variance assumption for the independent-samples t test. Additional parametric techniques involve using trimmed means, in which some percentage (usually 10 or 20 per cent) of the largest and smallest data values are removed from your data set, or various methods in which data values are removed based on their identification as outliers. It is important to understand that although these approaches are parametric, they estimate specialized parameters, such as a difference in *trimmed* means rather than the traditional difference in means, and they require special procedures for computing important values such as standard errors and confidence intervals. More information on robust statistical techniques can be found in Wilcox and Keselman (2003); Erceg-Hurn and Mirosevich (2008); Erceg-Hurn, Wilcox, and Keselman (2013); Hoaglin, Mosteller, and Tukey (2000); and Wilcox (1998, 2012).

Practical Tips for Specific Approaches to Data Analysis

1. Prior to gathering your data, understand the type of data you will collect (e.g., means, counts) and what statistical methods are appropriate (e.g., t test, χ^2 test).

2. As the first part of your analysis, always compute descriptive statistics and create visual displays of your data.

3. Check the assumptions of your statistical tests and, in particular, identify values that might be considered outliers.

4. Compute effect sizes and, when appropriate, confidence intervals.

5. If appropriate, consider using non-parametric tests or robust parametric tests.

CHAPTER SUMMARY

In this chapter, we examined a variety of statistical methods that you have at your disposal when conducting research. As you conduct your analysis, you should inspect descriptive statistics and plot data in different ways, compute effect sizes, and use confidence intervals and inferential statistical tests to help you draw conclusions. Although you should have a good sense of how your data analysis will proceed prior to even collecting your data, do not apply statistical tests rigidly.

The specific statistical test you choose depends on your research question and measurement type. To examine patterns of means, you will typically use t tests, one-way ANOVA, or factorial ANOVA. To examine the relationships between variables measured on interval or ratio scales, you will most often use correlations. When inspecting counts or frequencies for categorical data, you will typically use a χ^2 test.

Once you have completed your data analysis, it is a good idea to develop a clear, concise summary of what you have found. A good place to start is to create visual displays that capture any of your key results. This process should help you understand what your results mean and help you interpret why your results may or may not have come out as you had expected. This is also a good time to write a formal paragraph that captures the design of your analyses and results, so that you can see the big picture that has emerged. In the next chapter, we lead you through the process of writing up your results in a way that conveys a narrative of your research most effectively.

End-of-Chapter Exercises

1. For each of the research scenarios presented below, indicate the type of statistical analysis you would need to conduct.

   a. You want to test a hypothesis that mean test scores between a sample of students who listened to music while studying was different from a sample of students who did not listen to music while studying.

b. You want to test a hypothesis that men and women have different preferences for alcoholic beverages (i.e., wine, beer, cocktails).

c. You are interested in whether there are differences in reported relationship satisfaction of married couples. You recruit 30 couples and have each rate their relationship satisfaction on a 7-point scale.

d. You want to test a hypothesis that there is a relationship between hours of sleep and number of mistakes made on a memory task.

e. You want to test a hypothesis that sex and self-talk (positive versus negative) have an impact on video game performance (i.e., score on the game).

2. You are interested in whether the difference in siblings' ages is indicative of how well they get along. You collect information from 20 pairs of siblings in each of four age-difference categories (13–24 months, 25–36 months, 37–48 months, and 49–60 months). You have siblings provide ratings of how much they like each other on an 11-point scale

ranging from 0 to 10. How might you analyze your data? What statistics, visual displays, and so on would you like to see to help you understand and interpret your results?

3. Referring back to question 2, suppose that instead of numerical ratings, you have siblings simply indicate whether they like each other "not at all," "a little bit," "somewhat," or "a lot." How might you analyze your data? What statistics, visual displays, and so on would you like to see to help you understand and interpret your results?

4. Revisiting an example from Chapter 8, suppose you are interested in the effectiveness of directive versus non-directive therapy for patients who exhibit either high or low openness to therapy. Shown below are descriptive statistics, an ANOVA table, and box-and-whisker plots for hypothetical data, where the dependent variable is effectiveness of therapy measured on a scale from 0 to 100. How would you interpret these results? What other information would you like to see to help in your interpretation?

Descriptive Statistics

	Directive High Openness	Non-directive High Openness	Directive Low Openness	Non-directive Low Openness
Count	10	10	10	10
Mean	43.2	57.8	38.7	40.3
Median	43.0	58.0	41.5	40.5
Standard deviation	7.50	11.92	14.22	7.45

Analysis of Variance Table

	Sum of Squares	df	Mean Square	F	p
Therapy	656.1	1	656.1	5.75	.022
Openness	1,210.0	1	1,210.0	10.61	.003
Therapy × openness	422.5	1	422.5	3.71	.062
Residual	4,105.4	36	114.0		

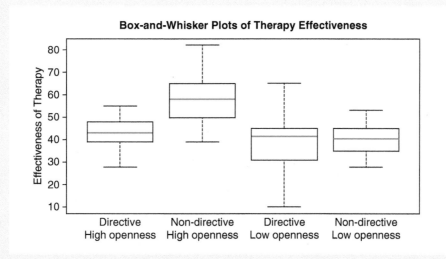

Box-and-Whisker Plots of Therapy Effectiveness

5. A teacher was interested in whether paper colour could have an impact on exam performance. She gave half of her class (n = 15) the exam printed on blue paper, and the other half (n = 15) got the exam printed on white paper. She found that the blue group had an average score of 80.60 per cent (SD = 8.71) and the white group had an average of 78.40 per cent (SD = 8.13). She got the following data analysis results:

t = 0.7168
df = 28
standard error of difference = 3.069
p value = .4794
the mean of group one minus group two equals 2.200
95% confidence interval of this difference: from −4.087 to 8.487
Summarize these results in APA style.

Key Terms

Writing Up Your Results

13

Chapter Contents

INSIDE RESEARCH: Patricia Coburn

I began my undergraduate studies majoring in history. I was particularly interested in the history of World War II and the former Soviet Union. I think my switch to psychology came about because of my desire to understand human behaviour: What factors lead people to commit atrocities or, alternatively, courageous acts in the face of disaster? I wanted to practise research in an applied setting, so I conducted my graduate training in the law and forensic psychology program at Simon Fraser University. Today, I am particularly interested in how people make decisions in a legal setting, although this can be a difficult area to conduct research in. In Canada, jurors are prohibited from discussing information pertaining to serving on a jury, and professionals working in the legal system may be reluctant to discuss how legal

Courtesy of Patricia Coburn

Sessional instructor, doctoral candidate, Simon Fraser University

continued

outcomes are determined. I therefore test my research questions through archival research and simulated juror experiments.

I use archival research, with judicial reasons for judgments, to study factors related to outcomes in legal contexts while maximizing ecological validity. This approach can be challenging, as there are inherent limitations to archival research, such as missing data and outliers. Importantly, while this type of research allows me to examine the relationship between variables, it does not allow me to make conclusions about the causes of phenomenon. For this reason I also conduct simulated juror experiments. This allows me to manipulate the variables I am interested in and control for extraneous variables. Between these two approaches, I have employed a wide variety of statistical tests, correlation, regression, chi-square analysis, and repeated-measures analysis of variance. My approach to data analysis is to stay open to learning a variety of statistical approaches. The questions you ask will dictate the type of analysis you need to do and may require you to try something new.

Patricia Coburn has received a Joseph-Armand Bombardier Canada Graduate Master's Scholarship and a Canada Graduate Doctoral Scholarship from the Social Sciences and Humanities Research Council of Canada to conduct research looking at factors related to decisions involving child witnesses and victims. She has presented her findings at relevant conferences in Canada, the United States, and Europe.

Research Focus: Factors related to legal cases involving child witnesses and victims with a focus on the effect of repeated event memory and cross-examination on the accuracy, consistency, and perceived credibility of children's reports

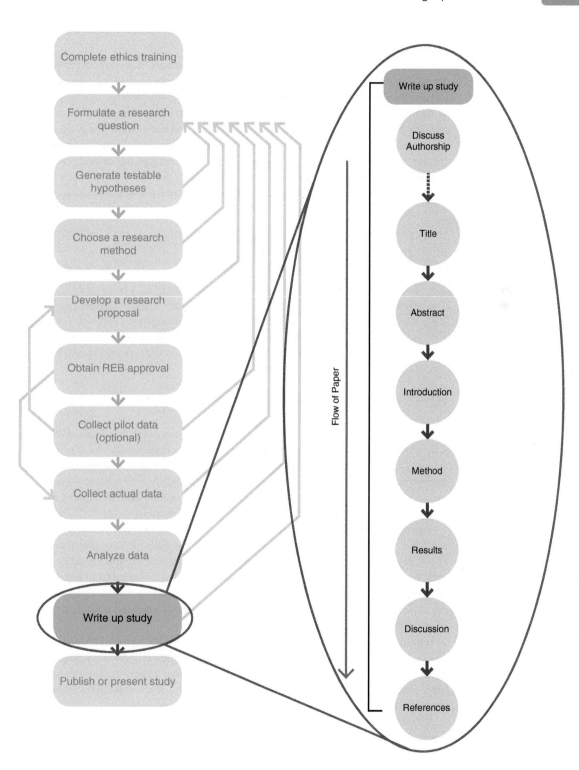

Chapter Abstract

Now that you have completed your study, you face the task of communicating your work to others. This involves crafting your hypotheses, experiments or observations, results, and conclusions into a readable article. In this chapter, we direct you through this process, which can be daunting but ultimately exhilarating. You will learn how to identify your target audience and how best to reach them. Next, you will discover the key elements of good scientific writing, as well as additional resources to help you with structure and style. We will conclude the chapter with some guidelines on how to create an academic poster or oral presentation as an alternative way to communicate your research.

LEARNING OBJECTIVES

By the end of this chapter, you should be able to:

- Describe the key elements of good scientific writing.
- Describe the hourglass organization of a quantitative research paper.
- Outline the basic sections of a quantitative research paper.
- Identify common mistakes researchers make in their writing.
- Briefly describe how a poster and oral presentation differ from a research paper.

DETERMINING YOUR AUDIENCE

Writing a research report is different from other kinds of writing, but, like any form of writing, it is a skill that can be improved with practice. Effective communication of research is a valuable skill that is transferable to many different fields and disciplines. Much of our advice in this chapter applies to scientific writing in general, although specific conventions differ by academic journal and field. Regardless, high-quality scientific writing requires knowing your audience and what readers expect to see in a research report.

One of the first questions you must answer when writing up your research is, Who will you write for? Most likely you will be writing up your research for your instructor as part of a course project, but if you were seeking publication of your work, you would need to consider your audience more closely. Will you write for individuals interested in general science, researchers within the broad discipline of psychology, or researchers within a specific area of psychology? The answer depends in part on you as a researcher and in part on the quality and originality of your research.

High-quality research with novel results will interest a broader audience (Gray & Wegner, 2013), whereas the best audience for work that is not quite so innovative might be readers of a journal focused on a subdiscipline of psychology. Most beginning researchers write for the latter group, which often includes both seasoned and novice researchers and perhaps a few interested non-researchers and journalists from the general public.

Although research reports can take several forms, in this chapter we focus primarily on writing up the results of a single study using APA style, because most beginning researchers start with this kind of paper. Although it is often best to write your report for the requirements of a specific journal, once you have collected the basic information and outlined the structure, it is usually not difficult to adapt the paper for another journal. You might consider using a paper that was recently published in a scientific journal you are considering for your own work as a model. You can also find example scientific papers in *The APA Publication Manual* and on many websites.

ELEMENTS OF GOOD SCIENTIFIC WRITING

The primary goal of scientific writing is to communicate. Scientific writing is designed to show why your research is interesting and important, why you conducted the particular study, what you did in the study, what you discovered, and implications that can be drawn from your results. Scientific reports are not meant to entertain or provide wild conjecture, but to provide the facts in a clear, concise, and relatively structured fashion. They are also meant to provide enough detail about the methods so that another researcher would be able to replicate your research (see Chapter 4).

Clear

Clarity is important to scientific writing because, first and foremost, scientists want other people to understand their work. The APA offers a number of tips in its sixth edition of the *Publication Manual of the American Psychological Association* (American Psychological Association, 2010, sections 3.09 and 3.11) for improving clarity in writing research reports. These include, among others, avoiding bias, being precise in your word choice, avoiding colloquial expressions, avoiding scientific jargon, making sure that pronouns have clear antecedents, and avoiding the third person when describing methodology or procedure. Bias, in particular, should be avoided by using language that is accurate and respectful, particularly around how labels are used; the focus should be on people, not on the labels. Using appropriate identifiers to refer to your research population will improve the clarity of your writing and minimize the likelihood of offending your readers. For example, instead of referring to your sample as an *elderly* or *learning disabled* population, they should be identified as *older adults* or *individuals with specific learning disabilities*. Similar sensitives need to be considered when referring to gender, race, ethnicity, sexual orientation, and other disabilities.

We also suggest the following tips for clarity in your writing: (1) Avoid artsy or flowery language (as in the APA's tip on jargon); (2) at the same time, avoid being dry and boring; and (3) write in readable, succinct sentences. Readers of scientific writing do not want to spend time and energy unpacking the meaning of long, complex sentences. Shorter, more direct sentences are best; there is no need to impress your audience with your extensive vocabulary. Also, be sure to define your terms and use them in a consistent manner throughout the manuscript.

Concise

Most researchers read a lot of research articles. They want to be able to grasp the gist of your article quickly and relatively easily. If you take 10 pages to say what you could say in 5, you will lose many readers. Gray and Wegner (2013) suggest that you should strive to be "clear, concise, and direct" (p. 552). Avoiding redundancy will help you to stay concise. Undoubtedly, you will have to mention some aspects of your research in different sections of the report.

What you write in later parts of the report, however, should build on what you have already said, not merely restate it. Also, journal editors frown on duplication of information provided in the text, tables, and figures, even if the information is provided in somewhat different formats.

Compelling

narrative A description of your research that flows from highly structured and organized ideas.

One of the most important aspects of good scientific writing is to provide a compelling narrative about your research—a description that flows from highly structured and organized ideas. Sternberg (1992) argues that high-quality scientific writing should "emphasize logical flow and organization" (p. 13). He also posits that a research article tells a story, and "like a story, it should capture readers' interest" (p. 13). We prefer the word "narrative" to "story," because the latter term can imply a form of creativity that does not belong in scientific writing. The goal is not to make up details, as Diederik Stapel did (see Chapter 1), but to state the facts in as unbiased a way as possible. We base many of the following suggestions on Sternberg's article, "How to Win Acceptances by Psychology Journals: 21 Tips for Better Writing," which appeared in the *APS Observer* in 1992 and still provides valuable insights about scientific writing.

Be Interesting.   Spell out clearly why the work is noteworthy and how it is novel, without being grandiose. As Sternberg (1992) suggests, "Tell readers why they should be interested" (p. 12). Also, without overstating the contribution or scope of your work, describe how your research fits with and builds on past work and moves our understanding of your topic forward. In addition, it is helpful to provide some concrete examples that highlight key concepts. But with each example, ask yourself, "Does the example clarify the concept?" and "Does it make my narrative more compelling?"

Use Logical, Evidence-Based Reasoning.   You should base your research and write-up on logical, evidence-based reasoning. The ideas you developed in the introduction should build on past research, which you should cite appropriately, meaning you must provide a citation to any ideas or research that are not your own. Your hypotheses, study design, analysis, results, and discussion should flow logically.

Start and End Strong.   The three most important parts of your research report are the abstract, the first paragraph, and the last paragraph. This is because readers usually use these three elements to determine whether they want to know more about your study. Gray and Wegner (2013) argue, "With writing, as with life, first impressions matter" (p. 551). Spend extra time drafting and redrafting these sections. Indeed, Gray and Wegner (2013) advocate that you "should spend hours and hours to make [the] first few sentences sing" (p. 552). But the end should "sing" too, so spend equal time drafting the last paragraph.

Use Active Voice.   One persistent misconception about scientific writing holds that researchers should write in the passive voice to emphasize objectivity. This misconception likely stemmed from a desire to de-emphasize the individual conducting the research. However, we wholeheartedly encourage you to reject the notion that the identity of researchers must be obscured behind awkward phrasing. Your high school English teacher would be happy to know that the most recent (sixth) edition of the *APA Publication Manual* explicitly directs writers to avoid passive voice in favour of more active phrasing and to use personal pronouns rather than the third person when describing researchers' methodology.

Write Multiple Drafts and Proofread.   Good writing takes time, energy, and a lot of rewriting. Some researchers complete as many as 10 drafts before sending a paper off for review. Just like faculty members who are annoyed by students who submit assignments with typos, grammatical errors, and missing sections, reviewers are annoyed by researchers who submit papers with these same issues. A research report that has many of these problems will likely receive negative reviews. Many seasoned researchers will ask a colleague to read over their papers before submitting them to a scientific journal. They want to make sure their arguments are convincing and that they have not missed an important detail. An unbiased reader or a new set of eyes will more easily catch flaws in logic or typos not caught by spell-checking software (e.g., "their" instead of "there").

OVERALL MANUSCRIPT FLOW AND ORGANIZATION

In this chapter, we focus on writing up quantitative research, in part because this perspective dominates contemporary psychology. Quantitative reports generally follow a similar, rather rigid template in contrast to qualitative reports, which follow a more narrative structure and have less strict guidelines regarding organization, flow, and content. Although it is important to create a compelling narrative in quantitative reports, this format generally has distinct subsections that are required by specific journals. Regardless of the type of research you conduct, however, when it comes to writing up that research, you must ensure that you have organized your paper in a logical, intuitive way and that you have included the right level of detail.

Hourglass Organization

The best way to envision the flow of the manuscript is to think of an hourglass. The wide top of the hourglass is your introduction—the place to present your general ideas and situate your work in the broader context of past research. Many beginning researchers start too broadly or reach too far back in time. How far back in time you need to go depends on the topic and how rapidly the information related to that topic has changed. Most of your readers will know the deep history of the topic, so cite it only if you can make an explicit, direct link to your current research. For example, if you are writing an experimental research paper, there is no need to cite Wilhelm Wundt as the first individual to have created an experimental psychology laboratory. The introduction should taper like an hourglass, ending with a set of precise hypotheses or goals.

The narrowest part of the hourglass represents the section that should contain the most specific details. These include a description of your method and procedures, followed by the analysis and results. This section tends to be less speculative and more cut and dried.

Finally, just as the hourglass begins to flare and then widens at the bottom, the discussion section should delve into specific results in detail and then broaden the scope of the discussion to include larger implications. As in the introduction, you want to avoid overreaching—the vast majority of studies do not produce earth-shattering results.

The Right Level of Detail

How much detail is necessary? Capturing the correct level of detail in a research report is a skill that takes practice. Your goal should be to provide enough detail that an independent researcher (i.e., someone from a different laboratory) could read the article and use the information to satisfactorily replicate your research. One question to consider as you are writing and revising is, "Does the reader need to know this?"

You will find that almost all articles, even the simplest of studies, miss some important detail regarding participant selection, methods, measures, or data analyses. If you have been using the same type of methods repeatedly, you might mistakenly assume that certain aspects are "understood" by other researchers and not even consider describing them in your report. This is why a second set of objective eyes is so important before submitting a paper for review. A good practice, then, is to ask a peer to read your "final" draft for clarity, logic, and appropriate level of detail.

Some beginning writers provide far too much information about the cited author or authors and their institutions. We have encountered numerous write-ups that contain sentences such as the following: "Professor Benjamin Franklin of the Department of Psychology at the University of Toronto in 1776 wrote a paper titled 'Psychological Effects of Getting Struck by Lightning' published in the *Journal of Early Canadian Psychology*." What's wrong with that sentence? Much of the detail is unimportant for readers to know, can be said more concisely, or belongs in other places, like the reference section. In addition, generally you should only use the last names of researchers. A more appropriate sentence is "Franklin (1776) examined the impact of getting struck by lightning on a number of psychological processes, including . . ." You would then include details about Franklin's paper in the reference section.

BASIC SECTIONS OF A QUANTITATIVE RESEARCH PAPER

Quantitative research reports have a highly formulaic structure. You should be able to open any psychology journal and quickly determine whether the article is a report of empirical research, a review paper, or a commentary. Although this structure may seem constraining to a novice research report writer, it helps readers and reviewers find the important details quickly and efficiently.

Most empirical articles published in psychology journals will contain the following key elements: title page, abstract, introduction, methods and procedures, results and analysis, general discussion, and references. Here, we discuss each of these using sections of Stella Christie's award-winning article as an example (Christie & Gentner, 2010). We use a published paper as an example for a number of reasons. First, it should be the goal of any research project, even one conducted by an undergraduate, to produce high-quality research that could be published in an academic journal. Second, highlighting a published article provides another opportunity to discuss the reading of and thinking about research articles (see Chapter 3). Keep in mind that different journals—and even individual editors—may have slightly different preferences about the structure of manuscripts submitted to their journals.

Most psychology journals follow the sixth edition of the *Publication Manual of the American Psychological Association* (American Psychological Association, 2010) for writing an APA-style manuscript. The APA manual provides extensive information about the formatting, organization of content, reference citations, and writing style required, and it promotes consistency within the discipline. There are specific details for all the sections required in an empirical research report or review article. A number of excellent online resources also provide tips and guidelines that help with APA formatting. The Online Writing Lab (OWL) at Purdue University is one of the best and most extensive websites on APA-style writing: https://owl.purdue.edu/owl/research_ and_citation/apa_style/apa_formatting_and_style_guide/general_format.html. In addition to providing guidance on how to properly cite your sources and structure your paper, there are also several examples of fully formatted APA-style papers. Many other colleges and universities provide similar, but often less detailed, information about formatting and writing papers in APA style, and you should consult with your own school library for available resources.

As we go through each of the sections of a quantitative research paper below, we will highlight some of the most common APA-style requirements.

Title Page

Although it may seem obvious, we like to start with the title page when we write a research report. The title informs the reader of the content of the report. Many journals have specific word or character limits for titles. Some editors and journals want clear, direct, informative titles, such as "Low Self-Control Promotes the Willingness to Sacrifice in Close Relationships" (Righetti, Finenaur, & Finkel, 2013), whereas others encourage cute or humorous titles, such as, "Rising Stars and Sinking Ships: Consequences of Status Momentum" (Pettit, Sivanathan, Gladstone, & Marr, 2013). Think carefully about the title and how others will perceive it. We often start with a "working title," or even a couple of alternative titles, and modify it as we write our paper. Like the rest of the paper, it is not a bad thing to revise, rethink, and rewrite titles to arrive at one that is clear and effective.

The title page includes the authors' names and their professional affiliations (see Figure 13.1). Sometimes journals want both the department and the college or university affiliation, whereas others want only the latter. The title page should also list contact information for the corresponding author—the individual who submits the manuscript to a journal and who is responsible for all communication with the journal editor. For most multiple-author research projects, the corresponding author is the most senior author, who is most likely to be at the same institution through the review and publication process. However, in the case of articles based on a senior thesis or dissertation, which sometimes include multiple authors, the student may be the most appropriate corresponding author.

The title page for multiple-author papers also provides an opportunity to discuss each author's contribution and the order of authors of the paper. The convention in psychology is to list the individual who did the most work on the paper first and then the other authors, in order of decreasing contribution to the paper. In contrast, in some other disciplines, such as engineering, the convention is to name the senior author or individual who made the largest contribution last.

Before deciding the order of authors, it is important to determine who should be considered an author at all. The APA offers a number of resources about what constitutes a contribution substantial enough to be listed as an author on a paper (Graf et al., 2007). These include making significant conceptual or intellectual contributions to the paper, playing a role in the design of methods, conducting the primary data analyses, and writing substantial aspects of the paper. Scheduling participants, collecting data, and entering data are not considered intellectual contributions that warrant authorship. Many journals now require the contribution of each author to be explicitly stated when the manuscript is submitted for consideration. Some journals also publish this information along with the actual paper.

FIGURE 13.1   Title page in APA style based on Christie and Gentner (2010).

In our view, determining authorship and order of authors is rarely straightforward. People often overestimate their own contributions and underestimate those of their colleagues. We advocate open, frank conversations about authorship beginning with the initial planning of the project. Over time, these discussions should be repeated with all members of the research team to discuss changes in individual effort that might warrant adding or subtracting authors or changing the order of authorship.

Abstract

The abstract provides a brief summary of the research. Although different journals specify different lengths, most abstracts range from about 150 to 250 words. Stay within the limits. The abstract for single research study reports should state the following:

- The purpose of the research: one or two sentences
- Why the research is important: one or two sentences
- Who the participants were: usually one sentence
- What the participants did: about three sentences
- What the results revealed: one or two sentences
- An interpretation of the results: one or two sentences
- Any implications that can be drawn from the study: one or two sentences

Not all abstracts will contain all of these points, especially abstracts for articles that contain more than one study, because it may be difficult to fit in all the details of the research. It may be easy for some studies to combine aspects of the research, such as the participant population and what the participants did, in a short phrase (e.g., "A sample of 221 young adults [65 per cent female] completed a 20-minute survey assessing happiness.").

Many readers will read only the abstract, so you want it to be succinct and interesting and to capture the essence of your study. Many researchers will write the abstract last, after they have completed the rest of the paper, because it is often easier to do after the entire narrative has been spelled out.

Figure 13.2 shows the abstract written by Christie and Gentner for their article that explores how preschoolers' learning changes when they compare different spatial representations of objects and animals.

In just 158 words comprising seven sentences, Christie and Gentner effectively describe the goal of their experiments, their participants, the methods they used, the results, and their interpretation. They use simple language and the first person. A few terms in this abstract may stand out to non-experts as jargon: "exemplar" and "structural alignment processes," which refer, respectively, to specific examples and the cognitive process where an individual might make comparisons in an analogy. Although it is best to avoid jargon as much as possible, sometimes you will have to use standard terms. Overall, this abstract promises readers interested in this field an investigation into the cognitive mechanisms that preschoolers use to form hypotheses.

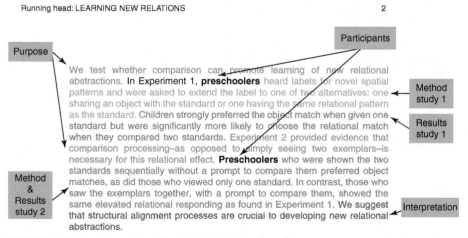

FIGURE 13.2   Abstract from Christie and Gentner (2010).

Source: Reproduced by permisssion of Taylor & Francis Ltd. from Christie, S., & Gentner, D. (2010). Where hypotheses come from: Learning new relations by structural assignment. *Journal of Cognition and Development, 11,* 356–73.

Some journals, especially those in more medically oriented areas of psychology, will require highly structured abstracts that contain a number of specific sections corresponding to the aspects of the paper, such as the objective, the design, the participants, the outcome measures, the results, and the conclusion. Again, if the journal requires this format, you should follow it or the editors may reject your paper without ever sending it out for review. Many journals request that a short list of keywords be included on the abstract page. It is a good strategy to also include one or more of these keywords in the title to make it easier for other researchers to find your published article through literature searches. When choosing your keywords, think about how you would conduct a search to find a paper like your own.

Spend time on the abstract. Think of it as your chance to convince casual readers that they want to learn more about your research. If people never read beyond your abstract, you are not doing an effective job of describing your work, and ultimately your work will not have the impact you would like.

The abstract starts on the second page of the manuscript with the heading "**Abstract**" in bold. Another feature of APA style is a specific system for headings to separate and categorize the manuscript sections. There are five heading levels in APA. Each main section of the paper starts with the highest level of heading (level 1). As subheadings are used within each main section, the next level of heading is used. The format for each level is presented in Table 13.1.

Introduction

Your introduction starts on the third page of your manuscript. The title is centred and bolded at the top of the page. Do not put "Introduction" at the start of this section. Your introduction should accomplish three main goals. First, it should clearly articulate the purpose of your research. In the first paragraph of their introduction, Christie and Gentner set the stage by asserting the significance of their topic—relational abstractions—and then move quickly to their overall goal of studying the process by which children learn it (see Figure 13.3).

Second, the introduction should make clear to readers why they should be interested in your research. In the paragraph shown in Figure 13.4, a few pages into the introduction, Christie and Gentner put their research into a larger context to help readers understand its relevance.

Christie and Gentner back up each of their points in this paragraph with citations to other research. Although the citations make the paragraph more difficult to read, they provide important information for other researchers reading the article. These citations also need to be

Level	Format
Table 13.1	**Five heading levels for APA-styled papers.**
1	**Centred, Boldface, Uppercase and Lowercase Heading**
2	**Left-aligned, Boldface, Uppercase and Lowercase Heading**
3	**Indented, boldface, lowercase heading with a period.**
4	***Indented, boldface, italicized, lowercase heading with a period.***
5	*Indented, italicized, lowercase heading with a period.*

Why topic is important

Learning relational abstractions is fundamental to the development of knowledge. Children must learn to categorize and reason over functional relations (X is edible), biological causal relations (X needs water to grow), mechanical causal relations (X can move things), and spatial relations such as those that underlie the meanings of prepositions and many verbs (X is moving upwards–*ascending*–or X is located *above* another object.) A critical question is how children achieve this learning.

Specific goal

FIGURE 13.3   First paragraph from Christie and Gentner (2010).

formatted in a specific way. They are cited by the author's last name(s) and the date of publication in brackets at the end of the sentence; do not include any first names or initials (e.g., Rusticus, 2019). If you are citing a direct quotation, you must also include the page number (e.g., Rusticus, 2019, p. 8). When you have groups of three or more authors, you must cite all the authors the first time you cite the source. For example, the first citation from Figure 13.4 is Gentner, Loewenstein, & Thompson, 2003. If you were to cite those same authors again later in the paper, you can cite them as Gentner et al., 2003. Sometimes you may cite the source directly within the sentence; in this case the author(s) are included within the sentence and only the date of publication is in brackets, right after the author(s). See if you can spot an example of this in Figure 13.4.

Some journals may limit the number of references you have in your paper, in which case you need to cite only the most relevant ones. Some journals may not allow you to cite work that is "in press," as is the case for the last citation. The "in press" label indicates that a manuscript has undergone peer review and been accepted for publication, but it has not yet been formally published. These journals want citations to research that has been formally published.

The third goal for your introduction is to situate your research in the context of past studies and current trends in your *specific* research area. For most empirical papers, it is not necessary to write an exhaustive history of the field (that level of depth and breadth belongs in a major review paper). Rather, you want to get to the issues relatively quickly, providing summaries of the methods and conclusions most relevant to your own research (Sternberg, 1992). Your literature review should also articulate how your research builds on past research, complements

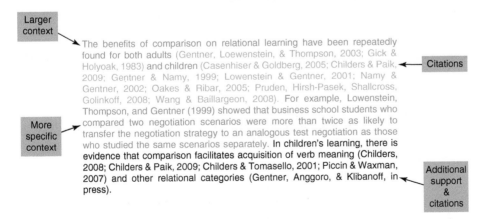

Larger context

More specific context

The benefits of comparison on relational learning have been repeatedly found for both adults (Gentner, Loewenstein, & Thompson, 2003; Gick & Holyoak, 1983) and children (Casenhiser & Goldberg, 2005; Childers & Paik, 2009; Gentner & Namy, 1999; Lowenstein & Gentner, 2001; Namy & Gentner, 2002; Oakes & Ribar, 2005; Pruden, Hirsh-Pasek, Shallcross, Golinkoff, 2008; Wang & Baillargeon, 2008). For example, Lowenstein, Thompson, and Gentner (1999) showed that business school students who compared two negotiation scenarios were more than twice as likely to transfer the negotiation strategy to an analogous test negotiation as those who studied the same scenarios separately. In children's learning, there is evidence that comparison facilitates acquisition of verb meaning (Childers, 2008; Childers & Paik, 2009; Childers & Tomasello, 2001; Piccin & Waxman, 2007) and other relational categories (Gentner, Anggoro, & Klibanoff, in press).

Citations

Additional support & citations

FIGURE 13.4   Paragraph from Christie and Gentner (2010).

In a study that relates to the present work, Gentner and Namy (1999) taught 4-year-olds a new name for a pictured object (e.g., a bicycle) and asked them to choose another with the same name. The alternatives were a perceptually distinct match from the same category (e.g., a skateboard) or a perceptually similar object from a different category (e.g., eyeglasses), thus pitting perceptual similarity against conceptual commonalities. When children saw a single standard, they tended to choose the perceptually similar alternative, consistent with prior studies (Baldwin, 1989; Imai, Gentner, & Uchida, {3} 1994; Landau, Smith, & Jones, 1988). In contrast, children who initially compared two standards (e.g., bicycle and tricycle) showed a greater preference for the conceptual match. This was a striking result, because the two standards always shared the same properties with each other as they did with the perceptual alternative, so on a feature-overlap account, comparison should have led to *more* perceptual responding rather than less. **Gentner and Namy concluded that structural alignment between the two standards fostered noticing common (hitherto implicit) relational structure (such as "both can be ridden"; "both stay in the garage," etc.) and thus pointed the children toward the category choice.**

> Highlighting a past study directly relevant to current one

> Highlighting a striking finding that leads to current study

> Presenting a hypothesis from previous work to be examined in current study

FIGURE 13.5   Paragraph highlighting past research directly relevant to the current study and setting up arguments for the current research from Christie and Gentner (2010).

that work, and moves beyond it in important ways. Figure 13.5 illustrates how Christie and Gentner highlight past research and set up additional questions the research raises to be examined in the current study.

In papers focusing on a single study or experiment, the introduction will often end with a brief paragraph that outlines the specific hypotheses investigated in the research. Papers that contain multiple experiments will often introduce each separate experiment with a brief paragraph that presents issues specific to that experiment. Christie and Gentner present two studies in their 2010 paper. The first study is introduced in a separate section with a new heading (see Figure 13.6). Careful reading of this paragraph along with the introduction will indicate some redundancy across sections. Although you should generally avoid repetition, sometimes it is necessary to repeat information across sections to ensure clarity.

Methods

In principle, the main goal of the methods section is to provide enough information so that your study could be replicated. It includes a description of participants, materials used, and procedures followed, each addressed in its own subsection. As described earlier, exact replication is

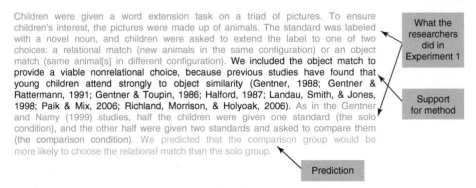

Children were given a word extension task on a triad of pictures. To ensure children's interest, the pictures were made up of animals. The standard was labeled with a novel noun, and children were asked to extend the label to one of two choices: a relational match (new animals in the same configuration) or an object match (same animal[s] in different configuration). **We included the object match to provide a viable nonrelational choice, because previous studies have found that young children attend strongly to object similarity (Gentner, 1988; Gentner & Rattermann, 1991; Gentner & Toupin, 1986; Halford, 1987; Landau, Smith, & Jones, 1998; Paik & Mix, 2006; Richland, Morrison, & Holyoak, 2006).** As in the Gentner and Namy (1999) studies, half the children were given one standard (the solo condition), and the other half were given two standards and asked to compare them (the comparison condition). We predicted that the comparison group would be more likely to choose the relational match than the solo group.

> What the researchers did in Experiment 1

> Support for method

> Prediction

FIGURE 13.6   Introductory paragraph to the first experiment from Christie and Gentner (2010).

likely impossible for a variety of reasons, unless it is done in the same laboratory with the same experimenters. However, if that level of replication is necessary to produce the psychological effect of interest, then it is time to worry about the generalizability of your findings.

Participants. In the participants subsection, you should provide details about how you recruited participants and their age, sex, and racial or ethnic background. These details aid the reader in considering how well the results might generalize beyond the participant population studied. It is also important to provide details about any compensation provided to participants. Compensation can aid in recruiting a more diverse sample or ensure a higher retention rate, and if another researcher attempts to replicate your work, the amount of compensation could be an important factor.

Christie and Gentner described their participants in Experiment 1 in the paragraph shown in Figure 13.7. This description of participants contains a few details specific to the *Journal of Cognition and Development*, in which the article appeared. First, the specification of ages, such as "3-year-olds ($M = 3;8$, range = $3;6–4;2$)," is a convention indicating that the average or mean age of the children is three years and eight months with a range of ages from three years and six months to four years and two months. Conventions such as this may vary somewhat from journal to journal, so be sure to follow the "Author Guidelines" or "Instructions to Authors," which are often found on the front or back covers of print versions of journals or online at the journal submission website. Second, the description of participants as "white middle- to upper-middle-class families in the greater Chicago area" tells the readers important details about the participant population. One detail missing from this participant description is the breakdown by sex—specifically how many boys or girls participated in the study. Even if there is no reason to expect that the results would differ for males or females, it is a good idea to include this information, broken down by any subgroups (e.g., age, condition) that are used in the study.

Another detail to include is the rate of participation—the number of individuals who agree to participate versus those who were initially contacted. Participation rates are influenced by a number of factors, including the research focus, the time commitment required by the study, and whether the researcher provides some type of incentive for participation. Related to rates of participation is the attrition rate, the number of participants who started the study but for some reason eventually dropped out. This is mostly an issue with longitudinal research, but information about the number of participants who began the study and the number who complete it should be included in your write-up. On the one hand, high dropout rates may indicate potential problems with recruiting or result in a final sample that is not representative. On the other hand, low dropout rates may indicate a successful recruiting strategy or potential fraud.

In a study such as Christie and Gentner's (2010) that involves relatively old preschool children, it is likely that all children whose parents had provided consent and who were approached by the experiments agreed to participate and completed the study. In many areas of psychology, including developmental psychology, participation rates are not commonly

---

Participants. Twenty-six 3-year-olds ($M = 3;8$, range = $3;6—4;2$) and thirty 4-year-olds ($M = 4;8$, range = $4;5—5;1$) participated. The children were from predominately white middle- to upper-middle-class families in the greater Chicago area.

FIGURE 13.7 Participant section from Christie and Gentner (2010).

reported. However, in areas where attrition is common, such as with research with young infants, researchers should provide information about the drop rate. For example, it is not uncommon in studies of infants to have "dropout" because they become hungry or fussy or fall asleep.

Researchers conducting studies involving highly technical equipment may also drop some participants because of "equipment malfunction" or "experimental error." You should report this information. Finally, participation rates are also commonly reported in survey research where many people may be contacted but only a subset of them agree to participate. For example, a researcher may send out 200 surveys, but receive only 45 completed surveys.

Here's an example of why participation rates are important to report. Participation rates that were much higher than those found in similar research ultimately led to researchers uncovering fraud in a widely reported study in *Science* that found that views of gay marriage could be changed through door-to-door canvassing (NPR, 2015). The fraud was revealed in part because a researcher from another laboratory was surprised at the reported participation rate and asked the original investigator how he had been so successful. Attempts to replicate the recruiting strategy failed to yield similar rates, and as the researchers delved more deeply into the study, they eventually found convincing evidence of fraud. The paper was ultimately retracted.

Materials.   In the materials subsection, you will need to describe any materials used in your study, including any apparatus that presents stimuli, the stimuli themselves, and any questionnaires and surveys. If you are using standard equipment, surveys, or questionnaires that are commonly used by researchers and have been described in other published works, you need to cite those studies and provide a brief description that is tailored to and relevant to your own research. This should include the number of items in the survey, how the items are responded to, how the items are scored, and the reliability (alpha) of the survey data for your sample. If you have developed new materials, then you must describe them in detail.

As shown in the paragraph in Figure 13.8, Christie and Gentner constructed their own stimuli for use in their study and described the stimuli in a clear fashion; they also provided a

---

Materials. There were eight sets of colored animal pictures, each consisting of two standards, plus an object match and a relational match. Each picture depicted two or three animals configured in a novel spatial relation (e.g., a black cat directly above an otherwise identical white cat). The second standard within a given set showed different animals in the same spatial configuration (e.g., a black dog above a white dog). The object match contained an exact animal match from each standard but in a different relational pattern (e.g., a black dog diagonally above a black dog). The relational match was composed of new animals in the same relational configuration as the two standards (e.g., a black bird directly above a white bird; Figure 2). Children were randomly assigned to either the solo condition (single standard) or the comparison condition (two standards presented together, as shown in Figure 2). Within the solo condition, which standard children saw was counterbalanced.

FIGURE 13.8   Description of materials used from Christie and Gentner (2010).

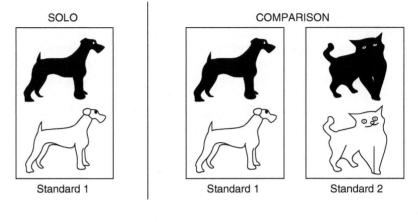

FIGURE 13.9 Stimuli in Experiment 1 from Christie and Gentner (2010).

figure (see Figure 13.9, corresponding to Figure 2 in the original article) in the manuscript to clearly show how they presented stimuli to the children.

Procedures. The final part of the methods section, the procedures subsection, describes the actual procedures completed by participants (see Figure 13.10). Specifically, describe what the participants did, the order of any tasks or conditions, and why you used that particular order. It is also important to clearly state your variables and how they were operationalized. Christie and Gentner provide the exact wording of the questions the children were asked and explicitly describe the different steps of the experimental procedure, providing a level of detail that should make it relatively easy for other researchers to understand what was done and potentially replicate the methods.

Note that the researchers refer to a previous study (Gentner & Namy, 1999) to justify some of their procedures. Although it is entirely appropriate, and often necessary, to explain why you chose particular procedures, you can also refer to previous research for more details about particular methods and procedures; this approach can help keep the procedure section relatively short and concise. A growing number of journals are also asking authors to make many of the details of methods and procedures available as online resources connected to a particular journal.

> *Procedure.* Children were seated across from the experimenter. In the solo condition, the experimenter laid out a single standard and labeled it with a novel count noun: "Look, this is a jiggy! Can you say jiggy?" The experimenter then placed the two alternatives side by side below the standard and asked the child, "Can you tell me which of these two is a jiggy?" After the child made a choice, the experimenter continued with a new standard from a new set.
>
> The comparison condition began in the same way: The experimenter presented and labeled the first standard. Then the experimenter placed the second standard near the first one. Half the standard pairs were laid out horizontally (side by side), the other half vertically. The experimenter named the second standard with the same label as the first and encouraged the child to repeat the word and to compare the two standards: "Can you see why these are both jiggies?" (As in Gentner and Namy's (1999) studies, no answer was required; the idea was to invite children to think about it.) Then the two alternatives were presented as in the solo condition.
>
> Eight different novel labels were used, one for each relational pattern. The order of novel words and the item order were varied in four semi-random orders, counterbalanced within each condition. Left-right placement of the two alternatives was also counterbalanced.

FIGURE 13.10   Procedure section from Christie and Gentner (2010).

Results

You may find the results section one of the most difficult sections to write well. The difficulty arises from the problem of providing a clear, logically organized narrative about sometimes dry and complex statistical analyses. Three strategies can enhance readability of the results section:

1. Divide the analyses into sections addressing particular hypotheses or issues.
2. Provide brief explanations throughout the results section to clarify statistical statements (which often look more like math text), but save interpretation of the results for the discussion.
3. Consider placing some of the key results in tables or figures to reduce the density of the text (number of sentences) in the results section.

Many researchers begin their results section with a brief descriptive overview of the data before starting on a more specific discussion of the statistical analyses used. The start of a results section might include a report of overall means and standard deviations between groups to give a summary of the data obtained.

The results section should provide sufficient detail about the statistical tests you conducted, both the type of statistical test that was conducted and the results of the test. Remember that your goal in a research report is to provide a narrative; in general, you should include statistical analyses that directly address your goals or hypotheses, as well as any statistical tests that could be done to rule out potential alternative hypotheses. You should report both tests that revealed statistically significant results and those that did not result in significant findings, especially if these results go against your stated hypotheses and predictions. You must also decide whether to present the results of your tests in a table/figure format, or within the actual written narrative of the results section. It is unnecessary, and repetitive, to do it both ways. If you are presenting a single analysis, including the results in the written section will likely be the more efficient option. If you are presenting the results of several analyses, then a table may be the better choice.

The beginning of Christie and Gentner's results section states, "Figure 3 shows the mean proportion of relational matches selected by 3- and 4-year-olds in the solo and comparison conditions." This statement effectively orients the reader to the figure (shown here as Figure 13.11), and the figure provides a clear and effective overview of the results.

As Christie and Gentner make clear in the caption, the figure presents data from two different experiments. Often researchers will include data from two or more studies in a figure to facilitate comparison of the results across related studies. It may be better to present the results of the initial study in a figure and then provide the comparison in a second figure that comes later in the paper. In the example presented in Figure 13.11, readers will not understand the statement "with two intervening fillers" until they have read the procedures reported in Experiment 2a. When deciding whether to combine data across studies in a single figure, think about the narrative you are telling. Does this approach help clarify the results, or does it make the results section more confusing?

Christie and Gentner also provide information about statistically different means in a non-cluttered way by providing "*" and "ns" labels. The "*" indicates that the means are statistically different at $p < .05$ level (as mentioned in the caption). The "ns" label stands for "non-significant," indicating that the means that are bracketed with that label do not statistically differ from one another. These are common conventions used to indicate when means are

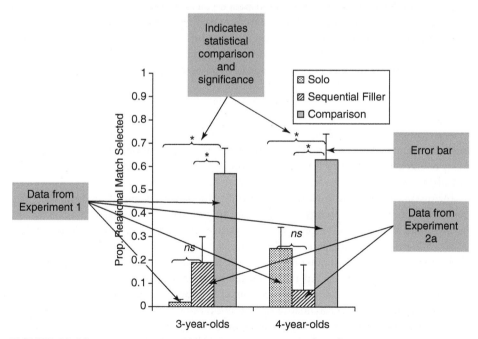

FIGURE 13.11   Figure reproduced from Christie and Gentner (2010). Providing the "mean proportion of relational responses in solo and comparison (Experiment 1) and in the sequential—with two intervening fillers—condition (Experiment 2a). *$p < .05$."

error bar A graphical representation of the amount of variability of a sample statistic, such as a mean.

similar to or different from one another. Another common convention is to provide **error bars** that depict the amount of variability in the sample. Figure 13.11 contains error bars, but the authors do not provide information about whether the error bars indicate the standard deviation or standard error of the means. This information should be provided.

After the introductory sentence of the results described earlier, Christie and Gentner provide the following sentence: "A 2 (condition: solo and comparison) × 2 (age: 3-year-olds and 4-year-olds) analysis of variance (ANOVA) revealed a significant main effect of condition, $F(1, 52) = 23.83, p < .001, \eta^2 = .30$."

This statement tells the reader that the researchers included two factors (condition and age) in the analysis, evaluated potential differences between conditions using an ANOVA, and found that the main effect of the condition was statistically significant. The "η^2" refers to the effect size, a measure of the strength of the effect. The effect size reported by the authors indicates a large effect (Cohen, 1988). As described in Chapter 11, effect sizes provide an indication of the magnitude of the difference between groups. According to Christie and Gentner, the analysis revealed they did not find a significant main effect of the age factor and they did not find a significant interaction between their two factors. Although the authors then describe their results in more detail, this initial analysis successfully tests their key hypotheses involving condition and age.

Sternberg (1992) argues that you should briefly explain what the results mean rather than leaving the interpretation up to the reader. Christie and Gentner (2010) do exactly this in the following sentence in their results section: "The fact that children in the comparison condition chose relational matches more than twice as often as those in the solo condition is consistent with the claim that structural alignment is an effective way to induce children to focus on common relational structure" (p. 363). Although you will need to present a more detailed analysis of your results in the discussion section, these brief explanations make the results section more readable and improve readers' understanding of the findings. One way to organize these explanations is to refer the reader back to your hypotheses by indicating which of your results support (or fail to support) specific hypotheses.

Discussion

The discussion section is analogous to the bottom of the hourglass. Start with a review of your most important and specific results and then present the general implications of your research. Many researchers end the discussion with ideas about what kinds of future research are needed or with more practical applications of the research findings.

The discussion section provides an opportunity to include secondary findings that relate peripherally to your main findings. Although we advocate presenting alternative explanations in the results section, in some cases you can consider them in the discussion section. When you do this, however, tell readers why these alternative explanations fall short of your primary explanation. Christie and Gentner do this in their discussion, stating, "A key question here was whether our results could be explained by cross situational learning, without invoking comparison, by assuming that children formed a set of hypotheses when they saw the initial standard and then used the other standard to filter these guesses. Contrary to this account, children showed relational insight only when they saw the standards simultaneously and were invited to compare them" (Christie & Gentner, 2010, p. 369). If the results are equivocal, you should be honest, but if you do not take a stand in your discussion, your work will never be published.

Remember, the goal is to tell a compelling, accurate narrative of your study. This narrative should provide the facts, an interpretation of what the facts mean, an acknowledgment of problems or limitations, an explanation of why these limitations do not undermine the overall conclusion, and a statement about the direction the research should take in the future.

Christie and Gentner discuss their findings and suggest areas for future research in the paragraph shown in Figure 13.12. This paragraph effectively states their main finding ("that relational abstraction requires structural alignment"), defines the scope of the finding, situates their research in the context of other research with adults and children, provides suggestions about how a researcher might further explore this area of research, and provides implications of predicted findings.

An important issue to consider is that authors cannot always control how the popular press and other researchers will interpret their work (see "Media Matters: When Research Is Misrepresented"). Providing a clear, objective interpretation of your own results, however, improves the chances that others will capture your work accurately. In addition, if you do not plainly define your participant categories up front, you can leave your work open to wild misreading.

As with the overall paper, you should start and end strong. The first and last paragraphs of the discussion section are two of the paper's most important paragraphs. Spend time on them. Make sure they are clear and convey why your work is interesting and important. Highlighting the importance of your final paragraph, Gray and Wegner (2013) write, "The conclusion should not be a restatement of the results but instead a grander statement, one that ideally takes the reader back to the first paragraph or the opening quote or one that links the findings to some famous idea" (p. 552). As they note, based on the work of Kahneman and colleagues (Kahneman, Frederickson, Schreiber, & Redelmeier, 1993), people tend to form the strongest memories of the last part of a narrative they encounter. Make it sing like your introductory paragraph.

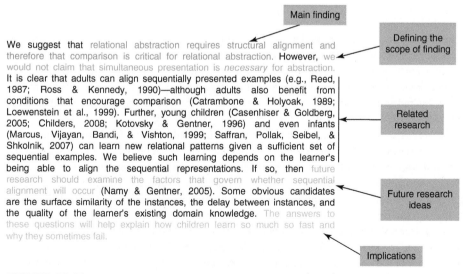

FIGURE 13.12   Discussion section from Christie and Gentner (2010).

MEDIA MATTERS

When Research Is Misrepresented

Any serious researcher knows the importance of writing up research results honestly, without distortion, overreaching inferences, or false claims. Yet even the most experienced researchers cannot always predict how the media will react to their papers. Consider the example of Dr. Steffanie Strathdee, a researcher at the British Columbia Centre for Excellence in HIV/AIDS, who had been awarded a young investigator award in 1997 for her research on a needle exchange program (NEP) in Vancouver, which was intended to help reduce incidences of disease.

However, the study revealed that despite the program, incidences of HIV had become more prevalent in Vancouver. The researchers concluded that their results "do not argue against the overall effectiveness of NEP as an intervention, but rather, they lead us to propose that without adequate and appropriate community-wide interventions . . . stand-alone NEP may be insufficient to maintain low HIV prevalence and incidence" (Strathdee et al., 1997, p. 63). However, this was not how it was reported in the media; and according to Strathdee, media in the United States in particular touted the uselessness of NEPs (Hrvatin, 2018). This resulted in the US Congress, in 1999, citing the study as a reason to ban NEPs. This news was devastating to Strathdee, who commented that "For years afterwards I was presenting the data over and over again, trying to set the record straight. I met with cops and the press and policy officials just trying to undo the damage" (Hrvatin, 2018).

Unfortunately, this is not an isolated case, and others have shared similar experiences where misrepresentations in research have led to serious repercussions (Hrvatin, 2018). In 2014, Sumner and colleagues (2014) conducted a study looking at the accuracy of press releases and found that over one-third contained exaggerated advice, exaggerated causal claims, or exaggerated inferences of animal research. Further, they found that when press releases exaggerated the results, news stories also showed similar exaggeration. And as noted by Dr. Christopher Chambers, a cognitive neuroscientist, "It's not just about exaggerating the findings of a particular study, it's about distorting the way science really works" (quoted in Hrvatin, 2018).

References

All articles cited in the text should appear in the reference section, and all articles listed in the reference section should be cited in the main text. Reviewers will often go back and forth between the text and the references to learn more about the area you are studying. In fact, one of the reasons for being a reviewer is to keep up on the latest research in a particular area, and reviewers will look up references of which they were not aware. As a reviewer, it is frustrating to get excited about an idea discussed in a citation, but then be unable to find the paper in the reference section.

The reference section should follow the format dictated by the journal and the discipline. For most psychology journals this means following APA format guidelines (as outlined in the *APA Publication Manual*), although non-APA journals vary in requiring this format. You can usually find guidelines regarding references on the journal website. If you do not follow these guidelines, do not bother submitting your work, because it will most likely be rejected without being sent out for review.

The reference section starts on its own page and lists all of the sources that were cited in the manuscript. The sources are presented in alphabetical order according to the last name of the first author of the cited source. Each reference begins on a new line using a hanging indent—the first line is flush with the left margin and the subsequent lines are indented. Titles of books

References

Askay, D. (2017). Communication. In D. Levi (Ed.), *Group dynamics for teams* (pp. 105–132).

 Thousand Oaks, CA: Sage.

Braun, V., & Clarke, V. (2006). Using thematic analysis in psychology. *Qualitative Research in*

 Psychology, 3(2), 77–101. doi: 10.1191/1478088706qp063oa

Chapman, K. J., Meuter, M., Toy, D., & Wright, L. (2006). Can't we pick our own groups? The

 influence of group selection methods on group dynamics and outcomes. *Journal of*

 Management Education, 30(4), 557–569. doi:10.1177/1052562905284872

Felder, R. M., Felder, G. N., & Dietz, E. J. (1998). A longitudinal study of engineering student

 performance and retention versus comparisons with traditionally-taught students. *Journal*

 of Engineering Education, 87(4), 469–480. doi:10.1002/j.2168-9830.1998.tb00381.x

Grzimek, V., Marks, M. G., & Kinnamon, E. (2014). Do differences in GPA impact attitudes

 about group work? A comparison of business and non-business majors. *Journal of*

 Education for Business, 89(5), 263–273. doi:10.1080/08832323.2013.872591

Joo, M., & Denna, V. P. (2017). Measuring university students' group work contribution: Scale

 development and validation. *Small Group Research, 48*(3), 288–310.

 doi.org/10.1177/1046496416685159

Michaelsen, L. K., Knight, A. B., & Fink, L. D. (2004). *Team-based learning: A transformative*

 use of small groups in college teaching. Sterling, VA: Stylus Publishing.

FIGURE 13.13   Example of a reference page. Included here are example references for books and journal articles.

and journals and the volume number of journals get italicized. The titles of the journal articles and book titles have the first word capitalized and the first word following a colon, plus any proper nouns. See Figure 13.13 for an example of a reference page.

Figures and Tables

As you decide which tables and figures to include in your article, you should always ask yourself the following questions: Are they necessary? Do they replicate information in the text? Do they capture the data in a compelling and interesting way that magnifies the results? Or do they state the obvious and really add nothing to information in the text? The *APA Publication Manual* has advice about how best to present information in both figure and table formats. Do not try to do too much in any one figure or table. Too much information can appear cluttered and overwhelm the reader. Well-formatted tables and figures can effectively simplify a section of otherwise dense text (as noted earlier in the results section), but use them judiciously.

COMMON ISSUES TO CONSIDER

Beginning researchers tend to make a number of mistakes in their write-ups. Here we present a few additional guidelines for avoiding some of the most common mistakes.

Avoid Using the Word "Prove."   One of the most common mistakes is to include a statement to the effect that the results prove something. No single research study or collection of studies can actually prove anything, so avoid using that word. "The results indicate that . . ." or "The results suggest that . . ." are better ways to present your findings.

Do Not Anthropomorphize.   It is not uncommon for authors to state that "The research found . . ." or "The data revealed . . ." suggesting that research or data are real actors in the world. It is better to say "We found . . ." or "Our inspection of the data revealed . . ." Give credit where credit is due.

Report Data in a Meaningful Manner.   We have encountered papers where students have coded males and females as 1s and 2s in the data file and report a mean for this variable of 1.7. Although a statistical package will easily calculate a mean for this category, calculating means for categorical data is not appropriate. Consider whether your data are categorical or continuous and report the data appropriately.

Be Careful How You Report Your Statistics.   When writing a description of your data and data analysis, APA recommends that you should round to two decimal places rather than to all the decimals that might be generated by a calculator or statistical program, as this level of accuracy is rarely meaningful. In some cases, however, greater precision is needed; p values, for instance, should be reported to three decimal places (e.g., $p = .004$).

   You also need to be mindful of when to report a leading zero (a zero that is placed before a decimal point). According to APA, you should include a zero before a decimal if the value you are reporting has the potential to exceed 1. For example, a standard deviation or a t value, can be larger than 1, but if your value is less than 1, you should report it with a zero (e.g., $SD = 0.76$). If a number cannot exceed 1, such as a p value or a correlation coefficient, then you should not include a zero in front of the decimal place (e.g., $p = .115$).

Provide Enough Detail about the Statistical Test Used to Examine the Data.   Another common mistake is not providing enough detail about the statistical test used to examine the data. This is particularly true in students' reporting of their use of ANOVA. Rather than merely stating "An ANOVA was conducted to examine difference between groups," you should provide details about the ANOVA. How many groups or conditions did you use? Was it a one-way ANOVA or a multivariate ANOVA? Did you have any covariates? Did you repeat any measures? Did you examine within- and between-subjects effects?

Discuss Hypotheses and Limitations.   Sternberg (1992) encourages researchers to consider alternative interpretations of the data and results in the results section. This is not only a highly effective way to convince your audience of the value of your research, but also fair and ethical because it acknowledges that no single study in psychology definitively establishes a key finding as fact. If you bring up an alternative interpretation of the data in the results section, then it is appropriate to examine and potentially rule out that alternative using appropriate statistical procedures. If you bring up alternative interpretations in the discussion section, be sure to explain why they may or may not be plausible.

All research studies have limitations, and many journals require authors to state a study's limitations in the final section of the written report. Some journals may even have a special section or sections where limitations must be listed. Although it is appropriate and, for many journals, necessary to list limitations, do not stop with merely listing them. Rather, discuss how the limitations might have influenced the results obtained and conclusions drawn from the research. Yet remember that you must advocate for your research, so be sure to discuss the limitations in ways that do not undermine the value of the research you have just completed. In some cases, it might be appropriate to point out how potential limitations might be addressed in future research.

VARIATIONS FROM A SINGLE-EXPERIMENT PAPER

Empirical research reports are not the only types of articles produced by psychologists and other social scientists. Here, we briefly describe multiple-experiment papers and qualitative research reports because they are the most common for beginning researchers to write.

Multiple-Experiment Papers

Multiple-experiment papers are common in psychology, and the more prestigious journals will rarely accept a single-experiment paper. However, the preference for single or multiple experiments varies by journal and the discipline of psychology. In fact, many journals have begun to publish rapid reports of only one study or experiment in addition to more traditional, longer, multiple-experiment papers.

The organization and structure of a multiple-experiment paper is similar to that of a single-experiment paper. The main difference is that there is generally a separate brief introduction to each study or experiment, with each study followed by a brief discussion. The manuscript then ends with a final discussion that summarizes and integrates the findings from all of the research reported in the manuscript.

For more experienced researchers, deciding whether to "package" experiments together or submitting one or more rapid research reports can take considerable thought and deliberation with co-authors. Although it is not ethical to divide up a study solely for the purpose of publishing more than one paper, often the narrative works better in either a short report or a multiple-experiment paper. The narrative that you want to tell should ultimately drive this decision.

Qualitative Research Reports

Although a quantitative research report is by far the most common form of article in psychology, a significant number of qualitative researchers in psychology write up their research in a completely different manner. These two approaches differ not only in how they are written, but also in their research designs (see Chapter 4).

As with quantitative reports, qualitative reports should strive to be clear, direct, and accurate (Kirkman, 1992; Strong, 1991). A number of excellent sources provide detailed guidance in conducting and writing up qualitative research (e.g., Denzin & Lincoln, 1998a, 1998b;

Flyvbjerg, 2006; Holliday, 2001; Kidder & Fine, 1997; Robson, 2002: Willig, 2008), so we will provide only a brief description of a qualitative research report here.

Qualitative research reports vary to a much greater extent than quantitative research reports in terms of structure and style. For this reason, it is important to determine before you start writing who you want your audience to be. Then you can tailor your writing for that audience (and the specific journal that will reach that audience).

Generally, the difference between a qualitative and a quantitative report can be found as soon as you look at the title. Whereas few quantitative reports will use the term "quantitative" in the title, because this is the default assumption, it is not uncommon for qualitative reports to include the term "qualitative" or some other related term (e.g., "narrative," "personal meanings," "social construction") that distinguishes the report as qualitative in nature.

In terms of the actual content, qualitative reports rarely, if ever, report any type of statistical analysis, which is at the heart of most quantitative reports. Instead, many qualitative reports include relatively lengthy narrative accounts of interviews or observations. In addition, direct quotes from participant interviews will generally be interspersed throughout. This is in contrast to quantitative reports that rarely include quotes, except in the final discussion to highlight an important finding.

We have presented only a brief overview of qualitative reports here. If your real interest is in qualitative research and methods, you should explore some of the many books and articles devoted to this topic (e.g., Denzin & Lincoln, 2005; Fischer, 2006; Forrester, 2010).

ALTERNATIVE WAYS TO COMMUNICATE RESEARCH RESULTS

Although writing a research paper is the primary outcome of a research project, there are two other common ways that researchers can communicate their work: poster presentations and oral presentations, both of which typically occur at a research conference. While the full research paper will present and discuss the entire research study in detail, both poster and oral presentations provide a more concise representation of the research, each presented in their own unique format. In this next section, we briefly provide some guidelines for creating these two types of presentations. See Chapter 14 for a more detailed discussion of conferences.

Poster Presentations

A poster presentation is a concise snapshot of your research. It needs to provide enough detail to give the context and main message of your research, but is brief enough that someone can scan your poster in a few minutes and understand what your research is about. Posters are generally five feet wide and three feet tall, but the exact dimensions can vary. Although the author or authors decide on a particular design and style, most posters include all the sections found in a formal paper—an introduction or background, methods, results, and conclusions (see Figure 13.14). Researchers vary in whether they include an abstract or the references. Posters are a highly visual presentation of your work and it is better to present the information in figures and tables as much as possible, rather than with detailed text. When using text, it should be used sparingly, and it is typically used in point form. The highly attractive visual presentation format of a poster is designed to catch the attention of your audience while also enabling them to determine the main message of your poster quickly.

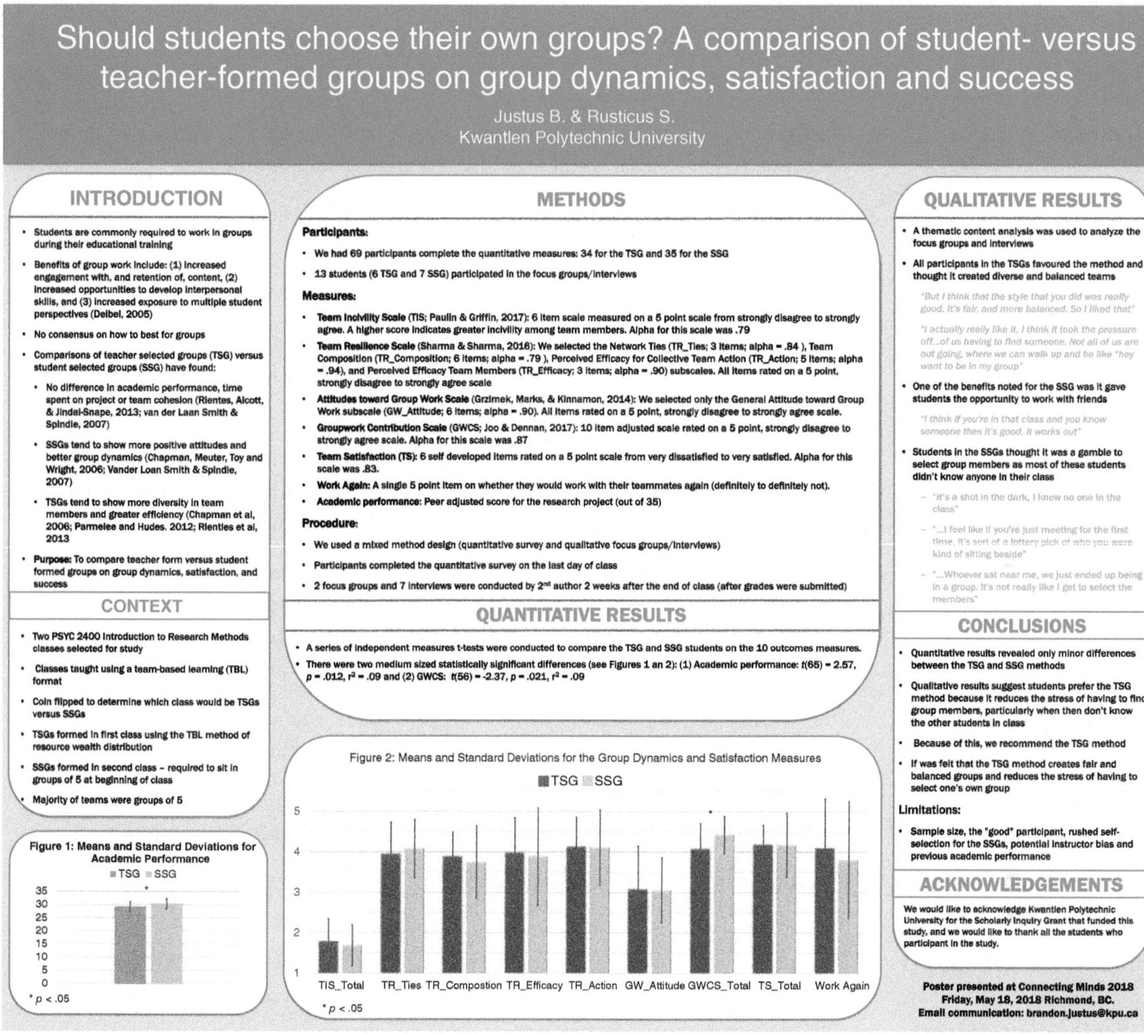

FIGURE 13.14   Example of a poster presentation by Justus and Rusticus (2018).

Summarized in Table 13.2 are 10 rules, drawn from Erren and Bourne (2007) for preparing and presenting a good poster. Overall, these rules encourage authors to strategically design their posters so they will capture an audience's attention through compelling titles, concise and appropriate levels of detail, and eye-catching, organized, and easy to read layouts. Plenty of online resources are available on the technical requirements of a poster (for an example, see www.apa.org/gradpsych/2011/01/poster).

Oral Presentations

An oral presentation is a short talk, typically 10 to 15 minutes, on your research. It is also more concise then a research paper, but will still include the main sections of a paper—introduction/background, methods, results, and discussion. Oral presentations are supplemented by some sort of slideshow (e.g., a PowerPoint presentation) so that the audience is able to both see and hear

Table 13.2   Ten rules for creating effective posters (Erren & Bourne, 2007).

Rule	Guideline
1. Define the purpose	Think about what impact you want your poster to make; are you wanting to share your research or spark interest in future research or collaborations?
2. Sell your work in 10 seconds	Aim to create a good first impression of your poster. You need to catch the attention of your audience.
3. The title is important	Use a compelling title to encourage your audience to want to view the rest of your poster.
4. Poster acceptance means nothing	Just because a poster has been accepted for presentation, this is not an endorsement of the poster.
5. Many of the rules for writing a good paper apply to posters, too	You need to consider your audience in gauging the scope and level of detail to include on your poster. All main sections of a paper should also be included on a poster (e.g., introduction/background, hypothesis, methods, results, and discussion).
6. Good posters have unique features not pertinent to papers	Your posters must present the results of your study in a concise and visual way, while still getting your main message across. You also have the advantage of being there with the poster to expand on the details not included on the poster. You can also provide handouts of your poster to help communicate your work.
7. Layout and format are critical	The visual appeal of your poster is of vital importance. You need to present your work in a format that is easy to follow, easy to read, and catches the interest of your audience.
8. Content is important, but keep it concise	You need to minimize the amount of text you use while still getting your message across. Use figures, graphs, and tables to easily communicate large amounts of data.
9. Posters should have your personality	Use your own personal flair to make your poster more attractive.
10. The impact of the poster happens both during and after the poster session	How you interact with your audience when giving a poster presentation is important. Don't hassle people, but also be prepared to answer questions and speak about your work.

about your research. Delivering a good and engaging presentation requires good oral communication skills and a well-designed slideshow. Good presenters are able to share information by telling the audience about their research, while supplementing this with text, figures, tables, pictures, or other forms of media. The amount of information presented in the slideshow should be minimal, and only contain key messages. As the presenter, you are there to expand on these key points orally. An oral presentation typically concludes with a short question-and-answer period. This can provide a valuable source of feedback that could further, and strengthen, your research.

Summarized in Table 13.3 are 10 rules, drawn from Bourne (2007), for preparing and delivering a good oral presentation. Overall, these rules encourage authors to strategically plan their presentations to engage with the audience and present a concise, structured, and appropriately detailed summary of your research. Plenty of online resources are also available on the technical requirements of an oral presentation (for an example, see https://elearningbrothers.com/blog/6-tips-creating-effective-powerpoint-presentation).

Table 13.3   Ten rules for creating effective oral presentations (Bourne, 2007).

Rule	Guideline
1. Talk to the audience	Consider who your audience is and create your presentation to target that audience.
2. Less is more	Presentations should be clear and concise. Focus on the main message of your presentation and do not overload your slides or your presentation.
3. Only talk when you have something to say	You do not need to include everything in your presentation. Focus only on the key details needed to get your message across.
4. Make the take-home message persistent	Consider what main points you want to get across in your presentation and make sure these are emphasized.
5. Be logical	Your presentation should tell a story. Ensure you have a clear beginning, middle, and end.
6. Treat the floor as a stage	Aim to make your presentation engaging (e.g., using humour or stories), but don't overdo it.
7. Practise and time your presentation	Practise your presentation. This will help determine how much time it will take and make the final presentation smoother.
8. Use visuals sparingly but effectively	Use visuals to help clarify material and emphasize your points. Visuals, such as graphs and charts, are especially effective for presenting large amounts of data.
9. Review audio or video of your presentation	Reviewing your presentation can help identify where you need to make improvements.
10. Provide appropriate acknowledgments	If appropriate, acknowledge people or organizations who contributed to the project.

Source: © 2007 Philip E. Bourne. Creative Commons Attribution License (CC BY)

Practical Tips for Writing Up Your Results

1. Write clearly and concisely.

2. Be sure to cite research that your work builds on.

3. Cite other researchers for any ideas that are not your own.

4. Avoid repetition. Avoid repetition.

5. Never think that a first draft is sufficient. Revise, edit, and rewrite often.

6. Find someone who can read and comment on your final draft. This person can help you make sure that your narrative flows logically, that you have not left out steps in an argument, and that your writing is clear and concise.

7. Writing well takes effort and practice. Try to schedule time for writing into every work day.

CHAPTER SUMMARY

Although writing your first research report or creating your first presentation can be intimidating, remembering the rules for good scientific prose will keep you in good stead. Tell the narrative of your research in language that is clear, concise, and engaging. Be careful to organize your information into appropriate sections, particularly for quantitative papers: title page, abstract, introduction, methods and procedures, results, discussion, and references, while also being mindful of the amount of detail to include for your chosen presentation format. Above all, adhere to the requirements of the journal or conference to which you are submitting. Now, you should be ready to tackle the final stage of your research—submitting your article for presentation at a conference or in the pages of a journal (see Chapter 14).

End-of-Chapter Exercises

1. Find a journal in your area of interest. Go to that journal's website and review their guidelines for authors. Does this journal follow APA style? Does the journal have specific requirements on page lengths and number of tables/figures? What other requirements does this journal have for manuscript submissions?

2. This chapter primarily focuses on writing up results for an academic journal in psychology, often the "first stop" for research findings for both novice and experienced researchers. Imagine that you have just successfully published your first peer-reviewed article that demonstrates a promising new intervention to boost reading fluency in young children. The local press catches wind of your research and wants to run a story on your findings. What should be the primary considerations in terms of how much detail you provide to the reporter about your research? What are the benefits of a more detailed (and technical) press report? What are the hazards? How would you think about striking the right balance between technical details and accessibility to your audience?

3. You are an undergraduate student who has just completed your honours thesis after an arduous year of work. As you prepare to apply to graduate school, you seek to publish a manuscript based on a portion of your thesis. As you ready your submission, your former adviser insists that he be listed as the first author on the manuscript, noting that the research was entirely funded by a multimillion-dollar grant that he had secured and that all of the equipment used in the study was from his laboratory. You also used several survey instruments authored by your adviser, but you wrote the entire manuscript. What are the considerations in determining authorship? Does your adviser have a valid claim to first authorship? To any authorship at all?

4. Below are several poorly written sentences. Rewrite these sentences using the guidelines presented in this chapter.
   a. This study hypothesized that attachment style in childhood would predict relationship satisfaction in adulthood.
   b. In this study, a t test was conducted to examine performance scores between participants who were in the distracted and non-distracted learning conditions.
   c. The data from this study proved that individuals in the high-stress condition performed more poorly than individuals in the low-stress condition.
   d. This research concluded that using emojis in text messages reduced the potential for miscommunication.

5. Given the story of the media's misrepresentation of Steffanie Strathdee's research regarding needle exchange programs (see "Media Matters: When Research Is Misrepresented"), what measures do you think researchers should take to minimize the risk of their research being misrepresented? Many researchers say that you should not make outlandish claims, but since Strathdee did not do so in the case of her research and her work was *still* misreported, are there any further measures to be taken?

Key Terms

error bar, p. 292

narrative, p. 278

Appendix

READING A RESEARCH ARTICLE—KEY QUESTIONS

As noted in Chapter 3, you can use this document to take notes on the key points as you read a research article.

Introduction

1. What are the problem areas—both broad and specific—that have led the researchers to study this problem and generate hypotheses? Why does the topic matter?
2. What are the central research questions?
3. What is the research hypothesis (or hypotheses)?

Method

1. Who is being studied (sample size and demographics)?
2. What are the key variables that were measured in the research? If the study is experimental, you should also be able to identify the independent and dependent variables.
3. How have the researchers operationalized those variables (i.e., defined them in measurable terms)?
4. What methods are used to collect the data, and what sorts of controls are in place to deal with potential error and false variables? How do the methods allow for distinguishing among various possibilities?

Results

1. What are the methods of data analysis (broadly speaking): qualitative, quantitative, or both?
2. Based on the analyses, what did the researchers find with reference to each of their hypotheses? Were their hypotheses supported?

Discussion

1. What are the major conclusions of the authors? What are the implications for this area of research?
2. Are the conclusions reasonable and well grounded in the actual findings?
3. What are the caveats and major limitations of the research?

Glossary

ABAB design A type of single-case experimental design that involves a baseline measurement (A), a treatment/intervention measurement (B), a measurement following removal of the treatment/intervention (A), and finally a second treatment/intervention measurement (B).

abstract A brief summary of a research article's purpose, methods, and major findings. Abstracts are typically about 150 to 300 words in length.

accommodation A concept of Piaget's (a cognitive developmental psychologist) that refers to a process where internal mental structures change as a function of maturation and taking in new information (assimilation).

acquiescence bias Errors in testing where the participant responds affirmatively to every question or to every question where they are unsure of the correct response.

active deception The giving of false information to study participants.

aging Changes, both positive and negative, associated with the latter part of the lifespan (e.g., from adulthood to death).

alternate forms reliability Correlation of the scores from two different versions of the same measure that is taken by the same group of respondents.

amblyopia A developmental visual disorder that arises when the inputs to the two eyes are not well correlated in young infants and children.

analysis of variance (ANOVA) A statistical technique to test for differences among means. (See also **one-way ANOVA, repeated-measures one-way ANOVA, two-way ANOVA**.)

anchoring A heuristic that leads individuals to use a particular value as a base for estimating an unknown quantity and adjust their estimate based on that quantity, even if the value given is entirely arbitrary.

ANOVA table A table used to organize and display the results of analysis of variance.

anterior cingulate A region of the brain involved in processing any kind of aversive state—for example, it is active when people make errors, when they experience pain, and when they exert hard mental effort.

applied research Research that generally seeks to address a practical issue or problem.

archival research The study of data that have been previously collected.

assimilation A concept of Piaget's (a cognitive developmental psychologist) that refers to a process where internal mental structures take in new information and fit it in with existing structures (schemas).

attention control group A type of control group in which participants receive everything the experimental group receives (e.g., the same amount of time and attention), with the exception of the "active ingredient" of the intervention or treatment.

attrition The loss of research participants prior to completion of a study.

availability heuristic A cognitive process that leads individuals to overestimate the likelihood of events that come easily to mind.

basic research Research that strives to advance knowledge within a particular area of science.

between-subjects design A type of experimental design in which the experimenter assigns individual participants or groups of participants to one of several conditions to detect differences *between* groups of participants, with each group exposed to a separate condition. Also called between-groups or independent-groups design.

bidirectionality In a cause-and-effect relationship between two variables, both variables can act as the causal variable. For example, higher intelligence may cause one to be in a higher socio-economic bracket and being in a higher socio-economic bracket may cause one's intelligence to increase; the effect goes both ways.

bimodal A data set with two distinct peaks in the distribution of data.

bivariate statistics Numerical values that characterize the relationship between two variables.

BOLD response Blood oxygen level–dependent response. Oxygenated blood has different magnetic properties than blood that is deoxygenated. Higher levels of oxygenated blood compared with deoxygenated blood are found in brain regions that are active.

boredom effect Participants begin to perform more poorly as the experiment goes on as a consequence of repeated exposure to experimental conditions in a within-subjects design. Also called a fatigue effect.

box-and-whisker plots A visual display that uses a box to represent the interquartile range and whiskers to represent the minimum and maximum values of the data set. Often simply called box plots.

Canadian Council on Animal Care (CCAC) The national organization responsible for protecting the health and well-being of animals being used in research, teaching, and testing throughout Canada.

case study A detailed examination of a single individual over a period of time.

causal design A research design that seeks to understand what causes or explains a certain phenomenon.

causality bias The tendency to assume that two events are causally related because of proximity of time and place, when in fact no such causal relation exists.

ceiling effect Occurs when scores on a measure cluster at the upper end (the "ceiling") of the measure.

cell A combination of one level from each factor in the experiment. The number of cells in a factorial design equals the number of levels of the different factors multiplied by each other. For example, a 2×2 design would have 4 cells, whereas a 3×4 design would have 12 cells.

central limit theorem A theorem that says with a large sample size, the sampling distribution of the mean will be normal or nearly normal in shape.

central tendency A description of the typical or average values of the data.

change over time A general way to capture temporal changes, particularly changes brought about by learning and experience.

clinical psychology The area of psychology that integrates science, theory, and practice to treat patients' psychologically based distress.

closed-ended response item A survey item/question that requires respondents to choose from a number of predetermined responses.

coding The process whereby data are categorized to facilitate analysis.

coercion The act of taking away someone's voluntary choice to participate through either negative or positive means.

cognitive bias An approach to thinking about a situation that may lead you to respond in a particular manner that may be flawed.

cognitive dissonance The idea that we are uncomfortable holding conflicting thoughts simultaneously and that we are motivated to reduce this discomfort (or "dissonance") by changing our existing thoughts to bring about a more consistent belief system.

cognitive miser model A cognitive bias that leads individuals to attend to only a small amount of information to preserve mental energy.

cognitive neuroscience Research with the goal of furthering a brain-based understanding of the mind.

Cohen's *d* A standardized effect size that is defined as the raw effect divided by its standard deviation.

cohort effect Differences that emerge between different age groups resulting from shared characteristics or experiences that impact an entire group of individuals (e.g., the invention of smartphones).

concealment A strategy for handling participant reactivity by keeping observers or recording equipment hidden from participants.

concurrent evidence The degree to which test scores predict a criterion variable measured at the same point in time.

condition The intervention or treatment in an experiment given to a particular group of participants.

confederate A person (accomplice) who is part of an experiment or study (but unknown to the participants) and plays a specific role in setting up the experimental situation.

confidence interval A range of values around the effect size obtained in a sample that is likely to contain the true population effect size with a given level of plausibility or confidence.

confidentiality The identity of participants, and any information that participants share with researchers, cannot be shared with anyone else (unless consent is given).

confirmation bias The tendency to give the most weight to information that supports your theory, potentially discounting or ignoring data that go against your strongly held theoretical bias.

conflict of interest A situation in which financial or other considerations may compromise or appear to compromise a researcher's judgment in conducting or reporting research.

confounding variables Variables that are not accounted or controlled for in your study that could act as an alternative explanation for your research findings.

confounds Extraneous variables that change with the independent variable(s) in your experimental design and could account for effects that you find.

congruent trials In a flanker task, trials where the target and distractor items face in the same direction ($<<< < <<<$).

construct irrelevant variance A construct is measured too broadly and its measurement includes aspects that are not part of the construct.

construct underrepresentation A construct is measured too narrowly and its measurement does not include all relevant aspects of the construct.

contingency table A tabular display for representing categorical or nominal level data. Also called a cross-tabulation table.

contrast effect When a participant's performance in a prior experimental condition influences the results of following experimental conditions. Also called a simple order effect.

control group In an experimental design, the set of participants who do not receive the experimental treatment (or who receive an inert version). This group is compared with the experimental group.

convenience sampling A method of sampling that makes use of the most readily available group of participants.

convergent design A mixed methods research design that collects and analyzes the quantitative and qualitative data separately, but then integrates the results together.

convergent evidence The degree to which two constructs that theoretically should be related to one another are related.

converging evidence Results from multiple research investigations that provide similar findings.

correlational design A research design that seeks to understand how different variables are related to one another.

counterbalancing A strategy that ensures control for the order of experimental interventions. The experimenter calculates all the possible orders of interventions and confirms even distribution of the different order combinations across participants.

Cramer's V A correlation-like measure used to summarize data in contingency tables.

Cronbach's alpha (α) A measure of the internal consistency of a set of scale items.

cross-sectional research designs The most common types of studies across age and time, involving simultaneously assessing a number of different age groups.

cross-sequential research design An approach that combines aspects of both cross-sectional and longitudinal designs where multiple age groups or cohorts are studied over time.

dark triad A cluster of three antisocial personality traits: Machiavellianism, narcissism, and psychopathy.

data blitz A 1- to 10-minute oral presentation that uses one or two slides to convey the essence of research and data in a fast, clear way at a conference.

data cleaning The process of checking that your measurements are complete and accurate prior to any analysis.

data map A region in an fMRI image that shows BOLD changes correlated with changes in activation pattern.

debrief To give participants study information that was initially withheld and the reasons why the information was withheld.

Declaration of Helsinki Formalized in 1964, this international proclamation broadened the Nuremberg Code guidelines from 1947, stating "It is the mission of the doctor to safeguard the health of the people."

deidentified data Data for which any information that can be used to identify participants (e.g., name, address, phone number) has been removed.

demand characteristics Features of the experimental design itself that lead participants to make certain conclusions about the purpose of the experiment and then adjust their behaviour accordingly, either consciously or unconsciously.

dependent variable The factor of interest being measured in the experiment that changes in response to manipulation of the independent variable.

descriptive statistics Numerical values that summarize the data and give a sense of the shape and spread of the data or the extent to which two variables are related to one another.

development Multidirectional changes that occur over the lifespan (e.g., from conception through old age).

diffusion-weighted imaging (DWI) An imaging technique that uses an MRI machine to measure the diffusion of water molecules in different brain regions. Combined with anatomical images and three-dimensional modelling, researchers are able to identify pathways in the brain. Also called diffusion-weighted magnetic resonance imaging.

discounting base-rate information A cognitive bias that leads individuals to favour anecdotal evidence over more detailed information that is available.

discriminant evidence A lack of correlation between two constructs that should not be related to one another.

domain specific The idea that knowledge or expertise in different areas is not based on an underlying general capability, but rather determined by particular capabilities or experiences within an area.

double-barrelled question A question that refers to more than one issue but requires or expects only one response. Also known as a compound question.

double-blind design Both the participants and the experimenters collecting the data are unaware of the condition to which participants have been assigned.

ecological validity A measure of the degree to which the conclusions drawn from a research study can be applied to real-life situations.

editorial board A group of researchers who make decisions about what a specific journal will publish.

effect size The magnitude of an effect (such as a difference of means or a relationship between two variables).

electroencephalography (EEG) A non-invasive technique for measuring brain activity that involves attaching electrodes to a participant's scalp and recording ongoing electrical signals from the brain.

environmental manipulation A manipulation that alters the participants' physical or social context for each level of the independent variable.

equivalent measures Methods that are equally good at measuring a behaviour of interest for different age groups in a sample.

error bar A graphical representation of the amount of variability of a sample statistic, such as a mean.

eta squared (η²) An effect size measure for one-way analysis of variance.

event sampling Observing and recording each occurrence of a targeted behaviour or event; shows how frequently a behaviour or event occurs.

event-related potential Brain activity measured in response to a particular stimulus or event using electroencephalography.

evidence based on consequences of testing Evidence that examines the interpretations and uses of test scores and their resulting intended and unintended consequences.

evidence based on internal structure The degree to which test items and components match the structure of the underlying construct.

evidence based on relations to other variables The degree to which a test/construct is related to other external variables.

evidence based on response processes The degree to which the mechanisms underlying what people think, feel, or do when responding to test items or tasks matches the construct the test or task is trying to measure.

evidence based on test content The degree to which the content of a test measures what it is intended to measure.

executive control The management of cognitive processes involved in planning, problem solving, reasoning, and switching between tasks.

exempt research Research that does not require research ethics board review.

experimental group In an experimental design, the set of participants that receives the intervention or treatment with the goal of determining whether the treatment impacts the outcome.

explanatory design A mixed methods research design that first collects and analyzes quantitative data then follows up the findings with a more in-depth qualitative study.

exploratory design A mixed methods research design that first collects and analyzes qualitative data then uses these findings to inform the quantitative data collection.

external validity A measure of the degree to which the conclusions drawn from a particular set of results can be generalized to other samples or situations.

extraneous variable Any variable that is not part of your research study that could influence your results. These variables should be controlled to reduce variability in your data and to prevent confounds.

factor A variable manipulated by the experimenter.

factor analysis A statistical technique that examines the relationships between items in a scale. This approach is useful for determining whether a scale measures a single variable or multiple ones.

factorial ANOVA A statistical technique for comparing means when the experimental design includes two factors.

factorial design An experimental design that has more than one independent variable.

falsifiable The concept that researchers can test whether the hypothesis or claim can be proven wrong.

fatigue effects Negative effects on survey responses or completion resulting from participants tiring of the survey. Can also occur in experiments as a consequence of repeated exposure to experimental conditions in a within-subjects design, where it is also called a boredom effect.

file-drawer problem Bias in published research resulting from the issue that studies that do not exhibit statistical significance are less likely to be published (or even submitted for publication) than findings that do exhibit statistical significance.

flanker task A test that measures attention and inhibitory control by asking the participant to focus on a particular stimulus (<) while ignoring other stimuli surrounding it (>>>> < > >>>>).

floor effect Occurs when scores on a measure cluster at the lower end (the "floor") of the measure.

focus group A small group of 6 to 10 individuals who are interviewed in a group setting.

fractional anisotropy A measure of the spatial pattern of diffusion. Basically, it describes whether diffusion is occurring equally in all directions or is greater in one direction or another.

framing effect A cognitive bias caused by seemingly inconsequential differences in wording in a question or problem that lead respondents to vary their choices.

Friedman test A non-parametric alternative to repeated-measures one-way analysis of variance.

functional magnetic resonance imaging (fMRI) A neuroimaging technique that, by measuring changes in blood flow, enables researchers to obtain images of the brain while the brain processes information.

funnel debriefing During the debriefing session, the researcher asks the participant a series of questions, starting broad and getting more specific, to identify if the participant had any suspicions about the true nature of the study.

general conference A professional meeting that covers many areas within a particular subject, such as psychology.

general factor of personality A single dimension of personality.

greater than minimal risk research Research that may pose substantial risk to participants and requires a full REB review.

Greenhouse–Geisser correction A statistical adjustment to account for violation of sphericity in repeated-measures analysis of variance.

habituation Diminished response to a stimulus that comes about through repeated exposure to that stimulus.

Hawthorne effect Participants in an experiment modify their behaviour as a result of knowing they are being observed. Also called the observer effect.

hemodynamic response Changes in blood flow in the brain. Increased blood flow to regions of the brain is associated with increased activity in that brain region.

heuristic Mental shortcuts that assist people in finding adequate but often imperfect solutions to difficult problems.

higher-order factorial design A design that includes more than two independent variables. For example, a $2 \times 2 \times 2$ design, with three factors, two levels for each factor, and eight cells or conditions.

histogram A visual display that uses bars to show the frequency of responses in the data set.

hypothesis A statement that predicts the outcome of your research study. It specifies a predicted answer to your research question.

Implicit Association Test A test of implicit cognition that measures participants' reaction time to investigate the strength of association between people's mental representations.

incongruent trials In a flanker task, trials where the target and distractor items face in a different direction (<<< > <<<).

independence of observations A measurement obtained on an observation (e.g., from a participant) in the experiment does not depend on the measurements obtained on other observations (e.g., from other participants). The responses are *independent* of one another.

independent variable A variable manipulated by the experimenter to observe its effect on a dependent variable.

inferential statistical tests Statistical methods such as t tests or χ^2 tests that enable researchers to use sample data to draw conclusions about the population of interest.

informed consent Agreement of a participant to take part in a study, having been made aware of the potential risks.

instructional manipulation A manipulation that provides different instructions for each level of the independent variable.

interaction Occurs when the differences on one factor depend on the levels of at least one other factor.

interaction chart A diagram that represents different combinations of the presence or absence of main and interaction effects.

interaction effect A measure of the extent to which the effect of one factor depends on the levels of the other factor.

internal consistency The degree to which the items within a measure assess various aspects of the same construct.

internal validity An assessment of whether a particular variable is the actual cause of a particular outcome.

interquartile range The range of values from the 25th percentile to the 75th percentile; the middle 50 per cent of values.

inter-rater reliability Correlation of the ratings made by two different raters observing the same behaviour.

interval scale A scale containing rank order information, as well as the property of equal intervals between points; it does not contain an absolute zero point.

interview A data collection technique in which researchers ask participants questions orally, either in person or over the phone.

interviewer effects Influences that the interviewer may have on responses, including the way in which they ask and respond to questions, tone of voice, or facial expressions. All of these may be interpreted by the interviewee as positive or negative evaluations of their responses and may lead the respondent to alter their answers.

invasive manipulation A manipulation that uses the administration of drugs or surgery to create physical changes within the participant for each level of the independent variable.

invited talks Discussions lasting between 60 and 90 minutes that are led by established researchers or up-and-coming stars at a conference.

journal impact factor A measure of how often other researchers cite papers published in a particular journal.

keynote address A speech delivered at a conference by an important researcher who presents groundbreaking research and ideas to inspire attendees to think about how they can extend their own research in interesting directions.

Kruskal–Wallis test A non-parametric alternative to one-way analysis of variance.

kurtosis A measure of the shape of a distribution that assesses how flat or peaked the distribution is relative to the normal distribution.

Latin square A type of counterbalancing technique in which each participant receives different experimental conditions in a systematically different order.

leading question A question that suggests a particular answer to the question because of the way it is phrased.

learning Changes tied to specific instruction or experiences over relatively short periods of time.

levels The values taken on by an independent variable or factor. For example, in a drug effectiveness study, you may have a factor of "treatment," which has levels of "placebo" and "drug."

Levene's test A test of the equality of two variances.

lie scale A set of survey items used to determine whether participants are taking the task seriously and not simply responding in such a way as to present themselves in the best possible light.

Likert response format An ordered range of responses used to measure particular attitudes or values. Response options usually include three to seven options that vary from "strongly disagree" to "strongly agree."

Likert scale The sum of responses to multiple questions intended to measure the same variable using the Likert response format.

Likert-type ratings Items that ask participants to rate their attitudes or behaviour using a predetermined set of responses that are quantified. An example would be a 5-point rating scale that asks about level of agreement from 1 (strongly disagree) to 5 (strongly agree).

literature review A summary of previous research that has been done on the topic, typically located in the introduction of the paper.

loaded question A question that contains an assumption about the respondent that might not be justified and can make the question difficult to answer.

longitudinal research designs Designs that track groups of participants over a period of time with two or more assessments of the same individuals at different times.

MacArthur Scale of Subjective Social Status A measure of subjective social standing, obtained by having respondents place themselves on a socio-economic "ladder."

magnetic resonance imaging (MRI) A neuroimaging technique that uses powerful magnets to create images of anatomical structures in the brain.

main effect The overall effect of a single factor on the dependent variable, averaging over the levels of all other factors.

manipulation check Assesses whether the manipulation of the independent variable was effective and elicited the expected differences between the experimental conditions.

Mann–Whitney U test (Wilcoxon rank-sum test) A non-parametric alternative to the independent-samples t test.

matched-group design A type of experimental design in which experimenters assign separate groups of participants in each condition and "twin" a participant in each group with a participant in another group.

maturation Growth and other changes in the body and brain that are associated with underlying genetic information.

Mauchly's test of sphericity A test of the sphericity assumption in repeated-measures analysis of variance.

mean A measure of central tendency that is calculated by summing all of the values in a data set and then dividing by the number of values in the data set. Also called the arithmetic average.

mean diffusion A measure of how fast water molecules move, or diffuse, through brain regions.

measurement error The difference between the actual or true value of what you are measuring and the result obtained using the measurement instrument.

median A measure of central tendency that is the middle value of all the data points; 50 per cent of the values are below the median and 50 per cent are above.

meta-analysis A statistical technique that combines results across a number of previous studies.

method The tools that are used to collect research data (e.g., surveys).

methodology The specific procedures or techniques that are used to identify, collect, and analyze information about a topic.

microgenetic design An approach that attempts to observe changes as they occur and to understand the process involved in any observed changes by focusing on a key transition point or dramatic shift in the behaviour of interest.

midpoint The centre value of a scale with an odd number of response possibilities. An example of a midpoint on a scale of agreement is "neither agree nor disagree."

minimal risk research Research that does not pose risks that are greater than risks encountered in daily life.

mixed factorial design A design that includes both within- and between-subjects factors.

mixed methods research Research that uses both quantitative and qualitative data within a single study.

mode A measure of central tendency that is the most common value in the data set.

moderating variable A variable that influences (but does not causally explain) the direction or strength of relationship between two other variables.

motion artifacts Data that are caused by the movement of the participant rather than a response to the stimuli of interest.

multiple baseline design A series of AB designs that are systematically staggered over time to examine the effect of the intervention or treatment across participants, settings, or behaviours.

narrative A description of your research that flows from highly structured and organized ideas.

naturalistic observation Looking at phenomena as they occur (naturally) in the environment.

near-infrared spectroscopy (NIRS) A neuroimaging technique for assessing brain function; a near-infrared light is shone through the scalp using optical fibres that are placed in a cap and reflected back to detectors in the cap.

neuropsychology A term generally used to refer to studies of individuals with brain damage.

nominal scale The most basic measurement, when scale points are defined by categories.

non-equivalent groups design A between-groups quasi-experimental design in which participants are not randomly assigned to conditions.

non-experimental methods A group of research approaches that do not attempt to manipulate or control the environment, but rather involve the researcher using a systematic technique to examine what is already occurring.

non-parametric test A statistical test that makes few assumptions about the population distribution and may be applied to nominal and ordinal measurements.

non-probability sample A sample in which members of the population are not all given an equal chance of being selected.

non-response bias Errors introduced into sampling that occur when individuals who are contacted and choose to complete a survey differ in some ways from others who are contacted but choose not to participate.

normal distribution A unimodal pattern of data, with the mode occurring in the centre of the distribution and values dropping off sharply in a symmetrical pattern on both sides of the mean.

null hypothesis Typically, a statement of "no effect" in your results. For example, a null hypothesis might suggest no difference in mean responses for different experimental conditions or zero correlation between two variables.

null hypothesis significance testing (NHST) A traditional approach to inferential statistical tests that attempts to determine whether a specific hypothesis (the null hypothesis) can be rejected at a given probability level.

Nuremberg Code of 1947 A group of 10 standards that guide ethical research involving human beings.

objectivity Approaching knowledge as a quest for the truth, rather than as an attempt to find results that support one's own beliefs or theory.

observational methods A class of research techniques that involve gathering information by observing phenomena as they occur.

omnibus null hypothesis In analysis of variance, the null hypothesis that all group means are equal.

one-way analysis of variance (ANOVA) A statistical technique to test for differences of means on a single factor.

open-ended response item A survey item/question in which answers are not provided and respondents are able to answer the question in their own words.

operational definition A clearly specified definition of your variables, stated in observable and measurable terms.

operationalizing The process by which a researcher strives to define variables by putting them in measurable terms.

order effect When a participant's performance in a within-subjects experiment is affected by the order in which the participant receives the experimental conditions. Also called a carryover effect.

ordinal scale A scale possessing the properties of identity and magnitude such that each value is unique and has an ordered relationship to the other values on the scale.

outliers Extreme values that do not match the pattern of the rest of the data.

oversampling The intentional overrecruitment of underrepresented groups into a sample to ensure there will be enough representation of those groups to make valid research conclusions.

page proofs Copies of the accepted paper that include questions from the copy editor for the authors to address.

parallel forms reliability A measure of survey reliability that examines the consistency of responses of respondents across two versions of a survey, with items in both surveys having been designed to probe the same variables. Also called alternate forms reliability.

parametric test A statistical test that requires that the measurement scale of your data be interval or ratio and makes strong assumptions about the distribution of measurements in your population.

participant observation An individual who is part of the environment observes and records a behaviour of interest (e.g., a parent making observations of a child during their normal interactions).

participant variable A pre-existing characteristic (e.g., sex, age, or ethnicity) to which a participant cannot be randomly assigned.

passive deception The withholding of some study details from participants.

Pearson's r A bivariate statistic that measures the extent of the linear relationship between two interval or ratio level variables and ranges from -1 to $+1$. The full name is the Pearson product-moment correlation coefficient.

peer-reviewed journals Scholarly journals whose editors send any submitted article out to be evaluated by knowledgeable researchers or scholars in the same field.

p-Hacking The process of deliberately manipulating factors in your research to maximize your chance of uncovering a statistically significant finding ($p < .05$).

phi (φ) A correlation-like measure used to summarize data in 2×2 contingency tables.

pilot study A "prestudy" conducted before your actual study to assess your survey/interview instrument or test a methodology.

placebo effect A result of treatment that can be attributed to participants' expectations from the treatment rather than any property of the treatment itself.

point-biserial correlation A measure that describes the degree to which a binary variable (e.g., yes/no) relates to a continuous variable.

population The entire group of individuals relevant to your research.

positive psychology An area of psychology that focuses on studying the strengths and virtues that enable individuals and communities to thrive.

poster symposia A meeting at a conference in which researchers present thematically linked posters and take part in a moderated discussion.

post-structural feminism A theoretical perspective that seeks to explore and understand how individuals are shaped and experienced through cultural and social norms.

practical significance The differences between groups are large enough that they represent a meaningful difference in a real-world context.

practice effect The result of a participant's performance in one experimental condition leading to improved performance on following experimental conditions due to increased familiarity and experience with the task.

predictive evidence The degree to which test scores predict a criterion variable measured at a future point in time.

presidential address A speech given at a conference by the head or president of the hosting society or organization, who discusses the collective body of research to be found at the conference within a historical context and presents ideas for future research.

pretest–posttest design A within-subjects quasi-experimental design in which participants are tested before and after an experimental treatment or condition is introduced.

primary source An article or reference that describes the results of original research that was conducted by the author(s) of the article.

priming The presentation of cues to push thinking in a certain direction.

probability sampling Sampling methods for which the probability of a person being selected into a sample is known.

probability value (p value) Indicates how likely it would be to see results at least as extreme as those observed under the assumption that the null hypothesis is true.

prospective power analysis A series of computations that help you to determine the number of participants you will need to successfully detect an effect in your research.

pseudoscience Practices, beliefs, or claims that are presented as scientific but do not have a scientific basis or empirical support.

PsycINFO A database specific to psychology journals and related references.

QQ plot A graphical technique to identify deviations from normality in a data set. Also called a normal quantile–quantile plot.

qualitative research Research that results in data that are non-numerical and are analyzed for meaning or patterns.

quantitative research The use of numerical data and statistical techniques to examine questions of interest. Or, research that results in data that can be numerically measured.

quasi-experimental design A design that is similar to a true experiment but does not randomly assign participants to conditions or randomly assign the order of the conditions.

quasi-random assignment The experimenter assigns equal numbers of participants with key characteristics (e.g., sex, age, or ethnicity) across the experimental and control conditions.

questionnaire A set of questions that may be part of a survey or interview.

radiofrequency coils Part of the magnetic resonance imaging machine that is used to produce radiofrequency pulses. These coils are also used to measure the energy given off by protons as they return to the state they were in prior to the radiofrequency pulse.

radiofrequency pulse A short burst of a high-wavelength, low-energy electromagnetic wave that is produced by radiofrequency coils in a magnetic resonance imaging machine to alter the alignment of protons.

random assignment The assignment of participants to different conditions in an experiment by methods that rely on chance and probability so that potential biases related to assignment to conditions are removed.

random sampling A method in which every member of a given population has an equal chance of being selected into a sample.

random selection The process by which experimenters recruit participants from the population into an experiment that involves each participant having a prespecified probability of being selected into the sample.

range The maximum value minus the minimum value in a data set.

ratio scale A scale sharing all the properties of an interval scale (rank order information and equal interval), but also containing a meaningful absolute zero point, where zero represents the absence of the thing that is being measured.

raw effects Straightforward measures of effect size, such as the difference in the means for two samples. Also called unstandardized effects.

reactivity A shift in an observed individual's normal behaviour as a result of the knowledge that they are being observed.

relaxation A measure used with magnetic resonance imaging that assesses the time it takes for protons to return to their original state following a radiofrequency pulse that altered their alignment.

reliability The idea that an investigation or measurement tool should yield consistent findings if researchers use the same procedures and methods repeatedly.

repeated-measures one-way ANOVA A statistical technique for testing differences of means across a single factor in which the same participants provide measurements for each level of the factor.

replication The process through which either the original researcher or the researchers from an independent laboratory repeat the investigation and obtain the same or highly similar results.

representative sample A sample that shares the essential characteristics of the population from which it was drawn.

researcher bias In survey/interview research, errors in testing that are introduced by the way in which experimenters ask questions (related to framing effects).

research ethics board (REB) A committee, consisting of faculty and community members, that has been established to review and approve research proposals within a university.

research question The central question(s) you are seeking to answer in your research study. It may ask what, how, or why something is happening.

response bias Errors in testing that are introduced into participants' responses to interview or survey questions because of such considerations as a desire to respond in a way the participant believes the researcher would want, an unwillingness to provide sensitive information, or a tendency to always respond positively when unsure about a question.

response set The tendency for a participant to respond to survey items with a consistent pattern of responses regardless of the question being asked (e.g., answering "strongly agree" to a long string of questions).

retrospective power analysis A series of computations that help you determine how much power you had in a study after the fact.

reversal design (ABA design) A type of single-case experimental design in which baseline measurements are initially taken (A), a treatment/intervention is then implemented and measurements are taken (B), and finally the treatment/intervention is removed and measurements are taken one last time (A).

risk–benefit analysis A comparison of the risks and benefits associated with a research study. It is used to determine whether the study is worth conducting or if the risks are too high.

robust statistical methods Statistical tests that are not greatly affected by conditions that violate the assumptions of standard parametric tests, for example, the assumption that population values are normally distributed.

sample A subset of individuals drawn from the population of interest.

sampling distribution of the mean The pattern of mean values obtained when drawing many random samples of a given size from a population and computing the mean for each sample.

sampling error Differences in the measurements observed in a data set and what would be expected from the population values.

sampling interval The amount of time elapsed between different data collection points in a developmental study.

scatterplot A method for simultaneously displaying the values for two or more variables that is useful for investigating the relationship between those variables.

scientific method An approach that seeks to generate explanations for observable phenomena with an emphasis on objectivity and verifiable evidence.

secondary source An article or reference in which the author describes research that has previously been published.

selection bias Errors in sampling resulting from a selected sample not being representative of the population of interest. This may come about because of under- or oversampling of particular types of respondents, respondent self-selection, or respondent non-response.

selective attrition Attrition resulting from certain types of participants dropping out of the study; can threaten the validity of the study.

self-selection An instance where participants electively place themselves into a particular sample (or they opt out of participation).

self-selection bias Errors introduced into sampling when it is completely up to potential respondents whether they participate in a survey.

shape Refers to whether the data values are normally distributed, have a flat or sharp peak, or are skewed to one end or the other of the data range.

single-blind design Either the participants or the experimenters collecting the data are unaware of the condition to which participants have been assigned.

single-case experimental design A design in which experimental methodology (e.g., manipulation of a variable and experimental control) is typically applied to a single participant or small group of participants using repeated measurements.

skepticism The process of applying critical thinking in evaluating the truth of a claim.

skewness A measure of how asymmetric a distribution of values is.

snowball sampling A method of sampling in which participants are asked to help recruit additional participants.

social constructionism A theoretical perspective that examines how participants derive meaning from their lived experiences.

social desirability bias The tendency of respondents to provide answers that will be viewed favourably by others.

socially desirable responding The tendency of individuals to respond in a way that will be viewed favourably by others.

specialized conference A professional meeting that focuses on a particular branch of a discipline, such as social or developmental psychology, or on particular research or statistical methodologies, such as methods for analyzing longitudinal data.

specimen record Observing and making a detailed record of a targeted behaviour during a given time period.

sphericity An assumption for repeated-measures analysis of variance that requires the variances of the differences between all pairs of groups be approximately equal.

standard deviation A measure of the variability of a data set that indicates how far, on average, data points deviate from the mean.

standard error The standard deviation of a sampling distribution. This value is calculated by dividing the standard deviation by the square root of the sample size.

standardization The designing of interview questions such that they are used in a consistent manner by all interviewers.

standardized effect Adjusts the raw effect based on the amount of variability in the data.

statistical control In analyzing experiment results, the experimenter makes a statistical adjustment that accounts for the influence of a specified third variable and allows for the analysis of results with the influence of that third variable eliminated.

statistical power The probability that your study will be able to detect an effect in your research, if such an effect exists.

statistical significance An indicator of the probability of obtaining an effect size as large as (or larger than) the one you obtained; also indicates that the differences between groups are not due to sampling error.

statistical significance level A conventional probability value, usually .05 or .01, used to assess whether the null hypothesis in NHST should be rejected.

stereotype threat The activation of a negative belief about a particular group that influences members of that group to underperform in certain situations.

stimulus manipulation A manipulation that uses different stimuli for each level of the independent variable.

stratified random sampling A technique whereby a population is divided into homogeneous groups, called strata, along some key dimension (e.g., race/ethnicity), and then random samples are drawn from within each of the strata.

structured observation An observational approach where researchers exert greater control over the setting in which the observation is occurring.

subjectivity Approaching knowledge from the standpoint of an individual's own beliefs, experiences, and interpretations.

subscales Distinct parts of a larger instrument that measure different aspects of a variable.

sums of squares Mathematical quantities that measure the amount of variability in data. These include between-subjects, within-subjects, and total sums of squares.

survey A set of questions administered to a group of respondents, usually via paper or online, to learn about attitudes and behaviour.

symposia Twenty-minute talks given by researchers at a conference that contain an overlapping theme and focus on a particular research study or studies.

***t* test** A statistical approach that compares the difference between the means of two groups.

***t* test, independent samples** A statistical test for comparing the means of two independent samples.

***t* test, matched pairs** A statistical test for comparing the means of two matched samples. The samples may represent two different measurements from the same participants or different participants matched on some criteria (e.g., academic achievement).

***t* test, one sample** A statistical test for comparing the mean of a single sample to a specified value.

T1-weighted image A weighted magnetic resonance image that is produced as energy is emitted from the protons as they recover their original magnetization. In these images, tissues with high fat content, such as the white matter of the brain, appear bright and sections of the brain filled with water appear dark.

T2-weighted image A weighted magnetic resonance image that captures energy emitted as excessive spin induced by the radiofrequency pulse returns to the steady state. In these images, tissues with high fat content look dark, and those areas with high water content appear light in shading.

Tesla (T) A measure of the strength of a magnetic field produced by a magnet. Higher numbers indicate a stronger magnetic field.

test–retest reliability Correlation of the scores from the same measure that is taken by the same group of respondents at two different points in time.

test statistics Computed values associated with particular approaches designed to test hypotheses.

Three Rs The principles of replacement (avoiding use of animals), reduction (minimizing use of animals), and refinement (modifying treatment of animals) that guide research being conducted with animals.

time sampling Observing and recording behaviours during predetermined units of time; for instance, one minute at the start of every five-minute period.

tractography A three-dimensional modelling technique used to visualize the neural pathways.

transcranial magnetic stimulation (TMS) A method that uses a strong magnet to cause a small group of neurons to fire in the brain. When used in concert with other neuroimaging techniques, researchers can study the impact of the activation on cognitive function.

transition point The point in development where key changes occur; often the focus of microgenetic designs.

Tri-Council Policy Statement First developed in 1998 and revised in 2010 and again in 2014 and 2018, it is a series of basic ethical principles to guide researchers as they perform studies with human participants.

trimmed mean A mean computed after removing some fixed percentage (often 10 or 20 per cent) of the largest and smallest values in a data set.

two-way ANOVA A statistical technique for comparing means when the experimental design includes two factors.

type I error Occurs if a researcher rejects the null hypothesis when, in fact, the null hypothesis is true.

type II error Occurs if a researcher fails to reject the null hypothesis when, in fact, it is false.

unimodal A data set with a single peak in the distribution of data.

univariate statistics Numerical values that summarize one variable at a time.

validity Overall, this concept refers to the idea that your measurements and methodology allow you to capture what you think you are trying to measure or study.

variability Refers to how spread out data values are in a sample.

variance A measure of the dispersion of a data set; the average squared deviation of values from the mean value.

voxels In functional magnetic resonance imaging, the smallest volume for which it is possible to compute a blood oxygen level–dependent response.

waves Repeated periods of data collection in a cross-sequential design.

Welch's *t* test A version of the independent-samples *t* test that takes into account unequal variances between the two groups.

Wilcoxon rank-sum test A non-parametric alternative to the independent-samples *t* test.

Wilcoxon signed-rank test A non-parametric alternative to the one-sample or matched-pairs *t* tests.

within-subjects design A type of experimental design in which the experimenter assigns each participant to all possible conditions. Also called a within-group or repeated-measures design.

References

Chapter 1

The aftermath of an unfounded vaccine scare in Britain. (2013, May 22). *New York Times* [editorial board]. Retrieved from https://www.nytimes.com/2013/05/23/opinion/the-aftermath-of-measles-vaccine-scare-in-britain.html

Aldhous, P. (2011, November 2). Psychologist admits faking data in dozens of studies. *NewScientist*. Retrieved from http://www.newscientist.com/article/dn21118-psychologist-admits-faking-data-in-dozens-of-studies.html

Armstrong, K., Schwartz, J. S., Fitzgerald, G., Putt, M., & Ubel, P. A. (2002). Effect of framing as gain versus loss on understanding and hypothetical treatment choices: Survival and mortality curves. *Medical Decision Making, 22,* 76–83.

Brody, J. (2012, June 25). Having your coffee and enjoying it too. *New York Times*. Retrieved from http://well.blogs.nytimes.com/2012/06/25/having-your-coffee-and-enjoying-it-too

Chai, C. (2014, March, 25). Anti-vaccination movement means preventable diseases making a comeback. *Global News*. Retrieved from https://globalnews.ca/news/1229059/anti-vaccination-movement-means-entirely-preventable-diseases-are-making-a-comeback

Chai, C. (2017, January 10). Weekend warrior? Your two-day exercise is just as good to reap health benefits: Study. *Global News*. Retrieved from https://globalnews.ca/news/3171697/weekend-warrior-your-two-day-exercise-is-just-as-good-to-reap-health-benefits-study

Deer, B. (2011, January 6). How the case against the MMR vaccine was fixed. *British Medical Journal, 342,* 77–84. doi:10.1136/bmj.c5347

Fiske, S. T., & Taylor, S. E. (2013). *Social cognition: From brains to culture* (2nd ed.). Thousand Oaks, CA: Sage.

Gilovich, T., Griffin, D., & Kahneman, D. (2002). *Heuristics and biases: The psychology of intuitive judgment*. Cambridge, UK: Cambridge University Press.

Gross, L. (2009, May 26). A broken trust: Lessons from the vaccine-autism wars. *PLoS Biology*. Retrieved from http://journals.plos.org/plosbiology/article?id=10.1371/journal.pbio.1000114/

Hannaford, A. (2013, April 6). Andrew Wakefield: Autism Inc. *The Guardian*. Retrieved from http://www.theguardian.com/society/2013/apr/06/what-happened-man-mmr-panic

Health Canada. (2018). Survey for the development of the childhood vaccination campaign. Retrieved from http://epe.lac-bac.gc.ca/100/200/301/pwgsc-tpsgc/por-ef/health/2018/022-17-e/report.pdf

Higgins, E. T. (2000). Making a good decision: Value from fit. *American Psychologist, 55,* 1217–30.

Hiltzik, M. (2014, January 20). The toll of the anti-vaccination movement, in one devastating graphic. *Los Angeles Times*. Retrieved from http://www.latimes.com/business/hiltzik/la-fi-mh-antivaccination-movement-20140120-story.html

Ingraham, C. (2015, January 22). The devastating impact of vaccine deniers, in one measles chart. *Washington Post*, Wonkblog. Retrieved from http://www.washingtonpost.com/blogs/wonkblog/wp/2015/01/22/the-devastating-impact-of-vaccine-deniers-in-one-measles-chart

Kahneman, D. (2011). *Thinking, fast and slow*. New York, NY: Farrar, Straus and Giroux.

Kahneman, D., Slovic, P., & Tversky, A. (1982). *Judgment under uncertainty: Heuristics and biases*. Cambridge, UK: Cambridge University Press.

Kahneman, D., & Tversky, A. (1979). Prospect theory: An analysis of decision under risk. *Econometrica, 47,* 263–91.

Northcraft, G. B., & Neale, M. A. (1987). Experts, amateurs, and real estate: An anchoring-and-adjustment perspective on property pricing decisions. *Organizational Behavior and Human Decision Processes, 39,* 84–97.

Reid, O. (2010, December 30). Stanford doctors face down ghost-writing, money scandals. *College Fix*. Retrieved from http://www.thecollegefix.com/post/5490

Robinson, M. (2016, July). Canadian researchers who commit scientific fraud are protected by privacy laws. *The Star*. Retrieved from https://www.thestar.com/news/canada/2016/07/12/canadian-researchers-who-commit-scientific-fraud-are-protected-by-privacy-laws.html

Rosengren, K. S., & French, J. A. (2013). Magical thinking. In M. Taylor (Ed.), *The Oxford handbook of the development of imagination* (pp. 42–60). New York, NY: Oxford University Press.

Stanovich, K. E. (2012). *How to think straight about psychology* (10th ed.). Boston, MA: Allyn & Bacon.

Steig, C. (2019, July, 12). Should you swap your regular coffee for green coffee extract? *Refinery, 29*. Retrieved from https://www.refinery29.com/en-us/what-is-green-coffee-extract

Szabo, A., Szemerszky, R., Dömötör, Z., Gresits, I., & Köteles, F. (2017). Laboratory investigation of specific and placebo effects of a magnetic bracelet on a short bout of aerobic exercise. *Journal of Sport Behavior, 40*(4), 410–22.

Taubes, G. (1993). *Bad science: The short life and weird times of cold fusion*. New York, NY: Random House.

Tversky, A., & Kahneman, D. (1974). Judgment under uncertainty: Heuristics and biases. *Science, 185,* 1124–31.

Weathers, C. (2015, January). Quackwear: Big pseudoscience wants to sell you wearable metal to improve your health. *Raw Story*. Retrieved from https://www.rawstory.com/2015/01/quackwear-big-pseudoscience-wants-to-sell-you-wearable-metal-to-improve-your-health

Weight Loss Pills Network. (2016). Dr. Oz green coffee bean extract: What does he recommend? Retrieved from http://www.weightlosspillswork.com/dr-oz-green-coffee-bean-extract

Wheeler, T. (2017, May). What is magnetic field therapy? *WebMD*. Retrieved from https://www.webmd.com/pain-management/magnetic-field-therapy-overview

Chapter 2

Albertson, B., & Gadarian, S. (2014, July 1). Was the Facebook emotion experiment unethical? *Washington Post*. Retrieved from https://www.washingtonpost.com/news/monkey-cage/wp/2014/07/01/was-the-facebook-emotion-experiment-unethical/?noredirect=on

Baumrind, D. (1964). Some thoughts on ethics of research: After reading Milgram's "Behavioral Study of Obedience." *American Psychologist, 19*, 421–3.

BBC Horizon. (2005). Dr. Money and the boy with no penis. Retrieved from http://www.bbc.co.uk/sn/tvradio/-programmes/horizon/dr_money_prog_summary.shtml

Blum, B. (2018, June). The lifespan of a lie. *Medium*. Retrieved from https://medium.com/s/trustissues/the-lifespan-of-a-lie-d869212b1f62

Brannigan, A., Nicholson, I., & Cherry, F. (2015). Introduction to the special issue: Unplugging the Milgram machine. *Theory & Psychology, 25*(5), 551–63. doi: 10.1177/0959354315604408

Burger, J. M. (2009). Replicating Milgram: Would people still obey today? *American Psychologist, 64*, 1–11.

Canadian Institutes of Health Research, Natural Sciences and Engineering Research Council of Canada, and Social Sciences and Humanities Research Council of Canada. (2018). *Tri-Council Policy Statement: Ethical Conduct for Research Involving Humans: TCPS 2 2018*. Retrieved from http://www.pre.ethics.gc.ca/eng/documents/tcps2-2018-en-interactive-final.pdf

Colapinto, J. (2000). *As nature made him: The boy who was raised as a girl*. New York, NY: HarperCollins.

Colapinto, J. (2004, June 3). Gender gap: What were the real reasons behind David Reimer's suicide? *Slate Magazine*. Retrieved from http://www.slate.com/articles/health_and_science/medical_examiner/2004/06/gender_gap.html

Gapp, K., Jawaid, A., Sarkies, P., Bohacek, J., Pelczar, P., Prados, J., ... Mansuy, I. M. (2014). Implication of sperm RNAs in transgenerational inheritance of the effects of early trauma in mice. *Nature Neuroscience, 17*, 667–9.

Grant, K. (2017, June). The pressure of big pharma. *Globe and Mail*. Retrieved from https://www.theglobeandmail.com/news/national/the-pressure-of-big-pharma-financial-conflicts-of-interest-common-on-medical-guidelinepanels/article35389639

Haney, C., Banks, C., & Zimbardo, P. (1973a). A study of prisoners and guards in a simulated prison. *Naval Research Reviews, 26*(9), 1–17.

Haney, C., Banks, C., & Zimbardo, P. (1973b). Interpersonal dynamics in a simulated prison. *International Journal of Criminology and Penology, 1*, 69–97.

Harris, B. (1988). Key words: A history of debriefing in social psychology. In J. Morawski (Ed.), *The rise of experimentation in American psychology* (pp. 188–212). New York, NY: Oxford University Press.

Katz, J. (1972). *Experimentation with human beings*. New York, NY: Russell Sage Foundation.

Koocher, G. P. (1977). Bathroom behavior and human dignity. *Journal of Personality and Social Psychology, 35*(2), 120–1.

Leaning, J. (1996). War crimes and medical science. *British Medical Journal, 313*, 1413–5.

Middlemist, R. D., Knowles, E. S., & Matter, C. F. (1976). Personal space invasions in the lavatory: Suggestive evidence for arousal. *Journal of Personality and Social Psychology, 33*(5), 541–6.

Milgram, S. (1963). Behavioral study of obedience. *Journal of Abnormal and Social Psychology, 67*, 371–8.

Millum, J. (2012). Canada's new ethical guidelines for research with humans: A critique and comparison with the United States. *Canadian Medical Association Journal, 184*(6), 657–61. doi: 10.1503/cmaj.111217

Money, J., & Ehrhardt, A. (1972). *Man & woman, boy & girl: Gender identity from conception to maturity*. Northvale, NJ: Aronson.

Mosby, I. (2013). Administering colonial science: Nutrition research and human biomedical experimentation in Aboriginal communities and residential schools, 1942–1952. *Social History, 46*(91), 145–72.

Raina, S. A., Wolfson, C., Kirkland, S. A., Griffith, L. E., Oremus, M., Patterson, C., ... Brazil, K. (2009). The Canadian Longitudinal Study on Aging (CLSA). *Canadian Journal on Aging, 28*, 221–9. doi:10.1017/S0714980809990055

Russell, W. & Burch, R. (1959). *The principles of human experimental technique*. London, UK: Methuen.

Samson, N. (2018, July 11). How a scholarly association is helping Indigenous writers to thrive. *University Affairs*. Retrieved from https://www.universityaffairs.ca/news/news-article/how-a-scholarly-association-is-helping-indigenous-writers-to-thrive

Silva, D. S., Matheson, F. I., & Lavery, J. V. (2017). Ethics of health research with prisoners in Canada. *BMC Medical Ethics, 18*(31), 1–7. doi: 10.1186/s12910-017-0189-6

Speaking of Research. (n.d.). Facts. Retrieved from https://speakingofresearch.com/facts

Steele, C. M., & Aronson, J. (1995). Stereotype threat and the intellectual test performance of African Americans. *Journal of Personality and Social Psychology, 69*, 797–811.

Sullivan, G. (2014). Cornell ethics board did not pre-approve Facebook mood manipulation study. *Washington Post*. Retrieved from http://www.washingtonpost.com/news/morning-mix/wp/2014/07/01/facebooks-emotional-manipulation-study-was-even-worse-than-you-thought

Unger, D. (2011). Research ethics. In *The Canadian bioethics companion* (Chapter 8). Retrieved from http://canadianbioethicscompanion.ca/the-canadian-bioethics-companion/chapter-8-research-ethics

Walker, J. (2004, May 24). The death of David Reimer: A tale of sex, science, and abuse. *Reason.com*. Retrieved from https://reason.com/archives/2004/05/24/the-death-of-david-reimer

Zimbardo, P. G. (1999). Stanford Prison Experiment. Retrieved from http://www.prisonexp.org

Enhancing cognitive and social-emotional development through a simple-to-administer mindfulness-based school program for elementary school children: A randomized controlled trial. *Developmental Psychology, 51*(1), 52–66. doi: http://dx.doi.org/10.1037/a0038454

Seligman, M. E. P., & Csikszentmihalyi, M. (2000). Positive psychology: An introduction. *American Psychologist, 55*, 5–14.

Spelke, E. S. (1985). Preferential-looking methods as tools for the study of cognition in infancy. In G. Gottlieb & N. Krasnegor (Eds.), *Measurement of audition and vision in the first year of postnatal life: A methodological overview* (pp. 323–63). Norwood, NJ: Ablex.

Watson, J. B. (1913). Psychology as the behaviorist views it. *Psychological Review, 20*, 158–77.

Chapter 3

Allen, C. (2015, January). Mindfulness-based program in schools making a positive impact: UBC study. *UBC News*. Retrieved from https://news.ubc.ca/2015/01/26/mindfulness-based-programs-in-schools-making-a-positive-impact-ubc-study

Chi, M. T. H. (1978). Knowledge structure and memory development. In R. Siegler (Ed.), *Children's thinking: What develops?* (pp. 73–96). Hillsdale, NJ: Erlbaum.

DeLoache, J. S., Pierroutsakos, S. L., Uttal, D. H., Rosengren, K. S., & Gottlieb, A. (1998). Grasping the nature of pictures. *Psychological Science, 9*, 205–10.

DeLoache, J. S., Uttal, D. H., & Rosengren, K. S. (2004). Scale errors offer evidence for a perception-action dissociation early in life. *Science, 304*, 1027–9.

Elsa, E. (2018, February). Goldie Hawn: MindUP and be happy. *Gulf News Government*. Retrieved from https://gulfnews.com/business/sectors/government/goldie-hawn-mind-up-and-be-happy-1.2171843

Festinger, L. (1957). *A theory of cognitive dissonance.* Palo Alto, CA: Stanford University Press.

Festinger, L., & Carlsmith, J. M. (1959). Cognitive consequences of forced compliance. *Journal of Abnormal and Social Psychology, 58*, 203–10.

Kanter, S. (2018, October). Goldie Hawn and Kate Hudson team up to drop a fashion collection ahead of new baby arrival. *People*. Retrieved from https://people.com/style/goldie-hawn-kate-hudson-fabletics-collection-mindup

Locke, L. F., Silverman, S. J., & Spiruduso, W. W. (2010). *Reading and understanding research* (3rd ed.). Los Angeles, CA: Sage.

Neale, M. C., & Cardon, L. R. (1992). *Methodology for genetic studies of twins and families.* Dordrecht, Netherlands: Kluwer Academic Press.

Pomerantz, D. (2014, May). How Goldie Hawn is helping kids focus in school. *Forbes*. Retrieved from https://www.forbes.com/sites/dorothypomerantz/2014/05/15/how-goldie-hawn-is-helping-kids-focus-in-school/#307c4a22bbf7

Schonert-Reichl, K. A., Oberle, E., Lawlor, M. S., Abbott, D., Thompson, K., Oberlander, T. F., & Diamond, A. (2015).

Chapter 4

American Educational Research Association, American Psychological Association, National Council on Measurement in Education [AERA/APA/NCME]. (2014). Standards for educational and psychological testing. Washington, DC: American Educational Research Association.

Blazer, C. (2011). Unintended consequences of high-stakes testing. *Information Capsule: Research Services, 1008*. Retrieved from https://files.eric.ed.gov/fulltext/ED536512.pdf

Bornstein, M. H., Mash, C., Arterberry, M. E., & Manian, N. (2012). Object perception in 5-month-old infants of clinically depressed and nondepressed mothers. *Infant Behavior & Development, 35*, 105–57.

CCFC. (2007, December 6). Disney no longer marketing *Baby Einstein* videos as educational. Press release. Retrieved from http://www.commercialfreechildhood.org/blog/disney-no-longer-marketing-baby-einstein-videos—educational

Creswell, J. W., & Poth, C. N. (2018). *Qualitative inquiry and research design: Choosing among five approaches* (4th ed.). Thousand Oaks, CA: Sage.

DeLoache, J. S., Chiong, C., Sherman, K., Islam, N., Vanderborght, M., Troseth, G. L., . . . O'Doherty, K. (2010). Do babies learn from baby media? *Psychological Science, 21*, 1570–4.

DeVellis, R. F. (2017). *Scale development: Theories and applications* (4th ed.). Los Angeles, CA: Sage.

Gardner, H. (1983). *Frames of mind: The theory of multiple intelligences.* New York, NY: Basic Books.

Greenwald, A. G., McGhee, D. E., & Schwartz, J. K. L. (1998). Measuring individual differences in implicit cognition: The Implicit Association Test. *Journal of Personality and Social Psychology, 74*, 1464–80.

Horn, J. L., & Cattell, R. B. (1967). Age differences in fluid and crystallized intelligence. *Acta Psychologica, 26*, 107–29.

Hubley, A. M., & Zumbo, B. D. (2017). Response processes in the context of validity: Setting the stage. In A. M. Hubley & B. D. Zumbo (Eds.), *Understanding and investigating response processes in validation research* (pp. 1–12). Switzerland: Springer.

Lewin, T. (2003, October 29). A growing number of video viewers watch from crib. *New York Times.*

Martin, J. (2011, June 30). UW battle over *Baby Einstein* settled, maybe. *Seattle Times.*

Mclean, J. (2009, October). Disney to refund *Baby Einstein* DVDs in Canada. *The Star.* Retrieved from https://www.thestar.com/life/health_wellness/2009/10/26/disney_to_refund_baby_einstein_dvds_in_canada.html

Pankratz, H. (2007, August 8). *Baby Einstein* may be harmful, study says. *Denver Post.* Retrieved from http://www.denverpost.com/2007/08/07/baby-einstein-may-be-harmful-study-says

Rice, C. (2007). Becoming "the fat girl": Acquisition of an unfit identity. *Women's Studies International Forum, 30,* 158–74. doi:10.1016/j.wsif.2007.01.001

Sireci, S. G. (2016). On the validity of useless tests. *Assessments in Education: Principles, Policies & Practice, 23*(2), 226–35. doi: 10.1080/0969594X.2015.1072084

Spearman, C. (1904). "General intelligence," objectively determined and measured. *The American Journal of Psychology, 15,* 201–92.

Stanovich, K. E. (2013). *How to think straight about psychology* (11th ed.). New York, NY: Pearson.

Tinbergen, N. (1951). *The study of instinct.* Oxford, UK: Clarendon Press.

Willig, C. (2012). Perspectives on the epistemological bases for qualitative research. In H. Cooper (ed.), *APA handbook of research methods in psychology: Vol. 1. Foundations, planning, measures, and psychometrics* (pp. 5–21). Washington, DC: American Psychological Association.

Yang, Y., DeCelle, S., Reed, M., Rosengren, K. S., Schlagel, R., & Greene, J. (2011). Subjective experiences in older adults practicing taiji and qigong. *Journal of Aging Research, 2011,* Article ID 650210. doi:10.4061/2011/650210

Yong, E. (2012, October 3). Nobel laureate challenges psychologists to clean up their act. *Nature.* Retrieved from http://www.nature.com/news/nobel-laureate-challenges-psychologists-to-clean-up-their-act-1.11535

Zimmerman, F. J., Christakis, D. A., & Meltzoff, A. N. (2007). Associations between media viewing and language development in children under age 2 years. *Journal of Pediatrics, 151,* 364–8.

Chapter 5

Beauchet, O., Allali, G., Annweiler, C., Berrut, G., Maarouf, N., Herrmann, F. R., & Dubost, V. (2008). Does change in gait while counting backward predict the occurrence of a first fall in older adults? *Gerontology, 54*(4), 217–23.

Beck, A. T., Ward, C. H., Mendelson, M., Mock, J., & Erbaugh, J. (1961). An inventory for measuring depression. *Archives of General Psychiatry, 4,* 561–71.

Bennett, J., & Lanning, S. (2007, August). The Netflix prize. *Proceedings of the KDD Cup and Workshop.* San Jose, CA.

Bootsma-van der Wiel, A., Gussekloo, J., de Craen, A. J. M., van Exel, E., Bloem, B. R., & Westerndorp, R. G. J. (2003). Walking and talking as predictors of falls in the general population: The Leiden 85-Plus Study. *Journal of the American Geriatric Society, 51*(10), 1466–71.

Brookshire, B. (2013, May 8). Psychology is WEIRD. *Slate Magazine.* Retrieved from http://www.slate.com/articles/health_and_science/science/2013/05/weird_psychology_social_science_researchers_rely_too_much_on_western_college.html

Buhrmester, M., Kwang, T., & Gosling, S. D. (2011). Amazon's Mechanical Turk: A new source of inexpensive, yet high-quality, data? *Perspectives on Psychological Science, 6,* 3–5.

Carifio, J., & Perla, R. (2008). Resolving the 50-year debate around using and misusing Likert scales. *Medical Education, 42,* 1150–2. doi:10.1111éj.1365-2923.2008.03172.x

Cooper, C. A., McCord, D. M., & Socha, A. (2011). Evaluating the college sophomore problem: The case of personality and politics. *Journal of Psychology, 145,* 23–7.

Difallah, D., Filatova, E., & Ipeirotis, P. (2018). Demographics and dynamics of Mechanical Turk workers. In *Proceedings of WSDM 2018: The Eleventh ACM International Conference on Web Search and Data Mining.* Marina Del Rey, California, February 5–9, 2018. https://doi.org/10.1145/3159652.3159661

Downey, G. (2010, July 10). We agree it's WEIRD, but is it WEIRD enough? Neuroanthropology.net. Retrieved from http://neuroanthropology.net/2010/07/10/we-agree-its-weird-but-is-it-weird-enough

Giridharadas, A. (2010, August 25). A weird way of thinking has prevailed worldwide. *New York Times.* Retrieved from http://www.nytimes.com/2010/08/26/world/americas/26iht-currents.html

Henrich, J., Heine, S. J., & Norenzayan, A. (2010). The weirdest people in the world? *Behavioral and Brain Sciences, 33*(2/3), 1–75.

Jamieson, S. (2004). Likert scales: How to (ab)use them. *Medical Education, 38,* 1217–8. doi:10.1111/j.1365-2929.2004.02012.x

Lohr, S. (2009, June 26). And the winner of the $1 million Netflix prize (probably) is . . . *New York Times.*

Moberg, P. E. (1982). Biases in unlisted phone numbers. *Journal of Advertising Research, 22*(4), 51–5.

Neider, M. B., Gaspar, J. G., McCarley, J. S., Crowell, J. A., Kaczmarski, H., & Kramer, A. F. (2011). Walking and talking: Dual-task effects on street crossing behavior in older adults. *Psychology and Aging, 26,* 260–8.

Roslow, S., & Roslow, L. (1972). Unlisted phone subscribers are different. *Journal of Advertising Research, 12*(August), 35–8.

Scherpenzeel, A. C., & Bethlehem, J. G. (2011). How representative are online panels? Problems of coverage and selection and possible solutions. In M. Das, P. Ester, & L. Kaczmirek (Eds.), *Social and behavioral research and the Internet* (pp. 105–32). New York, NY: European Association of Methodology.

Simmons, J. P., Nelson, L. D., & Simonsohn, U. (2011). False positive psychology: Undisclosed flexibility in data collection and analysis allows presenting anything as significant. *Psychological Science, 22,* 1359–66.

Statistics Canada. (2017). Postsecondary enrolments, by program type, credential type, age groups, registration status and sex. Table 37-10-0015-01.

Taylor, S. (2003). Telephone surveying for household social surveys: The good, the bad and the ugly. *Social Survey Methodology Bulletin, 52*, 10–21.

Van Buskirk, E. (2009, September 22). How the Netflix prize was won. *Wired*. Retrieved from https://www.wired.com/2009/09/how-the-netflix-prize-was-won

Watters, E. (2013, February 25). We aren't the world. *Pacific Standard*. Retrieved from https://psmag.com/we-aren-t-the-world-535ec03f2d45

Chapter 6

Adelson, J. L., & McCoach, D. B. (2010). Measuring the mathematical attitudes of elementary students: The effects of a 4-point or 5-point Likert-type scale. *Educational and Psychological Measurement, 70*, 796–807.

Adler, N. E., Epel, E. S., Castellazzo, G., & Ickovics, J. R. (2000). Relationship of subjective and objective social status with psychological and physiological functioning: Preliminary data in healthy white women. *Health Psychology, 19*, 586–92.

Armstrong, R. L. (1987). The midpoint on a five-point Likert-type scale. *Perceptual and Motor Skills, 64*, 359–62.

Badarudeen, S., & Sabharwal, S. (2010). Assessing readability of patient education materials: Current role in orthopaedics. *Clinical Orthopaedics and Related Research, 468*(10), 2572–80. http://doi.org/10.1007/s11999-010-1380-y

Best Travel Destinations. (2016). Traveleye.com. Retrieved from http://traveleye.com/travel-guide/top/top-100-travel-destinations

Carifio, J., & Perla, R. J. (2007). Ten common misunderstandings, misconceptions, persistent myths and urban legends about Likert scales and Likert response formats and their antidotes. *Journal of Social Sciences, 3*(3), 106–16.

Carlsmith, K. M., & Chabot, H. F. (1997). A review of computer-based survey methodology. *Journal of Psychological Practice, 3*, 20–6.

Cronbach, L. J. (1951). Coefficient alpha and the internal structure of tests. *Psychometrika, 16*(3), 297–334.

Cundiff, J. M., Smith, T. W., Uchino, B. N., & Berg, C. A. (2013). Subjective social status: Construct validity and associations with psychosocial vulnerability and self-rated health. *International Journal of Behavioral Medicine, 20*, 148–58.

Enders, C. K. (2010). *Applied missing data analysis*. New York, NY: Guilford Press.

Erdreich, B. L., Slavet, B. S., & Amador, A. C. (1994). *Sexual harassment in the federal workplace: Trends, progress and continuing challenges*. Washington, DC: U.S. Merit Systems Protection Board.

Floyd, F. J., & Widaman, K. F. (1995). Factor analysis in the development and refinement of clinical assessment instruments. *Psychological Assessment, 7*, 286–99.

Folstein, M. F., Folstein, S. E., & McHugh, P. R. (1975). Mini-mental state: A practical method for grading the cognitive state of patients for the clinician. *Journal of Psychiatric Research, 12*, 189–98.

Fowler, F. J. (2002). *Survey research methods*. New York, NY: Sage.

Furr, R. M., & Bacharach, V. R. (2014). *Psychometrics: An introduction* (2nd ed.). Thousand Oaks, CA: Sage.

Gardner, D. G., Cummings, L. L., Dunham, R. B., & Pierce, J. L. (1998). Single-item versus multiple-item measurement scales: An empirical comparison. *Educational and Psychological Measurement, 58*, 898–915.

Gillie, B. (2012, October 12). New survey exposes most absurd reasons for skipping work. Examiner.com. Retrieved from http://www.examiner.com/article/new-survey-exposes-most-absurd-reasons-for-missing-work

Goodman, E., Adler, N. E., Kawachi, I., Frazier, A. L., Huang, B., & Colditz, G. A. (2001). Adolescents' perceptions of social status: Development and evaluation of a new indicator. *Pediatrics, 108*(2), E31.

Gorvine, B. J. (2002). *Fathers and father figures of Head Start children: A study of the effects of involvement on children's socioemotional development*. Ann Arbor, MI: University of Michigan.

Inflation remains in check—Except for the tooth fairy. (2013, August 31). *Chicago Tribune*. Retrieved from http://articles.chicagotribune.com/2013-08-31/business/chi-tooth-fairy-amount-08302013_1_jason-alderman-single-tooth-young-parents

Jamieson. D. G., (2006). Literacy in Canada. *Paediatrics & Child Health, 11*(9), 573–4.

Jerman, P., & Constantine, N. A. (2010). Demographic and psychological predictors of parent–adolescent communication about sex: A representative statewide analysis. *Journal of Youth and Adolescence, 39*, 1164–74.

Kozicka, P. (2015, August 18). Survey reveals Tooth Fairy's going rates across Canada. *Global News*. Retrieved from https://globalnews.ca/news/2171237/survey-reveals-tooth-fairys-going-rates-across-canada

Likert, R. (1932). A technique for the measurement of attitudes. *Archives of Psychology, 140*(1), 44–53.

Likert, R., & Hayes, S. P. (1957). *Some applications of behavioural research*. Paris, France: UNESCO.

Lit, L., Schweitzer, J. B., & Oberbauer, A. M. (2011). Handler beliefs affect scent detection dog outcomes. *Animal Cognition, 14*, 387–94.

McAuliffe, W. E., Geller, S., LaBrie, R., Paletz, S., & Fournier, E. (1998). Are telephone surveys suitable for studying substance abuse? Cost, administration, coverage and response rate issues. *Journal of Drug Issues, 28*, 455–81.

Miller, J. (2018, September 5). Demand for pot will be much higher than anyone anticipated after legalization, says report commissioned for Health Canada. *Ottawa Citizen*. Retrieved from https://ottawacitizen.com/news/local-news/demand-for-pot-will-be-much-higher-than-anyone-anticipated-after-legalization-says-report-commissioned-for-health-canada

Oakes, J. M., & Rossi, P. H. (2003). The measurement of SES in health research: Current practice and steps toward a new approach. *Social Science & Medicine, 56*, 769–84.

Parsian, N., & Dunning, T. (2009). Developing and validating a questionnaire to measure spirituality: A psychometric process. *Global Journal of Health Science, 1*, 1–11.

Pew Research Center. (n.d.). Question wording. Retrieved from http://www.people-press.org/methodology/questionnaire-design/question-wording

Pfungst, O. (1911). *Clever Hans (The horse of Mr. von Osten): A contribution to experimental animal and human psychology* (Trans. C. L. Rahn). New York, NY: Holt.

Pisani, J. (2013, August 30). Tooth fairy inflation: Price of a tooth nears $4. *ABC News.* Retrieved from http://abcnews.go.com/Business/wireStory/tooth-fairy-inflation-price-tooth-nears-20114599? singlePage=true

Schonfeld, Z. (2013, July 2). Wives are cheating 40% more than they used to, but 70% as much as men. *The Wire.* Retrieved from http://www.theatlanticwire.com/national/2013/07/wives-cheating-vs-men/66800

Schwartz, Z. (2016, February 24). Canada's top party schools 2016: Full results. *Maclean's.* Retrieved from https://www.macleans.ca/education/canadas-top-party-schools-2016-detailed-results

Straus, M. A. (1979). Measuring intrafamily conflict and violence: The Conflict Tactics (CT) Scales. *Journal of Marriage and the Family, 41*, 75–88.

Straus, M. A., Hamby, S. L., Boney-McCoy, S., & Sugarman, D. B. (1996). The revised Conflict Tactics Scales (CTS2): Development and preliminary psychometric data. *Journal of Family Issues, 17*, 283–316.

Tooth fairy gives Canadian kids a raise this year. (2015, August 17). Retrieved from https://www.visa.ca/en_CA/about-visa/newsroom/press-releases/tooth-fairy-canadian-kids.html

Top universities in Canada 2018. (2018). Retrieved from https://www.topuniversities.com/university-rankings-articles/world-university-rankings/top-universities-canada-2018

Visa. (2013). *Financial literacy for everyone*: Practical money skills for life. Retrieved from http://www.practicalmoneyskills.com/resources/polls

Ward, M. K. (2015). Careless responding on internet-based surveys: Humanizing the process may improve data quality. *APS Observer, 28*(2), 37–9.

Weng, L. (2004). Impact of the number of response categories and anchor labels on coefficient alpha and test-retest reliability. *Educational and Psychological Measurement, 64*(6), 956–72.

Wolff, L. S., Acevedo-Garcia, D., Subramanian, S. V., Weber, D., & Kawachi, I. (2010). Subjective social status, a new measure in health disparities research: Do race/ethnicity and choice of referent group matter? *Journal of Health Psychology, 15*, 560–74.

Chapter 7

Anderson, K. J., & Revelle, W. (1994). Impulsivity and time of day: Is rate of change in arousal a function of impulsivity? *Journal of Personality and Social Psychology, 67*, 334–44.

Asch, S. E. (1951). Effects of group pressure on the modification and distortion of judgments. In H. Guetzkow (Ed.), *Groups, leadership and men* (pp. 177–90). Pittsburgh, PA: Carnegie Press.

Christensen, L. (2012). Types of designs using random assignment. In C. Harris, P. M. Camic, D. L. Long, & A. T. Panter (Eds.), *APA handbook of research methods in psychology, Vol. 2* (pp. 469–88). Washington, DC: American Psychological Association.

Dehue, T. (2001). Establishing the experimenting society: The historical origin of social experimentation according to the randomized controlled design. *American Journal of Psychology, 114*, 283–302.

Dwyer, R., Kushlev, K., & Dunn, E. (2018). Smartphone use undermines enjoyment of face-to-face social interactions. *Journal of Experimental Social Psychology, 78.* doi 10.1016/j.jesp.2017.10.007

Emmons, R. A., & McCullough, M. E. (2003). Counting blessings versus burdens: An experimental investigation of gratitude and subjective well-being in daily life. *Journal of Personality and Social Psychology, 84*(2), 377–89. doi: 10.1037/0022-3514.84.2.377

Hellerman, C. (2013, December 26). You may not be better off after knee surgery. *cnn.com.* Retrieved from http://www.cnn.com/2013/12/26/health/knee-surgery-study

Jaslow, R. (2013, December 26). Common arthroscopic knee surgery no better than "sham" version, researchers say. *CBS News.* Retrieved from http://www.cbsnews.com/news/common-arthroscopic-knee-surgery-not-effective-no-better-than-sham-researchers-say

Joffe, V., & Varlokosta, S. (2007). Patterns of syntactic development in children with Williams syndrome and Down's syndrome: Evidence from passives and wh-questions. *Clinical Linguistics & Phonetics, 21*, 705–27.

Keppel, G., & Wickens, T. D. (2004). *Design and analysis: A researcher's handbook.* Upper Saddle River, NJ: Pearson.

Kirsch, I., & Sapirstein, G. (1998). Listening to Prozac but hearing placebo: A meta-analysis of anti-depressant medication. *Prevention and Treatment, 1*, Article 2a.

Landsberger, H. A. (1958). *Hawthorne revisited: Management and the worker.* Ithaca, NY: Cornell University Press.

Marion, S. B., & Burke, T. M. (2017). Altruistic lying in an alibi corroboration context: The effects of liking, compliance, and relationship between suspects and witnesses. *Behavioral Science & the Law, 35*(1), 37–59. doi: 10.1037/t17832-000

Master, S. L., Eisenberger, N. I., Taylor, S. E., Naliboff, B. D., Shirinyan, D., & Lieberman, M. D. (2009). A picture's worth: Partner photographs reduce experimentally induced pain. *Psychological Science, 20*, 1316–8.

McGrath, P. J. (2018). Pioneer paper: An accidental scientist: Chance, failure, risk-taking, and mentoring. *Journal of Pediatric Psychology, 43*(7), 716–22.

Milgram, S. (1963). Behavioral study of obedience. *Journal of Abnormal and Social Psychology, 67*, 371–8.

Orne, M. T. (1962). On the social psychology of the psychological experiment: With particular reference to demand characteristics and their implications. *American Psychologist, 17*, 776–83.

Price, D. D., Finniss, D. G., & Benedetti, F. (2008). A comprehensive review of the placebo effect: Recent advances and current thought. *Annual Review of Psychology, 59*, 565–90.

Revelle, W., Humphreys, M. S., Simon, L., & Gilliland, K. (1980). The interactive effect of personality, time of day, and caffeine: A test of the arousal model. *Journal of Experimental Psychology: General, 109*, 1–31.

Sihvonen, R., Paavola, M., Malmivaara, A., Itälä, A., Joukainen, A., Nurmi, H., Kalske, J., & Järvinen, T. L. N. (2013). Arthroscopic partial meniscectomy versus sham surgery for a degenerative meniscal tear. *New England Journal of Medicine, 369*, 2515–24.

Stanovich, K. E. (2011). *How to think straight about psychology* (10th ed.). Boston, MA: Allyn & Bacon.

Zannad, F., Stough, W. G., McMurray, J. J. V., Remme, W. J., Pitt, B., Borer, J. S., Geller, N. L., & Pocock, S. J. (2012). When to stop a clinical trial early for benefit: Lessons learned and future approaches. *Circulation: Heart Failure, 5*, 294–302.

Chapter 8

Channelling Superman: Avatars and real-world behaviour. (2014, February 5). *The Economist.* Retrieved from http://www.economist.com/blogs/babbage/2014/02/avatars-and-real-world-behaviour

Chi, M. T. H. (1978). Knowledge structure and memory development. In R. Siegler (Ed.), *Children's thinking: What develops?* (pp. 73–96). Hillsdale, NJ: Erlbaum.

Dallery, J., Cassidy, R. N., & Raiff, B. R. (2013). Single-case experimental designs to evaluate novel technology-based health interventions. *Journal of Medical Internet Research, 15*(2), e22. doi:10.2196/jmir.2227

DeLoache, J. S., Uttal, D. H., & Rosengren, K. S. (2004). Scale errors offer evidence for a perception-action dissociation early in life. *Science, 304*, 1027–9.

Herbert, W. (2014, January 21). Know thy avatar: Good and evil in the gaming world. *Huffington Post.* Retrieved from http://www.huffingtonpost.com/wray-herbert/know-thy-avatar-good-and_b_4644183.html

Jhangiani, R. S., Dastur, F. N., Le Grand, R., & Penner, K. (2018). As good or better than commercial textbooks: Students' perceptions and outcomes from using open digital and open print textbooks. *Canadian Journal for the Scholarship of Teaching and Learning, 9*(1). https://doi.org/10.5206/cjsotl-rcacea.2018.1.5

Nowakowski, M. E., Rogojanski, J., & Antony, M. M. (2014). Specific phobia. In S. G. Hofmann, D. J. Dozois, W. Rief, & J. A. Smith (Eds.), *The Wiley handbook of cognitive behavioral therapy* (pp. 979–99). Boston, MA: Wiley–Blackwell.

Raiff, B. R., & Dallery, J. (2010). Internet-based contingency management to improve adherence with blood glucose testing recommendations for teens with type 1 diabetes. *Journal of Applied Behavioral Analysis, 43*(3), 487–91. doi:10.1901/jaba.2010.43-487

Raven, K. (2014, February 19). Can avatars bring out the good in gamers? *Reuters Health.* Retrieved from http://www.reuters.com/article/2014/02/19/us-can-avatars-gamers-idUS BREA1I21L 20140219

Rizvi, S. L., & Nock, M. K. (2008). Single-case experimental designs for the evaluation of treatments for self injurious and suicidal behaviors. *Suicide and Life-Threatening Behavior, 38*(5), 498–510.

Vincent, J. (2014, February 11). Do you play as Voldemort or Superman? Study shows virtual roleplay affects behaviour. *The Independent.* Retrieved from http://www.independent.co.uk/news/science/do-you-play-as-voldemort-or-superman-study-shows-virtual-roleplay-affects-behaviour-9121831.html

Witt, M. R., Stokes, T. F., Parsonson, B. S., & Dudding, C. C. (2018). Effect of distance caregiver coaching on functional skills of a child with traumatic brain injury. *Brain Injury, 32*(7), 894–9.

Yoon, G., & Vargas, P. (2014). Know thy avatar: The unintended effect of virtual-self representation on behavior. *Psychological Science, 25*(4), 1043–5.

Chapter 9

Arthur-Banning, S., Wells, M. S., Baker, B. L., & Hegreness, R. (2009). Parents behaving badly? The relationship between the sportsmanship behavior of adults and athletes in youth basketball games. *Journal of Sport Behavior, 32*, 3–18.

Blurton Jones, N. (1972). *Ethological studies of child behavior.* New York, NY: Cambridge University Press.

Boller, K., Sprachman, S., and the Early Head Start Research Consortium. (1998.) Time-sampling coding form. *The NICHD Study of Early Child Care and Youth Development.* Retrieved from https://www.nichd.nih.gov/publications/pubs/documents/seccyd_06.pdf

Borenstein, M. (2012). Effect size estimation. In H. Cooper (Ed.), *APA handbook of research methods in psychology: Vol. 3. Data analysis and research publication* (pp. 131–46). Washington, DC: American Psychological Association.

Carter, R. (1999). Artistic savants tune in and tune off. *New Scientist, 2207*, 30–4.

Charlesworth, W. R. (1986). Darwin and developmental psychology: 100 years later. *Human Development, 29*, 1–35.

Chatterjee, A. (2004). The neuropsychology of visual artistic production. *Neuropsychologia, 42*, 1568–83.

Christensen, A., & Hazzard, A. (1983). Reactive effects during naturalistic observation of families. *Behavioral Assessment, 5*, 349–62.

Cooper, H. (2010). *Research synthesis and meta-analysis—A step-by-step approach* (4th ed.). Thousand Oaks, CA: Sage.

Corkin, S. (1984). Lasting consequences of bilateral medial temporal lobectomy: Clinical course and experimental findings in H. M. *Seminars in Neurology, 4*, 249–59.

Corkin, S. (2002). What's new with the amnesic patient H. M.? *Nature Reviews: Neuroscience, 3,* 153–160.

De Bruin, A., Treccani, B., & Della Sala, S. (2015). Cognitive advantage in bilingualism: An example of publication bias? *Psychological Science, 26,* 99–107.

Drake, J. E., & Winner, E. (2011). Superior visual analysis and imagery in an autistic child with drawing talent. *Imagination, Cognition, and Personality, 31,* 9–29.

Eibl-Eibesfeldt, I. (1967). Concepts of ethology and their significance in the study of human behavior. In H. Stevenson, E. H. Hess, & H. Rheingold (Eds.), *Early behavior: Comparative and developmental approaches* (pp. 127–46). New York, NY: Wiley.

Fortner-Wood, C., & Henderson, B. B. (1997). Individual differences in two-year-olds' curiosity in the assessment setting and in the grocery store. *Journal of Genetic Psychology, 158,* 495–7.

Galanes, P. (2013, June 14). The mother of all housewives. *New York Times.*

Heffernan, V. (2011, April 17). Too much relationship vérité. *New York Times.*

Henley, D. (1989). Nadia revisited: A study into the nature of regression in the autistic savant syndrome. *Art Therapy: Journal of the American Art Therapy Association, 6,* 43–56.

Jacob, T., Tennenbaum, D., Seilhamer, R. A., Bargiel, K., & Sharon, T. (1994). Reactivity effects during naturalistic observation of distressed and nondistressed families. *Journal of Family Psychology, 8,* 354–63.

Johnson, S. M., & Bolstad, O. D. (1975). Reactivity to home observation: A comparison of audio recorded behavior with observers present or absent. *Journal of Applied Behavior Analysis, 8,* 181–5.

Kaczynski, A. T., Potwarka, L. R., & Saelens, B. E. (2008). Association of park size, distance, and features with physical activity in neighborhood parks. *American Journal of Public Health, 98,* 1451–6.

MacKay, D. G., James, L. E., Taylor, J. K., & Marian, D. E. (2007). Amnesic H. M. exhibits parallel deficits and sparing in language and memory: Systems versus binding theory accounts. *Language and Cognitive Processes, 22,* 377–452.

Maerz, M. (2011, April 21). You haven't heard the last of the Louds. *Los Angeles Times.*

Martin, R. C., & Allen, C. (2012). Case studies in neuropsychology. In H. Cooper (Ed.), *APA handbook of research methods in psychology: Vol. 2. Research Designs* (pp. 633–46). Washington, DC: American Psychological Association.

Messer, S. C., & Gross, A. M. (1995). Childhood depression and family interaction: A naturalistic observation study. *Journal of Clinical Child Psychology, 24,* 77–88.

Moens, E., Braet, C., & Soetens, B. (2007). Observation of family functioning at mealtime: A comparison of families of children with and without overweight. *Journal of Pediatric Psychology, 32,* 52–63.

Mottron, L., Limoges, E., & Jelenic, P. (2003). Can a cognitive deficit elicit an exceptional ability? A case of savant syndrome in drawing abilities: Nadia. In C. Code, C. Wallesch, Y. Joanette, & A. R. Lecours (Eds.), *Classic cases in neuropsychology: Vol. II* (pp. 323–40). East Sussex, UK: Psychology Press.

NICHD Early Child Care Research Network. (1996). Characteristics of infant child-care: Factors contributing to positive caregiving. *Early Childhood Research Quarterly, 11,* 269–306.

NICHD Early Child Care Research Network. (2003). Does quality of child care affect child outcomes at age 4½? *Developmental Psychology, 39,* 451–69.

O'Dougherty, M., Story, M., & Stang, J. (2006). Observations of parent–child co-shoppers in supermarkets: Children's involvement in food selections, parental yielding, and refusal strategies. *Journal of Nutrition Education and Behavior, 38,* 183–8.

Ogden, J. A., & Corkin, S. (1991). Memories of H. M. In W. C. Abraham, M. Corballis, & K. G. White (Eds.), *Memory mechanisms: A tribute to G. V. Goddard* (pp. 195–215). Hillsdale, NJ: Erlbaum.

Pariser, D., & Zimmerman, E. (2004). Learning in the visual arts: Characteristics of gifted and talented individuals. In E. W. Eisner & M. D. Day (Eds.), *Research and policy in art education* (pp. 379–408). Mahwah, NJ: Erlbaum.

PBS Video. (2013, September 26). *An American Family*: Revisit the Loud family [Video file]. Retrieved from http://video.pbs.org/video/2045835722

Piaget, J. (1926). *The language and thought of the child.* New York, NY: Harcourt, Brace, & World.

Piaget, J. (1952). *The origins of intelligence in children.* New York, NY: International University Press.

Ramachandran, V. S. (2002). *The artful brain.* London, UK: Fourth Estate.

Reyns, B. W. (2015). A routine activity perspective on online victimisation: Results from the Canadian General Social Survey. *Journal of Financial Crime, 22*(4), 396–411. https://doi.org/10.1108/JFC-06-2014-0030

Roberts, B. W., Walton, K., & Viechtbauer, W. (2006). Patterns of mean-level change in personality traits across the life course: A meta-analysis of longitudinal studies. *Psychological Bulletin, 132,* 1–25.

Rosengren, K. S., Gutiérrez, I. T., Anderson, K. N., & Schein, S. S. (2009). Parental reports of children's scale errors in everyday life. *Child Development, 80,* 1586–91.

Rosengren, K. S., Schein, S. S., & Gutiérrez, I. T. (2010). Individual differences in children's production of scale errors. *Infant Behavior and Development, 33,* 309–13.

Scoville, W. B., & Milner, B. (1957). Loss of recent memory after bilateral hippocampal lesions. *Journal of Neurology, Neurosurgery and Psychiatry, 20,* 11–21.

Selfe, L. (1977). *Nadia: A case of extraordinary drawing ability in an autistic child.* New York, NY: Academic Press.

Selfe, L. (2011). *Nadia revisited: A longitudinal study of an autistic savant.* New York, NY: Psychology Press.

Shields, D. L., Bredemeier, B. L., LaVoi, N. M., & Power, F. C. (2005). The sport behavior of youth, parents, and coaches: The good, the bad, and the ugly. *Journal of Research in Character Education, 3*, 43–59.

Shores, K. A., & West, S. T. (2010). Rural and urban park visits and park-based physical activity. *Preventative Medicine, 50*, S13–7.

Stenovec, T. (2013, March 14). Google Glass ban underscores privacy concerns months before futuristic specs are even released. *Huffington Post*. Retrieved from http://www.huffingtonpost.com/ 2013/03/14/google-glass-ban-privacy-concerns_n_2856385.html

Valentine, J. C. (2012). Meta-analysis. In H. Cooper (Ed.), *APA handbook of research methods in psychology: Vol. 3. Data analysis and research publication* (pp. 485–99). Washington, DC: American Psychological Association.

Von Hofsten, C. (1993). Studying the development of goal-directed behavior. In A. F. Kalverboer, B. Hopkins, & R. Geuze (Eds.), *Motor development in early and later childhood: Longitudinal approaches* (pp. 109–24). Cambridge, UK: Cambridge University Press.

Winer, L. (2011, April 25). Reality replay. *The New Yorker*.

Chapter 10

Adolph, K. E., & Robinson, S. R. (2011). Sampling development. *Journal of Cognition and Development, 12*, 411–23.

Adolph, K. E., Robinson, S. R., Young, J. W., & Gill-Alvarez, F. (2008). What is the shape of developmental change? *Psychological Review, 115*, 527–43.

Aldwin, C. M., & Igarashi, H. (2015). Successful, optimal, and resilient aging: A psychosocial perspective. In P. A. Lichtenberg & B. T. Mast (Eds.), *APA handbook of clinical geropsychology: Vol. 1. History and status of the field and perspectives on aging.* Washington, DC: American Psychological Association.

Azad, M. B., Vehling, L., Lu, Z., Dai, D., Subbarao, P., Becker, A. B.,... Sears, M. R. (2017). Breastfeeding, maternal asthma and wheezing in the first year of life: A longitudinal birth cohort study. *European Respiratory Journal, 49*. https://doi.org/10.1183/13993003.02019-2016

Bak, T. H., Nissan, J. J., Allerhand, M. M., & Deary, I. J. (2014). Does bilingualism influence cognitive aging? *Annals of Neurology, 75*, 959–63. doi:10.1002/ana.24158

Berger, K. S. (2011). *The developing person through the life span* (8th ed.). New York, NY: Worth Publishers.

Berger, S. E., & Adolph, K. E. (2007). Learning and development in infant locomotion. *Progress in Brain Research, 164*, 237–55.

Bialystok, E., Craik, F. I., & Freedman, M. (2007). Bilingualism as a protection against the onset of symptoms of dementia. *Neuropsychologia, 45*, 459–64.

Boker, S. M., & Nesselroade, J. R. (2002). A method for modeling the intrinsic dynamics of intraindividual variability: Recovering the parameters of simulated oscillators in multiwave panel data. *Multivariate Behavioral Research, 37*, 137–60.

Burke, D. M., & Shafto, M. A. (2004). Aging and language production. *Current Directions in Psychological Science, 13*, 21–4. doi:10.1111/j.0963-7214 .2004.01301006.x

Caspi, A., Hariri, A. R., Holmes, A., Uher, R., & Moffitt, T. E. (2010). Genetic sensitivity to the environment: The case of the serotonin transporter gene and its implications for studying complex diseases and traits. *American Journal of Psychiatry, 167*, 509–27.

Champagne, F. A., & Mashoodh, R. (2009). Gene–environment interplay and the origins of individual differences in behavior. *Current Directions in Psychological Science, 18*(3), 127–31.

Cohen, P. (2012, January 19). A sharper mind, middle age and beyond. *New York Times*. Retrieved from http://www.nytimes.com/2012/01/22/education/edlife/a-sharper-mind-middle-age-and-beyond.html

Colcombe, S., & Kramer, A. F. (2003). Fitness effects on the cognitive function of older adults: A meta-analytic study. *Psychological Science, 14*(2), 125–30.

Collins, L. M., & Graham, J. W. (2002). The effects of the timing and spacing of observations in longitudinal studies of tobacco and other drug use: Temporal design considerations. *Drug and Alcohol Dependence, 68*, S85–S93.

Crawley, P. (2019, January 31). Globe editorial: Don't go baby boomers! The economy still needs you. *Globe and Mail*. Retrieved from https://www.theglobeandmail.com/opinion/editorials/article-globe-editorial-dont-go-baby-boomers-the-economy-still-needs-you

Crowley, B. L., Clemens, J., & Veldhuis, N. (2010, June 25). The Canadian century: What the United States could learn from its northern neighbor. *Foreign Policy*. Retrieved from https://foreignpolicy.com/2010/06/25/the-canadian-century

Dennis, W. (1940). The effect of cradling practices upon the onset of walking in Hopi children. *Journal of Genetic Psychology, 56*, 77–86.

Gatehouse, J. (2010, December 1). What the boomers are leaving their children: Fewer jobs. Lower pay. Higher taxes. Now the screwed generation is starting to push back. *Maclean's*. Retrieved from https://www.macleans.ca/news/world/what-the-boomers-are-leaving

Granott, N., & Parziale, J. (2002). *Microdevelopment: Transition processes in development and learning*. Cambridge, UK: Cambridge University Press.

Gustavson, K., von Soest, T., Karevold, E., & Roysamb, E. (2012). Attrition and generalizability in longitudinal studies: Findings from a 15-year population-based study and a Monte Carlo simulation study. *BMC Public Health, 12*, article number 918.

Hess, R., Kashigawa, K., Price, G. G., & Dickinson, W. P. (1980). Maternal expectations for mastery of developmental tasks in Japan and the United States. *International Journal of Psychology, 15*, 259–71.

Karasik, L. B., Tamis-LeMonda, C. S., & Adolph, K. E. (2011). Transition from crawling to walking and infants' actions with objects and people. *Child Development, 82,* 1199–209.

Leslie, M. (2000, July/August). The vexing legacy of Lewis Terman. *Stanford Magazine.* Retrieved from https://alumni.stanford.edu/get/page/magazine/article/?article_id=40678

MacWhinney, B. (1987). *Mechanisms of language acquisition.* Hillsdale, NJ: Erlbaum

Manuck, S. B., & McCaffery, J. M. (2014). Gene–environment interaction. *Annual Review of Psychology, 65,* 41–70.

Piaget, J. (1964/1997). Development and learning. In R. E. Ripple & V. N. Rosckcastle (Eds.), *Piaget rediscovered* (pp. 7–20). Reprinted in M. Gauvain & M. Cole (Eds.), *Readings on the development of children* (2nd ed.). New York, NY: Freeman.

Raina, P. S., Wolfson, C., Kirkland, S. A., Griffith, L. E., Oremus, M., Patterson, C. . . . Brazil, K. (2013). The Canadian Longitudinal Study on Aging (CLSA). *Canadian Journal of Aging, 28,* 221–9. doi:10.1017/S0714980809990055

Rosengren, K. S. (2002). Thinking of variability during infancy and beyond. *Infant Behavior and Development, 25,* 337–9.

Rovee-Collier, C. (1999). The development of infant memory. *Current Directions in Psychological Science, 8,* 80–5.

Scheve, T., & Venzon, C. (2015). 10 stereotypes about aging (that just aren't true). HowStuffWorks: Health. Retrieved from http://health.howstuffworks.com/wellness/aging/aging-process/5-stereotypes-about-aging.htm#page=0

Siegler, R. S. (2006). Microgenetic analyses of learning. In D. Kuhn & R. S. Siegler (Eds.), *Handbook of child psychology: Vol. 2. Cognition, perception, and language* (6th ed., pp. 464–510). New York, NY: Wiley.

Siegler, R. S. (2007). Cognitive variability. *Developmental Science, 10,* 104–9.

Siegler, R. S., & Crowley, K. (1991). The microgenetic method: A direct means for studying cognitive development. *American Psychologist, 46,* 606–20.

Siegler, R. S., & Jenkins, E. (1989). *How children discover new strategies.* Hillsdale, NJ: Erlbaum.

Sleek, S. (2013, August 28). Science reveals the benefits of an aging workforce. *Psychological Science.* Retrieved from http://www.psychologicalscience.org/index.php/news/minds-business/science-reveals-the-benefits-of-an-aging-workforce.html

Taylor, A., & Kim-Cohen, J. (2007). Meta-analysis of gene–environment interactions in developmental psychopathology. *Development & Psychopathology, 19,* 1029–37.

Terman, L. M. (1925). *Mental and physical traits of a thousand gifted children, I.* Stanford, CA: Stanford University Press.

Terman, L. M. (1930). *The promise of youth, follow-up studies of a thousand gifted children: Genetic studies of genius, III.* Stanford, CA: Stanford University Press.

Terman, L. M. (1947). *The gifted child grows up, twenty-five years follow up of a superior group: Genetic studies of genius, IV.* Stanford, CA: Stanford University Press.

Tugend, A. (2013, July 26). Unemployed and older, and facing a jobless future. *New York Times.* Retrieved from http://www.nytimes.com/2013/07/27/your-money/unemployed-and-older-and-facing-a-jobless-future.html

Tun, H. M., Konya, T., Takaro, T. K., Brook, J. R., Chari, R., Fields, C. J., . . . Kozyrskyj, A. L. (2017). Exposure to household furry pets influences the gut microbiota of infants at 3–4 months following various birth scenarios. *Microbiome, 5*(4). https://doi.org/10.1186/s40168-017-0254-x

Vygotsky, L. S. (1978). Chapter 6: Interaction between learning and development. In M. Cole, V. John-Steiner, S. Scribner, & E. Souberman (Eds.), *Mind in society: The development of higher psychological processes* (pp. 79–91). Cambridge, MA: Harvard University Press.

Winerip, M. (2013, January 13). Documenting a generation's fall. *New York Times.* Retrieved from http://www.nytimes.com/2013/01/14/booming/set-for-life-documents-crisis-among-baby-boomers.html

WHO Multicentre Growth Reference Study Group. (2006). WHO Motor Development Study: Windows of achievement for six gross motor development milestones. *Acta Paediatricia, Suppl. 450,* 86–95.

Zelazo, P. D., & Bauer, P. J. (2013). National Institutes of Health toolbox cognition battery (NIH Toolbox CB): Validation for children between 3 and 15 years. *Monographs of the Society for Research in Child Development,* Serial No. 309, *78,* 1–149.

Chapter 11

Carver, R. P. (1978). The case against statistical significance testing. *Harvard Educational Review, 48,* 378–99.

Carver, R. P. (1993). The case against statistical significance testing, revisited. *Journal of Experimental Education, 61,* 287–92.

Cohen, J. (1962). The statistical power of abnormal social psychological research: A review. *Journal of Abnormal and Social Psychology, 65,* 145–53.

Cohen, J. (1988). *Statistical power analysis for the behavioral sciences* (2nd ed.). Hillsdale, NJ: Erlbaum.

Cohen, J. (1990). Things I have learned (so far). *American Psychologist, 45,* 1304–12.

Cumming, G. (2012). *Understanding the new statistics: Effect sizes, confidence intervals, and meta-analysis.* New York, NY: Routledge.

Fraley, R. C., & Vazire, S. (2014). The N-pact factor: Evaluating the quality of empirical journals with respect to sample size and statistical power. *PLoS ONE, 9*(10), e109019. doi:10.1371/journal.pone.01909019

Furr, R. M., & Bacharach, V. R. (2014). *Psychometrics: An introduction* (2nd ed.). Thousand Oaks, CA: Sage.

Gigerenzer, G. (2004). Mindless statistics. *Journal of Socio-Economics, 33,* 587–606.

Hagen, R. L. (1997). In praise of the null hypothesis statistical test. *American Psychologist, 52,* 15–24.

Harris, R. J. (1997). Significance tests have their place. *Psychological Science, 8,* 8–11.

Hubbard, R., & Lindsay, R. (2008). Why *p* values are not a useful measure of evidence in statistical significance testing. *Theory & Psychology, 18,* 69–88.

Inzlicht, M. (2016, February 29). Reckoning with the past. [Blog post]. Retrieved from http://michaelinzlicht.com/getting-better/2016/2/29/reckoning-with-the-past

Krueger, J. (2001). Null hypothesis significance testing: On the survival of a flawed method. *American Psychologist, 56*(1), 16–26.

Kwak, J. (2013, February 9). The importance of Excel. *The Baseline Scenario.* Retrieved from https://baselinescenario.com/2013/02

Leyser, O., Kingsley, D., & Grange, J. (2017, March 15). The science "reproducibility crisis"—and what can be done about it. *The Conversation Canada.* Retrieved from https://theconversation.com/the-science-reproducibility-crisis-and-what-can-be-done-about-it-74198

Lloyd, R. (1999, September 30). Metric mishap caused loss of NASA orbiter. *cnn.com.* Retrieved from http://www.cnn.com/TECH/space/9909/30/mars.metric.02

Loftus, G. R. (1996). Psychology will be a much better science when we change the way we analyze data. *Current Directions in Psychological Science, 5*(6), 161–71.

Maxwell, S. E. (2004). The persistence of underpowered studies in psychological research: Causes, consequences, and remedies. *Psychological Methods, 9,* 147–63.

Meyer, M. N., & Chabris, C. (2014, July 31). Why psychologists' food fight matters. *Slate.* Retrieved from http://www.slate.com/articles/health_and_science/science/2014/07/replication_controversy_in_psychology_bullying_file_drawer_effect_blog_posts.html

Mone, M. A., Mueller, G. C., & Mauland, W. (1996). The perceptions and usage of statistical power in applied psychology and management research. *Personnel Psychology, 49,* 103–20.

Nyhan, B. (2014, September 18). To get more out of science, show the rejected research. *New York Times.* Retrieved from http://www.nytimes.com/2014/09/19/upshot/to-get-more-out-of-science-show-the-rejected-research.html

Rossi, J. S. (1990). Statistical power of psychological research: What have we gained in 20 years? *Journal of Consulting and Clinical Psychology, 58,* 646–56.

Rozeboom, W. W. (1960). The fallacy of the null-hypothesis significance test. *Psychological Bulletin, 57,* 416–28.

Rusticus, S. A., Wilson, D., Casiro, O., & Lovato, C. Y. (2019). Evaluating the quality of health professions learning environments: Development and validation of the Health Education Learning Environment Survey (HELES). *Evaluation and the Health Professions.* doi: 10.1177/0163278719834339

Savory, P. (2008). How do you interpret a confidence interval? *Industrial and Management Systems Engineering, Instructional Materials.*

Schmidt, F. L., & Hunter, J. E. (1997). Eight common but false objections to the discontinuation of significance testing in the analysis of research data. In L. A. Harlow, S. A. Mulaik, & J. H. Steiger (Eds.), *What if there were no significance tests?* (pp. 37–64). Mahwah, NJ: Erlbaum.

Sedlmeier, P., & Gigerenzer, G. (1989). Do studies of statistical power have an effect on the power of studies? *Psychological Bulletin, 105,* 309–16.

Wainer, H. (1999). One cheer for null hypothesis significance testing. *Psychological Methods, 6,* 212–3.

Wilkinson, L., & the Task Force on Statistical Inference, APA Board of Scientific Affairs. (1999). Statistical methods in psychology journals: Guidelines and explanations. *American Psychologist, 54,* 594–604.

Chapter 12

Briggs, M. (2013, October 1). Use the wrong *p*-value, go to jail: Not a joke. [Web log comment]. Retrieved from http://wmbriggs.com/blog/?p=9308

Brown, D. (2013, September 23). The press release conviction of a biotech and its impact on scientific research. *Washington Post.* Retrieved from http://www.washingtonpost.com/national/health-science/the-press-release-crime-of-a-biotech-ceo-and-its-impact-on-scientific-research/2013/09/23/9b4a1a32-007a-11e3-9a3e-916de805f65d_story.html

Callaway, E. (2013, October 2). Uncertainty on trial. *Nature.* Retrieved from http://www.nature.com/news/uncertainty-on-trial-1.13868

Cohen, J. (1988). *Statistical power analysis for the behavioral sciences* (2nd ed.). Hillsdale, NJ: Erlbaum.

Cohen, J. (1992). A power primer. *Psychological Bulletin, 112*(1), 155–9.

Erceg-Hurn, D. M., & Mirosevich, V. M. (2008). Modern robust statistical methods: An easy way to maximize the accuracy and power of your research. *American Psychologist, 63*(7), 591–601.

Erceg-Hurn, D. M., Wilcox, R. R., & Keselman, H. J. (2013). Robust statistical estimation. In T. Little (Ed.), *The Oxford handbook of quantitative methods* (Vol. 1). New York, NY: Oxford University Press.

Hoaglin, D. C., Mosteller, F., & Tukey, J. W. (Eds.). (2000). *Understanding robust and exploratory data analysis.* New York, NY: Wiley.

Hoekstra, R., Kiers, H. A. L., & Johnson, A. (2012). Are assumptions of well-known statistical techniques checked, and why (not)? *Frontiers in Psychology, 3,* 137. doi:10.3389/fpsyg.2012.00137

Mewhort, D. J. K., Kelly, M., & Johns, B. J. (2009). Randomization tests and the unequal-*N*/unequal-variance problem. *Behavior Research Methods, 41*(3), 664–7.

Norman, G. (2010). Likert scales, levels of measurement and the "laws" of statistics. *Advances in Health Sciences Education, 15,* 625–32.

Pallant, J. (2016). *SPSS survival manual: A step by step guide to data analysis using IBM SPSS* (6th ed.). New York, NY: McGraw-Hill.

Tabachnick, B. G. & Fidell, L. S. (2013). *Using multivariate statistics* (6th ed.). Boston, MA: Pearson.

Wilcox, R. R. (1998). How many discoveries have been lost by ignoring modern statistical methods? *American Psychologist, 53*, 300–14.

Wilcox, R. R. (2012). *Introduction to robust estimation and hypothesis testing* (3rd ed.). Waltham, MA: Academic Press.

Wilcox, R. R., & Keselman, H. J. (2003). Modern robust data analysis methods: Measures of central tendency. *Psychological Methods, 8*, 254–74.

Yates, D., Moore, D., & McCabe, G. (1999). *The practice of statistics.* New York, NY: Freeman.

Chapter 13

American Psychological Association. (2010). *Publication manual of the American Psychological Association* (6th ed.). Mountain View, CA: Mayfield.

Bourne, P. E. (2007). Ten simple rules for making good oral presentations. *PLoS Computational Biology, 3*(4), 593–4. doi:10.1371/journal.pcbi.0030077

Christie, S., & Gentner, D. (2010). Where hypotheses come from: Learning new relations by structural assignment. *Journal of Cognition and Development, 11*, 356–73.

Cohen, J. (1988). *Statistical power analysis for the behavioral sciences* (2nd ed.). Hillsdale, NJ: Erlbaum.

Denzin, N. K., & Lincoln, Y. S. (1998a). *Strategies of qualitative inquiry.* Thousand Oaks, CA: Sage.

Denzin, N. K., & Lincoln, Y. S. (1998b). *Collecting and interpreting qualitative materials.* Thousand Oaks, CA: Sage.

Denzin, N. K., & Lincoln, Y. S. (2005). *The Sage handbook of qualitative research* (3rd ed.). Thousand Oaks, CA: Sage.

Erren, T. C., & Bourne, P. E. (2007). Ten simple rules for a good poster presentation. *PLoS Computational Biology, 3*(5), 777–8. doi:10.1371/journal.pcbi.0030102

Fischer, C. T. (2006). *Qualitative research methods for psychologists: Introduction through empirical studies.* Amsterdam: Elsevier/Academic Press.

Flyvbjerg, B. (2006). Five misunderstandings about case-study research. *Qualitative Inquiry, 12*, 219–45.

Forrester, M. A. (Ed.). (2010). *Doing qualitative research in psychology. A practical guide.* London, UK: Sage.

Gentner, D., & Namy, L. (1999). Comparison in the development of categories. *Cognitive Development, 14*, 487–513.

Graf, C., Wager, E., Bowman, A., Fiack, S., Scott-Lichter, D., & Robinson, A. (2007). Best practice guidelines on publication ethics: A publisher's perspective. Retrieved from http://www.apastyle.org/manual/related/best-practice-guidelines.pdf

Gray, K., & Wegner, D. M. (2013). Six guidelines for interesting research. *Perspectives on Psychological Science, 8*, 549–53.

Holliday, A. (2001). *Doing and writing qualitative research.* London, UK: Sage.

Hrvatin, V. (2018, February 13). Fake science: Who's to blame when the media gets research wrong? *National Post.* Retrieved from https://nationalpost.com/news/world/fake-science-whos-to-blame-when-the-media-gets-research-wrong

Justus, B., & Rusticus, S. (2018, May). Should students choose their own groups? A comparison of student- versus teacher-formed groups on group dynamics, satisfaction and success. Presented at Connecting Minds, Richmond, British Columbia.

Kahneman, D., Fredrickson, B. L., Schreiber, C. A., & Redelmeier, D. A. (1993). When more pain is preferred to less: Adding a better end. *Psychological Science, 4*, 401–5. doi:10.1111/j.1467-9280.1993.tb00589.x

Kidder, L. H., & Fine, M. (1997). Qualitative enquiry in psychology: A radical tradition. In D. Fox & I. Prillentensky (Eds.), *Critical psychology: An introduction.* London, UK: Sage.

Kirkman, J. (1992). *Good style: writing for science and technology.* London, UK: E & FN Spon.

NPR. (2015, May 24). Author says researcher faked gay marriage opinion study. Retrieved from https://www.npr.org/2015/05/24/409210207/author-says-researcher-faked-gay-marriage-opinon-study

Pettit, N. C., Sivanathan, N., Gladstone, E., & Marr, J. C. (2013). Rising stars and sinking ships: Consequences of status momentum. *Psychological Science, 24*, 1579–84.

Robson, C. (2002). *Real world research* (2nd ed.). Oxford, UK: Blackwell.

Righetti, F., Finenaur, C., & Finkel, E. J. (2013). Low self-control promotes the willingness to sacrifice in close relationships. *Psychological Science, 24*, 1533–40.

Sternberg, R. J. (1992, September). How to win acceptances by psychology journals: 21 tips for better writing. *APS Observer,* 12–3, 18.

Strathdee, S. A., Patrick, D. M., Currie, S. L., Cornelisse, P. G. A., Rekart, M. L., Montaner, J. S. G., . . . O'Shaughnessy, M. V. (1997). Needle exchange is not enough: Lessons from the Vancouver injecting drug use study. *AIDS, 11*(8), 59–65.

Strong, W. (1991). *Writing incisively: Do-it-yourself prose surgery.* New York, NY: McGraw-Hill.

Sumner, P., Vivian-Griffiths, S., Boivin, J., Williams, A., Venetis, C. A, Davies, A., . . . Chambers, C. D. (2014). The association between exaggeration in health related science news and academic press releases: Retrospective observational study. *British Medical Journal, 349*, 1–8. doi: 10.1136/bmj.g7015

Willig, C. (2008). *Introducing qualitative research in psychology* (2nd ed.). Buckingham, UK: Open University Press.

Chapter 14

Amin, M., & Mabe, M. (2000). Impact factors: Use and abuse. *Perspectives in Publishing, 1*(2), 1–6.

Banobi, J., Branch, T., & Hilborn, R. (2011). Do rebuttals affect future science? *Ecosphere, 2*(3), 37. Retrieved from https://esajournals.onlinelibrary.wiley.com/doi/pdf/10.1890/ES10-00142.1

Bhattacharjee, Y. (2013, April). The mind of a con man. *New York Times Magazine.*

Brainard, J. & You, J. (2018, October, 25). What a massive database of restricted papers reveals about science publishing's "death penalty." *Science Magazine.* Retrieved from https://www.sciencemag.org/news/2018/10/what-massive-database-retracted-papers-reveals-about-science-publishing-s-death-penalty

Clarivate Analytics. (2018). *Journal citation reports.* Retrieved from https://clarivate.com/blog/science-research-connect/the-2018-jcr-release-is-here

Gladstone, B. (2013, July 5). Retraction Watch revisited. *On the Media.* Retrieved from http://www.onthemedia.org/story/304647-retraction-watch-revisited

Naik, G. (2011, August 10). Mistakes in scientific studies surge. *Wall Street Journal.* Retrieved from http://online.wsj.com/news/articles/SB10001424052702303362710457641185066658 2080

Oransky, I. (2013, December 24). Doing the right thing: Yale psychology lab retracts monkey papers for inaccurate coding. *Retraction Watch.* Retrieved from http://retractionwatch.com/2013/12/24/doing-the-right-thing-yale-psychology-lab-retracts-monkey-papers-for-inaccurate-coding

Reaction Watch. (2018). The Retraction Watch leaderboard. Retrieved from https://retractionwatch.com/the-retraction-watch-leaderboard

Chapter 15

Allen, B., Spiegel, D. P., Thompson, B., Pestilli, F., & Rokers, B. (2015). Altered white matter in early visual pathways of humans with amblyopia. *Vision Research, 114,* 48–55. doi:10.1016/j.visres.2014.12.021

Aslin, R. N. (2012). Questioning the questions that have been asked about the infant brain using near-infrared spectroscopy. *Cognitive Neuropsychology, 29,* 7–23.

Bigelow, H. J. (1850). Dr. Harlow's case of recovery from the passage of an iron bar through the head. *American Journal of Medical Sciences, 20,* 13–22.

Cacioppo, J. T., Berntson, G. G., & Nussbaum, H. C. (2008). Neuroimaging as a new tool in the toolbox of psychological science. *Current Directions in Psychological Science, 17,* 62–7.

Carey, B. (2005, May 31). Watching new love as it sears the brain. *New York Times.* Retrieved from http://www.nytimes.com/2005/05/31/health/psychology/watching-new-love-as-it-sears-the-brain.html

Casarotto, S., Lauro, L. J. R., Bellina, V., Casali. A. G., Rosanova, M., Pigorini, S., . . . Massimini, M. (2010). EEG responses to TMS are sensitive to changes in the perturbation parameters and repeatable over time. *PLoS ONE, 5*(4), e10281. doi:10.1371/journal.pone.0010281

Chung, E. (2011, May 25). Blind people echolocate with visual part of brain. *CBC News.* Retrieved from http://www.cbc.ca/news/technology/blind-people-echolocate-with-visual-part-of-brain-1.1012642

Damasio, H., Grabowski, T., Frank, R., Galaburda, A. M., & Damasio, A. R. (1994). The return of Phineas Gage: Clues about the brain from the skull of a famous patient. *Science, 264,* 1102–5.

Eisenberger, N. I., Lieberman, M. D., & Williams, K. D. (2003). Does rejection hurt? An fMRI study of social exclusion. *Science, 302,* 290–2.

Farar, M. (2002). Emerging ethical issues in neuroscience. *Nature Neuroscience, 5,* 1123–9.

Finkel, M. (2011, March). The blind man who taught himself to see. *Men's Journal.* Retrieved from http://www.mensjournal.com/magazine/the-blind-man-who-taught-himself-to-see-20120504

Fleischman, J. (2004). *Phineas Gage: A gruesome but true story about brain science.* New York, NY: Houghton Mifflin Harcourt.

Giedd, J., Raznahan, A., Alexander-Bloch, A., Schmitt, E., Gogtay, N., & Rapoport, J. L. (2015). Child psychiatry branch of the National Institute of Mental Health longitudinal structural magnetic resonance imaging study of human brain development. *Neuropsychopharmacology, 40,* 43–9.

Harlow, J. M. (1848). Passage of an iron rod through the head. *Boston Medical and Surgical Journal, 39,* 389–93.

Hillman, C. H., Buck, S. M., Themanson, J. R., Pontifex, M. B., & Castelli, D. M. (2009). Aerobic fitness and cognitive development: Event-related brain potential and task performance indices of executive control in preadolescent children. *Developmental Psychology, 45,* 114–29.

Illes, J. (2006). "Pandora's box" of incidental findings in brain imaging research. *Nature Clinical Practice Neurology, 2*(2), 60–1.

Kulkarni, H. (2009). MRI: What, why, and when? *Health & Medicine, Technology.* http://www.slideshare.net/keshrad/basics-of-mri

Lin, T. (2012, June 4). Hitting the court, with an ear on the ball. *New York Times.* Retrieved from http://www.nytimes.com/2012/06/05/science/a-game-of-tennis-tests-notions-of-blindness.html

Lloyd-Fox, S., Blasi, A., & Elwell, C. E. (2010). Illuminating the development brain: The past, present and future of functional near infrared spectroscopy. *Neuroscience and Biobehavioral Reviews, 34,* 269–84.

Macmillan, M. (2000). *An odd kind of fame: Stories of Phineas Gage.* Cambridge, MA: MIT Press.

Maguire, E. A., Woollett, K., & Spiers, H. J. (2006). London taxi drivers and bus drivers: A structural MRI and neuropsychological analysis. *Hippocampus, 16,* 1091–101.

Mai, X., Xu, L., Li, M., Shao, J., Zhao, Z., Lamm, C., . . . Lazoff, B. (2014). Sounds elicit relative left frontal alpha activity in 2-month-old infants. *International Journal of Psychophysiology, 94,* 287–91.

Miller, L., & Spiegel, A. (2015, January 22). Batman Pt. 1. *National Public Radio, Invisibilia.* Retrieved from http://www.npr.org/2015/01/23/379134306/batman-pt-1

Ratiu, P., Talos, I. F., Haker, S., Lieberman, D., & Everett, P. (2004). The tale of Phineas Gage, digitally remastered. *Journal of Neurotrauma, 21,* 637–43.

Richeson, J., Baird, A. A., Gordon, H. L., Heatherton, T. F., Wyland, C. L., Trawalter, S., & Shelton, N. (2003). An fMRI investigation of the impact of interracial contact on executive function. *Nature Neuroscience, 6*(12), 1323–8.

Schaefer, P. W., Grant, P. E., & Gonzalez, R. G. (2000). Diffusion-weighted MR imaging of the brain. *Radiology, 217*(2), 331–45.

Thaler, L., Arnott, S., & Goodale, M. (2011). Neural correlates of natural human echolocation in early and late blind echolocation experts. *PLoS ONE.* Retrieved from http://journals.plos.org/plosone/article?id=10.1371/journal.pone.0020162

Underwood, E. (2014, November 11). How blind people use bat-like sonar. *Science.* Retrieved from http://www.sciencemag.org/news/2014/11/how-blind-people-use-batlike-sonar

Van Horn, J. D., Irimia, A., Torgerson, C. M., Chambers, M. C., Kikinis, R., & Toga, A. W. (2012). Mapping connectivity damage in the cage of Phineas Gage. *PLoS ONE, 7*(5), e37454. doi:10.1371/journal.pone.0037454

Weisberg, D. S., Keil, F. C., Goodstein, J., Rawson, E., & Gray, J. R. (2008). The seductive allure of neuroscience explanations. *Journal of Cognitive Neuroscience, 20,* 470–7.

Willems, R. M., Van der Haergen, L., Fisher, S. E., & Francks, C. (2014). On the other hand: Including left-handers in cognitive neuroscience and neurogenetics. *Nature Reviews Neuroscience, 15,* 193–201.

Author Index

Subject Index